Tocqueville

Tocqueville

THE ARISTOCRATIC SOURCES OF LIBERTY

Lucien Jaume

Translated by Arthur Goldhammer

PRINCETON UNIVERSITY PRESS

Princeton & Oxford

World copyright © 2008 by Librairie Arthème Fayard
English translation copyright © 2013 by Princeton University Press
Published by Princeton University Press, 41 William Street, Princeton,
    New Jersey 08540
In the United Kingdom: Princeton University Press, 6 Oxford Street,
    Woodstock, Oxfordshire OX20 1TW

press.princeton.edu

Jacket Art: Théodore Chassériau (1819–56), *Alexis de Tocqueville*, 1850,
    Oil on canvas, 163.0 × 130 cm. Photo: Arnaudet. Chateaux de
    Versailles et de Trianon, Versailles, France. Photo credit: Reunion des
    Musées Nationaux / Art Resource, NY.

Library of Congress Cataloging-in-Publication Data

Jaume, Lucien.
    [Tocqueville. English]
    Tocqueville : the aristocratic sources of liberty / Lucien Jaume ; translated
by Arthur Goldhammer.
        p. cm.
    Translation of: Tocqueville : les sources aristocratiques de la liberté
biographie intellectuelle. Paris : Fayard, c2008.
    Includes bibliographical references and index.
    ISBN 978-0-691-15204-2 (acid-free paper) 1. Tocqueville, Alexis de,
1805–1859. 2. Historians—France—Biography. 3. Democracy—Philosophy.
4. Political science—France—History—19th century. I. Goldhammer,
Arthur. II. Title.
    DC36.98.T63J3813 2008
    320.092–dc23   2012032469

British Library Cataloging-in-Publication Data is available

Ouvrage publié avec le soutien du Centre national du livre –
    ministère français chargé de la culture.
This work is published with support from the French Ministry of Culture /
    Centre national du livre.

This translation is published with the support of Sciences Po, Paris.

This book has been composed in Garamond Premier Pro

Printed on acid-free paper. ∞

Printed in the United States of America

10 9 8 7 6 5 4 3 2 1

For Françoise Mélonio, who believed in this book long before it became a reality.

Opposite him was a young man with a pale face and somewhat sickly appearance. . . . In his manners there was a grace and politeness that the present generation in France seems to value less than the previous generation. "Who is that young man?" I asked the person I was with, because he had made an impression on me. "That is Monsieur de Tocqueville," came the answer. "He has just published a quite remarkable book about democracy in the United States." That book has enjoyed an unusual fate: all the parties like it. The liberals and Carlists approve of it, and the juste-milieu spares it from attack. . . . He is sought after and admired: all the salons want him. He is descended from an old family yet animated by a strong love of liberty. He belongs to the nobility by birth, to liberty by the activity of his mind.

—*Tocqueville in the salon of Madame Récamier,*
by Édouard Gans, 1836

Contents

Introduction   1

PART ONE. WHAT DID TOCQUEVILLE MEAN BY "DEMOCRACY"?   15

1. Attacking the French Tradition: Popular Sovereignty Redefined in and through Local Liberties   21

2. Democracy as Modern Religion   65

3. Democracy as Expectation of Material Pleasures   82

PART TWO. TOCQUEVILLE AS SOCIOLOGIST   95

4. In the Tradition of Montesquieu: The State-Society Analogy   101

5. Counterrevolutionary Traditionalism: A Muffled Polemic   106

6. The Discovery of the Collective   115

7. Tocqueville and the Protestantism of His Time: The Insistent Reality of the Collective   129

PART THREE. TOCQUEVILLE AS MORALIST   145

8. The Moralist and the Question of *l'Honnête*   147

9. Tocqueville's Relation to Jansenism   159

PART FOUR. TOCQUEVILLE IN LITERATURE: DEMOCRATIC LANGUAGE WITHOUT DECLARED AUTHORITY   193

10. Resisting the Democratic Tendencies of Language   199

11. Tocqueville in the Debate about Literature and Society   226

PART FIVE. THE GREAT CONTEMPORARIES: MODELS AND COUNTERMODELS   249

12. Tocqueville and Guizot: Two Conceptions of Authority   251

13. Tutelary Figures from Malesherbes to Chateaubriand   291

      Conclusion   319

Appendix 1. The Use of Anthologies and Summaries in Tocqueville's Time   327

Appendix 2. Silvestre de Sacy, Review of Democracy in America   328

Appendix 3. Letter from Alexis de Tocqueville to Silvestre de Sacy   335

Index   337

Tocqueville

Introduction

There is, in many respects, a Tocqueville enigma.

Why did Tocqueville write *Democracy in America*? The question might seem incongruous.[1] In fact, it is the key to understanding both the work and the man. Today we know that America was not the sole subject of the book that Tocqueville published in two volumes in 1835 and 1840. America was merely the pretext for studying modern society and the woes of France. What is more, the author's intention remains ambiguous and controversial, as does the precise scope of the book he had in mind. *Democracy in America* has become a world classic (especially in the United States, Italy, and France), yet anyone who reads it slowly and reflectively will notice that its careful prose incorporates a number of curious *signs*: the author never discloses his opinion straightaway but rather turns it over in his mind, modifies it, and on occasion contradicts himself.[2] His position on

---

[1] No one asks why Cézanne painted Mont Sainte-Victoire, because the masterpiece speaks for itself.

[2] To the point that Jon Elster often finds his thought to be incorrigibly incoherent: see *Political Psychology* (Cambridge: Cambridge University Press, 1993). Citations from *De la démocratie en Amérique* are from the 1981 Garnier-Flammarion edition, as follows: *DA* I, for the 1835 text, *DA* II, for the 1840 text, followed by a page number; citations to specific chapters take the form *DA* I.2.5, for example, to indicate the fifth chapter of book 2 of volume 1. English translations are taken from Arthur Goldhammer's translation, published in one volume by the Library of America in 2004 (hereafter cited as AG). For other texts I refer to the Gallimard edition of the *Œuvres complètes*. For example, *OC* VIII-1, p. 72, indicates page 72 of book 1 of volume 8, which contains the correspondence with Gustave de Beaumont in three books. When necessary I also cite the Pléiade edition as follows: *Œuvres*, La Pléiade, followed by the volume and page. This edition includes numbered excerpts from drafts and manuscripts of *DA* I, *DA* II, and *L'Ancien Régime et la Révolution* (*ARR*). Volume 3 (*ARR*) is the result of a collaboration between François Furet and Françoise Mélonio. Volume 1 was edited by André Jardin with the collaboration of Françoise Mélonio and L. Queffélec. Volume 2 was edited by Jardin with the collaboration of J.-C. Lamberti and James Schleifer. English quotations from this text are from the translation by Arthur Goldhammer, published by Cambridge University Press in 2012 and hereafter cited as AG2. There are also numerous references to the manuscripts of *DA* I and *DA* II in the Eduardo Nolla edition, published by Vrin in 1990. The reading of the manuscripts is not always reliable, but I owe a great deal to this edition, which also gives the reactions of Tocqueville's family. This is cited as Nolla I and Nolla II, followed by the page; the Nolla text is also available in a bilingual French-English edition, translated by James Schleifer (Indianapolis: Liberty Fund, 2010); page citations to the latter version are indicated by JS, but the translations given here are Arthur Goldhammer's. Other anthologies are also cited below. In general, if a place of publication is

the great modern phenomenon that he baptized "democracy" is difficult to pin down: sometimes he praises it (human dignity, personal responsibility, feelings of sympathy and sociability), but at other times he describes its worrisome flaws (selfishness, social dissolution, mediocre leadership, materialism of private interests, tyranny of majorities, oppressiveness of the welfare state). Readers are thus led to ask themselves what they ought to think. And that is indeed what Tocqueville wanted, for he shared the view of his master Montesquieu that "the problem is not to get people to read but to get them to think."[3]

The careful reader will therefore ask herself another question: "But what did Tocqueville think about what he was describing?" Tocqueville was usually at pains to conceal precisely this, however. He even made this a principle of composition, as members of his family who read and commented on his manuscripts knew well.[4] One of his two brothers, Édouard de Tocqueville, reminded him of this rule and scolded him a bit for seeming to reveal his opinion of centralization in France compared with what he called administrative decentralization in the United States.[5]

"The author," Édouard reminded his brother, "should remain behind the curtain and content himself with producing conviction without commanding or stating it. Here, for my part, is the conclusion I draw from all this."[6] Is there a "curtain" in Tocqueville's writing? Why should authors wear masks?[7] Apparently the issue is a pedagogical one: the reader must be gently guided and allowed to form his own opinion, as if he had discovered it on his own. Tocqueville himself stated this view on several occasions: the purpose of *Democracy in America* was to persuade without being too obvious about it.[8] Furthermore, to be a "great" writer, Tocqueville (again taking Montesquieu as his model) believed that one had to be capable of revealing society to itself, of enabling people to see clearly what they thought obscurely: "The success

---

not given, it is Paris. English translations of many of Tocqueville's letters can be found in Olivier Zunz, ed., *Alexis de Tocqueville and Gustave de Beaumont in America: Their Friendship and Their Travels*, trans. Arthur Goldhammer (Charlottesville: University of Virginia Press, 2010), cited hereafter as GZ.

[3] Montesquieu, *De l'esprit des lois*, XI, 20, in *Œuvres complètes*, ed. Oster (Paris: Le Seuil, 1964), p. 598.

[4] Many of these notes have been preserved and can be readily consulted in the Nolla edition cited above.

[5] In fact, the term corresponded to nothing of the kind in America, as we will see in part 1.

[6] Letter of June 15, 1834, to Alexis de Tocqueville, cited in Nolla I, p. 69, n. c.

[7] Descartes: "In the theater of the world, I make my way masked" (*larvatus prodeo*).

[8] Another purpose of the work was to assist Tocqueville in embarking on a career in politics. He published his book in 1835 in the hope of being elected deputy, a goal he did not realize until 1839. He published the second volume with the express hope of enhancing his reputation for competence in the art of modern government. Hence in a sense the book was an action manifesto.

of a book depends more on thoughts that were already in the reader's head than on those that the writer expresses."[9] This is a key observation, which tells us a great deal about Tocqueville's "secret thought" (or *pensée de derrière*, to quote his other master, Blaise Pascal).

Édouard's letter was not confined to the pedagogical aspects of writing, however. Another reason for Alexis to disguise his opinions and preferences was to raise his thinking to a level of generality that would enable it to escape its historical context and partisan conflict: "In this final chapter, I find that you are on stage too much;[10] you enter the lists armed with your personal opinion. You apply your principles to France; you get into politics.[11] .... Bear in mind that your book should not be stamped with the date 1834 or even with the colors of France. If it is to live for posterity, it should be free of the influence of time and place."

The problem, then, was to achieve a level of theoretical generality that would enable Tocqueville to deal with the problems of society and government while at the same time allowing the reader to occupy the place of the invisible author, who would meanwhile take pains to hide not only his personal opinions but also his role as mentor. The author's goal was to enable the reader to escape the context of 1834, even though that context formed the basis of the comparison between the French *commune* and the Massachusetts town.

There was also the realm of political opinion: Édouard reminded his brother that in the years after the July Revolution of 1830, many things had been called into question. Indeed, as Tocqueville well knew, change had been constant since the "Great Revolution" of 1789. These changes informed his celebrated distinction between aristocratic and democratic societies. Once again, however, the careful reader may find herself perplexed, for Tocqueville did not always use the word *democracy* in the same way. How many meanings did he ascribe to it? Three, five, eleven—estimates vary according to the commentator.[12]

Furthermore, this carefully maintained vagueness about the word *democracy*—which, as François Furet has noted, would disappear from *The*

[9] Letter to Mme Swetchine, January 7, 1856, *OC* XV-2, p. 269.

[10] Again we find the idea of a "curtain." In part 3 we will see that Tocqueville himself used the image of a *veil*, because truth is in any case veiled (like the God of the Jansenists), and good writing will preserve the veil that separates man from the inaccessible truth of his being.

[11] This was in 1834, when decentralization of *communes* was being debated. In the Chamber of Deputies, Thiers was resisting the demands of Odilon Barrot. Tocqueville made notes on the debate in his manuscripts.

[12] In this book I retain one meaning with three constituent elements: democracy as local power, democracy as a substitute for religion or "public religion," and democracy as a promise of "material enjoyments."

Ancien Régime and the Revolution—was not unrelated to the personal views of Tocqueville the man.

Tocqueville the man—and this book is also a study of him as well as his work—must be distinguished from Tocqueville the author, or, to put it another way, from the *rules* of style and expression that Tocqueville set for himself. People nowadays love to speak of "positioning themselves" in every possible way. If we ask how the author Tocqueville wanted to believe that he "positioned himself," or at any rate how he tells us he positioned himself, the answer is: in the center.

"Amid the swirl of divisive and contradictory opinions, I have tried for a moment to forget the sympathies and antipathies that each of them may inspire in me."[13] In other words, the rule was not to reveal oneself as a defender of traditional monarchy or an aristocratic society based on privilege, nor as a systematic adversary. It was not to appear republican in the French sense (that is, all too often in favor of the bloody tyranny of 1793 and of extralegal political action) or even in the American sense, by disclosing the innumerable reservations and criticisms that popular sovereignty might inspire. Tocqueville often refers to this stance as one of *impartiality* (the word appears one line before the quoted passage), a notion to which he was particularly attached. He fell into a cold rage when Silvestre de Sacy, writing in the *Journal des débats*, claimed to uncover his personal contradictions, thereby denying Tocqueville the impartiality that he claimed.[14]

Clearly, we have already discovered quite a bit of ambiguity in a work celebrated as one of the monuments of political thought. Who was Tocqueville the man? What did the author conceal behind what he revealed? And finally, *why* did he write this book?

As mentioned earlier, there is also another ingredient: to those with ears to hear, *Democracy in America* speaks about a country other than the United States, namely, the France of the July Monarchy, Napoleon, Louis XIV, and Philip the Fair. The author himself tells us this in a note that anticipates an important section of his 1856 work, *The Ancien Régime and the Révolution*.[15] It was not the Revolution that created administrative centralization in France, and the comparison with the New England town was supposed to

---

[13] *DA* II, preface, 6; AG, p. 480.

[14] Silvestre de Sacy's review can be found in the appendix. He was a paragon of liberal literary criticism, the scion of a family of prominent scholars and religious leaders. Tocqueville's mordant reply, a hitherto unpublished draft of a letter, is also reproduced in the appendix (with the kind permission of the comte d'Hérouville).

[15] See note K of *DA* I, p. 557: "It is not accurate to say that centralization stemmed from the French Revolution."

lead back to the medieval commune in Europe and especially France, before the monarchy imposed centralization.[16]

To his cousin, confidant, and sometime collaborator, Louis de Kergorlay, Tocqueville disclosed that "although I very seldom spoke of France in that book, I did not write a page without thinking about France or without having France in a manner of speaking before my eyes.... The constant, unspoken comparison with France was in my opinion one of the main reasons for the book's success."[17] To believe Tocqueville, the book's first readers had no difficulty grasping its message: they were able to penetrate the secret of the work and make the comparison that the man "behind the curtain" intended them to make.

And yet the work has remained a fundamental landmark *in America* for Americans wishing to learn about their own country. Is this paradoxical, or is it a sign of Tocqueville's splendid success? In any event, the foreign author who has excelled all others in teaching Americans about themselves wrote a book that again and again addressed itself to French readers and spoke to them of France. Was this yet another mask, or, to use Tocqueville's preferred image, a "veil"? Tocqueville's America was above all a mirror of France, but France's image was so elegantly encoded that we should speak of it as an *anamorphosis* rather than an image.[18] To carry the metaphor still further, one might say that Tocqueville's portrait had several implied viewers (or readers).

❧

The question on which our understanding of Tocqueville depends is therefore not simply "Why did he write *Democracy in America?*" but also "For whom did he write it?" The two questions are linked in that the existential situation of the man—a young aristocrat in conflict with the beliefs of his milieu—inspired the position and style of the author.

Before continuing, I must make one thing clear. I had long felt that I could not analyze *Democracy in America* (a text I have been studying for twenty-five years) until I had explored the intellectual and ideological landscape of French liberalism in the nineteenth century, in order to understand the

---

[16] Indeed, it was supposed to lead back to Guizot's course on the *Histoire de la civilisation en France*, which, as we will see later, Tocqueville would transform and challenge in his *L'Ancien Régime et la Révolution*. Tocqueville attended Guizot's lectures and took notes, which have been preserved (and published by Gallimard).

[17] Letter to Kergorlay, 1847, *OC* XIII-2, p. 209; GZ, p. 587.

[18] Recall that an anamorphosis is a visual representation in which an object cannot be perceived from certain angles and becomes visible only if the spectator occupies a certain position. The spectator's gaze is incorporated into the structure of the painting, as Roland Barthes noted in the case of another stylistic exercise, the painting of Arcimboldo (see part 3). The reader may wish to consult Jurgis Baltrusaitis, *Anamorphoses ou magie artificielle des effets merveilleux* (Paris: Olivier Perrin, 1969).

contemporary issues in the background of Tocqueville's work. The "liberal" label is not misplaced, because Tocqueville described himself as a liberal ("of a new type," to be sure, but who would want to be an "old liberal"?). I published the results of my research in *L'Individu effacé ou le paradoxe du libéralisme français* (1997). But this was not enough. It also proved necessary to undertake a literal, internal interpretation of the text in order to understand the ideas and currents of opinion with which *Democracy in America* maintained a hidden dialogue (hidden in the sense that Tocqueville rarely cites any author by name; when he does cite a person or group—for example, the authors of the *Federalist*, or Thomas Jefferson—it means that the reference has no strong ideological valence). Yet the whole era is in the text, which bristles with contradictory voices: among them we find counter-revolutionaries (Bonald, de Maistre, Lamennais), liberal aristocrats (Montlosier, Chateaubriand), republicans (from Mme de Staël to Armand Carrel), the so-called *doctrinaires* (Guizot, Rémusat, Royer-Collard), and aristocrats such as Louis de Carné who threw in their lot with the middle class. In addition, Tocqueville's style was shaped in large part by seventeenth-century moralists, who were dear to the man as well as the author. Hence it was important to look again at the question (or myth) of Tocqueville's relation to Pascal and to Jansenism more generally.

The purpose of this book is therefore to combine a study of context with an internal reading. It is to offer not a *commentary* on *Democracy in America*—a much-practiced exercise in which the commentator paraphrases the text and comments on other commentators—but rather an *interpretation* based on signs, indices, and even stylistic turns of an author who revealed himself even as he attempted to draw a veil over his own views and who can also be heard speaking in a different register in his correspondence and manuscripts as well as in the accounts of his contemporaries.[19] To sharpen the intellectual portrait of Tocqueville the man, we need to identify the various *levels of meaning* contained in the text and the various audiences to which it was addressed. As Édouard de Tocqueville said, "to remain behind the curtain and produce conviction" presumes a *labor* of thought, rationalization, and even elocution by means of which Tocqueville the author was trying to persuade himself as well as his readers.[20] But what did he persuade himself of?

He convinced himself of precisely the same thing that he discussed with his father, Count Hervé de Tocqueville, his brother Édouard, his cousin

---

[19] This study is far from exhaustive. My goal is to open an avenue for exploring the meaning of the work and a method of interpretation that others may be able to follow.

[20] "Labor" here is to be understood in the sense of childbirth.

Kergorlay, and his friend Bouchitté when he had them read his manuscripts: namely, that "democracy" was already on the march and that the best one could do was to help it to understand itself and conduct itself wisely. There was no point in lamenting the bygone age of aristocracy.[21] Rather, one should try to *transfer* some of its noble values to a society driven by the powerful and irrepressible engine of equality. The young Alexis de Tocqueville did not reach this conclusion without pain. At the outset of his journey to America with Gustave de Beaumont, in Philadelphia, he offered the following plaintive observation, from which we gather how difficult it would be for him to attain the requisite level of abstraction, generality, and impartiality: "Tied to the royalists by shared principles and a thousand family connections, I see myself as somehow chained to a party whose conduct strikes me as often not very honorable and nearly always extravagant."[22]

With these various indications in mind, it becomes clear that if we are to fully grasp the meaning of *Democracy in America*, we would do well to approach it as the historian Lucien Febvre approached the work of Rabelais: "What could a contemporary reader of Rabelais understand," Febvre asked, "and which of our modern ideas would he certainly not have found in the work? Above all, what did sixteenth-century readers read between the well-justified lines of text?"[23] Indeed, we initially project onto the text our preoccupations, sentiments, and prejudices, even though the categories of the author's thought were different. What is more, if the author of these "well-justified lines of text" is named Tocqueville and has slipped in (or involuntarily emitted) signals to certain groups of readers, then we must make every effort to avoid anachronistic readings. In 2005, the bicentennial of Tocqueville's birth, how often did we read in the press of "Tocqueville our contemporary"?

---

[21] For Tocqueville, this meant the feudal era, as we will see: a time of honor, loyalty coupled with moral independence, chivalry in war, feudal patronage of the peasantry, etc.

[22] Letter to Ernest de Chabrol, October 18, 1831, quoted in Nolla I, p. xxi, n. 33. This letter will be published in the Gallimard edition of the *Œuvres complètes*.

[23] Lucien Febvre, *Le Problème de l'incroyance au XVIe siècle. La Religion de Rabelais* (Paris: Albin Michel, 1942), p. 7. The fine lesson in historical intelligence that Febvre gave with his *Rabelais* was repeated in a less well-known but even more audacious work on Marguerite de Navarre, *Amour sacré, amour profane. Autour de l'Heptaméron* (Paris: Gallimard-NRF "Idées," 1944). The following plea is worth quoting for an age like our own, which often believes that the past can easily be judged without studying it: "Let us be historians. Which means: let us not kill the dead a second time. Let us not deprive them of that which is far more precious than their material life, namely, their spiritual life—that which they thought, loved, and believed—which we do indirectly by replacing their true thoughts, beliefs, and loves with what we think of when we use the same words, what we believe when we utter the same incantations, and what we love with the same enthusiasm" (p. 356). In other words: how can we escape ourselves in order to interpret another era?

This book will *not* treat Tocqueville as our contemporary. It will seek rather to restore the distance between him and us, because Andrew Jackson's America and Louis-Philippe's France were not societies in any way contemporary with our own. Indeed, to measure the temporal distance between them and us, one would do well to begin reading those chapters of the second volume of *Democracy in America* that deal with literature, painting, architecture, and theater.[24] In these chapters, which most commentators avoid, we see clearly Tocqueville's relation to his own time and to what he calls "democratic literature," especially Romanticism. His critical discourse is one with which we are no longer familiar, quite conservative in its approach to art and language. Yet these attitudes constitute an important key to Tocqueville's work, since he wrote in the age of Victor Hugo, Lamartine, Walter Scott, and Chateaubriand, whom he had constantly in mind, along with the art criticism of Victor Cousin and Abel-François Villemain.

Make no mistake, however: just because Tocqueville is not "our contemporary" does not mean that he is of no use for understanding our time. Indeed, the contrary is true. By restoring *Democracy in America* to its era, with its own set of issues, we will see more clearly where and who we are. One of Tocqueville's most important ideas, "the authority of the social" (for which he was greatly indebted to Lamennais), can teach us a great deal about the growing power of civil society today, as well as about the proliferation of identity groups that compete for legitimacy with the traditional state. The force of public opinion—the great rival of states and governments, representing society's revenge on the state—is a subject that Tocqueville viewed through the lens of American communities and discussed at great length.

Having invoked the authority of Lucien Febvre concerning the question of historical interpretation, let me now quote Ernest Renan, who wrote in *L'Avenir de la science* "that true admiration is historical." Indeed, to enter Tocqueville's study (which he described in many manuscripts and letters) is in no way to disparage his work. Nor is it disparaging to show that, broadly speaking, none of the themes of *Democracy in America* was original to its author. He continually reworked themes that were circulating in the political, religious, and literary culture of his time yet drew from those themes a work that overshadowed much of the writing of his contemporaries and that stands with that of the best of them: Mme de Staël, Benjamin Constant, and François Guizot.

Henri-Dominique Lacordaire, a politically active Dominican friar whose Notre-Dame lectures Tocqueville attended along with the rest of the July Monarchy elite, imparted an important truth to his august audience:

---

[24]*DA* II, book 1, chaps. 9–21. This will be the principal subject of part 4 of the present work.

Perhaps you believe that you are self-made. You are wrong: it is the nineteenth century that made you. And what is the nineteenth century? It is the soul, which expresses itself in speech, which is transformed into public opinion, which lives in the air you breathe, which insinuates itself into your very marrow and governs you without your knowledge. . . . Even when you anticipate [the century], you are but its echoes and servants.[25]

All the themes that Tocqueville developed were being debated, and had already been debated, at the time he published his book. The idea of a "social state" was on everyone's lips. The difference between "administrative" and "political" centralization was a commonplace in legitimist circles. The tyranny of public opinion in a democracy was discussed by various people in the United States, including perhaps James Fenimore Cooper. Lamennais and Leroux recognized the religious dimension of democracy, and Constant, Guizot, Royer-Collard, and Chateaubriand all believed that greater equality was inevitable. Mme de Staël contrasted democratic literature and aristocratic literature. All these were recurrent topics, as was "democracy," which became a commonplace of French political discourse during the Restoration and July Monarchy, even if the meaning of the term varied considerably from author to author.

If we want to explore the palette of meanings in *Democracy in America*, we must therefore identify the plethora of hidden references in the text—references by means of which Tocqueville sought to educate his readers and at times to engage in polemic with the various parties in contention, as well as to elucidate the worldviews that animated their conflicts. We see this in particular in the opposition between the values of the Right and those of the liberals, because America—Protestant, republican, federal, deeply involved in commerce, and avid for wealth—provided an excellent case for Tocqueville to get his message across. Note that when Tocqueville entered the Chamber as a young deputy in 1839, he wanted to sit on the left but was actually seated with the center-left.

Since my goal was to draw an intellectual portrait of the young Tocqueville, who published the first volume of *Democracy* at the age of thirty and the second five years later, it would have been methodologically unwise to begin with his biography only to "discover" the more personal aspects of the text later on. With that type of approach, the interpreter invariably confirms what he already knew, whether right or wrong. It seemed better to proceed

[25] Henri-Dominique Lacordaire, 56th Notre-Dame lecture, "Sur la prophétie," 1849, in *Œuvres de Lacordaire* (Paris: Poussielgue-Rusand, 1861), 4:111. To be sure, Lacordaire said this to underscore his point that only God's word can set man free.

inductively: to try to understand the author by starting with what he said and the way he said it, recognizing the theories and ideas to which he was responding (usually implicitly) in order to influence his readers and only then (in part 5 of this book) to examine whether what we have learned about the author and perceived about the man can be linked to his entourage and education and to the people he chose as models and countermodels in his youth. In other words, since there is an enigma about Tocqueville, let us not try to understand who he was. Let us try rather to acquaint ourselves with his reflections on institutions, religion, literature, and so on.

The plan of the book is simple. The four parts that precede the final synthesis proceed in order of explanatory importance. We begin with the "publicist" (or political scientist, as we would say today) who explained the idea of democracy. We then turn to the sociologist, who has more to tell us about the logic of collective action. But the key to the analysis, the heart of the work, is to be found in the moralist, the admirer of La Bruyère and the seventeenth-century theorists of "self-love" (*amour de soi*). Then, in part 4, we study Tocqueville "in literature," that is, immersed in the language, writing, and conversation from which he drew the nourishment he deemed vital to sustain his anxious attitude toward existence.[26] By weaving together the strands contributed by the publicist, the sociologist, the moralist, and the writer and by delving into Tocqueville's rivalry with Guizot and debt to Chateaubriand, we will take the measure of Tocqueville's central problem, which he approached from various angles: namely, the problem of *authority*, or, more precisely, of its collapse, as well as of the new *forms* that it was already beginning to adopt. Tocqueville pursued the question of authority in a number of areas apart from the state: religion, civil society, literature, and the family. And the fact that authority was his central problem explains why, upon returning from America, where he expressed various reservations about the subject, he decided on the phrase "democratic social state" to describe the whole range of life styles, social relations, and modes of thought that together give rise to an authority *external* to the political sphere.

The "authority of the social" is Tocqueville's idea, but it was Lamennais who revealed it to him. The specific type of horizontal authority that he discovered in the democratic social state encourages group cohesion and identity but tends to destroy individual autonomy, individual and national

---

[26] The term "literature" in this period covered everything from philosophy to history to oratory. The reference here to literature will serve to clarify Tocqueville's understanding of what he called (in his introduction to the 1835 volume) the "new science" that he believed indispensable for democracy not to succumb to its demons.

identity, and freedom of judgment. In this sense, the political scientist, the sociologist, the moralist, and the "lover of language" all described the same thing but as seen through different lenses: "democracy" as the creator of new forms of authority but also as the source of a novel form of despotism, all the more alarming because there is a risk that it will go unnoticed. Or, as Tocqueville memorably put it in 1835: "Democratic republics transform despotism into something immaterial."[27]

In the draft of a parliamentary speech from 1844, Tocqueville noted his deep conviction and revealed the theme that obsessed both the man and the author: "After this carnage of all authorities in society, in hierarchies, in the family, and in the world of politics, one cannot live without authority in the intellectual and moral world. If it is absent there, it must be found elsewhere, where I do not want it, either in a new hierarchy or in a great political power. If beliefs are abolished, soldiers and prisons will be needed."[28] The need for beliefs (an idea that Tocqueville shared with Lamennais[29]) contained serious ambiguities, however: if democracies adopted strong beliefs, would they therefore grant greater freedom to individuals? On this basis Tocqueville developed his thinking about religion in America, which he called a political force, in a country that had separated church and state. The question of authority was the key to Tocqueville's reflection on religion: "When no authority exists in matters of religion, any more than in political matters, men soon become frightened in the face of unlimited independence."[30]

The question of authority and its avatars is so important to Tocqueville that he returns to it in *The Ancien Régime and the Revolution* in his covert polemic against Guizot, the historian and talented author of *La civilisation en France* (see part 5 of the present work). Finally, the question of authority sheds light on a distinction that is no longer clear to us today but that was still a burning question for the descendants of the great Malesherbes, who died on the revolutionary scaffold: the difference, even among those who remained loyal to the monarchy, between the *culture of absolutism* (in which the king "rules" by divine right, as Bossuet told the Protestant Pierre Jurieu) and the vision of *aristocratic liberalism*. This difference is yet another key to the thought of Tocqueville the man and perhaps one of his reasons for writing *Democracy in America*.

[27] *DA* I, p. 352; AG, p. 292.

[28] *OC* III-2, p. 551. André Jardin, *Alexis de Tocqueville, 1805–1859* (Paris: Hachette "Pluriel," 1984), p. 348, erroneously links this to a passage in an article published in *Le Commerce*.

[29] I will show that three years later Tocqueville wrote a letter of praise to a correspondent, who was very likely Lamennais, to whom he had sent a copy of *Democracy in America* in 1835.

[30] *DA* II.1.5, p. 31; AG, p. 503.

Clearly, then, there is no need to erect a Great Wall of China between *Democracy in America* and *The Ancien Régime and the Revolution*, as many commentators do. By the time he wrote the later work, Tocqueville had come to understand his own thought better than he had understood it in his youth, but there was no break in continuity.

Nor do we need to organize our investigation in terms of the differences between "the two *Democracies*," a theme that has (rightly) preoccupied Tocqueville specialists.[31] These differences appear in a new light once we focus our inquiry on the question of authority. This leads to a full appreciation of the fact that Tocqueville believed in a novel form of despotism specific to democracy and thus was able to identify new ways for "society to act upon itself" (to use his formulation). He also believed that despotism might reemerge in history and bestow new legitimacy on the classic tutelary state.[32] The problem of fusion of old and new, or of the kinship of the two, points to an obscure, mysterious reality to which Tocqueville returns again and again. This obsession was an aspect of his personality and the source of a number of arguments that might otherwise be considered enigmatic.

Despite the variety of subjects treated in this book, the reader should not expect to find an analysis of Tocqueville's views on Algeria. His numerous notes, letters, reports, and speeches on the subject provide rich material for such a study, enough to merit a separate work. Similarly, it was necessary to exclude the work of Tocqueville and Gustave de Beaumont on prisons and penal colonies. Furthermore, in investigating the sources of *Democracy in America*, I systematically favored Tocqueville's French influences, including his contemporary contacts and readings as well as his hidden dialogues with the writers of the seventeenth and eighteenth centuries, and did not

[31] The debate originated early (in the 1840s) and was revived by Jean-Claude Lamberti's *Tocqueville et les deux démocraties* (Paris: PUF, 1983), translated by Arthur Goldhammer as *Tocqueville and the Two Democracies* (Cambridge: Harvard University Press, 1989), as well as by the earlier work of Anna-Maria Battista between 1971 and 1985. The question was to what extent Tocqueville saw a contrast between (French-style) revolutionary democracy and an American democracy devoid of revolutionary passions, as well as to understand why the vision of power at the end of *DA* II is very different from the view of popular sovereignty given in *DA* I. These questions are clearly discussed in Francesco De Sanctis, *Tocqueville. Sulla condizione moderna*, rev. ed. (Naples: Editoriale Scientifica, 2005), pp. 244–50 (originally published in 1993). De Sanctis offered a new analysis of these issues in *Tempo di democrazia. Alexis de Tocqueville* (Naples: Editoriale Scientifica, 2005), pp. 81–117.

[32] The problem of French "democracy" was that it had emerged from monarchy (allied with the Gallican church), as can still be seen in many arguments advanced today. In the United States, local and central governing authorities are (constitutionally) "vested with" or (as Locke says) "entrusted with" power. In France, the head of state "incarnates" something. In the former the law is supreme, whereas in the later it is the person in whom power is embodied. For Édouard Laboulaye, writing on the eve of Louis-Napoléon Bonaparte's coup d'état, this exemplified France's Catholic heritage.

examine his American sources. Nor did I consider the accuracy of his analyses of America. The focal point of this book, it bears repeating, is *Democracy in America*, illuminated by its relationship with *The Ancien Régime and the Revolution*; my working hypothesis was that this would be enough to reveal Tocqueville the man in his intellectual, psychological, and moral dimensions. The research necessary to accomplish this task has already absorbed many long years.

‰

Among the documents used, Tocqueville's unpublished correspondence (roughly 1,200 letters) deserves special mention. Françoise Mélonio was kind enough to share these letters with me prior to their publication in the Gallimard edition of the *Œuvres complètes*.[33] I also want to thank Yann-Arzel Marc, who invited me to join the Lanjuinais project, which will publish all of Tocqueville's correspondence with Jules Dufaure and Victor Lanjuinais. Two excerpts from the correspondence with Lanjuinais were taken from the archives of the château de Pont-Chevron, with the kind permission of Bernadette de La Rochefoucauld.

‰

I also wish to thank everyone who helped me to clarify my ideas about Tocqueville, starting with Francesco M. De Sanctis, who invited me to teach at the École Européenne of Naples (Institut Suor Orsola Benincasa), and whose many books on Tocqueville stimulated my thinking.[34] Given the partly historical nature of my research, I profited greatly from my dialogues with the illustrious Italian school of Tocqueville studies, which includes a number of scholars well versed in the history of French political culture: Vittorio de Caprariis, Anna-Maria Battista, the late Nicola Matteucci, Dino Cofrancesco, Mario Tesini, and Regina Pozzi, to name a few. Among American scholars, Melvin Richter, equally adept at interpreting Montesquieu and Tocqueville, encouraged me to pursue the comparison of the two theorists.

‰

Obviously a study like this one, based primarily on what is explicit and implicit in the text of *Democracy in America*, could not take account of the hundreds of commentaries that have been published in the New World as well as the Old. To have done so would have made for a very different kind

---

[33] These letters are cited as "unpublished correspondence."
[34] See the two works cited in note 31 above.

of book. The work of Tocqueville specialists will therefore be invoked only if truly necessary to shed light on some question treated here. It turned out to be more appropriate to discuss the thought of Alexandre Vinet or to analyze the interpreters of Chateaubriand, Sainte-Beuve, and the literary historians than to engage in dialogue with the many published studies of Tocqueville, some of which are quite brilliant yet do not discuss, say, Vinet or Chateaubriand or comment on Guizot's *Washington*, published in 1839.

Of course, none of this work would have seen the light of day without the encouragement of an understanding family, and first and foremost my wife.

BIBLIOGRAPHIC NOTE

Anyone looking for an introduction to Tocqueville's work may wish to consult the very fine anthology edited by Charlotte Manzini, *Qui êtes-vous Monsieur de Tocqueville?*[35] The most accurate biography of Tocqueville (despite a few errors) is that of André Jardin, cited above. The best introduction to Tocqueville in his time is still Françoise Mélonio's *Tocqueville et les Français.*[36] For penetrating overviews of Tocqueville's work, see the chapter devoted to the author in Raymond Aron's *Les Étapes de la pensée sociologique*[37] and François Furet's preface to the Garnier-Flammarion edition of *De la démocratie en Amérique.*[38]

---

[35] Charlotte Manzini, *Qui êtes-vous Monsieur de Tocqueville?* (Saint-Lô: Archives départementales de la Manche, 2005), published in connection with the exposition at the Archives départementales de la Manche curated by G. Désiré Dit Gosset, archivist and paleographer.

[36] Françoise Mélonio, *Tocqueville et les Français* (Paris: Aubier, 1993); in English, *Tocqueville and the French*, trans. Beth Raps (Charlottesville: University of Virginia Press, 1998).

[37] Raymond Aron, *Les Étapes de la pensée sociologique* (Paris: Gallimard/Tel, 1967); in English, *Main Currents of Sociological Thought*, vol. 1, trans. Brian Anderson (New Brunswick, NJ: Transaction Publishers, 1998).

[38] Antoine Rédier's odd collection, *Comme disait M. de Tocqueville* (Paris: Perrin, 1925), deserves to be reprinted because commentators have often quoted it out of context or inaccurately, although Rédier was one of the first to make use of Tocqueville's archives, which he began to organize. Thanks to the support of the Conseil Général of La Manche, we now possess a numerical catalog of Tocqueville's archives prepared by Vanessa Gendrin (Archives départementales de la Manche, 2007). These documents can also be consulted at the Archives Nationales in Paris (under a different system of classification).

PART ONE

What Did Tocqueville Mean by "Democracy"?

In France, M. de Tocqueville saw only the state; in America, it was always the individual that he found before him.

—Édouard Laboulaye, *L'État et ses limites*, 1863

The republic is everywhere, in the streets as in Congress. If something obstructs a public road, the neighbors will immediately establish a deliberative body.

—Franz Lieber, conversation with Tocqueville in Boston, 1831

People here enjoy the most insipid prosperity imaginable. Political life consists in debating whether a road should be repaired or a bridge built.

—Letter from America to Eugénie de Grancey, October 1831

MODERN DEMOCRACY, A POLYMORPHOUS NOTION

The term *democracy* has multiple meanings in Tocqueville's work, as many commentators have pointed out. James Schleifer has identified as many as eleven.[1] Tocqueville's apparent tolerance of ambiguity has to this day allowed countless interpreters to develop their own ideas about "democracy in Tocqueville" because the elasticity of the notion fosters the illusion of sharing the view of the author himself while encouraging interpretations that are to one degree or another anachronistic. A victim of his success (as great authors often are), Tocqueville is often assumed to have had prophetic powers that enabled him to speak of society as we know it. The principal purpose of this book is first to examine the ways in which Tocqueville shared the

---

[1] James Schleifer, *The Making of Tocqueville's Democracy in America* (Chapel Hill: University of North Carolina Press, 1980), pp. 263–74. Schleifer argues that Tocqueville was uncertain and did not always make a clear choice. One of the meanings he adopted, but not the most frequent, identified democracy with the industrial middle class. As we shall see, he shared this with his contemporary Michel Chevalier.

preoccupations of his time and only then to ask what comparisons with the present are justified.

To begin, it is important to note that Tocqueville shared his era's passionate interest in "democracy," which in Restoration France meant the *civil equality* established by the Revolution and the Civil Code, as well as the increased *prosperity* of the social strata that had recently gained access to power or at any rate hoped someday to own enough property to qualify to vote (under the so-called censitary system), in anticipation of which they sought to influence public opinion.[2] Today it requires effort to understand how the leaders of the Restoration, in Tocqueville's youth, could have spoken of "democracy" at a time when the institutions of government established by the Charter of 1814 were anything but democratic: among these were a divine right monarchy, a lower chamber elected by voters subject to strict property qualifications, a hereditary upper chamber, and so forth. When, for example, Royer-Collard ironically adopted the comte de Serre's formula, "Democracy's cup runneth over," he meant that the *middle classes* had transformed the political landscape: "In contrast to aristocracy, or merely compared with it, I agree that democracy's cup runneth over in a France shaped by events and centuries. . . . Wealth has brought leisure; leisure has brought enlightenment; independence has given rise to patriotism. The middle classes have begun to take up public affairs. . . . They know that these are their affairs."[3] Here, "democracy" is a metonymy for a rising social group, whereas "aristocracy" refers to a stably situated group that had been deprived since the French Revolution of the lever of *privilege* in both civil society and institutions.[4]

After the revolution of 1830, Royer-Collard returned to this theme to indicate how history had moved still further in this direction: "Ten years ago, when my noble friend M. de Serre proclaimed that 'democracy's cup runneth over,' he was still referring only to society. . . . Today it is true of

[2] Writing to his cousin Camille d'Orglandes shortly before completing *DA* I, Tocqueville observed that democracy for him was not the republic but "a state of society"—an important early formulation—tending toward "absolute equality of conditions" and such that "everyone will participate in affairs to one degree or another" (November 29, 1834), in Tocqueville, *Lettres choisies. Souvenirs*, ed. Françoise Mélonio and Laurence Guellec (Paris: Gallimard, 2003), p. 310. This very important letter was first published by mistake in the correspondence with Louis de Kergorlay, *OC* XIII-1, pp. 373–75, an error that was pointed out by the editors of *Lettres choisies* and by Jean-Louis Benoît, *Tocqueville. Un destin paradoxal* (Paris: Bayard, 2005), p. 16, n. 19.

[3] Royer-Collard, speech on freedom of the the press, January 22, 1822. Baron de Barante, *La Vie politique de M. Royer-Collard* (Paris: Didier, 1861), 2:134.

[4] We will see later that various other writers employed the same metonymy, in particular the Saint-Simonian Michel Chevalier.

government."[5] Indeed, the issue of the day was the continuation of hereditary peerage. Despite Guizot's efforts, the Orleanist government could not maintain a distinction that was clearly associated with the perpetuation of great families exempt from the general rule of equality: the last aristocratic institution therefore fell, although the king continued to appoint peers, thereby maintaining a façade of continuity. As social equality increased because of equality before the law, political institutions also became more egalitarian.

Between 1815 and 1848, in other words, everybody talked about democracy but in a rather special sense that is no longer familiar to us. First, it was a question of equality before the law, created by the Revolution: civil equality rather than political equality.[6] Second, and relatedly, it referred to the rising power of the bourgeoisie, to the "middle classes" and the values they represented. Third, it designated a regime type, "democratic government," but as a historical effect and not a theoretical prerequisite. Fourth and last came the question of suffrage, and a fortiori its universal extension, generally advanced as a possible outcome but not a historically necessary or normatively desirable one. This, more or less, was the range of meanings of the word "democracy" with which Tocqueville the author was confronted.

Tocqueville reworked an idea that everyone was using but did not add to it anything truly new. Observing the American spectacle, he proposed to distinguish two different and often distinct aspects of democracy: the democratic regime aspect, which was a question of politics, and the social or sociological aspect. Modern democracy requires certain mores, manners,[7] and opinions as well as a certain perception of citizens by one another.[8] Tocqueville applied the term "democratic social state" to this second aspect, which he regarded as essential for equality.[9] In fact, Tocqueville's distinction

---

[5] Royer-Collard, speech of 1831, Barante, *La Vie politique*, 2:469. It was now a case of "royal democracy," the orator asserted in the same speech.

[6] In 1840 the constitutionalist and economist Pellegrino Rossi reviewed *DA* II. He said that democracy was a "social fact" and added that "democracy is civil equality, the same law for everyone" but not material equality or "equality of conditions." He criticized Tocqueville for perpetuating this confusion. *Revue des deux mondes*, September 15, 1840.

[7] For Tocqueville, a reader of Montesquieu, manners are the visible expression in society of mores, which are more in the nature of implicit and acquired behaviors.

[8] As usual, there is a certain vagueness in Tocqueville's ideas. He ascribes a fairly extensive meaning to the word "mores," for example: "But all these habits, opinions, usages, and beliefs—what are they, if not what I have been calling mores?" *DA* I, p. 416; AG, p. 350.

[9] There was nothing original about the idea of "social state." It can be found in Benjamin Constant, *Mémoires sur les Cent Jours*, 1829; in Guizot, *Essais sur l'histoire de France*, 1823, and *Histoire de la civilisation*; in Lullin de Châteauvieux in 1822, in Saint-Simon, etc. According to the Frantext database, "*democratic social state*" is Tocqueville's own invention (I thank Marie-France Piguet for this information). In fact, however, I have found the phrase in Bonald's writing as early as 1810 and in Guizot's *Washington*, 1839.

reinforced the well-known liberal distinction between civil society and government.

Tocqueville was more original in the status that he granted to the norm of equality and the effects it engendered. Instead of treating it as a fixed and purely abstract category (originating in law), he offered a profound analysis of the *representation of self and others* that equality fostered. In other words, he looked at the range of human emotional relationships that led to competition and cooperation. We will return to this because Tocqueville's idea of equality contains a number of complex subtleties.[10] For now, let me say simply that, for Tocqueville, democratic equality is not a de facto state: it is at once a historical dynamic, an internal motivation for action, and a collective norm. Thus, in the vision proper to the democratic world, the comparative adjective "more" (in the sense of greater wealth or greater achievement) became an *imperative* if man wished to move closer to an equality that was always receding into the distance.

Equality is therefore the perpetual motion machine (*perpetuum mobile*) of postaristocratic and postrevolutionary society. Hence "democracy"[11] can be seen as both a way of life and a mode of thought, or, if you will, a worldview, because democratic "thought" is not necessarily conscious of itself as theory or doctrine. The egalitarian aspiration becomes "natural."[12] "Democracy" is both a way of life in society and a regime based on popular sovereignty. What is more, the primary democratic passion—to achieve equality—can be furthered by a *despotic* regime. In Tocqueville's eyes, the suppression of liberty was quite compatible with a "social" democracy—as Louis-Napoleon's coup of 1851 would prove (to his chagrin). That is why, in the wake of that event, he threw himself into studying the origins of the French Revolution. In the foreword to *The Ancien Régime and the Revolution* (1856), he reaffirmed what he had said twenty years earlier about the possible alliance of equality with despotism: "Democratic societies that are not free[13] may yet be rich,

[10] These will emerge from our study of his relation to the seventeenth-century moralists in part 3.

[11] I use quotation marks henceforth to indicate that I am speaking of Tocqueville's concept of democracy.

[12] As we will see later, to the extent that equality sanctified majorities in the age of universal suffrage, it became almost synonymous with left-wing ideology. The Right believes that inequalities necessarily exist and always will exist on various scales and in different areas. The primary concern of the Left is "to combat inequality," whereas the Right focuses its attention elsewhere. We will therefore need to clarify Tocqueville's position. The dividing line between Right and Left was described in these terms by Le Brun de Charmettes in *Épître sur le libéralisme* in his 1831 anthology, which is reproduced in appendix 4 to the French edition of the present work.

[13] To today's reader, this formulation might seem contradictory, but it was perfectly acceptable to Tocqueville's contemporaries. He publicized it more than any of them.

refined, ornate, and even magnificent, powerful by dint of their homogeneous mass," but they will not have "great citizens, much less a great people," and "the common level of hearts and minds will steadily diminish as long as equality and despotism remain conjoined."[14]

Thus despotism is not the opposite of democracy but one of its possible avatars (in the Hindu sense of the word). It feeds on the quest for *material* pleasures (or comfort and consumption, in today's terms) that democracy inevitably encourages in the form of commerce and industry. Indeed, "it is of the very essence of despotism" to encourage and expand "the desire to enrich oneself at all cost, that taste for affairs, the love of profit, the search for well-being."[15] Ultimately, despotism encourages democratic individualism "because it deprives citizens of all common passion and mutual need.... It confines them, as it were, behind the walls of the private."[16] Indeed, nothing resembled free democracy more than despotic democracy. In the manuscript, Tocqueville wrote the following passage, which he later erased (but we can read it in Eduardo Nolla's edition): "Democracy is a manner of being of society. Popular sovereignty [is] a form of [or the essence of] government. They are by no means inseparable, because democracy is even more compatible with despotism than with liberty."[17]

The preface to *The Ancien Régime*, in which Tocqueville pointed out that he had been right in 1835 when he foresaw the danger inherent in modern democracy, reveals the complexity of his thought.[18] There is complexity in the idea of democracy (which is at once a psychological and a sociological reality and a form of power) and complexity of the democratic forces, which are sometimes egalitarian and hostile to liberty and sometimes liberal and apt to moderate the impulses of collective opinion. There is in any case a danger of calling "democratic" any behavior or cultural phenomenon that emerges in modern society—a danger that Tocqueville does not always

---

[14] Tocqueville, *ARR, OC* II-1, p. 75. This passage from 1856 follows the introduction to *DA* I (1835).

[15] Ibid., p. 74.

[16] Ibid. It was not without reason that Tocqueville applied to despotic depoliticization what Royer-Collard said about the press in a regime of liberty: private life must be "walled off." The formula, which had become famous, was boldly stood on its head by Tocqueville: Bonaparte or any other popular despot confined all the forces of individuality behind the walls of the private.

[17] Nolla I, p. 38; JS, p. 76.

[18] There is room for debate, however, about the identification after the fact of the Second Empire with the "tutelary power" predicted at the end of *DA* I. This issue was in fact the subject of a debate between Melvin Richter and Claude Lefort at the Centre Raymond Aron in the 1990s, in which I was fortunate to participate at the invitation of François Furet. See Melvin Richter, "Tocqueville and French Nineteenth-Century Conceptualization of the Two Bonapartes and Their Empires," in *Dictatorship in Theory and History*, ed. P. Baehr and M. Richter (Washington, DC: German Historical Institute, 2004).

escape in *Democracy in America*. When you try to grasp too many things at once, you come away with nothing very specific.

⊗⊙

If we really want to see what struck the young Tocqueville on his journey to America (forcefully enough to produce genuine illumination), we must study the implicit and explicit comparison with France in the first *Democracy*. We must attend carefully to what he says about local democracy, especially in the New England town,[19] which combined—in Tocqueville's own terms—popular sovereignty, administrative decentralization, and democratic mores and behavior. For the French reader, the critical force of this example derived from the way in which *popular sovereignty* was organized and practiced daily at the local level. In fact, what Tocqueville was attacking with muffled vehemence was the French conception of the state, which had confiscated the popular sovereignty so often proclaimed since 1789.

This will enable us to clarify one aspect of "democracy" according to Tocqueville, namely, its connection with decentralization. We will then turn to other aspects, such as democratic religion (chapter 2) and the taste for material pleasures that inevitably accompanies the development of democracy (chapter 3). In each case, we adopt the method of internal interpretation (how coherent is the argument and the text?) and comparison (to which other authors or currents of thought does Tocqueville refer in developing his arguments about decentralization, democratic religion, and material pleasure?). We will also describe in broad strokes the *reactions* of these other writers when *Democracy in America* appeared and attacked them without naming them. Tocqueville's thought is inseparable from his intellectual and political strategy and perhaps from his ideological strategy: he saw himself as a teacher and an engaged citizen who aspired to run for office, as he did not hesitate to admit once the book was published.

---

[19] [In *Democracy in America* Tocqueville employed the English word "township" as the translation of the French *commune*. Most translators have followed Tocqueville's usage, but as I explained in my translation of *Democracy in America*, the correct designation for the local government entity in New England is "town," not "township." Indeed, Tocqueville took most of his information about the structure of local government from a book entitled *The Town Officer*. For that reason, I prefer to use "town."—TRANS.]

Attacking the French Tradition

<small>POPULAR SOVEREIGNTY REDEFINED IN AND
THROUGH LOCAL LIBERTIES</small>

The Gap between France and America

When Tocqueville decided to introduce the United States to the French
public, he had no choice but to begin with what had been first the sphinx
of the French Revolution and then the nightmare of the moderates: popular
sovereignty. The fourth chapter of book 1 of the first volume of *Democracy
in America* was devoted to this overwhelming idea: "Any discussion of the
political laws of the United States has to begin with the dogma of popular
sovereignty."[1] The word "dogma" indicated how the question was to be approached. But this particular dogma gave rise to two very different religions,
as noted by one of Tocqueville's readers, Édouard Laboulaye, who taught a
course on the history of the United States at the Collège de France.[2] While
"the people reign over the American political world as God reigns over the
universe,"[3] the same was not true of France. It would be too simple to say that
the difference stemmed from the difference between a republic and a monarchy (the so-called July Monarchy of Louis-Philippe). Tocqueville knew
French history and knew that popular sovereignty had been brandished as
a banner by various forms of strong state: the Convention, the Terror, the
seizure of power by the men of Brumaire, and Napoleon's authoritarian rule.
The restored Bourbons had maintained administrative centralization, and
their Orleanist successors did little after 1830 to make government more
responsive to local concerns. The state therefore maintained its ascendancy
over the nominally sovereign people.

---

[1] *DA* I, p. 117; AG, p. 62.
[2] Édouard Laboulaye, *Histoire des États-Unis* (Paris: Charpentier, 1855–66), 3 vols. Quotes are from
the fifty-seventh edition, published in 1870.
[3] *DA* I, p. 120; AG, p. 65.

Napoleon is particularly significant in this regard because he claimed legitimacy as the representative of the sovereign people, in particular thanks to his use of the plebiscite. Later in French history, the popular sovereign was transformed into the *sovereign representative*, sometimes in the form of an elected assembly, sometimes as incarnated in the person of an individual in whom the nation saw its unity reflected. Despite the differences among them, Napoleon, Napoleon III, Thiers, and de Gaulle all fulfilled this role. It was in the apex of the pyramid of state that the people *recognized* themselves as sovereign, acknowledged and consulted as such. This way of thinking dated back to 1789, when an assembly of the common people declared itself first the National Assembly and then the Constituent Assembly. The assembly claimed legitimacy by proclaiming the sovereignty of the nation (as against that of the king) and by portraying the nation as one and indivisible (despite differences among corporations, privileges, the distinction between *pays d'État*, with their own representative "estates," and *pays d'élection*, without them, etc.). The united nation *fictively* sat on the benches of the assembly, where it embodied the national will represented nowhere else. The "general will" resided in the representative body, not outside it. The act of voting created the national will but did not express it.[4]

The *mystical* operation that allowed each deputy "to represent the entire nation" (as the Constitution of 1791 put it) and that gave rise to the general will within the walls of parliament transformed the sovereignty of the people into a sovereignty of the representative body and therefore of the state. As Abbé Sieyès put it on September 7, 1789, the people exists as political reality and can act (that is, legislate) only through its assembly, its representatives.

Sieyès's doctrine imparted a certain stability to this idea (which owed a great deal to the Church),[5] but it soon gave rise to repeated conflicts between the "will of the people" and representatives deemed to be "unfaithful." Competition to see who was the more authentic "representative" of the popular will marked all the challenges raised against the Constituent and Legislative Assemblies and the Convention. Between 1789 and 1793 the Jacobins took advantage of these conflicts, taking to heart Rousseau's celebrated words about the nonrepresentability of the general will, which resides in the individual citizen and in the citizens' assembly but not in a body of delegates speaking in the people's name.

---

[4] Again, only in so-called second-degree assemblies, according to the Constitution of 1791.

[5] The idea of representation as *metamorphosis* and source of sovereignty is also found in Hobbes's *Leviathan*. See Lucien Jaume, *Hobbes et l'État représentatif moderne* (Paris: PUF, 1996), and "La théorie de la 'personne fictive' dans le *Léviathan* de Hobbes," *Revue française de science politique* 33, 6 (December 1983): 1009–35.

The conflict between represented sovereignty and inalienable sovereignty has been responsible for various oscillations or swerves in French political history.[6] In Tocqueville's youth, "the sovereignty of the people" was a resounding battle cry: if it were to be realized in the streets, assemblies, or political clubs, would not the Revolution be reignited? As François Furet has shown, moderates throughout the nineteenth century were perpetually asking themselves how the Revolution could be stopped.

When Tocqueville sat down to write his masterpiece, the French faced two or three major problems linked to this historic conflict: (1) the fear of intermediate bodies, which were seen as a permanent invitation to revert to the corporatist society of the past, encouraging both the Church (via the law of congregations) and socialist agitation (worker defense); (2) the difficulty of conceiving popular sovereignty from below, as embedded in society and reflective of regional diversity (indeed, both the citizen and the political representative were highly abstract concepts owing to the requirements that had to be met in order to "raise oneself to the level of the general interest"); and (3) the question of executive power, a perpetual problem for republicans because of Louis XVI's failure to lead the Revolution and then the drama of the regicide, which left republicans saddled with obsessive fears that something like a monarchy might somehow be resurrected. To see this, one has only to glance at the debates that took place in the constituent assemblies of 1793, 1848, and 1871–75.

Tocqueville knew that these three problems were linked in French history, and he also knew that America had offered a novel solution by combining local government with federalism and administrative decentralization. Popular sovereignty was not embodied in the president of the United States, who was not a monarch (or even a republican monarch), because constitutional checks and balances subjected the unity of the political will to the corrective of moderation as virtue and negotiation as practice. Nor was popular sovereignty embodied in Congress, because the American representative was neither an undifferentiated *image* of the states (in the Senate) nor an image of the nation as a whole (in the House of Representatives). Popular sovereignty remained with the people. Hence to observe it one had to go to the base of society, the New England town, and look at the very concrete issues dealt with at that level (land use, law and order, education). The town was the primitive fact, the basic "cell" of the organism, as Tocqueville sometimes called it. It was in the first instance a collection of families and therefore

---

[6]These seem likely to be revived today. See my article "La représentation: une fiction malmenée," *Pouvoirs*, no. 120 (2006): 5–16.

possessed a natural and prepolitical reality.[7] In addition, it helped American independence to flourish: "Then came the American Revolution. The dogma of popular sovereignty emerged from the towns and took possession of the government.... It became the law of laws."[8]

Owing to this dual origin (quasi-natural primitiveness and revolutionary genesis), popular sovereignty in the United States worked not as in France, from the top down (and for the benefit of the state), but from the bottom up: "Sometimes the people as a body make the laws as in Athens; at other times deputies created by universal suffrage represent them and act in their name, under their almost immediate surveillance."[9]

Tocqueville was very struck by the fact that the New England town was governed by a town meeting rather than a council. Citizens were not represented but deliberated directly on the issues of the day.[10] This led him to a general proposition that implicitly condemned the way in which the French organized their political life: "Without local institutions, a nation may give itself a free government, but it will not have a free spirit."[11] Indeed, the French would debate decentralization interminably and endlessly discuss the advantages of "self-government" along English or American lines, but they would continue to worry about the fragmentation of sovereignty that might ensue. Tocqueville himself, in 1848, did nothing to push the issue in the National Assembly—a silence that astonished observers at the time.

In one of his manuscripts, Tocqueville observed that "in our minds, the word 'decentralization' stands for nothing but a host of petty sovereigns."[12] It was indeed a question of representations: the obsession with federalism dated back to the spring of 1789.[13] Antifederalist rhetoric would later legitimate

---

[7] This idea was common in nineteenth-century France, as we shall see, not only among traditionalist writers but also in the work of Royer-Collard. It was responsible for certain nostalgic tendencies, even among republicans and socialists, to say nothing of liberals like Benjamin Constant.

[8] *DA* I, p. 118; AG, p. 63. In *ARR* Tocqueville wrote: "Transported at one stroke far from feudalism and left as its own absolute master, the rural parish of the Middle Ages became the New England town." *OC* II-1, p. 120. The same passage shows how he discovered in the archives of an *intendance* the parish of the Ancien Régime, the portrait of which suddenly reminded him of features of the American town that he had observed twenty years earlier: civil and political life was played out in communal assemblies and not through the mediation of representatives.

[9] Ibid., p. 119; AG, p. 64.

[10] Historians have pointed out that the New England town of the 1830s did not really correspond to the French commune; in area it was closer to what the French call a *canton*.

[11] Ibid., p. 123; AG, p. 68.

[12] Nolla I, p. 79, n. e; JS, p. 164.

[13] Or, to take a somewhat later example, consider this speech by Sieyès on September 7, 1789: "I still maintain that France is not and cannot be a *democracy*. It must not become a *federal state* composed of a multitude of republics.... France is and must be *a single whole*, subject in all its parts to a common law and administration." *Archives parlementaires*, 1st series, 8:594. Emphasis in original.

the frontal assault first on the Girondins (who were attacked on May 31 and June 2, 1793) and then on the Terror (September–December 1793). But the Girondins were by no means federalists.[14] The real issue was the (largely imaginary) obsession with the idea that France might fracture as well as the fear that the Third Estate might lose the *unity* that its leaders needed in order to abolish privileged corporations. In France antifederalism and antipluralism both stemmed in large part from the monarchical and Catholic mindset, which the new ruling class refocused onto its aristocratic enemy.[15]

Under these conditions, the decentralization of power, even to decide issues of purely local interest, could be seen as inciting local resistance to Paris and encouraging "the parochial spirit" against the national spirit. Indeed, the very idea of local interests was problematic for major figures. When the Chamber of Deputies debated the municipal law in 1831, Guizot said: "Do not think, Gentlemen, that it is easy to separate local interests from general interests; this distinction is never as real as some imagine."[16] So when Benjamin Constant praised "municipal power" as a fourth branch of government, he was actually taking the risk of lending support to traditionalists and legitimists,[17] such as Joseph Fiévée, a friend of the Ultra party and for a while a candidate to lead it.[18] Almost until the adoption of the municipal law of 1884, there was a persistent idea in France of local government as part of the *administrative order*, so that the mayor was first of all an official of the executive branch, like the prefect. Tocqueville, writing about local government in the United States, wrote that "the [federal] state governs and does not administer,"[19] whereas in France the first move was to distinguish the administrative from the political and then to place both under the control of the state. From the time of Napoleon on, mayors were appointed by the central government, and their primary function was to enforce national laws and regulations rather than to represent local interests. In 1791 and Year III

---

[14] See Lucien Jaume, "Les Girondins: un conflit véritable, une interprétation faussée," in *Décentraliser en France*, ed. C. Boutin and F. Rouvillois (Paris: De Guibert, 2003), pp. 33–48.

[15] "One king, one law, one faith": this principle, which symbolized the attitude that led to the expulsion of the Protestants, was revived in the Terror. See Lucien Jaume, *Le Discours jacobin et la démocratie* (Paris: Fayard, 1989).

[16] François Guizot, *Histoire parlementaire de France* (Paris: Michel Lévy, 1863), 1:215. The same critique can be found in François Burdeau's analysis of countless debates about decentralization, *Liberté, libertés locales chéries!* (Paris: Cujas, 1983).

[17] Benjamin Constant, *Principes de politique* (1815), chap. 12.

[18] On Fiévée's bid for the leadership, see Lucien Jaume, "Questions d'interprétation: le texte comme producteur d'idéologie," in *L'Architecture du droit. Mélanges en l'honneur de Michel Troper* (Paris: Economica, 2006), pp. 519–37. See also Lucien Jaume, "Réflexion sur le sens et l'idéologie dans les textes d'intervention politique. Le cas Fiévée en 1815," *Revista de Estudios Politicos*, no. 134 (December 2006).

[19] *DA* I, p. 147; AG, p. 92. This was Fiévée's main theme among the Ultras of the Restoration.

there was lively debate about the dual role of "local administrators," as one said at the time. In 1841 Louis Blanc jestingly referred to the mayor as "a hermaphroditic power."[20]

For Tocqueville, the New England town represented a different vision. Rather than distinguish between the administrative and the political, the Americans availed themselves of a subtle "subsidiarity" between the private and the public, or between particular, local interests and general, national interests.[21] In his eyes, local democracy was a *school* in which the subject was political liberty: "Local institutions not only teach *the art of using noble political freedom* but also instill *a true taste* for liberty."[22] Like John Stuart Mill somewhat later, Tocqueville believed that when neighbors developed the habit of deliberating and negotiating with one another, they would also develop the ability and desire to take a larger view of politics: local democracy[23] could thus provide a way into political responsibility, collective decision making, and acceptance of majority rule. Tocqueville also insisted on local government as a form of civic education: "Local institutions are to liberty what elementary schools are to knowledge; they bring it within reach of the people."[24]

It was this idea of civic education on different levels that led Tocqueville to the distinction between political centralization, which he believed to be essential, and administrative centralization, which he believed sapped the spirit of liberty. Insofar as popular sovereignty was desirable, it would inevitably have to be "dispersed"[25] across pieces of the territory. There was nothing to fear in plural diversity if order was assured locally and political centralization was maintained. Yet in making this point, Tocqueville was aware of challenging the entire French conception of administrative centralization, which he would continue to attack in later years.[26] But what did "the state" mean on

---

[20] Quoted in Louis Blanc, *Questions d'aujourd'hui et de demain* (Paris: Dentu, 1873), 1:310.

[21] Here I draw on an idea of Stefano Mannoni in his excellent *Une et indivisible. Storia dell'accentramento amministrativo in Francia* (Milan: Giuffré, 1996), 2:217–24.

[22] Nolla I, p. 79, n. b. Emphasis in original.

[23] In France, on February 27, 2002, the government of Lionel Jospin adopted a law entitled "La démocratie de proximité," which established deliberative procedures in towns and neighborhoods to assist mayors in their decisions but not actually to vote new laws. The term seems apt to describe Tocqueville's thinking.

[24] *DA* I, p. 123; AG, p. 68.

[25] The French word is *éparpillé*, which Tocqueville used frequently: "Much artful care has been taken in American towns to . . . . *disperse* power in order to interest as many people as possible in public affairs." Ibid., p. 131; AG, p. 76. When we look in part 4 at Tocqueville's analysis of democratic literature, we will find him using this word again in association with what is vital in democracy.

[26] Especially in connection with the handling of conflicts between citizens and the administration. In 1856 *The Ancien Régime and the Revolution* renewed the battle launched by *Democracy in America* in

the other side of the Atlantic? "What most strikes the European who travels through the United States is the absence of what we would call government or administration.... Things seem to be in motion all around you, yet the force that drives them is not apparent. The hand that guides the social machinery constantly evades detection."[27]

A Frenchman, Tocqueville continued, expects to see "only one administrative official, the mayor," but he would find "in the New England town ... some nineteen town officials." He would also expect someone like a prefect to supervise local affairs on behalf of the central administration, but in America one sees "scarcely any trace of administrative hierarchy."[28] The conclusion of this passage is surprising ("Hence there is no central hub toward which the spokes of administrative power converge"), but it introduces a lengthy reflection on *judicial* power in the United States—a power that in Tocqueville's eyes was both judicial and administrative and therefore unacceptable in postrevolutionary France. Note, too, that in his manuscripts and correspondence, Tocqueville voiced worries about the mixing of functions.[29]

⊘⊘

The description of the American system in terms of towns and counties is one of Tocqueville's bravura passages. We will return to it later because it was in the self-governed town that Tocqueville saw the political, the moral, and the sociological coming together: this was the "living democracy" that he promised to show the French to make them think. Remember that in his eyes America was an example but not a model: he did not believe for a second that American institutions (such as federalism, judicial power, and perhaps decentralization) could be transplanted to French soil. Indeed, mores, history, and the "social constitution" (of which I will say more in a moment) were

---

1835 and carried on throughout the July Monarchy and Second Republic. See Jaume, *L'Individu effacé ou le paradoxe du libéralisme français*, pp. 367–79. Tocqueville attacked the special status and protective immunities granted to the Conseil d'État and, through it, to functionaries, who could not be taken to court without the prior agreement of the administrative judge; the Conseil d'État is the sole judge in the French administration.

[27] *DA* I, p. 134; AG, p. 79.

[28] Turning the tables, it is amusing to read the observations of an American in Paris in 1847: "In the constant surveillance of such a police force there is something incompatible with an American's idea of freedom. Yet at the same time there is a subtle and hidden charm in sensing the presence of security and order: an infallible and almost perfect order. This, in large part, accounts for the luxury of Parisian life, this calm in the midst of so much gaiety." Quoted in Berthier de Sauvigny, *Vus par les voyageurs américains, 1814–1848* (Paris: Flammarion, 1982).

[29] See, for example, *DA* I, Pléiade edition, vol. 2, n. a on p. 88, text on p. 963 (from Tocqueville's manuscript).

the primary factors, more powerful than laws.[30] American social philosophy, based on "self-interest properly understood," social relations among groups and families as a check on individualism, and the very structure of the political sphere (collective action without the state as the central axis) all converge in Tocqueville's text on one and the same reality: local life.

Tocqueville's Portrait of the New England Town: Passions, Interests, and Authority

Tocqueville's concept of local democracy was rather different from today's idea of "participatory democracy." And when politicians today speak of "decentralization," what they have in mind is usually to fortify their local electoral base.[31] For Tocqueville, by contrast, the local was the essence of the *democratic* spirit: "In the United States, therefore, local liberty is a consequence of the dogma of popular sovereignty itself."[32]

Yet Tocqueville also believed that the natural tendency of popular sovereignty was to increase centralization. He therefore set out to show (1) how popular sovereignty could exist in the routine tasks of local life, and (2) how what the French called "administrative" decentralization would serve to increase popular sovereignty defined in these pragmatic, quotidian terms.[33]

In the first volume of *Democracy in America*, Tocqueville combined the political and psychosociological points of view in his discussion of the town, while in the second volume, at the heart of a key chapter on social morality and self-interest properly understood, he returned to the town as model. It is impossible to understand his use of the concept of "self-interest properly understood"—a sort of disinterested self-interest—without relating it to "local liberties" and the "local spirit" (to borrow his terms): "Thus local liberties, in consequence of which large numbers of citizens come to value the affection of their neighbors and relatives, regularly bring men together, despite the instincts that divide them, and force them to help one another."[34]

The theme of obligatory togetherness (in answer to the great modern anxiety about the absence of any bond to hold together what Norbert Elias

---

[30] We will return to the summary given in *DA* I.2.9.

[31] France officially "decentralized" its 1958 constitution with the constitutional law of March 28, 2003.

[32] *DA* I, p. 128; AG, p. 173.

[33] Note that the term "decentralization" did not exist in America. According to the *Dictionary of American English* (Chicago, 1938), it did not appear until 1872, although "centralism" and "centralization" did exist as early as the 1830s. Used in French as early as 1835, the term was accepted by Littré in 1877 and by the *Dictionnaire de l'Académie* in 1878.

[34] *DA* II, p. 133; AG, p. 592.

called a society of individuals) was first treated in volume 1 of *Democracy in America* in the chapter on "the local spirit in New England." In Europe, Tocqueville tells us, by which he means France, leaders do not know how to create local spirit: "Their fear is that to allow towns to be strong and independent would be to divide social power and lay the state open to anarchy. Deprive a town of strength and independence, however, and its inhabitants cease to be citizens; they are reduced to mere subjects of an administration."[35] France, where mayors still address citizens as "*mes chers administrés*," is clearly the country he has in mind. What makes a citizen? "Civic spirit," Tocqueville tells us. And civic spirit is a product of obligatory togetherness: the state is remote, "obscure and tranquil," the federal government even more remote. Hence *ambition* must satisfy itself locally. As a result, self-interest, social prestige, and the acquisition of legitimate authority can go together: "It is in the town, amidst the ordinary relationships of life, that the desire for esteem, the needs stemming from vital local interests, and the thirst for power and notoriety come to be concentrated; these passions, which so often roil society, change in character when they find a vent close to home, in the bosom, as it were, of the family."[36]

This passage should be read carefully. Contemporaries might have taken it as coming from the pen of a traditionalist or at any rate a legitimist writer: local government, family life, passionate yet innocent activity—the usual litany.[37] As we will see, Tocqueville borrowed these themes and applied them, in altered form, to democratic and republican America. In a sort of pastoral meditation à la Rousseau, Bonald praised the French commune in 1816 as an "asylum for naïve mores, innocent labor, and frugal living."[38] He, too, saw

[35] *DA* I, pp. 130–31; AG, p. 75.

[36] Ibid., p. 131; AG, p. 75 (translation modified). To his father, Tocqueville wrote from America that "that is how they made the republic practical. Individual ambition finds within reach everywhere a small focus where it can act without danger to the state." *OC* XIV, pp. 113–14. See the excellent overview of Tocqueville's view of the local in Agnès Antoine, *L'Impensé de la démocratie* (Paris: Fayard, 2003), pp. 96–100.

[37] In the letter to his father cited in the previous note, Tocqueville reproached the Bourbons for failing in 1814 to seize the opportunity to introduce local government, as Joseph Fiévée had done in his pamphlets on decentralization. In the same year, Tocqueville argued to Kergorlay that "we are headed toward unlimited democracy" and that Louis XVIII's big mistake was to enshrine aristocratic institutions such as the peerage and royal administration in "political laws" while leaving "in civil laws a democratic principle so potent that it inevitably destroyed in short order the foundations of the structure he was trying to create." *OC* XIII-1, p. 233. Regarding the Bourbons, he added that "the local and departmental system should immediately have attracted their full attention" (p. 234). All these points (along with opposition to the Civil Code, mentioned in the same letter) were the specialty of Montlosier during the Restoration. For Chateaubriand, Montlosier was a liberal who saw the world through a Gothic window. Inwardly Tocqueville was not far from sharing this view when he set out on his journey in 1831.

[38] Debate of December 30, 1816, on the electoral law. *Archives parlementaires*, 2nd series, 17:770.

the commune as preventing modern individualism from fully blossoming because it was "the first and most natural of corporations."

By contrast, Tocqueville argued that sociability and the social spirit could flourish in the New England town because individual selfishness was cunningly channeled. When a citizen assumed an official role in his town, he experienced personal satisfaction. "There are also a great many offices, and a host of different officials, each of whom represents, within a limited sphere, the powerful corporation in whose name they all act. How many men thereby exploit the power of the town for their own benefit and take an interest in public affairs for reasons of their own!"[39]

Self-interest was not exclusively self-directed: one served oneself, but by serving the collectivity. This would later draw an angry reaction from the republican Charles Dupont-White, who opposed decentralization precisely because it gave free rein to local wheelers and dealers.[40] True, local independence was good for the "education of universal suffrage," but it was a "corrupt education, teaching the profits of power and the exploitation of sovereignty as a way of raking off gains."[41]

Tocqueville, probably drawing on Benjamin Constant's characterization of patriotism as primarily "a love of localities,"[42] argued that local implantation was the true basis of patriotism. The idea of a fatherland cannot thrive in an abstract symbol, and the general is built up from the particular. This point is central to Tocqueville's thinking about "democracy": it is in the realm of local liberties that he situates the emotional bond, the palpable connection *between the particular interest and the general interest*, which was Rousseau's great question and which remained an insoluble problem not only for the Jacobins but also for modern republicans.[43] Returning to the question in the second volume of *Democracy in America*, Tocqueville drove the point home: "Hence if the goal is to foster the interest of citizens in the public good and make them see that they need one another constantly in order to produce

[39] *DA* I, p. 131; AG, p. 76.

[40] On Dupont-White, see Sudhir Hazareesingh, *Intellectual Founders of the Republic* (Oxford: Oxford University Press, 2001).

[41] Charles Dupont-White, *La Liberté politique*, 1864, quoted in Mélonio, *Tocqueville et les Français*, p. 209.

[42] See Constant, *Principes de politique*, chap. 13. There is also a celebrated passage in Constant's pamphlet *De l'esprit de conquête et de l'usurpation:* "It is by defending the rights of parts (*fractions*) of the nation that one defends the rights of the nation as a whole, because it is apportioned among each of its parts." See part 1, chap. 13, "De l'esprit de conquête."

[43] See my discussion of the "obligation to be congruent with the general interest" in *Le Discours jacobin et la démocratie*, esp. pp. 203–9 (on the meaning ascribed to civic denunciation).

it, it is far better to give them responsibility for the administration of minor affairs than to put them in charge of major ones."[44]

This deflation of French discourse (especially in its republican version), advocating close involvement in "minor affairs" rather than exalting major ones, puts us in mind of Gambetta thirty-five years later, especially in regard to his ingenious construction of the Senate as the "grand council of the communes of France." Gambetta favored a prudent politicization of the countryside: universal suffrage, in two stages to be sure, might have a genuine conservative virtue, even though it had been previously regarded as destructive. Jules Ferry expressed a similar idea in a speech he gave in Bordeaux on August 30, 1885: "Never forget that if universal suffrage in the countryside confidently and resolutely chose the republican path, it did so with its own faculties and its own circumspect, not to say conservative, temperament.... The universal suffrage of the peasantry is a solid foundation for our society and, for the Republic, a granite base."[45]

In 1932 Albert Thibaudet issued a similar judgment: political liberals had nothing more to ask of the Republic after the law of 1884 authorized the election (rather than appointment) of mayors, thereby establishing local democracy. "The Republic," he wrote, "is the regime of the elected mayor. No other government has ever given up so much of its electoral and administrative power."[46] For Thibaudet, the synthesis between local life, on the one hand, and the primacy of the law and state, on the other, had been achieved. Further discussion of decentralization would therefore be unnecessary.

To return to Tocqueville, who still lived in the world of limited suffrage, his philosophical postulate was that the only way to obtain civic virtue was through local activity. Public virtue must be built atop private self-interest, the only moral capacity that one could assume modern democratic man possessed. "American legislators display relatively little confidence in human honesty, but they always assume that man is intelligent."[47] He seems, however, to have associated the virtue of intelligence with what the French call *notables*, the more prominent and well-to-do among the citizenry, although he was hostile to the July Monarchy and therefore reluctant to use the term

[44] *DA* II, p. 133; AG, p. 592.

[45] Jules Ferry, *Discours et opinions*, ed. P. Robiquet (Paris: Armand Colin, 1898), 7:37. See the historical overview in Jean-Pierre Machelon, "Les communes dans les débuts de la Troisième République. Administration et politique," *Revue administrative* (May–June 1989): 201–8, as well as the more developed thesis in *Les Communes et le pouvoir de 1789 à nos jours*, ed. L. Foubère, J.-P. Machelon, and F. Monnier (Paris: Presses Universitaires de France, 2002).

[46] Albert Thibaudet, *Les Idées politiques de la France* (Paris: Stock, 1932), p. 53.

[47] *DA* I, p. 144; AG, p. 88.

and loath to give it a positive value. But was it not the rural French *notable* he had in mind when he wrote that "with one spectacular stroke one can instantly win the favor of a people, but to earn the love and respect of one's neighbors takes a long series of small services and obscure favors, habitual and unremitting kindness, and a well-established reputation for impartiality"?[48]

Furthermore, Tocqueville himself practiced the art of patronage as a deputy of the July Monarchy and *conseiller général* of La Manche, as we know from a vast trove of recently published archival documents. When Tocqueville and Beaumont denounced corruption (or, more precisely, trafficking in influence), Françoise Mélonio observes, Tocqueville's "moral protestations elicited smiles."[49] In 1838, when he ran for deputy, he wrote to one of his agents, the notary Langlois: "It not only pleases me but is also in my interest to support in Paris all just requests from communes and other public institutions. It is also my intention, and I should add my duty, to support those of my compatriots who appear worthy of the government's favors and who are recommended to me by my friends."[50] In the same letter Tocqueville matter-of-factly detailed the network on which he knew he could count: "I have in each canton a small number of highly educated friends in whom I have full confidence and to whom I believe I have great obligations, etc."[51]

To return to the passage of the second *Democracy* cited earlier, Tocqueville bluntly described the exchange of "benevolence" for "reputation" (that is, the esteem of the beneficiaries) as a matter of class: in America, the rich know that they "always have need of the poor and that in democratic times one wins the loyalty of the poor more through manners than through benefactions."[52] For him, this was an important difference between the wealthy American and the French notable: because the bourgeoisie in France neglects *manners*, it risks losing everything. This chapter, on "free institutions" (*DA* II.2.4), reveals a feature of Tocqueville's thought that we will encounter often in what follows: a model of patronage (in the nineteenth-century sense), that is, a

[48] *DA* II, p. 133; AG, p. 592.

[49] Mélonio, *Tocqueville et les Français*, p. 90. In 1847 Tocqueville complained that the minister of finance "had compiled a list of all the requests that I had made or commented on over the past seven years ... to prove that the deputies of the opposition were not as virtuous as they wished to appear." Quoted by André-Jean Tudesq in Tocqueville, *Correspondance et écrits locaux, OC* X, preface, p. 17.

[50] Mélonio, *Tocqueville et les Français*, p. 87, January 4, 1838. See in Y. Déloye, *Sociologie historique du politique* (Paris: La Découverte, 1997), p. 97, the summary entitled "Les servitudes d'un notable: l'exemple d'Alexis de Tocqueville." The famous pages of the *Souvenirs* on the bourgeoisie's slicing up of the July government must therefore be reinterpreted in this light (as we will see later). Recall this passage: "In charge of everything as no aristocracy had ever been nor likely will be, the middle class, which should be called the governmental class, having ensconced itself in power and before long in selfishness, took on an air of private industry." Tocqueville, *Souvenirs, OC* XII, p. 31.

[51] *OC* X, p. 87, *Correspondance et écrits locaux*, letter of January 4, 1838.

[52] *DA* II, p. 133; AG, p. 592.

relation of protection and charity tinged with respect, which the British and French aristocracies shared but the French bourgeoisie did not. [53]

Tocqueville's liberalism, we have begun to see, was antibourgeois. This was the basis of his persistent rivalry with Guizot. He is therefore rather hard to place on the political spectrum: he never compromised himself by joining the legitimists, yet he also remained resolutely distant from the moderate and elitist republicanism of someone like Armand Carrel—an important contemporary of Tocqueville's who died young in 1836, the victim of a duel.

Tocqueville's commentators have generally overlooked the polemic against the bourgeoisie that runs throughout *Democracy in America*. In the *Souvenirs*, which he did not intend to publish before his death, his antibourgeois stance is unambiguous. But listen to the description of his French contemporaries in the second *Democracy*: "They readily consent to do good for the benefit of the people but prefer to keep them scrupulously at a distance. They think this is enough; they are mistaken. They could ruin themselves in this way without kindling any warmth in the hearts of the people around them. What is asked of them is not the sacrifice of their money; it is the sacrifice of their pride."[54]

Elsewhere, however, Tocqueville said much the same thing about great British landlords. When they began to hire hands rather than claim a share of what tenants produced, they "traded cash" for the *influence* they once possessed. "What they gained in money, they would soon lose in power," he prophesied.[55]

✌

Tocqueville's analysis of the town in the chapter entitled "How Americans Combat Individualism with Free Institutions"[56] thus leads us toward

[53] A picturesque example can be found in Talleyrand's memoirs. In the château de Chalais in the Périgord where Talleyrand spent his childhood, his grandmother received guests every Sunday after mass in the "apothecary." Neighbors came in search of remedies: "My grandmother pointed out the place where the remedy was kept. One of the nobles who had been at mass went to fetch it. Another brought a drawer full of linen. I took a piece of it, and my grandmother herself cut bandages and compresses as needed." After describing this ceremonial dispensation of relief to the suffering, Talleyrand derived the lesson: "The injured on whose wounds consolations had been poured and the sick to whom hope had been offered were quite prepared to be cured. Their blood circulated more easily, their humors grew purer, their nerves revived, sleep returned, and their bodies were reinvigorated. Nothing is as effective as trust, and it is most effective when it emanates from the ministrations of a great lady with whom ideas of power and protection are associated." See Talleyrand, *Mémoires*, (Paris: Jean de Bonnot, 1996), 1:11–12.

[54] *DA* II, p. 134; AG, p. 593.

[55] In 1818 Benjamin Constant expressed similar disappointment in a text that was reprinted in 1829: "They [the 'gentry'] believed that they could divest themselves of the responsibilities while keeping the benefits." See Jaume, *L'Individu effacé*, p. 305.

[56] *DA* II.2.4, pp. 131–35; AG, pp. 590–94.

social issues. The town as nexus of interests, public opinion as a check on individual behavior, the influence of notables, and the philosophy of moral utilitarianism—this was what Tocqueville meant by "democracy." What is problematic about this portrait is that the democratic liberalism it advocates is antibourgeois. We will return later to this powerful tension in Tocqueville's work, which both the author and the private man found difficult to manage.

For now, note simply that Tocqueville portrays the town as a self-managed institution that nevertheless required the dedication of notable citizens to function. If convinced by reason and self-interest of the need for charity, they could successfully negotiate a career in both the public and private spheres. They win the "hearts of the poor," or so we gather from Tocqueville's warning to legitimists: "An aristocracy that allows the heart of the people to slip through its fingers for good is like a tree whose roots have died."[57] Note the phrase "for good" (*définitivement*): the author seems to have abandoned hope in any specific group. Yet he believes that "free institutions" can give rise to social feeling (a sense of affable self-sacrifice and apparent disinterestedness). Indeed, he himself offered an unforgettable portrait of how a notable should behave toward the peasants on election day. The passage in the *Souvenirs* in which he describes the excitement in the *chef-lieu de canton* (county seat) is well-known: "All these men lined up in double-file by alphabetical order. I went to take the place to which my name assigned me, because I knew that in democratic countries in democratic times, one must allow the people to place oneself at their head and not assume the position on one's own."[58] So much for the parvenus of July, who failed to clamber aboard the speeding train in 1848. Tocqueville was fairly pleased by that election day: "The people had always been kind to me, but now I found them affectionate, and I have never been greeted with more respect than since the day that posters bluntly proclaiming equality began to cover all the walls." This is the language of the country squire.

In other words, even in democracy there exists a psychology of *authority*. Local democracy as Tocqueville understood it depended on a critique of two illusions: first, the illusion that elections would suffice to create the necessary authority, and second, the illusion that money can by itself produce obedience and deference. Tocquevillean democracy involved a conquest of the "heart." Its analysis therefore required the eye of a moralist[59] combined with that of a sociologist attuned to empirical data. Tocqueville therefore needed

[57] *DA* II, p. 232; AG, p. 680.
[58] *OC* XII (*Souvenirs*), p. 114.
[59] In the sense of La Bruyère, La Fontaine, and La Rochefoucauld: see part 3.

a sophisticated approach to writing in order to fully express his thought. He first had to distill his transatlantic experience in such a way as to take his distance from the legitimism of his family, and he had to combine that experience discreetly with his own deeply personal philosophy.[60] And then he had to incorporate his critique of the French bourgeoisie, albeit in attenuated form, while hiding the deeper meaning of his work behind any number of veils. Thus to decipher the meaning of *Democracy in America*, we must investigate Tocqueville's relation to the social milieu from which he sprang, a relation that he deliberately muted in his writing and mediated through his discussion of America. The young aristocrat *set out to educate his own*, for whom he painted a portrait of the new "democratic" world—but he did not entrust the keys to that world to the middle class.

Was it possible in 1835 or 1840 to praise popular sovereignty while rejecting both the bourgeoisie and socialism? We shall pursue this question throughout the book. Unlike Louis de Carné, another aristocrat of the same generation, Tocqueville refused to ally himself with such representatives of the bourgeoisie as the Doctrinaires or the followers of Thiers. He became a sort of republican of the mind, as he put it, while inwardly remaining fearful of the masses. Despite his abortive attempt to create a Young Left party, his political position was never clear. From this he derived a successful intellectual strategy, but political success eluded him.[61]

A COMPARISON: CONTEMPORARY CURRENTS

Legitimism and Authority (of the People / over the People)

Did legitimists read Tocqueville's message clearly? Although they could not accept the idea of popular sovereignty,[62] they nevertheless found in his

---

[60] As we will see, it was ultimately the moralist that clarified the thinking of the political scientist and the sociologist.

[61] He said as much in his correspondence when each of his books appeared: readers with firm opinions would mostly be disappointed. On November 29, 1834, for example, he wrote to Camille d'Orglandes: "[My position] is not likely to enlist the active sympathies of anyone. Some will find that at bottom I do not like democracy and treat it rather severely. Others will think that I am incautiously encouraging its spread." *Lettres choisies. Souvenirs*, p. 311; GZ, p. 563. As for Tocqueville's personal credo, which he jotted down on a piece of paper, we have it thanks to Antoine Rédier: "I have an intellectual taste for democratic institutions, but I am aristocratic by instinct, which is to say that I despise and fear the crowd. I love liberty, legality, and respect for rights with a passion, but not democracy. That is my innermost conviction." Rédier, *Comme disait M. de Tocqueville*, p. 48.

[62] Except, as we shall see, when it came to mobilizing the people against bourgeois notables and capitalists. Some legitimists, such as Chateaubriand, held that the king represented the national will by popular consent, which had been continually renewed since the time of Hugh Capet.

work one of their favorite themes: that "liberty" exists primarily in the form of local liberties, and that *community* held out hope of survival despite the atomizing forces of the market society. Some legitimists shared with Tocqueville what Louis Blanc would call "pained admiration" of American democracy. In a perceptive review, the republican and socialist leader thought he saw in Tocqueville a lack of faith in progress.[63] Like Tocqueville, legitimists often preferred the American republican system to the July Monarchy, which retained administrative centralization for the benefit of the middle class.[64] They combined nostalgia for the medieval commune with admiration for self-government.

The monarchists' dream of decentralization was based on the following principle: "Government to the king, administration to the country." Stéphane Rials, a specialist on the question, has shown that the monarchist movement was deeply divided over the idea of national sovereignty, which was in principle incompatible with the monarchist faith. Part of the movement responded to the traumatic experience of 1789 (when numerous liberal nobles sat in the Constituent Assembly) by embracing the idea of a state with a *monarchical executive*. In the struggle against Orleanism, the notion of "royal democracy" emerged, and southern royalists even formed a "white Mountain" (a reference to the politics of 1793).[65]

One of the most eclectic syntheses of the period can be found in the person of Antoine-Eugène de Genoude, a journalist who made the *Gazette de France* one of the leading newspapers of the Restoration. Claiming to combine popular sovereignty (via universal suffrage) with royal legitimacy, Genoude was ennobled by Louis XVIII in 1822. In 1834 he became a priest

---

[63] Louis Blanc: "Why did you stop in doubt as to coming things?" *La Revue républicaine* (April–May 1835), reproduced in Françoise Mélonio, *Tocqueville dans la culture française*, thesis (Paris X-Nanterre, 1991), 3:155–56.

[64] This was the basis of the so-called Carlo-republican alliance against the parliamentary monarchy, which proved to be powerful and durable. This was Guizot's nightmare as a minister. Tocqueville repeatedly defied this opposition, but intellectually he had much in common with the coalition of opposites: see Françoise Mélonio's shrewd remarks in *Tocqueville et les Français*, pp. 73–74. The alliance was electorally influential in two periods: 1830–1837 and 1848. In 1842 Guizot opposed a proposal to expand the vote on the grounds that it would have strengthened both the Carlists and the republicans. In the same speech he argued that the federal government was weak in the United States because it was based on universal suffrage. See Guizot, *Histoire parlementaire*, 3:561. Note that in the same year, 1842, Tocqueville judged that he had been elected deputy thanks to a Carlo-republican coalition, but that, as a person known for his "most moderate opposition," he was not beholden to it (Beaumont edition of the *Œuvres*, 7:201, to Eugène Stöffels, October 6, 1842).

[65] See Stéphane Rials, "Les royalistes français et le suffrage universel au XIXe siècle," in *Révolution et contre-révolution au XIXe siècle* (Paris: D.U.C. Albatros, 1987). See also Stéphane Rials, *Le Légitimisme* (Paris: Presses Universitaires de France, 1983).

but continued to work as a journalist. A strange personality, he sought to reconcile Carlists and republicans, and the resulting coalition met with success in several departmental and legislative elections.[66] In his manifestos of 1834 (*Déclaration royaliste*), 1837 (*Avis électoral*), and 1847 (*Congrès de la presse réformiste de droite*), the commune was conceived as both part of a decentralized administration and the site of the first stage of national voting because monarchists favored universal suffrage in several stages: the idea was to "purify" representation by moving up the ranks of a hierarchy, starting with the common people and ending with illustrious party leaders such as Antoine Berryer (the coalition's leading orator).[67] Genoude was backed by another energetic intellectual, Honoré Lelarge de Lourdoueix, who was made a baron in 1821 and who became owner and editor in chief of the *Gazette de France* when Genoude died in 1849.[68]

In 1832 the *Gazette* published a program advocating universal suffrage and support for the great achievements of 1789 (freedom of the press, property, religion, jury, etc.). Its project of decentralization, a common goal of legitimists, was based on the commune: "We regard France as having achieved the independence of communes and provinces with respect to local interests, along with the election of magistrates by taxpaying, domiciled citizens and free deliberation of freely elected councils in regard to administration of local affairs."[69]

With the assertion that there exist purely local interests that local elected officials are competent to deal with "independently," these monarchists took a step that the Orleanists in power refused to take. At about the same time, however, the duchesse de Berry launched her insurrection against the July Monarchy, in which Tocqueville's cousin and friend Louis de Kergorlay was directly involved.[70] This affair made a mockery of the legitimist cause, whose traditions include various conspiratorial plots.

[66] On the phases of this alliance and its electoral manifestos, see Hugues de Changy, *Le Mouvement légitimiste sous la monarchie de Juillet (1833–1848)* (Rennes: Presses Universitaires de Rennes, 2004). It bears emphasizing that this coalition was more than just opportunistic.

[67] See texts cited in ibid., pp. 47, 101, and 311. The text of 1834 mainly discusses the need to broaden the suffrage in order to rescue the legitimists from their refusal to accept the Orleanist "usurpation."

[68] An ardent apostle of universal suffrage for the benefit of the monarchy, Lourdoueix wrote *La Restauration de la société française*, 3rd ed. (Paris: Sapia, 1834), a passionate but theoretically feeble work.

[69] *Gazette de France*, March 28, 1832, reproduced in Stéphane Rials, *Textes politiques français* (Paris: Presses Universitaires de France, 1983), pp. 38–39.

[70] On March 9, 1833, Tocqueville represented Kergorlay at the royal court of Paris; see *OC* XIII-1, pp. 321–27. His cousin was charged with attempted subversion. In the (ardently monarchist) newspaper *La Quotidienne*, on February 2, 1833, Tocqueville published a protest, which he signed as "judge-auditor of Versailles" (a post he no longer held, because he had resigned after Gustave de Beaumont was sacked). He wrote: "The government would like to consider Mme la duchesse de Berry as a prisoner of war, which

Still, legitimist circles were quite divided, as the mixed reception of *Democracy in America* attests. Those who were open to the American experiment took that position mainly because they rejected the "usurper king" and the rise of the middle class. Berryer, the great orator of the movement, wrote that the middle class had to be steadfastly opposed and treated "as the monarchy . . . treated feudalism for three centuries."[71] The Carlo-republican alliance was deliberately aimed at the bourgeoisie and its detested instrument: the *cens*, or property qualification for the right to vote. Armand Carrel, the most brilliant republican of the day, Lafayette's heir, and an admirer of the United States, had to deny in *Le National* that he was working toward an alliance with the monarchists, especially after he proposed communal decentralization (which republicans associated with *La Tribune* firmly rejected).[72]

The *Gazette de France* received the first volume of *Democracy in America* coolly. In 1835 it published a particularly nasty review, which aimed most of its criticism at the United States. All the complaints about America that one still hears in France today (from both the Right and the Left) can be found in this lengthy review, which was published in two parts.[73] The United States is not a republic. There is no equality because the Indians are persecuted and exterminated, blacks are kept as slaves, money is king, and so forth. Tocqueville was accused of idealizing the American reality, which made him a "malefactor," a charge that would continue to be echoed on the right down to the time of Charles Maurras.[74] The *Gazette* wrote: "The American republic is a pure aristocracy, and the most ignoble of aristocracies, that of money. The people in America are sovereign in name only. They are reputed to make the laws, but in reality they are more subject to them than other classes."[75] Exactly the same point was made by the radical republicans, who, as René

---

the undersigned cannot accept." *Ibid. n.* 2, p. 319. When Tocqueville ran for office in these years (especially 1837 and 1839), he had a hard time denying that he was a "masked legitimist," as his opponents accused him of being. He was still denying this in 1848. See his response to the electoral committee in Valognes, *OC* III-3, p. 48. His awkward allies, the legitimist candidates, did not help matters by pretending to think as he did. For instance, Count Henri Duparc, in the spring of 1848: letter from Tocqueville to his wife, *OC* XIV, p. 514. Later (coup d'état of 1851) he would have to defend himself against his brothers. Unpublished and little-known documents show that in September 1837, at least, Tocqueville may have played a double game between the Orleanists and the legitimists (see part 5).

[71] Quoted in Rials, *Révolution et contre-révolution au XIXe siècle*, p. 154.

[72] On the charge that Carrel reached out to the *Gazette de France*, see the comments of his editor, Émile Littré, in *Œuvres politiques et littéraires de Carrel* (Paris: Chamerot, 1857), 3:421.

[73] Edifying reading: see Mélonio, *Tocqueville dans la culture française*, 3:77–90 (*Gazette*, February 2 and 13, 1835).

[74] Concerning the use of this term by Maurras, see below.

[75] Quoted in Mélonio, *Tocqueville dans la culture française*, 3:80.

Rémond has shown, turned hostile to America in 1835. Listen to Dr. Cerisé in *L'Européen*:

> This hideous collection of aristocratic bourgeois and bourgeois aristocrats, who so loudly proclaimed Christian liberty and rebelled against the mother country so as to avoid paying a few cents more for a pound of tea; this band of slave traders who speak of fraternity and equality yet engage in a shameful traffic in human flesh; this nation of ignorant shopkeepers and narrow-minded workers, who cannot boast of a single work of art across the vast extent of their continent....[76]

What is more, it is easy to see the influence of anti-Protestant sentiment and Catholic moralism in the legitimists and republicans who voiced such resentment. Cerisé continued: "Individualism in religion and morality, reflected in the Protestant spirit; individualism in politics and social economy, revealing itself in federalism.... This is solidly organized selfishness; it is regularized and systematized evil; it is, in short, the materialization of man's fate." Later, we will see that Tocqueville was not far from sharing such views (about individualism and ambient materialism), although the lessons he drew from them were of far better quality than these.

Tocqueville's affinity with the legitimists' most brilliant political thinker, Ferdinand Béchard, is clear.[77] Magistrate, deputy, local politician (*conseiller général*), journalist, and sophisticated theorist, Béchard published, soon after the appearance of the first volume of *Democracy in America*, a work in which he explored the consequences of Tocqueville's distinction between political centralization and administrative centralization. This *Essai sur la centralisation administrative* (1837) met with great success and was followed by a revised and expanded edition in 1845.[78] Béchard's best book, an in-depth treatment of local government in France, appeared in 1852: *De l'état du paupérisme en France et des moyens d'y remédier*.[79] His most important point, which captured the heart of the legitimist position, was that states must be built from the bottom up, by proceeding from the particular to the general and from local communities to the nation. Hence the social takes precedence over the political, mores over laws, and the local over the national. Domestic and communal mores are the basis of everything. For example, what is called public opin-

---

[76] Quoted in René Rémond, *Les États-Unis devant l'opinion française. 1815–1852* (Paris: Armand Colin, 1962), p. 671.

[77] For more on Béchard, see Jaume, *L'Individu effacé*, pp. 320–28.

[78] The revised edition was entitled *De l'administration de la France ou Essai sur les abus de la centralisation* (Paris: de Perrodil, 1845).

[79] Published in Paris by Charles Douniol, 1852.

ion is a source of error "in regard to that which transcends the local sphere," and it must be sought at the local level: "Do not listen to the voice of the people anywhere else; it is only there."[80] In other words, public opinion is not to be gleaned from the Paris newspapers or the parliamentary galleries. Like Tocqueville (whose study of the New England town he quotes and extends), Béchard set great store by "local democracy" (or *la démocratie communale*, as he called it), in which members of the local community exchanged views lent weight by the "personal reputation" of those who held them.

Still, Béchard's analysis was highly moralistic (without Tocqueville's praise for enlightened self-interest) as well as authoritarian, especially in regard to pauperism, which was the main subject of the book:

> Under the watchful eye of relatives and neighbors, the individual becomes a better person.[81] Everything is a reminder of duty and commands respect for oneself and others. The internal discipline of the family and town takes the place of police, and the fear of infamy is a more powerful motive than the fear of material punishment.... If you take people who have come down in the world, who abound in our cities, and put them back in their villages, you will have done a great deal for their moral regeneration.[82]

Although Béchard understood the importance of what Tocqueville called "democracy," he focused on the advantages of the democratic social state for preserving the family spirit, the corporatist spirit, and *l'esprit de cité*, all commonplaces in the work of Bonald, Montlosier, and other legitimist and traditionalist writers. Tocqueville used the term "civic spirit" (*esprit de cité*) only twice in the first *Democracy* and not at all in the second or in *The Ancien Régime and the Revolution*. He knew that it was closely connected with traditionalism, and his use of it in the first volume was a nod in the direction of the traditionalist camp.[83] Right at the beginning of *De l'administration de la France*, Béchard mentions these typically Bonaldian themes: "I would like to be able to revive the family spirit, the corporatist spirit, the civic spirit, the patriotic spirit, the religious spirit, and ultimately the public spirit, the soul

[80] Béchard, *De l'état du paupérisme*, p. 64.

[81] An optimistic view? Think of Tocqueville's own reflection on his parliamentary experience: "There is no one for whom approval is healthier than for me, and no one who needs the esteem and confidence of the public more.... Does my constant need to find, in a sense, the proof of myself in the thought of others come from true modesty? I believe rather that it comes from great pride." *OC* XII, p. 104. Tocqueville reflected on amour-propre in the sense of the seventeenth-century moralists.

[82] Béchard, *De l'état du paupérisme*, p. 66.

[83] See *DA* I.1.5, p. 154; *DA* I.2.6, p. 331. The nod is evident in the first passage: "I think that administrative centralization is likely only to weaken the peoples who are subjected to it, because it tends constantly to diminish *l'esprit de cité* among them." This was a legitimist commonplace.

of society, the source of its life, force, and progress."[84] Each of these "principles" is clearly constitutive of a social bond, a community transcending the
individual.

The intellectual (as opposed to political) affinity between Béchard and
Tocqueville is fairly extensive, in that the former extends the latter's effort
in *Democracy in America* to stand the classic French view on its head. In
France, as noted previously, the state was the real instigator of popular sovereignty. Hence the representative of the sovereign inherited the prestige of
the sovereign and the exercise of his powers. Béchard, in a very Tocquevillean move, distinguished between what he called the "system of power"
and the "system of authority." The latter was primordial, because it derived
from the base: "Resting on private and public mores, [it] seeks to constitute
the city through the family and the state through the city."[85] This is what
Tocqueville also seeks to do in the two *Democracies*. What I will henceforth call "the authority of the social" is his guiding thread in analyzing
the laws of inheritance and property, family mores, the status of American women, the spontaneous spirit of association, the genesis of a majority
spirit (common opinion), and so on. Béchard, for his part, observes that
"the system of power" wants to organize from the top down and must be
checked by decentralization. The legitimist axiom—"government to the
king, administration to the country"—remains fundamental for him, justified by the existence of *natural* communities: "In communal life, nothing is
in a sense individual: sentiments, thoughts, mores, even dress—everything
is collective."[86]

As a specialist in the courts and administrative law, Béchard saw the remedy not in the state but in what he called "Christian and municipal liberties." Communal life was supposed to fortify state power from the bottom
up. Thus Béchard was able to assert that the goal was both to restore authority *and* to establish liberty. Authority: order could be established only by
(plural) local *authorities*. Liberty: liberties were to be carefully metered out
and checked by local controls (modernized corporations, control of mobile
populations, local supervision of morality) as well as moderated by a multi-
level suffrage. Béchard understood Tocqueville's message, and when adapted
to France it would result in a conservative modernization:

---

[84] Béchard, *De l'administration de la France*, 2nd ed. (1845), 1:vii.

[85] Béchard, *De l'état du paupérisme*, p. 47. Think, too, of Lammenais's principle of authority or common sense (to use his terms). Indeed, "there is not authority or certitude except in society," according to
L'Essai sur l'indifférence, vol. 2.

[86] Béchard, *De l'état du paupérisme*, p. 64.

Liberty at the base and unity at the summit, or, in other words, the liberated commune and the centralized state: this is the twin principle of the administrative reform that must be implemented in the interest of both the government and the people, by entrusting purely local interests to administrators elected by their fellow citizens and by organizing the central government under conditions of hereditary and inalienable power.[87]

It is an irony of history that the monarchists of the period were clearly as cautious as the liberals and republicans: "local interests" must be clearly distinguished, they argued, to ensure that communes, cantons, and departments kept to their respective roles. They, too, feared the *politicization* of local entities. In theory the administrative and the political were supposed to be kept carefully separate. In practice things did not work out that way, as Hugues de Changy noted: on November 30, 1833, a circular from the minister of the interior went out to the prefects, calling for an official report (who was elected? with how many votes?). This was accompanied by a second, confidential circular: What was the elected official's social situation? What were his political leanings? So much for supposed "local interests"! This became a regular practice.[88] Tocqueville suggested blurring the boundary between local interest and political liberty because collective deliberation at the local level was the school in which the people learned to participate in politics. By contrast, the legitimists wanted both "local democracy" and politically neutral local officials. In a chapter entitled "On the Autonomy of the Communes, Principle of Liberty," Béchard remarked that the word *autonomy* "implies not political liberty, in the sense of participation in sovereignty, but rather civil liberty, in the sense of a right to attend to purely local interests."[89] Again, this confirms that in France the great fear was of dismemberment of the country and "federalism," which many people had denounced since 1789.[90]

Here, then, we have one of the most important points of contact between Tocqueville and the legitimist vision: local democracy as a marriage of the familial and the public. But we also have one of the major divergences, which drew protests from Tocqueville on numerous occasions: for Béchard, authority had to be democratic, in the sense that it emanated from the base and

---

[87] Ibid., pp. 77–78.

[88] See Hugues de Changy, *Le Mouvement légitimiste sous la monarchie de Juillet*, p. 32, n. 40. This practice made it possible for the historian to obtain "a veritable political snapshot of the *conseils généraux* under the July Monarchy."

[89] Béchard, *De l'état du paupérisme*, p. 117.

[90] This phobia has been revived lately by the European Union, whose precise configuration has never been clearly defined.

remained traditional, moralistic, and depoliticized. The revolutionary virus had to be eliminated.

These two schools of thought converged to a degree on one of the day's most troubling issues: pauperism. In an unpublished "letter on pauperism in Normandy," possibly intended for his brother Édouard (who owned a large estate in Baugy), Tocqueville proposed that communes implement strict measures to deal with unemployed workers and beggars who wandered the countryside in search of handouts. These were the people to whom Béchard referred, in a passage cited earlier, as "people who have come down in the world." But, Tocqueville argued, these strict measures should not be implemented until "associations for the elimination of vagabondage and begging" had been created. These were to be financed by well-to-do landowners on a voluntary basis as a sort of self-interested charity. Tocqueville wrote:

> Once an association has been established in a commune, the commune could then expel all alien indigents from its limits. Having taken responsibility for its own poor, it could then call upon all other communes to do the same. The residents of a commune with such an association would then be legally and rationally justified in refusing any assistance to beggars from elsewhere, and the mayor, using the powers granted to him under the law, could in all justice expel them from his territory.[91]

The idea that the commune had authority over "its" paupers was consistent with the thinking of legitimists and social Catholics as well as with the experience of the English under the Poor Law, about which Tocqueville knew a great deal. The main difference between him and Béchard lay in his rejection of the corporatist spirit: the associative initiative was to be free, despite the coercive power of the law, because it was the self-interest properly understood of the wealthy that would induce them to be generous. Indeed, "the rich [must] understand that Providence has decreed that there be *solidarity* between them and the poor," Tocqueville wrote. It was because the bourgeoisie neglected this obligation of the wealthy that socialism was a threat.

∾

Although Tocqueville was no less fearful of socialism than Béchard, he nevertheless had confidence in face-to-face interactions in small communities. He believed in public opinion and in the force of majorities, whereas Béchard, while lavishing praise on natural communities, reintroduced rather

[91] Tocqueville, *OC* XVI, p. 160.

oppressive agents of authority.[92] And even if Louis Blanc was right that Tocqueville did not believe in the future, he trusted in liberty sufficiently to make a wager that Béchard refused. The two men did not agree, except for brief intervals of political alliance (in 1848, for example). These were short-lived because, as became clear under the Second Republic, Tocqueville did not support the "party of order." He voted for Cavaignac, not Louis-Napoleon. He resigned his elective offices after the coup, while his brothers, especially Édouard, applauded the attempt to found a new dynasty.[93]

Legitimists found in *Democracy in America* support for their decentralizing demands. It is interesting to note that Louis de Carné, who was initially a friend of Tocqueville's and a Catholic legitimist who later threw in his lot with the July Monarchy and the middle class, was careful to exclude the decentralizing theses from his review of *Democracy in America*. He could not believe that Tocqueville would seriously defend the position of a party that had lost in 1830, and, what is more, a party that lacked the courage to choose a more decentralizing policy under the left-leaning Martignac government, the failure of which led to the Polignac reaction and then the July Revolution. After July, Carné explained, "provincial resurrection . . . was loudly prophesied by the legitimist party," but such illusions soon dissipated.[94] In France the central government relied on prefects and mayors, and while local officials might be chosen from among the elected members of the municipal council, they were often paid a salary by the state.

☧

Here we have a good example of the sort of partisan interpretation of *Democracy in America* that was common at the time of its publication. Was Tocqueville a champion of local liberties? Today's reader rightly takes the point for granted.[95] But the picture of the book painted by the liberal *Revue des deux mondes* was not so clear, particularly since Tocqueville himself, as deputy and minister, took no initiative in favor of decentralization under either the July Monarchy or Second Republic.

To be fair, he did strongly favor municipal liberties in Algeria, where he felt freer both politically and intellectually vis-à-vis party politics in the

[92] Great landowners, overseers of corporations, etc.

[93] On the modes of legitimation of this new dynasty, see Juliette Glikman, "L'imaginaire impérial et la logique de l'histoire. Étude des assises du régime du Second Empire," thesis, Université de Paris IV, 2007.

[94] Louis de Carné, "De la démocratie aux États-Unis et de la bourgeoisie en France," *Revue des deux mondes*, March 15, 1837, 9:674. The review appears on pp. 653–82.

[95] See the questions put to me in an interview by J.-M. Ohnet, "Tocqueville penseur des libertés locales," *Pouvoirs locaux* 67 (2005): 135–41.

Chamber. In a substantial 1841white paper, he wrote: "Make haste to secure the loyalty of the residents of this new land [the colony in Algeria] by
creating a forum for their collective interests and common action." In a parliamentary report on Algeria (1847), he pointed out the need to decentral-
ize the administration in relation to both Paris and Algiers on the grounds
that it was absurd, as well as historically unprecedented, to have colonization
without municipal life.[96] Tocqueville favored hasty election of municipal
councils. An 1847 ordinance did in fact create municipal governments in
Algeria, but nominations of the mayor and council members were left to the
king and the governor general.

The Saint-Simonian Michel Chevalier: American Anarchy and French Authority

For the followers of Henri de Saint-Simon, the question of state authority
in America was of great significance, and they approached it in an original
way. Saint-Simon aimed to transcend liberalism, which he believed had been
useful in its day but lacked the ability to "organize" (a key term among Saint-
Simonians). What France needed was not the Charter of Louis XVIII but an
"industrial constitution," which would establish a new hierarchy dominated
by industrialists in association with scientists and artists.[97] By socializing the
means of production and establishing a rational banking system, the state
could proceed with an industrial policy that would promote individuals
from the status of "subjects" to that of "partners" (sociétaires). It so happens
that Michel Chevalier, one of Saint-Simon's most brilliant disciples, applied
Saint-Simonian ideas to Jackson's America. In the wake of the notorious
trial of the Saint-Simonian leadership in August 1832 for activities hostile
to the social order, Chevalier, a young graduate of the École Polytechnique
and member of the Corps des Mines, was rescued from prison by the Molé-
Thiers government and sent to America to study transportation by water and
rail. The young engineer had already written about the crucial development
of railroads in France, as well as about the importance of a unified nation-
wide banking system, the potential for linking Egypt to Europe by rail, and

---

[96] See Tocqueville, "Travail sur l'Algérie," unpublished memorandum, October 1841, OC III, p. 277,
and "Rapport sur le projet de loi relatif aux crédits extraordinaires demandés pour l'Algérie," ibid., p. 352.
The first text followed a trip to Algeria in May–June 1841, while the second emerged from work on the
"African question" following another trip to Algeria in October–December 1846, which also led to two
other reports and a parliamentary committee.

[97] In Du système industriel (1821), Saint-Simon addressed himself directly to Louis XVIII in explaining what a "real charter" ought to look like.

the possibility of building canals in Suez and Panama. After Chevalier died in 1879, Jules Simon spoke of these visionary writings at the Académie des Sciences Morales et Politiques, to which Chevalier was elected in 1851.[98]

After spending six months in the United States, Chevalier published his *Lettres sur l'Amérique du Nord* in 1836. The letters had appeared earlier in the *Journal des débats* (between November 1833 and October 1835).[99] It is quite likely that Tocqueville (who published the first volume of *Democracy in America* in January 1835) read these texts in whole or in part, even though he forbade himself to read Chevalier's book when it was published in 1836, in keeping with his usual method when writing something of his own (in this case the second *Democracy*, which was not published until 1840).[100] He nevertheless questioned Beaumont about the work: "Have you laid eyes on it, and, if so, what do you think of it? What is the spirit of the book? Where does it go? Last but not least, what are people saying about it, and how might it be prejudicial to the philosophical and political text I am working on?"

These questions show that Tocqueville was keen to inform himself about the book even though he did not wish to read it. What clearly mattered to him was the *sense* of Chevalier's account of America ("Where is he going?"). The public's reaction also mattered. Chevalier's articles had apparently attracted considerable attention. The political and ideological moment called for an interpretation of what was happening in the United States: from the July Monarchy to the Second Empire, France was embroiled in debate about "democracy," complicated by a conflict between the controversial disciplines of ethics and economics, especially within the Institut de France (of which the Académie des Sciences Morales et Politiques was a part).

Toward the end of the century, the *Nouveau dictionnaire d'économie politique*, which reflected liberal economic thinking, described Chevalier's letters in the *Journal des débats* as having aroused "universal interest owing to the novelty of the portrait, the boldness and vividness of the composition, and the richness of the colors. The letters preceded Tocqueville's *Democracy in America*, a more systematic work written in a tone more in keeping with

---

[98] Jules Simon, "Notice sur Michel Chevalier," session of December 7, 1889 (online site of the Académie des Sciences Morales et Politiques, http://www.asmp.fr/travaux/notices/chevalier_simon.htm). See also the notice by E. Cheysson, *Livre du centenaire. École polytechnique* (Paris: Gauthier-Villars et fils, 1897), 1:509ff.

[99] Chevalier spent more than two years in the United States, Mexico, and the Antilles. He published his more technical observations separately (as Tocqueville and Beaumont did for their work on the prison system), in *Histoire et description des voies de communication aux États-Unis* (with atlas), while reserving his more philosophical and political remarks for the *Lettres sur l'Amérique du Nord*.

[100] Letter to Gustave de Beaumont, *OC* XVIII-1, p. 176. In fact, he refers to the book in the manuscript of *DA* II.

the ideas of the Doctrinaires, which were prevalent at the time."[101] I pass over the confusion between Tocqueville and the Doctrinaires (indeed, *Democracy in America* spurred an offensive by Doctrinaires from Guizot to Alletz and Carné). The dictionary goes on to describe Chevalier as having been more accurate than Tocqueville in his account of American institutions, mores, and beliefs, and not just economics (the domain in which Chevalier was reputedly more competent), but the article was written by the eminent Paul Leroy-Beaulieu, who also happened to be Chevalier's son-in-law.

The Chevalier-Tocqueville rivalry continued for quite some time. In 1838, when the respectable *Quarterly Review* dubbed Tocqueville "the Montesquieu of the present age," Chevalier sought to become a member of the Institute with the support of Beaumont and, if possible, the neutrality of Tocqueville.[102] Apparently, however, Tocqueville was unwilling to oblige. He noted that Chevalier had been convicted of a criminal offense and had been a follower of Saint-Simon.[103] The Académie des Sciences Morales et Politiques could not admit such a person! Chevalier would have to wait until 1851 to join the Institute, this time with Tocqueville's vote, which he obtained mainly because he and Tocqueville had common friends, the Circourts.[104]

∞

Why were French readers interested in Chevalier's articles? Because change was in the air: it seemed possible that there might at last be a role for the Saint-Simonians' elitist industrialism in the bourgeois July Monarchy. But Saint-Simonian elitism saw its mission as serving "the most numerous and poorest class" of society, as Saint-Simon put it late in life, in words often cited by his disciples.[105] This blend was part of the school's originality. In addition, the July Monarchy was seen as *parvenu* liberalism in power, which had relegated to the past the struggles of the Restoration (over parliamentary liberties, freedom of the press, the right to vote, the *carbonarism* of

[101] Léon Say and J. Chailley, eds., *Nouveau dictionnaire d'économie politique* (Paris: Guillaumin, 1891), 1:411.

[102] Chevalier also broke with Saint-Simonism in 1838. He quarreled with Prosper Enfantin in January 1837, after the latter's return from a fabulous expedition to Egypt.

[103] In August 1832 Enfantin, Duveyrier, and Chevalier were convicted of illegal association (art. 291 of the Penal Code). See S. Charléty, *Histoire du saint-simonisme (1825–1864)* (Paris: Paul Hartman, 1931), pp. 175–83. It was Molé who ordered that Chevalier be released six months early in order to proceed with his journey to America.

[104] On these various episodes, see *OC* VIII-1, pp. 301–2, 305, 481–82. In 1842 Beaumont explained that he preferred to vote for Duchâtel rather than Chevalier. See also *OC* VIII-2, pp. 312–14, 379. These episodes confirm that Chevalier was on Tocqueville's mind.

[105] See C. Bouglé and Élie Halévy, *Exposition de la doctrine de Saint-Simon* (Paris: Rivière, 1929), for the first year of public lectures by disciples.

the intellectual elite, and movements such as the Société Aide-toi et le ciel t'aidera). A rapprochement between Saint-Simonism and the July Monarchy was in fact what Chevalier was dreaming of in his letters from North America, if only in gratitude to his new protectors, Molé and Thiers.[106] Letter 29, entitled "Social Improvement," outlined a program for France: if only the monarchy could free itself from liberals who viewed the state as "an ulcer" and make good use of the "vast and powerful machine of centralization," the "principle of authority" could replace that of "individualism," a republican and Protestant idea.[107]

Chevalier, who, like Tocqueville and Beaumont, was sent to the United States on a government mission, inevitably saw American society through lenses of his own. Although they agreed on certain points (for instance, the invisibility of government in the United States), they drew different conclusions.[108] Whereas Tocqueville attempted to adopt a position of benevolent neutrality, Chevalier warned against various dangers, most notably economic (competition with America had to be anticipated) and political (republican and democratic regimes were enemies of the new aristocracies and therefore detestable). Chevalier aimed explicitly at reform in France and stated his recommendations forcefully, while Tocqueville's political goals were on an entirely different level and conceived in a liberal political context hostile to Chevalier. For the Saint-Simonian, liberty was historically a *means*, and only a means, never an end: this idea, frequently mentioned by Saint-Simonian writers, originated with Auguste Comte and led to a polemic between Benjamin Constant and Comte's allies in 1829. Chevalier's admiration for *military* organization as a model for France to emulate led Tocqueville to reject his thinking as absurd. What is more, it led Chevalier to take a highly critical attitude toward American lifestyles, modes of economic production, and political customs.

In 1832, writing in the *Globe*, a liberal newspaper that he and Pierre Leroux had taken over on behalf of the Saint-Simonians, Chevalier eagerly imagined the elaborate ceremony that he hoped the French would adopt to mark the construction of new railway lines: "The king and his family, the ministers, the supreme court, the royal court, and the two chambers would all take up

---

[106] The rapprochement drew protests from other Saint-Simonians, however: see Charléty, *Histoire du saint-simonisme*, pp. 238–39.

[107] Michel Chevalier, *Lettres sur l'Amérique du Nord*, 3rd ed. (Paris: Charles Gosselin, 1838), 2 vols. The quotations come from pp. 279, 283, and 285. Note that the title page is similar to that of *Democracy in America*, both having been published by Gosselin.

[108] The issue of which of the two influenced the other therefore becomes secondary (even though Chevalier cited Tocqueville in the fourth edition of his book, which came out after *DA* II).

shovels and pick-axes. Old Lafayette would be there . . . squadrons of workers would be led by engineers and polytechnicians in full uniform. . . . The most brilliant women would mingle with the workers to encourage them."[109]

The rivalry between Tocqueville and Chevalier was sustained by the fact that Chevalier dealt at length with the American economy and finances, areas that were relatively neglected in *Democracy in America*. But Chevalier did not receive nearly as many reviews as his rival, perhaps because he chose to publish first in a journal. However, his work was reprinted and translated abroad. As we will see later, Chevalier reviewed Tocqueville's book with eventual membership in the academy in mind, and Tocqueville eventually sent him a copy of the second volume of *Democracy in America*, but not until 1850, ten years after it was published.

It will be useful to consider a little more carefully why Chevalier's letters from North America might have struck readers as comparable to Tocqueville despite the considerable difference between the two thinkers.

What was democracy for Chevalier? Like Tocqueville, he played with the meaning of the word, but he tugged it in a somewhat different direction. By "democracy" he meant a social group that differentiated itself from the American bourgeoisie. In America, he argued, "there exist only two classes: the bourgeoisie and the democracy."[110] By "bourgeoisie" he meant industrialists, merchants, lawyers, and doctors. The democracy "includes *farmers* and *mechanics*. Farmers generally own their own land."[111]

Interestingly, this use of the term "democracy" is also frequent in another work of Chevalier's, *Des intérêts matériels en France* (1838).[112] "The democracy" here meant workers (proletarians) and, by extension, the poor (peasants). For instance, Chevalier wrote that "the democracy is thirsty, cold, and hungry," and for him this was the issue, *not political rights*. In the next sentence, "our democracy" refers to the "popular class": "We must therefore seek ways in which we can rapidly and reliably expand material interests and guarantee our democracy an appropriate share in the fruits of such improvements."[113] The clergy and the army were dependent on this democracy, moreover, because statistics showed that clergymen and soldiers

[109] Published in the *Globe* (April 1832) and quoted in Charléty, *Histoire du saint-simonisme*, p. 108. See also p. 102 (on centralization) and pp. 107–8 on Chevalier's economic and educational program.

[110] Chevalier, *Lettres sur l'Amérique du Nord*, letter 32, "On the bourgeoisie in America and in France," p. 331. This letter was reproduced by Guizot's acolyte Alletz in *De la démocratie nouvelle*, 1837.

[111] *Farmers* and *mechanics* were in English in the original. In another passage (in vol. 1 of the book), Chevalier added workers to this list.

[112] Michel Chevalier, *Des intérêts matériels en France* (Paris: Charles Gosselin and W. Coquebert, 1838). Chevalier sent Tocqueville a copy with a dedication.

[113] Ibid., p. 9.

were recruited among workers and peasants. Louis de Carné made a similar point,[114] inspired by Chevalier, in his previously cited 1837 review.[115] This usage is interesting because it confirms that the notion of a sociological democracy was in the political culture of the age and that Tocqueville drew on it in forging his concept of the "social state" characteristic of modern democracy.[116] As late as 1871, the word was still being used in Chevalier's sense.[117]

The debate in 1834–35 opposed people like Guizot, who rejected the term "democracy," and those who agreed with Tocqueville (or with republicans such as Carrel) that it represented the future. Note, however, that a writer like Alletz could change the terms of the debate while taking Guizot's side: ancient democracy was plebeian, and American democracy remained so; the "new democracy," with its 300,000 property-qualified voters, would be bourgeois and truly French.[118]

Chevalier, for his part, argued that a particular social group had seized power in America, a group heeded by politicians linked to President Jackson, who demagogically attacked the Bank of the United States. This "democrat party" was the servant of the "autocratic people,"[119] which not only posed a danger to America's future but might also presage the rise of something similar in Europe. Europe was in some respects bourgeois, in others aristocratic: "Political influence is today entirely in the hands of the American democracy, just as in France it belongs to the bourgeoisie" (p. 333). America had simplified the social structure: "Civilization, in passing from one continent to the other, rid itself of the proletariat and the idle bourgeoisie."[120] In America,

---

[114] Four years earlier, in an interesting critical summary of the Restoration, *Vues sur l'histoire contemporaine*, Carné did not use this notion.

[115] Carné, "De la démocratie aux États-Unis et de la bourgeoisie en France." Alletz, an acolyte of Guizot, mentioned both Carné and Chevalier in the appendix of his book on the middle classes.

[116] Jean-Jacques Ampère, a close friend of Tocqueville's, discussed the knighting of nonnobles in 1838: "Democracy participated in chivalrous sentiments and mores." "La chevalerie," *Revue des deux mondes*, 1838, part 2, pp. 423–57. The sentence may strike today's reader as unintelligible.

[117] See J. Dubois, *Le Vocabulaire politique et social en France de 1869 à 1872* (Paris: Larousse, 1962), p. 282. A communard poster, "To the proletarians," declared in April 1871 that "we call upon the democracy to organize itself immediately." This referred to a battalion of sharpshooters under the Commune.

[118] For Édouard Alletz, July "revealed the possibility of a monarchy without nobility, a democracy without universal suffrage, a new polycracy, mobile like democracy, an orderly democracy that called upon the wisest and most talented to manage the public's affairs." *De la démocratie nouvelle ou Des mœurs et de la puissance des classes moyennes en France* (Paris: Lequien, 1837), 2 vols., p. vii.

[119] Letter 4, p. 51: "Popular autocracy."

[120] This echoed a major Saint-Simonian theme: there would be no place for the idle in the future "society of organization." Cf. Saint-Simon's parable of the bees and the hornets. Chevalier's Letter 32 exhorted the "idle bourgeoisie" to "provide the people with leaders for their labors." The "25 million agricultural proletarians" were particularly in need of leadership, for otherwise the military threat might increase (as more peasants were recruited).

conflict pitted those who owned relatively little and were generally self-employed against well-to-do professionals and the highly educated.

Thus Chevalier's idea of democracy, like Tocqueville's, had two sides: it was a force, fed by envy and jealousy, that aimed for equality through leveling, while America proceeded toward "democracy or republic," a type of political regime that would be economically disastrous. For Chevalier, "egalitarian democracy" (an authentic pleonasm) did not represent the future of civilization in America, much less in Europe. In Letter 18, on public opinion,[121] Chevalier described America as Europe (read: France) turned upside down: "It is Europe with its head at the bottom and its feet on top" (p. 284). In other words, "the democracy" was at the summit and the bourgeoisie at the base: "The *farmer* and *mechanic* are the lords of the New World. Public opinion is *their* opinion. Public will is *their* will. The President is *their* choice, *their* representative, *their* servant."[122]

Except for the crudeness of the writing, Tocqueville could have said much the same thing, for this was the period of Jacksonian demagogy, but he could never have accepted the rest of the passage: "European society, in London and Paris as well as Saint Petersburg, in the Swiss republic as well as in the Austrian empire, is aristocratic, because it rests more or less predominantly on the principle of inequality or hierarchy. American society is essentially and radically a democracy, not of words but of things" (pp. 284–85). What Chevalier did not see was that the civil and legal equality that grew out of the French Revolution made it impossible to align Paris with London or the other places he mentioned. In France, neither the social structure nor the institutional spirit was aristocratic: the bourgeoisie was at work helping to bring forth democracy as a social state and political form. Indeed, Guizot would be forced to recognize this after the revolution of 1848, with exasperation as well as surprise: "Chaos is today hidden beneath the sovereign and universal word 'democracy,' which all parties invoke and seek to appropriate as a talisman. . . . The word democracy holds out infinite prospects and promises. It pushes in every direction; it speaks to every passion of the human heart. . . . *From now on, this is the social state*, the permanent condition of our nation."[123]

To be sure, Chevalier perceived a process of equalization of thought and action. "In the United States," he wrote, "the democratic spirit has found its

---

[121] Published December 22, 1834, before Tocqueville's book appeared.

[122] Chevalier, *Lettres sur l'Amérique du Nord*, p. 284. Emphasis in original.

[123] François Guizot, *De la démocratie en France* (Paris: Victor Masson, 1849), pp. 9, 12, 15. Emphasis added. The title of this pamphlet indicates that Guizot was responding to Tocqueville.

way into all national habits and customs. Through every pore it besieges and importunes the foreigner, who before landing on these shores had no idea of the degree to which his European upbringing had impregnated his fiber and nerves with aristocracy."[124]

Unlike Tocqueville, however, Chevalier never for a moment envisioned "mores" as a *new form of authority* located within society itself and creating a new type of collective organization. For him, the pressure of public opinion was merely pressure from one well-defined social group in tension with the "bourgeoisie." He had nothing approaching the subtlety of Tocqueville's concept of "tyranny of opinion" (which, as we shall see, Tocqueville actually borrowed from other writers).[125] Chevalier did not believe in the idea that guided all of Tocqueville's thinking, that *there was a social authority, a non-institutional authority* in America that might someday spread to European societies as well. He believed instead that authority was what America lacked because it could come only from *a new governing aristocracy*, which would have to be created (Letter 29). Chevalier's fourth letter (entitled "Democracy. The Bank"[126]) described America in terms of what it was missing:

> There is no government in the true sense of the word, which is to say, a guiding power. Everyone is on his own. This is self-government in all its purity. Here, this abnormal, monstrous development of the individual principle is not an evil.... It is the present condition of progress in the United States, because self-government is the only political regime that the American character as it exists today can tolerate.[127]

This, in Chevalier's eyes, was America's limitation, its weakness: it relied for the time being on the (Protestant) individual. This might change, perhaps, because "despite its egalitarian habits and laws, there is a sort of aristocracy based either on education or on high commercial positions" (p. 61). This was in fact the group that Chevalier also referred to as the bourgeoisie.[128] To be clear, Chevalier's position was that American society

---

[124]Chevalier, *Lettres*, p. 285. Note that René Rémond, in *Les États-Unis devant l'opinion française*, insisted that liberal (or, more precisely, Ideologue) criticism of America during the Restoration and Orleanist criticism during the July Monarchy were aristocratic in spirit. He quoted from Chevalier to bolster this point.

[125]See below my remarks on "democracy as modern religion" and, in part 2, on Tocqueville as sociologist.

[126]The title referred to President Jackson's attack on the Second Bank of the United States, which had precipitated a grave crisis.

[127]Chevalier, *Lettres*, p. 56.

[128]Chevalier predicted that America would develop industrially, and his view on this point had something in common with Tocqueville's perception of a "new industrial aristocracy" in *DA* II. But

lacked authority in the sense of an *organized* hierarchy. "The social bonds of opinion and religion, the only ones that subsist here," were not enough.[129] They could "make up for the absence of political bonds only by tightening to the point of tyranny."

To sum up, the Saint-Simonian argued that self-government was not a sign of locally implanted and fully developed authority and that the force of religion and public opinion did not amount to sovereignty of the people. For Tocqueville, popular sovereignty was *immanent* in civil society and mores. Indeed, the people hovered over American society "like God over the universe."[130] Consider two key propositions of the first *Democracy*: "Society acts by itself and on itself.... The people reign over the American political world as God reigns over the universe."[131] In these felicitous phrases, so different from Chevalier's cumbrous and turgid style, Tocqueville summed up the essential argument of his book. When Chevalier described democratic America as Europe stood on its head, he ignored the (historical and political) priority of the town over the state and failed to see that the locus of sovereignty was the New England town. He did not see that the people had been put in the place of the king, even as the king's place was eliminated. The reason for his blindness was that he took the American democratic spirit to be a product of Puritanism and of a social group that *failed to grasp the essential nature of the state* (or that had yet to grasp it, as though it were still a nascent people).

In Letter 34 ("Social Improvement"), Chevalier spelled out his vision of the state as an agent of authority and industry. America, he repeated, was Protestant, while France was Catholic. That is why the French understood the state: "Puritanism is absolute self-government in religion; it engenders

---

Tocqueville feared the appetites of the captains of industry and rejected the future that Chevalier hoped would come to pass.

[129] Chevalier, *Lettres*, p. 345. On this point, it is tempting to contrast Chevalier's judgment not only with Tocqueville's but also with Montesquieu's, because the spirit is the same: "Rome was a vessel held by two anchors in the storm: religion and mores." *De l'esprit des lois*, VIII, 13.

[130] Tocqueville studied ancient Greek society in the writings of historians and moralists. He was familiar with the historical reality that Hegel incorporated in his system as the concept of "objective morality" (*die Sittliche* or *die Sittlichkeit*) in *Principles of the Philosophy of Right*, or as the "ethical substance" of the Greek city-state in *The Phenomenology of Spirit*. Gobineau's distorted lectures on Hegel left Tocqueville unaware of Hegel's contribution, in addition to which Hegel was accused of pantheism, a convenient charge that made it possible for French thinkers to avoid reading the Germans. Tocqueville did not learn German until late in life, when he traveled to Prussia in the course of doing research for *The Ancien Régime and the Revolution*. His aptitude for language was quite astonishing, like that of Gide, who learned English after the age of forty.

[131] *DA* I, p. 120; AG, pp. 64–65.

self-government in politics. The United Provinces were Protestant. The United States is Protestant. Catholicism is essentially monarchical."[132]

In France, "the honor of improving the lot of the laboring classes ought to belong to the monarchy, once it has completed the dangerous mission of compelling them to respect law and order" (p. 273). The gendarme king must become a social and industrial king: "What we need in France, in the interest of all, is a supreme arbiter between the bourgeoisie and the popular classes" (ibid.). This prescient remark anticipated the reign of Napoleon III, whom Chevalier would serve as a friend and respected advisor. According to Leroy-Beaulieu, for instance, Chevalier was not only the instigator and drafter of the free-trade treaty of 1860 with England but also its *only* champion. Chevalier rallied to the side of Louis-Napoléon Bonaparte on the very day of the coup.

Chevalier thus stood for the freedom to associate, form coalitions, trade, and produce, but under the shadow of a tutelary state—a long way indeed from Jacksonian America. Tocqueville was well aware that such aspirations existed in France: he called them "despotism." Chevalier also expressed his desire for social reform led by a strong state in Letter 39, in which the explicit statement of his political preferences sheds light on his analysis of the United States. Napoleon, he noted, believed that "the people have only one representative: the emperor."[133] Chevalier's gloss: "I do not claim that Napoleon described things as they are, but I do not hesitate to assert that he described them as they ought to be" (p. 275). It would have been impossible to state his position more clearly. His warning to the July Monarchy was thus not that the king exerted too much influence over his government, as many claimed, but rather that he did not exert enough influence.

What Chevalier was calling for was therefore a form of Bonapartism, and fifteen years later his words would prove prophetic: "We have no more aristocracy. The spiritual power has been set aside. The only power left standing to which the cause of the numerical majority can be entrusted is the monarchy. Indeed, the only monarchy now possible in France is one prepared to assume the role of firm and devoted guide of the people."[134] He added that the French could do without "a highly organized moderating power" capable of reconciling the different classes of society if and only if (1) "all classes were and could be represented in deliberative assemblies," and (2) "we were made for

---

[132] Chevalier, *Lettres*, p. 272.

[133] This was the point of a piece published in the *Moniteur* and probably written by Napoleon himself to correct Joséphine's application of the word "representatives" to the Corps Législatif.

[134] Chevalier, *Lettres*, p. 274.

self-government." But this was not the case. Indeed, Saint-Simon's "industrial constitution," or representation of diverse interest groups, was unacceptable to the liberals in government, and local government had no historical roots in the French view. Hence a strong government would be needed because "the so-called minor classes[135] have just grievances to articulate, lengthy demands to propose, and stunning reparations to expect" (p. 275). Chevalier's version of socialism was thus an "emperor of the workers," and he looked forward to such a regime as a counter not only to liberalism and socialism but also to democracy as he understood it. "The French people will never put up with a simulacrum of government. They want to be well-governed, but they need to be much-governed" (p. 279). He predicted (almost as a threat) the synthesis of imperialism and democracy. Let America serve as a lesson, he argued: there, "the ties between individuals have been severed" (p. 286) and everything was in pieces. "The states are republics within the federation. The cities are republics within the states. A farm is a republic within the county. . . . The family is an inviolable republic within the city. Each individual is in himself a small republic within the family."

Clearly, nothing like this would work in France[136] because, Chevalier insisted, the French national genius was such as to "act in accordance with the principles of association and unity, which are characteristics of Catholicism and monarchy. France is the finest example of political and administrative unity that exists anywhere in the world" (pp. 286–87, Letter 39). Take French savings banks (*caisses d'épargne*), for example: "They form a perfectly *unified* whole without the slightest prejudice to their individual independence." The French "love independence but do not feel alive unless [they] are part of a whole." Hence it would be unwise to dream of seeing America reproduced in France. Remember that there existed at the time what was commonly known as "the American school," which revolved around the newspaper *Le National*, founded by Carrel. In fact, the republicans of *Le National* did not believe in a direct transplantation of American institutions.[137]

Continuing his praise of unity through association, Chevalier wrote that "the association must be hierarchical" because in France, "republican

[135] That is, the minority produced by property qualifications for voting.
[136] The language here is very archaic. The accusation of "federalism" harked back to the good old days of Jacobinism, when Robespierre argued that "sinister federalism" was morally responsible for the division of France into neighborhoods, families, etc.
[137] Laboulaye, who was just coming of age intellectually, would become the most accomplished political theorist of the American school. See Jean-Claude Lamberti, "Laboulaye et le droit commun des peuples libres," *Commentaire* 36 (Winter 1986–87), especially the table on p. 744, which contrasts French and American ideas of the constitution as expressions of popular sovereignty. The table is taken from Laboulaye's *Questions constitutionnelles*.

association degenerates into anarchy." Here he was referring to secret republican societies, which Tocqueville also feared,[138] and which became sources of resistance and insurrection under the July Monarchy, starting with the alliance with the *canuts* of Lyon in 1831 and 1834. The books of both Tocqueville and Chevalier came out shortly after a broad movement of strikes and insurrections gave rise to the Guizot and Broglie law of 1834, which prohibited newspapers from declaring themselves to be republican, thereby virtually eliminating freedom of association, which was already subject to strict controls.

Chevalier ended with a project of his own, in which he opposed the American *model*: social reform was necessary, he argued, but it should be led "primarily by institutions embodying both unity and hierarchical association and directly incorporated into the overarching association, which is the state—or else operating in the shadow of powerful secondary associations, themselves linked to the state" (p. 287). It would be hard to imagine a proposal more clearly antithetical to the view that Tocqueville would soon make famous, according to which American towns enjoyed a high degree of autonomy from both the state and federal government and civil society associations enjoyed free rein.

After 1848, however, Chevalier was obliged to retreat. In his review of *Democracy in America*, he wrote that "the century is democratic and will remain so."[139] Nevertheless, the popular-authoritarian synthesis that he was hoping for would arrive a few months later. Authoritarian democracy had found its incarnation, and Chevalier may have had a better claim than Tocqueville to have seen it coming (despite the preface to *The Ancien Régime and the Revolution*, which I quoted earlier).

It is amusing to note that when Tocqueville eliminated a crucial chapter from the second volume of *Democracy in America* (a chapter that would have changed the meaning of the book for many interpreters), he noted in the manuscript that Chevalier had already dealt with the question in greater depth. What was the subject of the suppressed chapter? "The necessity under 'certain circumstances' of an interventionist state."[140]

---

[138] "Unlimited freedom of association" is "the last that a people can tolerate. If it does not plunge them into anarchy, it often brings them close to it." *DA* II.2.7, pp. 151–52; AG, p. 608.

[139] Michel Chevalier, *Journal des débats*, review published October 1, 1851.

[140] For someone who "did not want to read," Tocqueville here recognized a serious problem. The chapter was to have followed chapter 5 of book 2 and was entitled "On the Way in Which American Governments Act with Respect to Associations." What might this have reminded him of? He wrote: "Men who live in democratic centuries need more than others to be allowed to do things for themselves and sometimes more than others to have things done for them. It all depends on the circumstances." This was in fact a dialectic of laisser-faire and dirigisme. See Nolla II, pp. 106–7 and n. t.

Was Tocqueville a liberal? Surely not in the simplistic sense in which he has sometimes been described as one from the nineteenth century on.

The Reception of the Traditionalists: Tocqueville Weakened the Principle of Authority

It is not always easy to separate the traditionalists from the monarchists, because in French history, resistance to innovation has generally involved nostalgia for the church-state alliance. Nevertheless, a number of strands of conservative opinion can be clearly distinguished from legitimism: for example, the school of Frédéric Le Play and the "social Catholic" current, which included such writers as Antoine-Frédéric Ozanam, Albert de Mun, and Augustin Cochin. Monarchist criticism of Tocqueville became increasingly harsh as the nineteenth century wore on. Traditionalists did not spare him either, particularly when it came to his views of democratic authority.

On this point, we must acknowledge that Tocqueville took seriously what some of his American interlocutors told him. From Josiah Quincy, the president of Harvard, for example, he learned that "in nearly all respects Massachusetts was as free before the revolution as it is today. For the king's name we substituted that of the people, but nothing else changed."[141] From this Tocqueville immediately deduced that "the absence of government" was a good thing and that "every man learns to think and act for himself without counting on the support of an outside force." This led him to the following formulation of the liberal ideal (which he included in the suppressed chapter of the second volume of *Democracy in America*): "The greatest concern of a good government should be to gradually accustom the people to do without it."

One might assume that the French also substituted the people for the king in 1792, 1795, 1799, 1848, and so forth. In fact, however, the locus of power remained the state—state power through centralization. In France, the idea was that *the people occupy the royal palace*: men elected by the people now either governed or appointed those who governed. On this score, Lanfrey, a republican of the American school, remarked that "in France, democracy has concentrated its passion almost exclusively on obtaining sovereignty.... As long as the people have the right to vote, we do not care if the expression of this right proves to be despotic. Our elected officials confiscate all our

---

[141] *Œuvres*, La Pléiade, 1:65 (travel notebooks); GZ, p. 236.

liberties, but they tell us that we are the sovereign people, and this consoles us for our loss."[142]

What Tocqueville did was to observe the American people in their primary place of activity (the towns) and to analyze the channels through which their power flowed, including that powerful ally of popular sovereignty, the *judicial power*. The same Josiah Quincy explained that in America, if you break a wagon axle, your first recourse as a citizen is to sue the town for failing to properly maintain the roads. The individual uses the law to assert his social and therefore political existence. In France, democracy was not only political and statist but also elitist, whereas in America, Tocqueville argued, it was not only "social" and jurisprudential but also oriented toward serving the individual.

These arguments irritated a number of French traditionalists. Claudio Jannet devoted half of *Les États-Unis contemporains* to refuting Tocqueville.[143] The latter's depiction of the United States did not correspond to reality, Jannet argued, because the reign of the professional politician, the politicization of local government, and the growing influence of corruption had already altered a picture that Tocqueville had in any case greatly idealized in his book. Furthermore, while it might be a good idea to refrain from drawing an abstract distinction between the municipal electorate and the political electorate,[144] who exactly were the "real people" in either France or the United States?[145] Drawing on conservative American political writers, Jannet insisted that the people had to be understood as "an organized moral being" for which the most descriptive word was "nation": "The *nation* does not refer to all or even the majority of the adult individuals in the country at any given time. The *nation* is the people organized into families, corporations, communes, and provinces, united by traditional customs, and in solidarity with past and future generations in such a way as to create *nationality* and *fatherland*."[146]

<hr/>

[142] P. Lanfrey, *Études et portraits politiques* (Paris: Charpentier, 1865), p. 161 (article on Armand Carrel in the context of the empire).

[143] Claudio Jannet, *Les États-Unis contemporains* (Paris: Plon 1876), subsequently revised and reprinted several times. Cf. Mélonio, *Tocqueville et les Français*, pp. 229–31.

[144] Jannet, *Les États-Unis contemporains*, p. 297, n. 2.

[145] This was an endless theme of debate in 1871–75 over the reform of universal suffrage. See Jaume, *L'Individu effacé*, pp. 334ff. In the correspondence in Royer-Collard's library, one finds a typical letter from Count Falloux to Paul Andral (Royard-Collard's son-in-law) concerning ways to reconstitute a true "people" for electoral purposes by calling on vestry councils in the churches, various groups of notables, etc.

[146] Jannet, *Les États-Unis contemporains*, p. 108.

A disciple of Le Play, Jannet sought to systematically destroy the image of America for which he held Lafayette and Tocqueville responsible.[147] In the preface Le Play himself recalled his long conversations with Tocqueville between 1840 and 1848, from which he drew the conclusion that Tocqueville suffered from the same illusions as the French liberals: "He convinced himself that electoral reform could be achieved in revolutionary France only by the lower class, instructed and guided by new men. That is why, in forming his view of America, he failed to take account of the deficiencies of the class in which he placed his hope."[148]

Although Tocqueville did not believe in direct suffrage, he was accused of using the term "democracy" to legitimate the rule of the multitude. "With their sophisms and illusions," Le Play argued, Lafayette and Tocqueville had helped to keep the revolutionary spirit alive—exactly the opposite of the goal that Tocqueville set for himself throughout his life.[149]

On the right, Tocqueville was frequently reproached for having flattered "the people." For the Action Française the case was open-and-shut. In 1903 Léon de Montesquiou called Tocqueville "a criminal," and in 1910 Maurras launched a virulent attack: "Tocqueville's responsibility cannot be passed over in silence. The mildest, most ingenuous, and most dangerous of philosophical malefactors contributed immensely to the general blindness."[150] How could he have sympathized as he did with America, "a pyramid of dollars, hardware, and delicatessen, which cannot even be compared with

---

[147] Le Play, born in 1806, was roughly the same age as Tocqueville (born 1805). An authoritarian Catholic, he was renowned for his travels throughout the world and for his social surveys, which enabled him to become the founder of a distinctive school of sociology. Under Napoleon III he served as an official expert. To this day he is considered the father of the social survey. See esp. *Études sociales*, no. 135–36 (2002), a special issue devoted to "the jurists of the Le Play school." In this issue an article by Jean-Luc Coronel de Boissezon, "L'État sans politique de Frédéric Le Play," is useful for a comparison with Tocqueville. See also *Études sociales*, no. 142–44, II/2005–06, a special issue devoted to "Frédéric Le Play. Anthology and correspondence." Tocqueville may have met Le Play in the salon of the Saint-Simonian Jean Reynaud, according to Antoine Savoye in the preface to Le Play, *La Méthode sociale* (Paris: Méridiens Klincksieck, 1989), p. 23. While Tocqueville was attempting to found the Young Left party in the Chamber, Le Play was for a few months active as an expert advisor to the government before 1848. Le Play said that he and Tocqueville had been brought together by their common friend, Victor de Lanjuinais, as part of a "reformist group" in July 1848. This group fell apart after the coup of 1851. See Le Play, *La Constitution essentielle de l'humanité* (Tours: Alfred Mame, 1881), pp. 238–39, 243. Under the Second Empire Le Play persuaded Tocqueville's cousin Louis de Kergorlay to join the Société d'Économie Sociale, of which Kergorlay served as president in 1863–64.

[148] Jannet, *Les États-Unis contemporains*, preface by Le Play, p. xix.

[149] Ibid., p. xxii.

[150] Charles Maurras, *L'Action française*, April 3, 1910. Cf. Mélonio, *Tocqueville et les Français*, pp. 257–58. More subtle—and penetrating—was the series of papers published by Pierre Boutang in *Aspects de la France* (1952). We will examine these later when we discuss *The Ancien Régime and the Revolution*, which Boutang reviewed when Gallimard issued a new edition as part of the *Œuvres complètes*.

Cheops' rock piles (which if nothing else have stood the test of time)" and yet pretended to rival "the columns of the Parthenon"? These were standard tropes of French anti-Americanism, which, as we saw earlier, was the monarchist equivalent of left-wing anticapitalism.

To return to the traditionalists, in his most important book, *La Réforme sociale en France,* Le Play frequently criticized Tocqueville's position on authority.[151] He challenged Tocqueville's account of the New England town and the notion of democracy itself. "His fine book" contained "many truths," Le Play conceded, but "he does not prove what he affirms, that government exclusively by the lower classes is responsible for the greatness that the United States has achieved today."[152] Michel Chevalier had a much clearer sense of the importance of large landowners in the South as well as in the federal government.[153] Like Guizot in *De la démocratie en France* (1849) or in his 1856 letter to Tocqueville, Le Play insisted that Tocqueville had failed to recognize who really wielded authority in the United States, namely, elites with an "aristocratic" profile. Le Play would return to this theme in a number of his works. For instance, in *La Méthode sociale* he wrote that Tocqueville "was completely wrong about the origin of American government. He failed to see that it stemmed from a fact rather than a principle."[154] Tocqueville was one of those innovators who for two centuries had been destroying "the ascendancy of the moral forces of the essential constitution." These writers neglected the Ten Commandments (for Le Play the only valid institutional code, always and everywhere), rejected paternal authority, despised religion, and believed in the sovereignty of the people: these were the four major errors that undermined "the essential constitution." By contrast, "Jefferson founded a democracy because in his day, the people, consisting of farmers obedient to the Ten Commandments, were the class most capable of choosing the *aristoi*. But he regarded this form of government as inappropriate for the *canaille* of the cities of Europe."

Le Play's critique of Tocqueville became the common view of conservatives and traditionalists. Even some liberal Catholics shared it (and we must be careful to distinguish them from social Catholics hostile to the Revolution). Although the liberal Catholics also sought a form of decentralized

---

[151] Frédéric Le Play, *La Réforme sociale en France* (1864), 2 vols. Six more editions appeared during Le Play's lifetime. Here I cite from the original edition, reprinted in facsimile by Slatkine in 1982.

[152] Ibid., p. 224, n. 1.

[153] Chevalier was related to Le Play by marriage of their children. On Le Play's refusal to consider the example of the town as conclusive for other countries, see ibid., pp. 284–87. For the demolition of Tocqueville's model of democracy, see pp. 221–24.

[154] Le Play, *La Méthode sociale,* p. 194, n. 1.

authority, as a glance at their newspaper, *L'Avenir*, in 1830 will show,[155] and although they gave priority to civil society over the state, they were for that very reason drawn to certain aspects of traditionalism. This is clearer in the case of Montalembert than in that of Lacordaire.[156] Montalembert, an enthusiastic reader of Le Play's social studies, wrote the author:

I do not hesitate to tell you that you have written the most original, most useful, most courageous, and in every respect *most powerful* book of this century. You are not more eloquent than the illustrious Tocqueville, but you are much more critically perceptive and above all morally courageous.... You are very clear about man's original fall, the doctrine that so deeply repels the servile pride of our contemporaries.[157]

In these circles, Tocqueville was seen as a legitimist who no longer dared to think in traditionalist terms, which is why he was accused of lacking courage. Montalembert made the same point to Augustin Cochin: "No more important or more interesting book has appeared since Tocqueville's great work on democracy, and Le Play is far more courageous than Tocqueville, who never dared to challenge any powerful prejudice."[158]

Tocqueville's principal "lack of courage" may have been his failure to heed Le Play's insistence that all restrictions on inheritances be lifted.[159] Tocqueville did not reject the argument out of hand; indeed, he paid a good deal of attention to laws of inheritance.[160] He had this to say about Le Play in a letter to Lanjuinais:

As for the substance of his ideas, I largely approve, but I think that the evil he attacks is invincible, and therefore I am not sure that one ought to attack it. The malady now affects the mind of the people more than the law. If we were to allow

[155]The commune was "the true political element," according to *L'Avenir*. The state was merely an extension of local governments. In 1848, as a member of the Constitutional Committee on which he sat with Tocqueville, Lamennais insisted that the family had to be "constituted" before the state. The commune was a "collection of families." Historically, "one proceeded from the family to the state," and not the reverse. These quotations come from the very useful book by Frédéric Lambert, *Théologie de la République. Lamennais prophète et législateur* (Paris: L'Harmattan, 2001), pp. 276–77, 281.

[156]Recall that Lacordaire succeeded Tocqueville in the Académie and praised *Democracy in America*. This was an excellent occasion for Guizot, who delivered the reception speech, to settle some scores with Tocqueville: see *OC* XVI, pp. 312–45, and part 5 below.

[157]Quoted in Father Lecanuet, *Montalembert*, 3rd ed. (Paris: Poussielgue, 1905), 3:424. This is the only biography of Montalembert, but it is a remarkable one.

[158]Letter of October 10, 1864, quoted in Sainte-Beuve, *Nouveaux Lundis (Paris: Calmann-Lévy, 1884)*, 9:196, n. 1.

[159]In addition, Le Play recommended institutionalizing the "stem family" as the source of everything, creating patronage, and restoring enlightened private charity.

[160]As we will see in part 2 on Tocqueville as sociologist.

a father to prefer his eldest son, the prejudices of his other children, of the public, and of other family members would prevent him from doing so.[161]

The familial authority that Le Play and most other traditionalists invoked was for Tocqueville a feature of aristocratic society. For him, the question was not whether he had the courage of his convictions; he saw the traditionalist position as a veritable *anachronism* likely to revive social conflict, as Peyronnet's proposed reform had done during the Restoration. Consider Le Play's definition of the "gentleman" in his "lexicon of social science": "In good social constitutions, [the gentleman] takes it upon himself, at his own cost, to serve the public interest of the Neighborhood, Commune, and Province."[162] Indeed, for a long time the English aristocracy assumed responsibility for local administration by establishing justices of the peace. Still, when Le Play's friend Jean Reynaud called on him in 1848 to participate in planning a National School of Administration, he agreed, despite his habitual preference for aristocratic patronage and what he called "natural Authorities" (as usual distinguished by a capital letter): "Individuals whose power is instituted in private Life by the nature of men and things [*sic*]. These authorities are: in the Family, the father; in the Workshop, the Employer; in the Neighborhood, the sage chosen by the affection and interest of the population."[163]

---

[161] Letter of March 3, 1856, to Victor Lanjuinais (archives of the château de Pont-Chevron, Fonds Lanjuinais, comtesse de La Rochefoucauld).

[162] Le Play, "Les 300 mots constitutifs du langage propre à la science sociale," in *Les Ouvriers européens*, vol. 1, *La Méthode d'observation*, 2nd ed. (Tours: Alfred Mame, 1879), p. 458. This book was reprinted by A. Savoye under the title *La Méthode sociale*, with the same pagination (see above). Note the capital letters in Le Play's text, a device he used frequently to indicate what he took to be quasi-sacred institutions in his constant search for "custom." Le Play used the term "social constitution" in much the same way that Tocqueville used "social state," to refer to mores, ideas, and customs. This point was made explicit by his disciple Demolin, the editor in chief of *La Réforme sociale* (quoted by F. Savoye in *La Méthode sociale*, p. 49). In *La Méthode d'observation* (vol. 1 of *Les Ouvriers européens*), Le Play wrote: "The true constitution of a people is in its ideas and in the mores and institutions of private life more than in the written laws by which new men nowadays pretend to govern all social relations" (pp. 180–81). In this respect, Tocqueville falls between the Montlosier moment of the Restoration (when this thesis first appeared) and the Le Play moment of the Third Republic. Note that Tocqueville seems wary of the expression "social constitution," which he never uses in *The Ancien Régime* and uses only once in *DA* II: "I have no doubt that the social and political constitution of a people fosters certain beliefs" (*DA* II, p. 180; AG, p. 634). This passage is not innocent, however, because it occurs in a context in which Tocqueville is discussing the "moralization of democracy by religion."

[163] Le Play, "Les 300 mots," p. 445. To be distinguished from "social Authorities," one echelon higher up, individuals who are models of social peace and can directly inspire social science. Le Play shared Guizot's dream of a "natural aristocracy," but on a very different basis. Le Play's contribution was nevertheless to undertake and encourage others to undertake field surveys of remarkable quality. He played "practically no role" in the inception of French sociology, however, according to Laurent Mucchielli, *La Découverte du social. Naissance de la sociologie en France* (Paris: La Découverte, 1998), p. 111, no doubt

∽

All things considered, it is not surprising that *Democracy in America* elicited these kinds of reactions from legitimists, traditionalists, and Saint-Simonians like Michel Chevalier. All admired authority and saw in the American republic *a powerful challenge to French history* and French political predilections. America stood for two ideas they feared: first, that a republic based on local liberties could do without a king, and second, that the French state, in which the administrative took priority over the constitutional, was not the realization of the divine that it took itself to be.

The Right criticized Tocqueville for proposing that a nation with a vibrant civil society might follow a different path of development. They also resented his efforts to educate conservatives. He might as well have been an out-and-out republican, and the fact that he took pains not to appear to be one was only a further source of irritation and embarrassment. Among his readers (whose various types we have begun to distinguish), he tried to enlist the sympathy of people of similar background, whom he hoped to persuade of the need to adapt to new times.

Indeed, the author of *Democracy in America* believed that it might soon be necessary to compromise with republicanism in France,[164] but it was even more important to win the cooperation of the people—and not to subjugate "the lower classes." These principles would guide Tocqueville's conduct in 1848: yes to the republican people, no to the socialist workers.

With respect to social and economic policy, Tocqueville believed that there was much to do in order to combat the utopians and gain the advantage over the Doctrinaires and Thiers: this was precisely the moment of the ephemeral "Young Left," and it was apparently at this point that Tocqueville paid close attention to what Le Play was saying. To his friend Dufaure he wrote:

> Since all political men nowadays harbor ardent personal ambitions and are eager, nay breathless, for success, they fail to see that not only the most legitimate but also the most durable way ... to obtain great political authority in a country where there are still as many things to be settled as there are in France is to find a good solution to a host of important issues that are not strictly speaking

---

because he and his school repudiated the universities of the Third Republic, unlike the Durkheimians, who achieved influence within them.

[164] To Ernest de Chabrol he wrote on October 26, 1831, that he had always thought that constitutional monarchy will lead to a republic. To Eugène Stöffels he wrote on October 5, 1836, that he favored a monarchy with substantial liberty granted to the provinces (Beaumont ed., 5:433–36).

political. . . . [The moral and material pleasures] of the people have thus far been abandoned either to the dreams and passions of the utopians or to the selfish and unintelligent contempt of the conservative majority that governs us, a species of new nobility that cares little for the people, or as M. *Desclozeaux* put it the other day in the Chamber, the *populace*.[165]

What traditionalists of various stripes failed to see and grasp in Tocqueville was that for him, the power of the people was above all a sociological and moral power, not an institutional one. *Democracy in America* offered a quite original conception of His Majesty the Majority, which was still called "the Public." In Tocqueville's eyes, the various organs of decentralized government—the communes (dominated by great landowners) of which the monarchists dreamed, the associations of families in Lamennais, the "social authorities" exalted by Le Play and his followers—made sense only in this context. The Public was not a phantom conjured up by political dreams—a liberal illusion that in Le Play's view stemmed from "the so-called principles of 1789." The Public was the new subject of history, or at any rate the quintessential totem of political action. Hence we turn now to this important new element of Tocqueville's concept of "democracy": the public as a moral personality.

[165] Letter to Dufaure, September 2, 1846, Dufaure family's papers, Beinecke Library.

Democracy as Modern Religion

> Human nature wants to believe.... [In the sixteenth century],
> authority, that is the right or faculty enjoyed by a reasonable being to
> be taken at his word, was the principal foundation of all belief.
>
> —Vinet, *Moralistes des seizième
> et dix-septième siècles*, 1856

THE "SUPERIOR WISDOM" OF THE PUBLIC

Just as the first volume of *Democracy in America* begins more or less with the New England town, the second volume begins with the other question that Tocqueville regarded as crucial: that of public opinion conceived as a form of *belief*. The chapter in question is entitled "On the Principal Source of Beliefs among Democratic Peoples."[1] This deserves to be read carefully, almost word by word, because in it Tocqueville sets forth one of his strongest intuitions, but in a complex style that proceeds from paradox to paradox.

Tocqueville's intuition is the following: that the "principal source" of what the citizens of a democratic society think takes on the form and power of an *authority*—an authority that everyone collectively exerts on each individual. But because "everyone" creates this authority without knowing it, individuals find themselves facing an entity that is not fragmented but monolithic and therefore omnipotent. Democratic public opinion becomes the god of modern times, a god strangely immanent in society (Tocqueville uses the word "pantheism"[2]) and with a face that changes daily. The present chapter is devoted to the mechanisms of this alienation,[3] which Tocqueville characterizes as "religious."

---

[1] *DA* II.1.2, pp. 15–20; AG, pp. 489–93.

[2] Of pantheism he wrote: "even though such a system destroys human individuality—or rather because it does—it will hold a secret charm for men who live in democracy." *DA* II, p. 42; AG, p. 512. Likewise, Benjamin Constant spoke of pantheism as a way out of "the individuality that oppresses us." See Constant, *De la religion*, ed. Tzvetan Todorov and E. Hofmann (Paris: Actes Sud, 1999), p. 257. The question of pantheism was fashionable at the time, if I may put it that way. It is likely (see part 2) that Tocqueville took his inspiration from *Exposition de la doctrine de Saint-Simon*, second year, 1830.

[3] I use "alienation" in a sense analogous to Feuerbach's in his reflections on Christianity to suggest that democratic man bows down before an authority that he himself produces but that he does not recognize as coming from him.

To study the text, it is best to follow its tortuous progression and numerous reversals before looking for intellectual affinities, primarily in the literature of counterrevolutionary sociology and Catholic thought.

ᴄᴀᴏ

Tocqueville begins by stating a number of axioms or theses drawn from his habitual intellectual baggage (or perhaps one should call it his ideology): (1) society cannot exist unless everyone accepts a certain number of common ideas; (2) this acceptance of certain ideas almost as facts of nature deserves to be called "authority"; and (3) in a democratic *society* (regardless of what the political regime may be), intellectual authority is vital:[4] "In any event, there must always be a place in the intellectual and moral world where authority exists. This place may vary, but it must exist somewhere.... Thus the question is not whether some form of intellectual authority exists in democratic ages but only where it resides [its *repository*[5]] and what its extent may be."[6] Over the course of history, in other words, it is not only the shape of intellectual authority that changes but also the site, the *locus*: in democracy, its locus is the society of individuals, and its official name is "public opinion" (Tocqueville also says "common opinion").

The term "repository" (*dépôt* in French) is quite important. Tocqueville uses it only three times in his work because its value is overdetermined: democratic authority has a "repository." Any French reader in 1840 would have been reminded of the "repository of faith" or "repository of truth," phrases that harked back to religious history, conciliar controversies, and debates about sects, especially Jansenism.[7] In each of the three places where Tocqueville uses the word in *Democracy in America*, the context has to do with religion. Just as in the case of the term "civic spirit" (see above), Tocqueville knew that he was taking a calculated risk in using a term with such heavy connotations. Why suggest that democratic public opinion might have something in common with religious authority or with a spiritual community such as Port-Royal?[8] Why indeed, since the next paragraph in fact denies the

---

[4] Instead of intellectual authority, one might say spiritual authority, but Tocqueville avoided the latter term because Comte and Saint-Simon used it. Even Lacordaire spoke of the Church as an "intellectual society" in his Notre-Dame sermons, presumably for the same reason.

[5] In French: *où en est le dépôt*. The word suggests a repository. This bears emphasizing.

[6] *DA* II, p. 16; AG, p. 490.

[7] On this point, see the appendix to part 1, where I cite the other passages in which Tocqueville uses the word. On Jansenism, see part 3.

[8] The chapter opens, moreover, with a discussion of "dogmatic beliefs." Tocqueville wrote: "It is impossible to eliminate dogmatic beliefs, by which I mean opinions that men accept on faith and without discussion." *DA* II, p. 15; AG, p. 489.

influence of the established religions, and even more of the new religions, on the democratic present and future: "a sort of instinctive incredulity about the supernatural" is widespread among the citizens of democracy, and "new prophets" will inevitably be mocked. Baffling our expectations, however, the chapter ends by identifying a religious phenomenon appropriate to the democratic spirit: "We may anticipate that faith in common opinion will become a sort of religion, with the majority as its prophet."[9]

In other words, democracy is in the process of establishing *a religion that does not know it is a religion*. But what is the object of this religion? It is a religion of democracy, of course, or, more precisely, of its sovereign, the Majority —or, to put it in more mystical, less numerical terms, the Public. The Public is the prophet that cannot be mocked, and public opinion indefatigably spreads its gospel.

Democracy engenders democratic religion. In other words, it worships itself: the Public celebrates itself through individuals who revere its word in the form of common opinion. This raises a new question: How does democratic *faith* work when democratic religion remains unaware that it is a religion? By way of response, Tocqueville seems to offer a second denial: modern individuals have "no faith in one another because of their similarity."

What does this mean? Equality simultaneously engenders a feeling of independent-mindedness ("I have my own ideas") and evidence of the similarity of all minds. Common sense is the most widely shared thing in the world, as Descartes said, and Tocqueville borrowed this formula when he saw how democratic citizens perceived themselves and others.[10] It might therefore seem that no democratic religion can exist because religion assumes some relationship to Transcendence, and democracy levels all transcendence. If all men are "equal and alike,"[11] who can be divinized? And who could accept such divinization in all sincerity? Here, for the third time, Tocqueville stands his thesis on its head: *it is precisely because equal individuals are incredulous that they will adhere to a powerful faith.*

Indeed, equal individuals exhibit "almost unlimited confidence in the judgment of the public." What matters is the object of faith: incredulity toward the other, but faith and confidence in the Public, with a capital P. This

[9] Ibid., p. 18; AG, p. 492.

[10] Tocqueville wrote on his manuscript that "Descartes is the greatest of democrats." Nolla II, p. 14, n. e.

[11] A constant formula in Tocqueville. Here we should understand "alike in aptitude," with aptitudes themselves sacralized as rights. Do we not say that "all opinions deserve respect"? In a Kantian spirit we should also rather say that all persons are worthy of respect, not all opinions, but democratic pride is sensitive on this point. One must often pretend to take even an idiotic opinion seriously, either out of respect (as on the radio) or for teaching purposes (in the schools).

Public arises, in fact, from the independence of which the individual is so proud,[12] because in representing himself as independent-minded, the individual cannot help representing himself as dependent on man collectively. He is inferior to the Whole, to the sum total of all those individuals in whose essential "resemblance" to himself, that is, his capacity to judge, he believes. Pride in equality immediately gives rise to its opposite: the feeling of inequality (between the part and the whole).

Thus, owing to equality and similarity, there exists a "judgment of the public," a subjective belief or imagination in the mind of the individual, which is invested with authority: "Public opinion holds that. . . ." It is common today to see politicians cowed by this judgment, which, far from being a "Last Judgment," is subject to constant, endless revision. Tocqueville explained why the Public has a force of its own: it exerts "a sort of immense pressure" on the mind of each individual, even though its repository is social rather than individual. To borrow Béchard's distinction, we might therefore say that the public is not a "power" but an "authority."

But we have already encountered another example of society's exercise of authority over itself, in the towns of North America and the concept of popular sovereignty. In America, the Whole acts on itself immanently, without *division*, without being crystallized in an incarnate figure, which in France might be called the king, emperor, republican monarch, Committee of Public Safety, the People United, the National Assembly, and so forth. For Tocqueville, the "public" is constituted from the bottom up through a process that never takes on an incarnate visage yet possesses a mouth and speaks with the force of law: "In the United States, the majority takes it upon itself to provide individuals with a range of ready-made opinions."[13]

But this brings us back to our question: Why do individuals accept this when they are so proud of being free and equal? The explanation lies in the religious aspect of democracy, namely, *the humility* of the equal individual when faced with the body composed of his equals. As Tocqueville puts it at the end of the second *Democracy* (when he discusses "mild and tutelary despotism"), "Each individual allows himself to be clapped in chains because he sees that the other end of the chain is held not by a man or a class but by the people themselves."[14] In the chapter under discussion here, which concerns democratic "beliefs," he shows that no one ties the citizen down; rather, he

---

[12] In "aristocratic centuries," as Tocqueville says, the individual knows that he is dependent on the knowledge, authority, and wisdom of others such as the lord, the bishop, the alderman, the provost, etc.

[13] *DA* II, p. 16; AG, p. 491.

[14] Ibid., p. 386; AG, p. 819 (chapter entitled "What Kind of Despotism Must Democratic Nations Fear?").

ties himself, he subjects himself voluntarily to the power of the majority. This is a transformation of what Étienne de La Boétie called "voluntary servitude," of the love of the despot that Claude Lefort analyzed as the cult of the One.[15]

Pursuing the *insinuation of the religious into the civil* (if I may put it that way), Tocqueville remarked that some ideas are accepted without examination, "upon the faith of the public." This was a splendid turn of phrase. To make his point, Tocqueville invested the familiar formula with a strong and unexpected meaning: when we repeat someone else's assertion or act on someone else's information, we say that we are doing so "upon the faith of what so-and-so said." But here, in the case of democratic opinion, this "faith" becomes truly prophetic and enlists the faithful (*fidèles*, from *fides*: confidence and faith). Thus one speaks *upon the faith of* what the majority thinks.[16] The individuals of the modern era, incredulous as they are, nevertheless have a belief.[17]

Democratic common sense is therefore both complex and lacking in self-awareness. But Tocqueville was not done with his wavering and reversals. He turned next to the necessary fate of religion in the strict sense, religion that exists as such, namely, American Christianity: "Indeed, if one looks into the matter closely, it becomes apparent that religion itself reigns [in the United States] far less as revealed doctrine than as common opinion." This assertion was addressed to French Catholics: in America, the Christian religion (not only in its diverse Protestant denominations but even in the Catholic Church) proceeds from the bottom up rather than from the church hierarchy down to the faithful, just as popular sovereignty does not "descend" from the representative state to society but thrives first of all in scattered communities. In short, Christianity, religion that knows itself as such, is absorbed by democracy, which does not know that it is a religion: in America, Christianity becomes an opinion.[18]

Furthermore (and I will return to this in part 3), religion is a *useful* opinion, a product of "self-interest properly understood," a concept to which Tocqueville would attach great importance in the second *Democracy*. But

[15] Claude Lefort, "Le nom d'Un," in Étienne de la Boétie, *Le Discours de la servitude volontaire* (Paris: Payot, 1976), reprinted in 2002.
[16] As we shall see, the majority is itself *what one thinks the majority is* (upon seeing certain signs): we create the Public.
[17] Durkheim later developed the following argument: "Generally speaking, there is no doubt that a society has everything it needs to awaken the idea of divinity by the way in which it acts on people's minds, because society is to its members what a god is to its faithful." Quoted by Juliette Grange in Comte, *Leçons de sociologie* (Paris: Garnier-Flammarion, 1995), p. 28.
[18] In other texts, moreover, Tocqueville observes and explains another fact that he found striking: the lack of formalism in the various denominations.

in his ironic formulation (borrowed from Montesquieu), one has to look into the matter very "closely" to see this because those who do not recognize the primacy of mores and of the sociology of democracy will not see what is distinctive about American religion: it is not revealed doctrine that counts but rather the heart, feelings spoken and sung in common. In other words, religion in Tocqueville's theory is the Public, which gives itself a body and observes itself as spectacle.

To recap, Tocqueville's argument runs as follows: there is a religion in the United States, because Christianity is openly proclaimed (even the president must swear on the Bible), but democracy has absorbed or ingested institutional faith and substituted the religion of democratic opinion: *the American way of believing*.

This astonishingly dense chapter concludes with a fourth and final reversal concerning this new entity, the Public. First, it is impossible to imagine any kind of transcendence in the future of democracy, whose citizens are "not inclined to locate the intellectual authority to which they submit outside and above mankind." But second, because of the difference between the individual and the "body" of his equals, the group (*grand corps*) tends to become differentiated and autonomous, a substantial presence in its own right, so that the individual "is immediately overwhelmed by his own insignificance and weakness."[19] The citizen asks himself, "If everyone thinks otherwise, who am I to doubt or contradict them?" But this means that the individual *believes* that everyone thinks in a certain way.[20] The image that each person has of the Majority institutes the latter as a separate and superior authority. Thus the democratic Public is constituted by each individual's conviction that the Public exists, which is reinforced by the fact that institutions and texts will speak of it as though it existed and as though its views needed to be taken into account.[21] On this point I differ with Pierre Manent, in that my analysis is couched in terms of "authority" rather than "social power."[22] To be sure, Tocqueville also uses the latter expression, but it does not designate the *figure* that confronts the individual; it is not a "repository of authority" or a personified Public. In the second volume of *Democracy in America*, for example, he mentions a "single social power" that opposes the tendency of individuals "to

---

[19] *DA* II, p. 17; AG, p. 491.

[20] The founder of French public opinion polling, Jean Stoetzel, argued that "public opinion" exists if, among other things, individuals believe that there is a "majority sentiment." In other words, public opinion engenders itself. See Jean Stoetzel, *Théorie des opinions* (Paris: Presses Universitaires de France, 1943), and Jaume, *La liberté et la loi* (chapter on opinion in Locke).

[21] Nowadays, of course, there are opinion polls to make the Public even more palpable.

[22] Pierre Manent, *Tocqueville et la nature de la démocratie* (Paris: Fayard, 1993), pp. 64–67.

want to judge for themselves."[23] But it suffices to consult *Democracy* II.4.5[24] to see that the social power, mentioned six times in the text, is "the sovereign power" in European nations, that is, the state. For Tocqueville, "social power" does not include every manifestation of the authority of the social.

We can now see what conditions must be met in order for a democratic faith to exist: an immanent form of transcendence (collective opinion), a superiority that humbles each individual, and a burning desire on the part of the individual to be recognized as both a bearer of truth and a member of society. In fact, the religion of public opinion is the religion of equality: Tocqueville drives this point home at the end of the chapter.[25] It is not political institutions that give the Public authority, because one would find the same type of behavior "in a democratic nation subject to a king," hence "the sources [of this influence must be sought] in equality itself."[26] Later he wrote that "equality fosters in each individual the desire to judge everything for himself. It inspires in him a taste for the tangible and the real in all things as well as contempt for tradition and forms."[27] The reversal of perspective is the same: the desire to judge is stopped short by the figure of the Public, the "repository" of Authority, because individuals are "almost always wracked by doubt."[28]

Equality, which creates a constitutive failure to recognize the democratic religion as such—the individual reveres what he constructs, pride of independence engenders submission— pushes men to hide their weakness from themselves: "There is no more inveterate habit of man than to recognize superior wisdom in his oppressor." The superior wisdom of the Public is the stubborn illusion of equal individuals. This can be put in the form of an equation: *the lived equality of I and Thou produces a feeling of inequality between I and All, between the Ego and the Public.* The mirror is a source of distortion: to the extent that the individual sees himself in the Whole, he is lost.

---

[23] *DA* II, p. 39; AG, p. 510.

[24] Ibid., pp. 369–81; AG, pp. 803–25.

[25] One might think that Tocqueville was describing something else: to suffer the pressure of the Majority and *to exalt* that suffering arises from (1) the spirit of Christiantiy, and (2) the ideology of the Left (which is not unrelated to Christianity). Might the Tocquevillean duality between aristocratic ethos and democratic ethos in fact be a Right/Left duality (of which Tocqueville was not explicitly aware)? If so, then Tocqueville would have described a current and type of opinion rather than modern society as such. On the ideology of the Right as the conviction that inequalities stem from the very condition of man, see Lucien Jaume, "Ministre, historien, candidat au leadership conservateur: le cas Guizot," *Jus politicum, Le droit politique* (Paris: Dalloz, 2009), no. 1 (2009). Mill already said that Tocqueville, mistaking his subject, confounded democracy with *civilization*.

[26] *DA* II, p. 18; AG, p. 492. The reference is to France under Louis-Philippe.

[27] Ibid., p. 53; AG, p. 522.

[28] Ibid., p. 89; AG, p. 553.

In other words, *thou* is a mirror of equality for *I*, but when *I* thinks of *them* (or addresses himself to *them*), the Public, sitting as a monarch on its throne, reflects an image of inequality. With this discovery of a "superior wisdom," a pure mirage of the egalitarian democratic mentality, Tocqueville believed that he had discovered a religious attitude—all the more worrisome in his eyes because it revealed itself in a society that did not recognize itself as religious (in the precise sense that I am ascribing here to "religious"). There were times when no society was more conformist than American society: "I know of no country where there is in general less independence of mind and true freedom of discussion than in America.... The majority erects a formidable barrier around thought"[29]

Then doubt takes hold, consensus crumbles, minds diverge in every direction, and individuals recover their liberty. But soon they will again celebrate the common opinion: the Public will have reconstituted itself, and for a time it will then reign in what might be called a state of grace.

Comparison: The Sociology of Opinion among the Counterrevolutionaries

At the time of Tocqueville's writing, France was rife with speculation about what might be called "the mystical body of the nation." On the socialist side, Pierre Leroux may be counted among the speculators,[30] but he was preceded by counterrevolutionary thinkers such as Joseph de Maistre or Frédéric de Lamennais, the author of one of the century's major best sellers, the *Essai sur l'indifférence en matière de religion*, which contains (especially in volume 2) numerous formulations similar to Tocqueville's.[31]

As both Auguste Comte and Émile Durkheim recognized, the fundamental idea of *sociology* was born, broadly speaking, among vehemently anti-individualist traditionalists. One of the basic concerns of nineteenth-century social thinkers was to find out whether individual thought and action could give rise to a different sort of a reality, an autonomous and active collective being.[32] Durkheim, following in this path, would later propose the idea of "collective consciousness."

---

[29] *DA* I, p. 353, AG, p. 293.

[30] More on Leroux will be found later.

[31] Félicité Robert de Lamennais, *Essai sur l'indifférence*, vol. 1 (1817), vol. 2 (1820). In all there would be four volumes, followed by a *Défense de l'Essai sur l'indifférence*. Tocqueville's library contained the third edition of the work.

[32] This perspective will be developed at length in part 2. For now I am interested only in characterizing "democracy" as a Tocquevillean concept.

Before examining this current of thought, however, it is important to recognize that what drew counterrevolutionaries to this way of thinking was the proposition that what they called *the social* is prior to and autonomous from the individual. For instance, Joseph de Maistre believed that if democracy survived, it would be "an association of individuals without sovereignty."[33] In his view, true sovereignty existed in the absolute monarchies of France and Spain: a sovereign is one who is separated from and dominates society.[34] De Maistre's question to republicans was the same as Bossuet's to Jurieu: if the people are called "sovereign," who will they dominate, since domination over oneself makes no sense? Popular sovereignty was therefore an absurdity, but for de Maistre this did not mean that the people could not exercise *authority*: the nuance is important, and in this respect de Maistre anticipated Tocqueville's thought. Since a republican people would be "a people less governed than any other," the Savoyard nobleman explained, the action of sovereignty "must be compensated by public spirit."[35] In this connection, he also mentions America and explains that "the spirit of voluntary association" and "the spirit of community" help to make up for the absence of a sovereign standing outside of society. It is striking to see how much the subsequent argument—explicitly intended to draw a contrast between the United States and European monarchies—anticipated what Tocqueville would say about American communities:

> Public force is less active and above all less visible than in the monarchies. One might say that it distrusts itself. A certain family spirit, which is more readily felt than expressed, means that sovereignty need not act in many circumstances in which it would intervene elsewhere. A thousand small things take care of themselves, *without knowing how*, as is commonly said, and order and harmony are everywhere apparent.[36]

---

[33] Joseph de Maistre, "De la démocratie," in "Étude sur la souveraineté," in *Œuvres inédites. Mélanges* (Paris: Vaton, 1870), p. 346. This text, written in 1794 or 1795, was published posthumously. Unless copies circulated, it is unlikely that Tocqueville knew it, but it is convenient to refer to it because it synthesizes a common body of thought. As Jean-Louis Benoît has pointed out, not only was de Maistre much admired in legitimist circles, but Tocqueville's tutor, the Abbé Lesueur, shared his main ideas: the Revolution was Satanic; liberalism aggravated the disorder; the mysterious workings of Providence guide history and will bring about the restoration of sovereignty. Tocqueville referred to de Maistre in *The Ancien Régime and the Revolution* to characterize a major body of opinion that did not analyze the Revolution but responded to it with passion. Gustave de Beaumont characteristically described de Maistre as a "superior mind" but added that he strongly opposed his "current of ideas." *OC* VIII-3, p. 459. See Jean-Louis Benoît, *Tocqueville moraliste* (Paris: Honoré Champion, 2004), p. 64.

[34] For my view of the concept of sovereignty, see Jaume, *Le Discours jacobin et la démocratie.* Sovereign comes from the superlative *superanus*, that which is above all.

[35] De Maistre, "Étude sur la souveraineté," p. 350.

[36] Ibid., p. 349.

Tocqueville of course said that "society acts by itself and on itself."[37] For him, this is the meaning of popular sovereignty. Where de Maistre expresses emotional surprise (how can one live without a sovereign?), Tocqueville transforms astonishment (which he shared, as his correspondence of 1830–31 attests) into theory: the "new political science" for which he called in the introduction to *Democracy in America*.

But the similarity does not end there. In the chapter entitled "On the National Soul," de Maistre searched for a form of *social* authority in democracy and explained that "political faith" was important if each person's "individual reason" was to find the authority that it needed. We will return later to the idea of individual reason, which Tocqueville also uses.[38] Recall that in the chapter of *Democracy in America* we just analyzed, the author said that every individual needs "dogmatic beliefs," which "men accept on faith and without discussion." The same is true on the scale of the entire community, where the same need for undisputed beliefs exists: "It is easy to see that no society can prosper without such beliefs . . . for without common ideas, there is no common action, and without common action, men may still exist, but they will not constitute a social body. If society is to exist . . . the minds of all citizens must be drawn and held together by certain leading ideas."[39]

Tocqueville did not invent this thesis, which was a commonplace among traditionalist thinkers (including Burke in England), all of whom were critical of the revolutionary idea of the tabula rasa. The point was that Cartesian rationalists sought to reconstruct the world of thought on the basis of methodical doubt, just as the social philosophers of the seventeenth and eighteenth centuries built society on a social contract among autonomous individuals (and the Civil Code on the autonomy of the individual will).[40] Hence it was no accident that Tocqueville repeated de Maistre's contention that man "needs beliefs. His cradle should be blanketed with dogmas, and when his reason awakens, he should find all his opinions readymade, at least with respect to anything that has a bearing on his behavior."[41] What Tocqueville called dogmatic beliefs, de Maistre called prejudices: "Do not take this

---

[37] *DA* I, p. 120; AG, p. 64. He also defines a republic as "the slow and tranquil action of society on itself." Ibid., p. 517; AG, p. 456.

[38] See the next chapter.

[39] *DA* II, p. 15; AG, p. 489.

[40] On political rationalism in politics, see Lucien Jaume, "Le Code civil avait-il pour finalité de terminer la Révolution française?" (2006), reprinted as "Terminer la Révolution par le Code civil ?" in *Les Penseurs du Code civil*, ed. Claude Gauvard (Paris : La Documentation française, 2005).

[41] De Maistre, "Étude sur la souveraineté," p. 246. Similar ideas can be found in Bonald.

word the wrong way. It does not necessarily refer to false ideas but only, as the etymology implies, to opinions adopted prior to examination."[42]

In other words, some prejudices are useful, namely, those that help to "mix and combine religious and political dogmas," which serve as firebreaks against the ravages of "individual reason" (also referred to as "particular reason"). To be sure, de Maistre pushes this argument toward an ideological destination that Tocqueville wants no part of (a theocratic state), but the starting point is similar for both writers: the vitality of social bonds fostered by dogmatic beliefs that individuals acquire and share without critical examination.

During the Restoration it was Lamennais who would repeat this argument again and again in his *Essai sur l'indifférence en matière de religion*, now in the form of "the authority of common sense" or "general reason," which imposes its articles of faith on the "particular reason" of individuals. Lamennais begins with the point that there can be no *society* without shared ideas: "True society exists only among intelligent beings. It is their essential mode of existence: the principle of society is therefore entirely spiritual."[43]

Guizot, who was also interested in the sociological organization of civilization, echoed this formula with an explicit reference to Lamennais.[44] Lamennais's second main point, for which he was vigorously criticized, was that the Catholic Church identified with what he called the historical progress of common sense (which is described in rather vague terms). What Lamennais has in mind is a theme that was very important to Bonald: "primitive revelation."[45] Common sense, or the Divine Word brought down to the level of human history, is also known as universal reason or general reason, which all Cartesians, Malebranche foremost among them, admitted as man's guide to knowledge of the truth. Man's temptation, in his prideful revolt, was to combat "the authority" of general reason and to prefer his own personal judgment to the universal judgment. "Madness consists in preferring one's

---

[42] The same definition can be found in Voltaire, "Préjugés," in *Dictionnaire philosophique*, ed. R. Pomeau (Paris: Garnier-Flammarion, 1964); and Bonald, "Sur les préjugés," text of 1810, in *Œuvres complètes de Bonald* (Paris: J.-P. Migne, 1859), 3:804–10. Think too of Burke, who often evoked "the hidden wisdom contained in prejudices." See Edmund Burke, *Reflections on the Revolution in France*. We know that Tocqueville read Burke carefully and repeatedly.

[43] Lamennais, *Le Conservateur*, 1819, 3:440.

[44] In his *Histoire de la civilisation en France*, Guizot wrote: "A common conviction, that is, a single idea recognized and accepted as true—that is the fundamental basis, the hidden bond of human society.... Everywhere and in all cases, association consists essentially in the adherence of individuals to the same philosophy.... A modern philosopher [in note: M. l'abbé de Lamennais] was right to say that society exists only among intelligences" (Paris: Didier, 1857), 1:307–8. Recall that Tocqueville attended Guizot's lectures and took notes on them. See *OC* XVI, *Mélanges*, pp. 441ff.

[45] See J.-R. Derré, *Lamennais, ses amis et le mouvement des idées à l'époque romantique* (Paris: Klincksieck, 1962), chap. 1.

own reason, one's individual authority, to the general authority or common sense."[46]

Therefore, Lamennais explained, two routes are open to man: those who believe in themselves, like Descartes, can choose the path of separation, which leads to individualism.[47] Those who heed the "reason of society" will choose the path of union, which is also the path of humility, or, to use Lamennais's term, the "social path of authority."[48]

Now we can understand where Tocqueville's idea of the "authority of the social" came from, as well as the intellectual background against which the traveler to America formed his own vision. Like Lamennais, he believed that authoritative common beliefs were necessary.[49] It was this authority that enabled society to assert its self-understanding through its influence on individual minds. Tocqueville departed from Lamennais, however, by interpreting this idea in a way that was more sociological and historical than theological.[50] For him, the path of "individual reason"[51] was the vector of democratic equality. The fear was not that it would oppose the "social path of authority," but rather that it would defer to social authority all too readily. He went beyond Lamennais's musings about the Church as the body of "common sense" (although Tocqueville's idea of a "repository" of opinion was rather similar), observing that in a democracy of individuals there existed a permanent tension between pride in personal independence and enforced servitude. In this new mode of existence, the democratic "social state," the Public was the elusive sovereign, anonymous and unstable (because its content was always changing) yet still powerful.

But was it really that powerful? Tocqueville expressed his own personal anxiety by saying that he feared the force of collective opinion while at the

---

[46] Lamennais, *Essai sur l'indifférence*, 2:160. We hear another echo of this in Guizot: "Although individual reason has the right to examine, it is subordinate to general reason, which serves as a measure and touchstone for all minds." Guizot, *Histoire*, p. 311.

[47] Lamennais, *Essai sur l'indifférence*, 2:2–3. It was common in this period to link Descartes to Protestantism.

[48] Ibid., 2:246.

[49] This point was clearly grasped by Anna-Maria Battista, who cites Lamennais's article in *L'Avenir* (October 18, 1830), entitled "De la séparation de l'Église et de l'État": "As has often been said, without common beliefs from which common duties derive, no stable society, indeed no society, is possible." See Anna-Maria Battista, *Studi su Tocqueville* (Florence: Centro Editoriale Toscano, 1989), p. 139 n. 65.

[50] Lambert, *Théologie de la République. Lamennais prophète et législateur*, p. 40, wrote that "if it was a question of sociology, it was more a social metaphysics or theology than a science of social facts." Lamennais was a theocrat (recognized as such by Joseph de Maistre) who became a monarchist, a liberal democrat, a republican, and a revolutionary. After 1834 (and his break with Rome), he looked for a people-as-king, as prophet and witness to Revelation in History.

[51] Tocqueville would borrow this phrase.

same time arguing that some form of social religion was necessary. We see this in the draft of a speech on freedom of education from October 1844.[52] There, Tocqueville set out to show that "after the carnage swept away so many different authorities in society, in the hierarchy, in the family, and in politics, we cannot survive without some kind of intellectual and moral *authority*. . . . If beliefs are abolished, we will need soldiers and prisons." This last formula is a leitmotif in Lamennais's writing from the period 1828–29, in which he criticized the inadequacy of liberalism while claiming to move toward it.

Tocqueville situated his search for a check to individualism somewhere between Christianity as authority (which he believed needed democratic roots) and democracy as "social authority." The school of Bonald, de Maistre, and Lamennais believed that the place to look for such a check was in the resources of society itself rather than in artificially created institutions. The military and the prison system counted among those artificial institutions: these were merely stopgap measures.

Note, moreover, that Tocqueville defined the social bond in terms of the power of certain types of *content* (opinions, beliefs, and even doctrines) rather than by the institutional vectors of these things.[53] The final chapter of the first *Democracy*, devoted to "the three races" that inhabit the United States, forcefully reaffirms this point. But a note in the manuscript is even more enlightening: "What really constitutes a society is not having the same government, the same laws, and the same language; it is having the same ideas and the same *opinions* on a great many points. The first things are all material. They are the means by which ideas and opinions reign. Note well that, if the despotic form (which needs a *society* least) is itself to last, it must rest on this foundation."[54]

As in Lamennais, social consensus is here presented as clearly intellectual or spiritual in essence, while laws and language are "material" realities: without a communion of thought, it is possible to have a common language and to constitute a historical nation-state without constituting a society. Here I use the term "communion" deliberately to indicate the point of convergence of two distinct theses concerning the relation between religion and

[52] *OC* III-2, p. 551. As I mentioned in my introduction, André Jardin, *Alexis de Tocqueville*, (p. 348) was mistaken in saying that this passage was published in the newspaper *Le Commerce*.

[53] But in *DA* II, p. 143; AG, p. 600, he thinks he has discovered an institutional vector for "common action," as he says in the same passage, as well as for common thought, namely, newspapers, because "only a newspaper can deposit the same thought in a thousand minds at once. . . . Hence the more equal men are and the more individualism is to be feared, the more necessary newspapers become." The newspaper thus offered a formal counterweight to individualism and could serve as an instrument for inculcating or instilling the force of its *content*.

[54] Nolla I, p. 286, n. y; JS, p. 598.

politics—theses that were hotly debated at the time. Following the Catholic tradition, many writers held that religion was in fact the ground of society.[55] For instance, Bonald: "Religion is the reason for any society . . . , the fundamental constitution of every state of society."[56] But other authors held a different view: that modern democratic society is a religious mode of existence, but of a distinctive kind.[57] To analyze this new phenomenon, one must therefore treat the religious as a psychological and social model, a revival that fails to comprehend its own nature.[58] Tocqueville favored this approach, and to that extent he took notice of the counterrevolutionary heritage. For him, in other words, Bonald, de Maistre, and Lamennais were writers who revealed not a theological truth about history—a view that Tocqueville did not share—but rather a *tradition*, that is, an unconscious transmission to which they were particularly sensitive. In modern democracy Tocqueville thus saw elements of communion that help to build community.

But things are not as simple as they appear because the author of *Democracy in America* covered his tracks: he asserted many times—in the introduction to his work, in the manuscripts, and in his correspondence[59]—that it was God's will that equality had become the irresistible motor of history, and this brought him close to Lamennais's political theology of the people as king.

---

[55] On the left, before and after Saint-Simon, a number of writers identified the "social" and the "religious" or, even more, "association" and "religion." See Michael Behrent, "Society Incarnate: Association, Society and Religion in French Political Thought, 1825–1912," Ph.D. dissertation, New York University, 2006. The term "association" is a source of great confusion, moreover: Leroux wrote that "the idea of society necessarily implies the idea of religion."

[56] Louis de Bonald, *Législation primitive*, in *Œuvres*, 4th ed. (Paris: Adrien Leclère, 1847), p. 185.

[57] The socialist Pierre Leroux argued that the "supposed separation of civil things and spiritual things" was a "pure illusion." He perhaps went the farthest in claiming to complete the spiritualization of society by modernity. In the same text he wrote: "Think about it a little: the Constituent Assembly was a council; the Convention was a council; Napoleon was pope." See "De la philosophie et du christianisme," 1832, in Pierre Leroux, *Aux philosophes, aux artistes, aux politiques*, ed. J.-P. Lacassagne (Paris: Payot et Rivages, 1994), p. 196, n. a. For a development of this thesis, see Pierre Leroux, *D'une religion nationale ou du culte* (Boussac: Imprimerie de Pierre Leroux, 1846) (new ed.), as well as *Du christianisme et de son origine démocratique* (Boussac, 1848), chapter on councils.

[58] Here it is necessary to distinguish between religion as traditional form and content (Christianity, for example) and the religious as a collective attitude and form of organization.

[59] Before publishing *DA* I, he wrote to his cousin Camille d'Orglandes: "I cannot believe that God has for centuries been pushing two or three hundred million men toward equality of conditions in order to bring them to the despotism of a Claudius or Tiberius. . . . Why is he taking us toward Democracy? I do not know; but, embarked on a vessel that I did not build, I am at least trying to make the best use of it in order to reach the nearest port." Tocqueville, *Lettres choisies. Souvenirs*, p. 311. An echo of this letter can be found in the introduction to *DA* I, p. 68; AG, p. 13: "God envisions a future calmer and more certain than the present. Though I cannot penetrate his designs."

Furthermore, Tocqueville, as is well known, believed that *religion*, as such, was indispensable in order for democracy to moderate itself. In the United States, he argued, the separation of church and state and the preservation of the religious in civil society taught citizens to consider the *limits* of human activity and to think of the future (life after death), thus balancing the tendency of democracies to live only in the present.

All in all, there are at least three Tocquevillean theses regarding "democratic religion," and he does not always clearly distinguish them: (1) the democracy of modern times, governed by the norm of equality, corresponds to God's plan; (2) democracy needs Christianity socially and morally; and (3) democracy creates a religion of the Public. Because of his own uncertainties and personal anxieties, Tocqueville often mixed these different themes, and his readers have also been confused. Here, for example, is a passage in which he "hits hard" but his meaning is unclear: "Unbelief is an accident; faith alone is the permanent condition of humankind."[60] This could be early Lamennais. Or again, here is a passage in the peremptory tone of the seventeenth-century moralists: "For my part, I doubt that man can ever tolerate both complete religious independence and total political liberty, and I am inclined to think that if he has no faith, he must serve, and if he is free, he must believe."[61] This alternative can be found in Benjamin Constant's *De la religion*, where it takes on its full meaning.[62] In Tocqueville, it seems to have nothing to do with the problem of "the religion of the Public." Why, then, does he hammer this opinion home so forcefully?

The common thread that holds Tocqueville's three theses together is the question of *authority*, and this is also what makes him receptive to the assumptions of counterrevolutionary sociology. The chapter just cited (*DA* II.1.5) is entitled "How Religion Uses Democratic Instincts in the United States," but a glance at the text reveals that the reverse is also true: democratic ideology uses religious instincts, because for Tocqueville, lack of faith is merely accidental.

Indeed, he argues in this chapter that (1) "common opinion seems increasingly to be the foremost of powers, and the most irresistible,"[63] and (2) "general ideas pertaining to God and human nature are therefore, of all ideas, the ones most appropriately shielded from the usual action of individual reason, and in which there is most to gain and least to lose in recognizing

---

[60] *DA* I, p. 403; AG, p. 342.

[61] *DA* II, p. 31; AG, p. 503.

[62] Constant, *De la religion* (Paris: Bossange, 1824), 1:89, wrote that "Some religious peoples may have been slaves; no irreligious people has remained free."

[63] *DA* II, p. 36; AG, p. 508.

an authority."[64] This says it all: like Machiavelli, Tocqueville was interested in the political effects of religion,[65] and his sociological cynicism anticipated an important idea of Durkheim, which might be summed up as follows: "To believe in religion is to believe in society." This was Lamennais's central intuition, and Tocqueville made it his own.[66]

Indeed, to believe "in religion" is not to have faith; it is not to believe *by way of* religion. From the standpoint of the observer of democratic society, it is rather to hold the view that there exists a deep *affinity* between two types of faith: the faith that the individual inevitably accords to the community of equals, and the faith that Islam and Christianity have historically inculcated. For Tocqueville, if the second faith disappears, the first will also be affected, and the social bond will wither: "When a people's religion is destroyed, doubt takes hold of the highest regions of the intellect and half paralyzes all the others."[67] Ultimately Tocqueville's personal attachment to Christianity was reinforced by what he deduced as a sociologist of religion: here again we see a hidden dialogue between the author and his milieu.

The commentators hesitate to assert that such a dialogue existed with Lamennais. Anna-Maria Battista notes that this can only be a presumption. Nevertheless, two unpublished documents confirm that Tocqueville at the very least wished to have Lamennais's good opinion. In a letter dated January 24, 1835, he offered Lamennais a copy of *Democracy in America*: "No one professes deeper respect or warmer admiration for your character and writings than I."[68] Another letter, dated April 23, 1847, and addressed to "Monsieur l'abbé," seems to have been intended for Lamennais. Tocqueville offered thanks for a pamphlet he had just received and added: "I have always

---

[64] Ibid., p. 30; AG, p. 502.

[65] According to a manuscript cited by James Schleifer, Tocqueville did not ask which religion could make men more honest or moral but rather which religion was more likely to be believed in a democratic age. See James Schleifer, "Tocqueville and Religion: Some New Perspectives," *Tocqueville Review* 4, 2 (Fall 1982): 311. In the same spirit, although he believed that Protestantism was more favorable to democracy than Catholicism, he observed several times that this dangerous path was best avoided. In the margin of one manuscript he noted: "This is a dangerous terrain, onto which I will venture only when necessary." See *Œuvres*, La Pléiade, 2:1141. Tocqueville also observed: "Religions inculcate the general habit of acting with an eye to the future. . . . This is one of their most salient political characteristics." *DA* II, p. 187; AG, p. 639.

[66] Pierre Leroux was also influenced by Lamennais. Leroux wrote in 1834: "We believe in individuality, personality, and liberty, *but we also believe in society*. . . . Yes, society is a body, but it is a mystical body." Emphasis added. At this point Leroux was arguing against both Saint-Simonian socialism and liberal individualism, hence his title, "De l'individualisme et du socialisme," reprinted in D. O. Evans, *Le socialisme romantique. Pierre Leroux et ses contemporains* (Paris: Marcel Rivière, 1948), p. 234. For Leroux, not to understand the essence of society was to succumb to a mentality dangerous for modern man.

[67] *DA* II, p. 30; AG, p. 502.

[68] Letter dated January 24, 1835, "Rue de Verneuil, no. 49," unpublished correspondence.

eagerly read your writings and greatly admired the most eminent talent they display." He also expressed pleasure that the recipient of the letter had joined him in the fight for freedom of education. The pamphlet could be the one that Lamennais published on January 9, 1847, entitled "À la démocratie européenne, la démocratie française."[69]

[69] Cf. F. Duine, *Essai de bibliographie de F. R. de La Mennais* (Paris: Garnier, 1923). The two Tocqueville letters will eventually be published in the Gallimard edition of the *Œuvres complètes*.

Democracy as Expectation of Material Pleasures

A Dividing Line between Aristocracy and Democracy

Most commentators on Tocqueville include equality as part of his definition of democracy, if they do not purely and simply equate the two. Hence it may seem surprising that the three elements of the definition of democracy I am using here are local power, the religion of the Public, and, now, the expectation of "material pleasures." I do not include equality, even though this term is omnipresent in both volumes of *Democracy in America*.

The reason for my choice is that equality is not a primary element in Tocqueville's definition of democracy. It is rather a *transversal* trait of human activities and representations in civil society and the state. Like popular sovereignty, Tocqueville's idea of equality is more correctly understood as practical experience than as principle.[1] Furthermore, when equality is considered in its own right (and not in relation to the passions or the law), it is, for Tocqueville, *not specifically democratic*. He took from Montesquieu (as well as Chateaubriand, as we will see later) the idea that a despot may rely on equality as a rule of conduct. Guizot and numerous other historians of the Restoration saw the despotic administrative monarchy of Louis XIV as France's initiation into the ways of equality, which the Third Estate then took as its ideal in 1789.

ဧ၁

By contrast, what Tocqueville indiscriminately referred to as the "taste for material pleasures" or the "passion for well-being" was a phenomenon directly linked to equality, which therefore became characteristic of "democracy." Here, then, we have a new facet of equality, different from the one we encountered previously in decentralized town government in America, where popular sovereignty achieved its concrete realization, and different

---

[1] Or as a principle in Montesquieu's sense: at once a norm and a passion (see chapter 1 on Tocqueville and Montesquieu).

too from the religion of the Public, in which the citizen is at once strong and weak because he must deal with "increasingly similar and equal men."

Equality works to stimulate and sustain the *expectation* of material pleasures. It moves democracy toward "equality of conditions," to use Tocqueville's well-known formula. It is noteworthy that while commentators often quote the formula, they rarely dwell on the expectation of pleasure that Tocqueville singles out as an important aspect of the material condition of democratic man. They seem embarrassed by what we might call "the imaginary of pleasure" or "comfort" that Tocqueville observed in the United States and therefore miss an essential feature of the *democratic spirit*. For Tocqueville, a democracy of frugality, which turned its back on what Aristotle (disapprovingly) called "chrematistics," cannot be a modern democracy. Democracy promises "the pursuit of happiness," but that happiness is necessarily material in the first instance (although it may to some extent be diverted toward artistic, intellectual, and spiritual goals).

Any definition of democracy that does not count pleasure in well-being as its foremost aim will fail to do justice to Tocqueville's thought. What is more remarkable still is the fact that the commentators' embarrassed silence is not a recent phenomenon: no serious analysis of this point can be found even in the first reviews.[2] To be sure, extremists of both the Left and the Right criticized the Americans' quest for wealth, the idea that "time is money," the shopkeeper spirit, and every other consequence of the utilitarian outlook (in the vulgar sense). Commentators such as Michel Chevalier and Louis de Carné discussed the role of the bourgeoisie in relation to France. But the social psychology of material possessions was not considered. Tocqueville was concerned, if I may put it this way, with moral man's quest for possession-consumption and with the representation of self implicit in this much-desired consummation.

To put it plainly, Tocqueville embarrasses his commentators because he draws on theological sources (the Church Fathers) and because he takes a

---

[2] Consider Guizot's protégé Rossi, an economist and jurist. In his view, Tocqueville overgeneralized: "America has brought civil equality closer to de facto equality in a distinctive way, which has not occurred and will not occur in our old societies." Furthermore, the United States will not continue to move toward greater equality of conditions; quite the contrary: "It is America that is in its own way moving toward Europe. Europe cannot become American." For the school of Guizot, equality of conditions was humanity's past, not its future. Tocqueville's concession to the socialists was a mistake. "As for equality of conditions," Rossi insisted, "it exists nowhere, has never existed, and will never exist, because it is contrary to human nature and contrary to law: it is injustice." See Rossi, review of *Démocratie en Amérique, Revue des deux mondes*, September 15, 1840, 23:904, 902.

disquietingly Jansenist view of the search for well-being.[3] Some say that he took little interest in the economy, but this is incorrect: his letters and manuscripts prove the opposite. But his interest was as a moralist and theorist of the consumerist imaginary, if I may put it in anachronistic terms.

&ego;

Why did Tocqueville believe that democracy was proceeding inexorably toward a greater equality of conditions rather than class inequality and division? This was one of the points on which he differed with the Doctrinaires. In his proposal to found a Young Left party in 1847, Tocqueville argued that wage increases, a more just apportionment of the tax burden, and worker participation should be immediate objectives, so as to hasten progress toward material equality and thus cut the ground out from under the socialist republicans he had encountered in 1828 and in July 1830.[4]

The response seems fairly simple because it was set forth in explicit detail in volume 1 of *Democracy in America*.[5] Tocqueville thought of "democracy" as an antiaristocracy, risen from the rubble of the previous social state. In other words, democracy would seek to diminish and even eliminate all hierarchies—even to the point of rejecting intellectual inequalities. He makes his case as a pedagogue, addressing the reader as if he were the tutor of a prince, a Fleury or a Fénelon, laying out a fundamental "choice" if the prince were somehow to become a social demiurge: "Do you wish to impart a certain loftiness to the human mind, a generous way of looking at the things of this world? Do you want to inspire in men a kind of contempt for material goods? Do you hope to foster or develop profound convictions and lay the groundwork for deep devotion?" From these principles flow certain consequences: a society regulated by etiquette ought to be able to subordinate the consumption of material goods to the display of "civilization." Clearly, he has the French and British aristocratic model in mind: "Is your goal to refine mores, elevate manners, and promote brilliance in the arts? Do you want poetry, renown, and glory?"

In foreign policy, this social model favors grandeur and memorable accomplishments. If this is what you want, the tutor says, "Do not choose democratic government, for it offers no guarantee that you will reach your goal."

---

[3] On Jansenism, see part 3 on material pleasures and Pascalian diversion. See also the three "libidos" of the Augustinians: the desire for knowledge, the desire to dominate, and the desire for sensual gratification.

[4] On the program for the Young Left, see *OC* III-2, pp. 729ff. In *Democracy in America*, the question of wage increases is analyzed in detail: "There is no issue more serious or more deserving of special attention from lawmakers than this." See *DA* II, pp. 235–37; AG, p. 684.

[5] *DA* I.2.6, p. 342; AG, p. 281. In what follows I quote from this page.

Then he considers the other possible option, inducing the governed to turn their minds to "the necessities of material life and . . . use their intelligence to improve well-being."

Here we have an image of democracy: "tranquil habits" will be preferred to "heroic virtues" and "vices" to "crimes," and people will desire "the greatest well-being for each individual member of society." In short, Balzac will supplant Corneille and César Birotteau will triumph over Le Cid and Polyeucte. If that is what you want, the prince's tutor concludes, "equalize conditions and constitute a democratic government."

Clearly, in Tocqueville's portrait of democratic society there is an anxious note of irony, as if an aristocratic moralist recognized democracy's intrinsic values without being able to work up much sympathy for them. In the second *Democracy*, moreover, this portrait would be abundantly fleshed out, but now with an insistence on the *contradictions* inherent in the democratic aspiration to well-being. To put it succinctly, production and commerce stem from liberty (including political liberty) but often end in a regime in which liberty is suppressed with the more or less tacit consent of the governed.

Tocqueville's principal thesis is formulated much more clearly at the beginning of the second volume: "Of all the passions that equality brings into being or encourages, there is, as we shall see, one that it causes everyone to feel with particular ardor, namely, the passion for well-being. The passion for well-being is a striking and indelible feature of every democratic age."[6]

In an even more pointed manner, Tocqueville explains in a very short chapter what differentiates the commercial and industrial bourgeoisie from the aristocratic class: "The passion for material well-being is essentially a middle-class passion. It grows and spreads with that class; it becomes preponderant when the class does. From there it reaches up into the upper ranks of society and descends among the people."[7]

Social legitimists (like Villeneuve-Bargemont) and "retrograde" Catholics had already said as much in similar terms: the bourgeoisie conveys its ideal of material civilization as well as its respect for money to the whole of society, and especially to the "popular" classes. In the same chapter, Tocqueville argues that wealthy aristocrats do not share this state of mind: for them, "material well-being is not the purpose of life. It is a way of living. They look upon it, in a sense, as synonymous with existence and enjoy it without thinking about it." Not that aristocrats do not share a "natural and instinctive taste

---

[6] *DA* II, p. 35; AG, p. 507.

[7] "On the Taste for Material Well-Being in America," *DA* II.2.10, pp. 161–63; AG, pp. 617–19, quote on p. 618.

for well-being": everyone does. But wealth in combination with their own values means that their "souls . . . turn elsewhere and harness themselves to some grander, more difficult undertaking." Aristocracy does not take unlimited consumption to be the goal of life.

If the pleasure of possession and consumption is so great in "democracy," it must inevitably influence the Christian religion as Tocqueville analyzed it. For him, as we have seen, Christianity becomes an "opinion," while the Public ensures that the religion of the majority will prevail. Similarly, well-being becomes *religious*, while the religious appeals to the common utilitarianism. In America, priests, confronting the desires of modern democratic man, "do not forbid the honest pursuit of prosperity in this [world]. Rather than show how these two things are distinct and contrary, they seek instead the point of contact and connection between them"[8]

Today, in fact, "churches of prosperity" are proliferating in the United States in the form of "megachurches," which are vast communal meeting places in which the spiritual is dispensed alongside such everyday amenities as supermarkets, service stations, hairdressers, tailors, and so on.

The use of religion as a source of comfort was already described by Tocqueville in a chapter I cited previously: the democratic taste for material pleasures goes along with a taste for order, good morals, and a tranquil existence, combined "with a kind of religious morality. People want to be as well off as possible in this world without renouncing their chances in the next."[9]

In this realm, Tocqueville is able to bring together many of the distinct aspects of his concept of democracy: the American priest, who lives in the community of "equals," is thoroughly familiar with the religion of the Public. He must therefore flatter the widespread taste for "comfort" if he wishes to speak of God: "In centuries of equality, kings often command obedience, but it is always the majority that inspires belief. Hence it is the majority that must be satisfied in all that is not contrary to faith."[10]

It is worth noting that Tocqueville was led to formulate one of his most striking observations ("it is always the majority that inspires belief") at the point where the factors of equality, community, religion, and material pleasure come together. This confirms our judgment that, for him, no definition of democracy as a *juridical* regime would do. Democracy is the expression of local liberties plus the cult of the Majority plus the expectation of ever greater wealth, or at any rate ever greater consumption. There is something

[8] *DA* II, p. 37; AG, p. 509.
[9] Ibid., p. 166; AG, p. 621.
[10] Ibid., p. 36; AG, p. 508.

religious in this expectation (in French the term is *espérance*, which has religious connotations), insofar as it influences the very content of the religious (at least in America). On this point, Tocqueville the man as well as Tocqueville the author had his doubts: the passage that describes "a kind of religious morality" in the search for well-being ends with the judgment that "a kind of moderate (*honnête*) materialism" threatens the future of democracy. This point really belongs to the study of Tocqueville as a reader and student of the classical moralists. Speaking for himself, he expressed his opinion as follows: "I reproach equality not for leading men into the pursuit of forbidden pleasures but for absorbing them entirely in the search for permitted ones."[11] This third aspect of democracy is thus very much concerned with the dynamics of equality. The democratic imagination of equality through rights is inseparable from a competition for material goods, but this competition will turn out to be potentially self-destructive.

Material Pleasures as Motivation and Self-Delusion

When one speaks of a "democratic dynamic" in Tocqueville (as he described it in the introduction to *Democracy in America*), it is clear in retrospect that this involved the economic "takeoff" of formerly agrarian societies, which produced a number socioeconomic effects. This dynamic was more than just a set of purely abstract rights or universal suffrage or the rights of man. In the introduction Tocqueville points out that the great issues of the future will involve property, its fruits, and the distribution of wealth: "The gradual development of the equality of conditions is therefore a providential fact. It has the essential characteristics of one: it is universal, durable, and daily proves itself to be beyond the reach of man's powers. Not a single event, nor a single individual, fails to contribute to its development."[12] God's providential plan, Tocqueville continued, served democracy itself: "To wish to arrest democracy would then seem tantamount to a struggle against God himself."[13] Of course this did not mean that the road ahead would be strewn with flowers. Democracy's promise of economic equality would prove difficult to fulfill, partly because competition spurred the search for ever greater satisfactions, and partly because material equality, though desired, is impossible to achieve. One of Tocqueville's most perceptive chapters on this

---

[11] Ibid., p. 167; AG, p. 622.
[12] *DA* I, p. 60; AG, p. 6.
[13] Ibid., p. 61; AG, p. 7.

issue was entitled "Why Americans Seem So Restless in the Midst of Their Well-Being."[14]

What was the source of the unsatisfying satisfaction that Tocqueville thought he discerned in the United States? First, competition among equals: "The same equality that allows each citizen to entertain vast *hopes*[15] makes all citizens individually weak. It limits their strength in every respect, even as it allows their desires to expand."[16] Here we see a logical equivalence (both positive and negative) with the right to judge discussed in the previous chapter: each individual is proud to make his own judgments but distressed if he finds himself in conflict with the judgment of the majority. His "vast hopes" may clash with the hopes of other individuals. In this competition, hope remains and may even increase, while concrete success becomes more and more uncertain: "When men are nearly all alike and follow the same route, it is quite difficult for any of them to move ahead quickly and break through the uniform crowd that surrounds them and presses in upon them."[17] Above all, progress toward economic and social equality, no matter how great, cannot *calm* human desire: "The desire for equality becomes ever more insatiable as the degree of equality increases."[18] Equality "recedes a bit further every day" as men pursue it; "it constantly eludes their grasp."

One might think that Tocqueville's moralistic tone led him to adopt a hypercritical style, a fashionable posture among Romantics. He writes that melancholy is becoming more common, that "disgust with life" overcomes men "in the midst of a comfortable and tranquil existence." Though he gives no statistics, he claims that the number of suicides in France is increasing. Another point, confirmed by many sociologists, reinforces this view of the modern condition: the cause of envious competition for greater riches is not the *great* inequality that one sees in aristocratic societies but rather the small differences that one finds in democratic societies. The more equal things are,

---

[14]*DA* II.2.13.

[15]Emphasis added. The French word is *espérances*, translated earlier as "expectations." The French word has both religious connotations and very mundane connotations: *l'espérance de vie* means "life expectancy," for example. It is etymologically related to *espoir*, which also means "hope."

[16]*DA* II, p. 173; AG, p. 627.

[17]Ibid. On this idea of a single route, a sort of democratic superhighway, Tocqueville might have read the following passage in Lamennais: "The character of democracy is continual mobility. Everything is constantly in motion, everything changes with frightening rapidity, buffeted by conflicting passions and opinions. There is nothing stable in principles, institutions, or laws. The power of time to establish, destroy, or modify is unknown. An irresistible force drives men and agitates them. Whatever they find on their way is trampled underfoot. They advance, retreat, and advance again, and for them the entire social order is nothing but a passageway." See Lamennais, *De la religion considérée dans ses rapports avec l'ordre politique et civil*, part 1, 1825, reprinted in *Œuvres complètes* (Paris: Daubrée et Cailleux, 1836–37), 7:17.

[18]*DA* II, p. 174; AG, p. 627.

the closer social conditions become, the more irritating becomes the *sight* of those differences that remain. In France, where salaries are kept secret and the word "privilege" is enough to trigger strikes, demonstrations, reforms, and backlash against reform, there is no need to belabor Tocqueville's point.

Indeed, the point can be generalized: what Tocqueville described was a contradiction inherent in democracy, which must therefore confront "social issues" as a permanent challenge.

Last but not least, according to Tocqueville, the expectation of material pleasures destroys the very basis of democracy, namely, the freedom of the individual. Despotic democracy is the result of a paradoxical competition in which "the passion for well-being then turns against itself."[19] The second volume of *Democracy in America* develops a new argument, according to which history demonstrates the existence of "a close and a necessary relation between... two things: liberty and industry."[20] At the time of writing, the word "industry" referred to any coordinated professional activity aimed at producing an economic good: agriculture, manufacturing, commerce, even banking and perhaps science (in the sense of applied research). One has only to consider the way in which the Saint-Simonians used the term *les industriels*. Tocqueville insisted that liberty was the source of economic development. When democratic despotism reared its head, it was "caviling and meddlesome"[21] and an impediment to economic activity. "Although a despotism of this kind does not trample humanity underfoot, it is diametrically opposed to the genius of commerce and the instincts of industry."[22]

In principle, then, democratic citizens must remain on their guard: they need both political and economic liberty to satisfy their passion for material goods, but economic development leads to a decline of interest in politics, elections, and legislation. Voters prefer to attend to profits and private life: "Exercise of their political duties strikes them as a troublesome inconvenience that distracts them from their private business."[23]

This political apathy is a serious failing because it can open the way to authoritarian government that will limit the freedom to produce and exchange: "The people who think this way believe that they are adhering to

[19] Ibid., p. 176; AG, p. 629. We are now into chapter 14, the most pessimistic in the book, which nevertheless ends by paying homage to the intelligence with which American society has recognized the danger.

[20] Ibid., p. 175; AG, p. 629.

[21] This passages suggests that Tocqueville did not think in terms of "two democracies": the tutelary soft despotism at the end of *DA* II is compatible with the description both in *DA* I and at the beginning of *DA* II. On this controversy in Tocqueville studies, see my conclusion.

[22] *DA* II, p. 176; AG p. 629.

[23] Ibid.; AG, p. 630.

the doctrine of self-interest, but their idea of that doctrine is crude at best, and in order to tend to what they call their affairs, they neglect the chief affair, which is to remain their own masters." This desertion by citizens leaves "the place of government . . . , in a sense, empty" and the way clear for a Bonaparte: "If, at this critical juncture, a shrewd and ambitious man happens to seize power, he will find nothing standing between him and every imaginable kind of usurpation."[24]

This possibility was in fact described by Benjamin Constant in *De l'esprit de conquête et de l'usurpation*, along with the conflict between the military spirit, bent on conquest and glory, and the commercial spirit, eager for peaceful exchange. Moreover, Montesquieu wrote that commerce was "the profession of equals." Unfortunately, as Tocqueville saw it, despotism also knew how to appeal to the material appetites, by promising order. No more strikes, riots, or risks of disturbance: this was the promise of absolute power in a democratic setting. Tocqueville described in specific and premonitory terms what he would observe with terror in 1851:

> As long as [the shrewd and ambitious usurper] devotes some time to making sure that material interests prosper, people will be quite ready to overlook everything else. He must uphold good order above all. Men whose passions run to material pleasures will usually be aware of the ways in which the unrest associated with liberty disrupts well-being before they notice how liberty helps to procure it.[25]

Ultimately, the passion for material pleasures goes through a depressing cycle, finally denying itself and escaping in a different direction. Along the way it abandons its companion, liberty, only to recover a certain form of equality, in submission and corruption: "A nation that asks nothing of government but the maintenance of order is already a slave in the depths of its heart; it is a slave of its well-being, ready for the man who will put it in chains."

Tocqueville thus completed his portrait of democracy, or at least of that aspect of democracy where economics, the social imaginary, and the history of the West came together. Again, however, democracy does not disappear: we know that for Tocqueville, there is no contradiction between "lack of liberty" and "democracy." The point to note, however, is that America, in Tocqueville's view, had contrived a way to counter this tendency of democracy: "An American will attend to his private interests as though he were alone in the world, yet a moment later he will dedicate himself to the public's

[24] Ibid.
[25] Ibid.

business as though he had forgotten them." Almost incredulous, he acknowledges his admiration for this great wisdom, which he finds in the community as well as the individual: "The human heart cannot be divided in this way," he adds, in a sort of exclamation.[26]

This Tocquevillean question is at the root of what we might call Tocqueville's sociology, which we will take up in the next part of the book. He argues that we must understand how the collective acts as both constraint and inspiration of informed self-interest. Here, too, we will find the interplay between liberty and modern forms of authority. The sociologist reinforces the political scientist.

APPENDIX TO PART ONE: THE TERM "REPOSITORY" AND ITS SEMANTIC FIELD

For contemporary readers, Tocqueville's formulation in the second volume of *Democracy in America* was rich in meaning: "Thus the question is not whether some form of intellectual authority exists in democratic ages but only where it resides [its *repository*] and what its extent may be." He may have been thinking of a famous passage from the *Encyclopedia*, written by Diderot, which also used the word "repository" in connection with legitimate authority: "It is from the general will that the individual must seek to find out how far he ought to be man, citizen, subject, father, and child and when it is appropriate for him to live or die. . . . But, you will say, where is the repository of this general will? Where can I consult it?"[27]

It is obvious that Jean-Jacques Rousseau found his own thought in this text: for him, to know "where" the general will "is" is to answer the question, "What or whom must I obey?" In *The Social Contract*, one must obey the the Whole, the sovereign People, not in the empirical sense of fluctuating majorities but rather the illumination that each individual finds in himself when he consults his reason (as citizen) rather than his particular interests (as man): the "general will" is not the "will of all." Indeed, obedience to the general will may lead to conflict with the Whole, as "will of all": hence the dilemmas of *The Social Contract* (because one cannot know in an assembly vote whether one is facing the pure general will or a "will of all" captured by special interests).

---

[26] *DA* II, p. 177; AG, p. 631.

[27] Diderot, "Droit naturel," in *Encyclopédie*, ed. A. Pons (Paris: Garnier-Flammarion, 1986), pp. 337–38.

Tocqueville, in describing the authority that the Public acquires over the mind of the citizen, rediscovers Rousseau's question, but as we have seen, he shifts the focus from the realm of reason and ideality to that of *belief* and, ultimately, to the intimidation of the part by the whole. He restores the very ancient and rich source of the idea of repository, namely, Catholic dogmatics. The Church was conceived as the "repository of truth," that is, as the institution to which Christ specifically assigned exclusive responsibility for transmitting his message and acting in his name. Pascal referred to the Jewish people as the group that God had previously chosen as "the repository of the prophecies." Massillon and Bossuet referred to the "repository of faith." Pontifical texts still use this very important formula: "The apostles and their successors are the authorized[28] guardians and witnesses of the repository of the truth vouchsafed to the Church, as well as the ministers of charity."[29] In the 1950 encyclical *Humani generis* opposing freedom in the interpretation of Scripture, Pius XII evoked "the Church that Christ instituted as the guardian and interpreter of the whole repository of divinely revealed truth." A repository is therefore that which is instituted by an authority and which thereby acquires authority of its own, thus ensuring permanence over time and enabling the community to transcend the limitations of mortality.

In Tocqueville's day, however, the idea of a repository had been revived and overlaid with two other types of discourse: the Jansenism of the eighteenth-century *parlements* and Montesquieu's opposition to monarchical despotism. Jansenism (and, in the view of some specialists, especially its *figuriste* tendency) drew on the theme of the "perpetuity of the repository of truth in the Church"—truth that could become the tool of an uncompromising oppositional minority.[30] The other type of discourse evoked the "repository of laws," a notion that Montesquieu made famous, even if he did not invent it. This, too, was a product of "enlightened" *parlementarisme* (a tradition to which Tocqueville was connected through his maternal ancestors, the Lamoignons), which warned of the danger of "despotism" on the part of the sovereign. Diderot, consulted by Catherine II of Russia, defined the repository of laws this way: "An institution in consequence of which the will of the sovereign is examined, authorized, published, and executed."[31]

---

[28] That is, endowed with authority.

[29] Benedict XVI, catechism of April 5, 2006, papal documents.

[30] In addition to the work of Catherine Maire cited in part 3, see her study "L'Église et la nation: du dépôt de la vérité au dépôt des lois, la trajectoire janséniste au XVIIIe siècle," *Annales ESC* 5 (1991): 1117–1205.

[31] Denis Diderot, *Observations sur l'instruction de S.M.I. aux députés pour la confection des lois*, in Diderot, *Textes politiques* (Paris: Éditions Sociales, 1971), p. 81. Cf. Monique Cottret, *Jansénismes et Lumières* (Paris: Albin Michel, 1998), p. 177.

As Montesquieu formulated the issue, a monarch needs to have a line beyond which the royal will cannot go. For that reason, "fundamental laws" are remembered and preserved. In despotic states, where there are no fundamental laws or repositories of law, religion "is usually so strong... [because] if creates a kind of repository and permanence" (*Esprit des lois* II.4). For Tocqueville, princely despotism is *analogous* to democratic popular despotism.[32] But at least democratic despotism—the authority of the Public and force of common Opinion—has a stabilizing virtue. For a time, people cease changing their minds and share the opinion of the majority. They are not forced to endure incessant conflict and loss of all confidence, which would be tantamount to the end of the very idea of society (as Lamennais argued). Democratic "belief" will inevitably be focused on the Public.

This is surely the sense in which Tocqueville used the term "repository." He turned away from the question of the general will as Diderot and Rousseau had posed it and turned toward democratic religion. And like Montesquieu, he imagined a "kind of permanence" as a necessary counter to democratic mobility. The citizen would encounter "the superior wisdom of the Public" and share in the religion of majoritarian despotism.

Is this interpretation correct? Tocqueville used the term "repository" three times, always in a religious context. He was conscious of the need to make himself intelligible to his readers at a time when Christian culture was ubiquitous (which does not mean that everyone accepted it or that most had a scholarly understanding of it). In addition to the cited passage from DA II, we also find the term in the section of *Democracy* I.2.9 entitled "On the Principal Causes of Religion's Power in America."[33] And we find it in the introduction as well: "Nobles, despite the vast distance that separated them from the people, took a benevolent and tranquil interest in their fate, much as the shepherd concerns himself with the fate of his flock. Without regarding the poor as equals, they watched over the destiny of those whose welfare had been entrusted to them by Providence (*un dépôt remis par la Providence*)."[34] To be sure, these nobles, described as pastors of the flock to whom a mission had been entrusted by Providence, offer a slightly ironic image of the Church. Tocqueville's compositional strategy left nothing to chance.

The reader was clearly meant to understand that if we no longer have the Church or the nobility, the new majesty can only be that invested in the Public. That, in any case, is what Americans *believe* in, in the strong sense of the word.

---

[32] As Chateaubriand suggested to him; this point will be developed in part 5.

[33] "I especially sought out the company of clergymen, who are not only the repositories of various beliefs but also have a personal interest in their duration." *DA* I, p. 402; AG, p. 341.

[34] Ibid., p. 63; AG, p. 8.

PART TWO

Tocqueville as Sociologist

Others have defended the religion of man; I defend the religion of society. Society is the sole and unique nature of man.

—Bonald, *Théorie du pouvoir*

Too much importance is ascribed to laws, too little to mores.

—Tocqueville, *Democracy in America*

In becoming the theorist of what he decided to call "democracy," Tocqueville also developed an expansive view of social life, as we have seen. He emphasized authority as intrinsic to society rather than imposed from outside, whether by religion (in the form of transcendence) or by an institution such as the state (in the classic sense of the term). Democracy for Tocqueville was both a "social state" and a political regime, a civil society and a government, because its unity depended, in a deep sense, on instances of authority within civil society itself. What were they? We have already considered public opinion and local government. Majority rule in the political sphere had its correlate in the social sphere as the "body" of the Public, or, to put it in more familiar terms, public opinion. A social dynamic thus complemented the political rule. Each reinforced the other because both stemmed from a common source: the reign of the people.

Tocqueville's sociology went much further, however. He pointed out that society creates paths to its own *ends*. He showed how not just individuals but mores and beliefs ensure the survival and reproduction of "democratic" society. Indeed, his goal was to lay bare the *logic of the social*, of which individuals are at least partially unaware. He thus anticipated the fundamental justification of the discipline of sociology, which Émile Durkheim and his school would later develop, namely, that there is a logic of the collective as such, a collective reality distinct from the reality seen by even the most lucid of individuals. Hence society deserves a science of its own, distinct from psychology, which is the science of the individual mind.[1]

---

[1] More recently, the question of "social psychology" has been raised. This discipline sometimes attempts to analyze the "collective consciousness" of the Durkheimians. As will emerge in what follows,

For Tocqueville, the existence of a distinct social wisdom followed from the "obvious fact" that societies are fundamentally *unified*. This idea he shared with, and to some extent borrowed from, Montesquieu: we will have to measure just how much he borrowed and how much was original. According to the author of *Democracy in America*, "everything is of a piece in the constitution of moral man,"[2] just as for Montesquieu, knowing "the general spirit of a nation" enables the observer to master the bewildering diversity of social phenomena.

Although Montesquieu provided Tocqueville with one set of analytic tools, he also drew on a range of traditionalist and counterrevolutionary thinkers. They furnished his raw material, if one may put it that way, but it was raw material that he subsequently modified and transformed. To get an idea of the state of opinion in traditionalist circles at the end of the Restoration, we can turn to an article that appeared in the first issue of the *Mémorial catholique* (1824), entitled "On Spiritual Authority in Relation to the Political Order."[3] The journal sought to explain to its readers a choice they had in fact already made, between, on the one hand, intellectual, moral, and political individualism, for which Protestantism bore most of the blame, and, on the other hand, Catholicism as a principle of order: "The governments of Europe . . . must choose between an individualistic Christianity as Protestantism has made it, essentially independent and therefore necessarily anarchic; . . . and a general Christianity, as the Catholic Church preserves it, which is *eminently social* because it subjects minds to common beliefs and

---

the argument developed here, linking Tocqueville to Durkheim, differs from that advanced by Raymond Boudon from a methodological individualist perspective. See Raymond Boudon, *Tocqueville aujourd'hui* (Paris: Odile Jacob, 2005). The main point of contention is that our methodological principles differ. Boudon writes: "Tocqueville *correctly anticipated* [my italics] the phenomena of disenchantment, secularization, and privatization, which are characteristic of the evolution of modern religions" (p. 59). He adopts the standpoint of the present and of sociological *science*. I interpret *Democracy in America* in relation to its time and as a function of the issues of the day, not from a teleological point of view. Furthermore, as to the substance of the argument, contrary to what Boudon often states, Tocqueville *also* made allowance for "causes acting without the knowledge of the subject" (p. 91 and passim) This is the central theme of this part of this book. As for secularization in democracy, in some respects, as we have seen, the opposite is true (democracy is a modern religion). At the same time, however, Christianity did become "one opinion" among others.

[2] Manuscript: Nolla II, p. 182, n. c; JS, pp. 1072–73.

[3] From January 1824 to December 1829, the *Mémorial catholique* served as apologist for the counterrevolution around the ideas of Lamennais and Bonald. In opposition to this, Leroux and Dubois founded *Le Globe*, which used the same printer but represented the young liberal school, which enjoyed the sympathy of Cousin and Guizot. After July the *Mémorial* was replaced by *L'Invariable* (October 1831–41), which was published in Fribourg, Switzerland, by some of the same editorial team but without Lamennais, who had gone over to the left with *L'Avenir*.

duties and thus ensures, by obedience to spiritual authority, the basis of the political order."[4]

What Tocqueville discovered in America six years later was a Protestant Christianity that was nevertheless "social." Obedience to spiritual authority did not require either hierarchy or tradition (Church Fathers, Catholic dogma, councils). Indeed, the denominational Christianity that Tocqueville encountered was "social" in two senses: religion had become more democratic while "democracy" (as Tocqueville interpreted it) was becoming the *modern form of religion.*

The traditionalists were right to worry about a crisis of authority in the modern world,[5] but they failed to see that a society of equal individuals produces its own form of regulation and, in particular, its own regulative *belief.* Hence to return to an alliance of throne and altar, so unpopular in France at that time, was the worst possible error.[6] There was reason to worry about the emergence of new religious doctrines in Europe,[7] but it was inevitable that democracy would discover new forms of religiosity: on this point, Tocqueville concurred with any number of French socialists.[8]

The same errors of diagnosis can be found in Louis de Bonald, whose major work, *Théorie du pouvoir politique et religieux* (1796), Tocqueville probably knew. Bonald, whose ideas influenced the "sociological" thinking of Auguste Comte and Émile Durkheim, was interested in what he called social man: the individual defined by his status, language, and national religion. In his view, the individual was also socialized by his position in a "corporation" (civil society) and, in the political sphere, as a subject of the monarchy. This led Bonald to contrast republic and monarchy: "In a monarchy, everything is social: religion, *power*, distinctions. In the people's state, everything is individual: each person has his religion, each has his *power*, each wants to distinguish himself or dominate by dint of talent or *force*."[9] This "people's state" (which is obviously not the Greek or Roman republic but the United

---

[4] *Mémorial* (1824): 1:23. Emphasis added.

[5] As Tocqueville wrote, "I doubt that man can ever bear complete religious independence and total political liberty." See part 1.

[6] According to Lacordaire and others, by the end of the Restoration a priest could no longer walk in the streets of Paris in his cassock.

[7] Tocqueville mentioned modern forms of pantheism, an observation that would subsequently be confirmed by the appearance of Abbé Maret's *Essai sur le panthéisme* in 1840.

[8] Such as Pierre Leroux, Saint-Simon (*Le Nouveau Christianisme*), Buchez (a Christian socialist), Pecqueur, and others. In Célestin Bouglé and Elie Halévy, *Exposition de la doctrine de Saint-Simon* (Paris: Rivière, 1929), p. 97, one can read this: "To raise all men in their quality as men, that is, as social or religious beings," with this note: "These two terms [religious and social], for us, are synonymous."

[9] Louis de Bonald, *Théorie du pouvoir politique et religieux dans la société civile démontré par le raisonnement et par l'histoire* (Paris: Le Clère, undated), 1:383, emphasis in original.

States) is again presented as a product of Protestant individualism. In this form of government and society, society is in fact "deconstituted," to borrow a term that Bonald liked: "The republic considers man outside of society, or natural man. . . . It is not appropriate to either society or man."[10]

Only a monarchy, and indeed a Christian monarchy, could be a *society*, in Bonald's view.[11] Tocqueville disposed of this tenuous partisan argument. In the United States, he discovered the "social" character of "individuality"—of an individuality, that is, that heeded its own judgment in matters of opinion and enjoyed self-government in matters of politics. Again, Tocqueville's object of study was doubly "social" in the sense of Bonald and Lamennais: not only did a democracy of equal individuals *constitute* (in Bonald's sense) an authentic "social state," but, in addition, society deeply informed the individuality of the individual. This was the basis of Tocqueville's theory of "thinking in common" (to borrow an expression of his that Durkheim would later adopt). As we will see shortly, Tocqueville also attacked the traditionalists on their notion of "individual reason." He showed that individual reason was by no means antithetical to society but rather one of its resources. Thus did he effectively "transcend" traditionalist political philosophy.[12] He discovered the *logic of the collective*, which traditionalists had circled around for a long time but never actually embraced because powerful prejudices prevented them from doing so.

How did Tocqueville explain this collective logic in *Democracy in America*? First, he showed how collective authority could be established through individual interaction, not by *contractual consent*, as the philosophers imagined, it, but involuntarily.[13] Without intending to or knowing that they are doing so, individuals proud of their autonomy *engender* the power to which they subject themselves. Or, as Marx would say (in incorporating this idea into his theory of commodity fetishism), the creature commands the creator.[14]

---

[10] Ibid., p. 384.

[11] In England, however, "there exists a constituted or monarchical political society," on the one hand, but on the other "a commercial society, the most extensive in the world. . . . The commercial society will be powerful because it will be rich; the political society will be powerful because it will borrow its strength from the wealth of the other society." Ibid., pp. 449, 450.

[12] Here, I use "transcend" in the strong Hegelian sense, to mean "eliminate the autonomy of and destroy by subsumption."

[13] Traditionalist thinkers incessantly attacked Rousseau and contractualism, but the true sociological perspective did not have to deal with this problem. Tocqueville avoided the whole debate, whereas Guizot and Constant had been obliged to respond to it during the Restoration.

[14] For Marx, it was the movement of commodities (the market in action) that masked the actual movement of reality, just as the sun seems to move around Earth: "The process of production, which is [the workers'] own creation, takes the appearance of a process of things, controlling them, not controlled by them." Karl Marx, *Capital*, vol. 1, chap. 1, sect. 4, "The Fetishism of Commodities and the Secret Thereof."

What Tocqueville observed, then, was this powerful hold of the collective and authority of society (represented by the public). This idea was not entirely original,[15] but he was able to put his finger on the key issue: the majority, as he put it, became "the only guide left to individual reason."[16] We knew this already, but the most original point of his analysis was to place the power of the majority at the heart of the social bond itself, as the force of opinion, disseminated everywhere and requiring no explicit adhesion to obtain the respect of the individual. Tocqueville discovered what Durkheim would later call the constraining power of the social fact.

[15] See below for American critiques of conformism, from James Fenimore Cooper, for example.
[16] *DA* II, p. 18; AG, p. 491.

In the Tradition of Montesquieu

THE STATE-SOCIETY ANALOGY

Tocqueville is known to have read Montesquieu often, although opinions differ as to the time he spent on the history of the Romans and the *Esprit des lois*. Here, I am interested mainly in Tocqueville's conviction that American society exhibited a *unified* spirit. This emerges clearly from a manuscript included in the Nolla edition of *Democracy in America*:

> There are a thousand ways to judge the social state and political laws of a people once one has thoroughly understood the various consequences that flow naturally from these two distinct things. A traveler's very scrupulous observations can lead you to the truth about this point just as well as the profoundest thoughts of the philosophers. Everything is of a piece in the constitution of the *moral man*, as well as in his physical nature, and just as Cuvier could take a single organ and reconstruct the entire body of the animal, a man who knows some of the opinions and habits of a people might often, I think, conceive a fairly complete portrait of the people itself.[1]

The analogy that Tocqueville uses is taken from the natural history of his time: if Cuvier could reconstitute a vanished animal from a small piece of its anatomy, it should be possible, Tocqueville argues, to do the same for aspects of "moral man" that cannot be observed directly. Tocqueville was rather proud of this approach, although he was aware of the risks, for it was of course entirely possible that a people might exhibit any number of allogenic or contradictory traits. In 1836, pleased with Edward Everett's review of the first volume of *Democracy in America*, he wrote to his friend Beaumont: "As you know, I worked on America in almost the same way that Cuvier worked on his antediluvian animals, making constant use of philosophical deductions

---

[1] Nolla II, p. 182, n. c. Emphasis added.

and analogies. I was therefore afraid that I might at times be making monumental errors, principally in the eyes of the people of the country."[2]

Tocqueville was so convinced that "everything is of a piece" that in writing *Democracy in America* he tried to *verify* his belief, and when evidence from the field was absent, he looked for examples.[3] The use of philosophical deductions and analogies confirms Tocqueville's proximity to Montesquieu: for instance, Montesquieu offered an a priori typology of regimes before turning to history for evidence. Consider the distinction among three types of government (republic, monarchy, despotism). Each was associated with a "principle" (virtue, honor, and fear, respectively), and everything was expected to *flow* from this principle. In education, for example, each principle would determine a different set of rules: "In monarchies, the object [of the rules] will be honor; in republics, virtue; in despotism, fear."[4] Concretely, however, there might be exceptions or anomalies since the principles in question do not describe any actually existing society but rather refer to an ideal type in the sense of Max Weber.

Montesquieu puts this rather nicely: he was not describing what is, he explained, but what ought to be, because "it is not proven that . . . in a certain monarchy honor exists or that in a particular despotic state people are afraid; what is described is rather what would be necessary, that without which the government would be imperfect."[5] *What would be necessary*: a nice formula for a sociologist (one of the founders of the discipline according to Raymond Aron), but a sociologist with a philosophical and rationalist cast of mind. Tocqueville's reasoning is often similar to Montesquieu's, antideterministic,[6] yet he takes it for granted that societies are internally coherent once one identifies what he sometimes calls the "basic fact" (*fait générateur*), "generative principle" (*principe générateur*, an expression that Tocqueville rarely uses, to which I will return later), "fundamental source of laws and mores" (*cause génératrice des lois et des mœurs*), or "fundamental idea" (*idée mère*).[7] Is what Tocqueville has in mind anything like Montesquieu's "general spirit of a

[2] *OC* VIII-1, p. 175; GZ, p. 572. The same idea can be found in a letter to Reeve, *OC* VI-1, p. 36.

[3] For example, he wrote to Beaumont: "I began, in the very structure of my book, by showing that the ideas and feelings of democratic peoples naturally led them . . . toward concentration of all power in the hands of a central authority. . . . Now, *I want to prove with actual facts that I was right*. I already have many general facts . . . but I would like more." *OC* VIII-1, p. 311, letter of July 8, 1838. Emphasis added.

[4] Montesquieu, *De l'esprit des lois*, VI, 4, sec. 1, p. 540.

[5] Ibid., II, 3, sec. 11, p. 540.

[6] He is contemptuous of explanations based on climate, geography, and race. In addition to his public and private statements on these themes, he engaged in an impassioned polemic with Gobineau, whose racial theory disappointed him greatly.

[7] Four of these five phrases occur in the introduction to *DA* I.

people"? Raymond Aron thought so, as did Georges Benrekassa.[8] Book 19 of *L'Esprit des lois* is devoted to the notion of the general spirit. Note, however, that for Montesquieu there seems to be an explanatory *principle* that ranks higher than (or is more profound than) the general spirit. The very title of book 19 says as much: "Laws in Relation to the *Principles* [my italics] That Shape the General Spirit, Mores, and Manners of a Nation." Furthermore, the general spirit is the *product* of several factors rather than a fundamental cause: "Several things govern men: climate, religion, laws, maxims of government, examples of past things, mores, manners; from which a general spirit is formed, which is the result of these things."[9] Finally, one of these factors may predominate, marking the general spirit with signs of its influence.

For these three reasons, what emerges from the concept of general spirit is the idea of unity of the social whole (rather than the idea of a universal cause). Do we find the same idea in Tocqueville? Note first that the notion of "social state" plays the same role in Tocqueville's writing as the concept of "general spirit" does in Montesquieu's. Contrary to what any number of commentators have said, this notion was commonplace at the time. For example, we find it in the writing of Benjamin Constant and in the Saint-Simonian newspaper *Le Producteur*.[10] Of course, Tocqueville inflected it in his own way. Here is a passage in which he is close to Montesquieu: "The social state is ordinarily the result of a fact, sometimes of laws. . . . If one would know a people's legislation and mores, one must therefore begin by studying its social state."[11]

The social state, as Dino Cofrancesco has shown, is a set of economic, social, and cultural (or symbolic) facts. As such, it might seem to be quite similar to Montesquieu's general spirit.[12] But Tocqueville seems to have relied

---

[8]Raymond Aron, *Dix-huit leçons sur la société industrielle* (Paris: Gallimard, 1962), pp. 69, 70; Georges Benrekassa, *Montesquieu. La liberté et l'histoire* (Paris: LGF, 1987), pp. 170–71. See Benrekassa's discussion under the head "Le tout social: les implications d'une causalité globale." The distinguished Montesquieu and Tocqueville scholar Melvin Richter agrees: "The Uses of Theory: Tocqueville's Adaptation of Montesquieu," in *Essays in Theory and History* (Cambridge: Harvard University Press, 1970).

[9]*Esprit des lois*, XIX, 4, p. 641.

[10]For an excellent review of this point, see Dino Cofrancesco, "*Assieto sociale* e dominio aristocratico," in *Il teatro della politica*, ed. F. Mioni (Reggio Emilia: Edizione Diabasis, 1990), pp. 44–46. Following Larry Sidentrop, *Tocqueville* (New York: Oxford University Press, 1994), a number of authors have argued that "social state" came from Guizot. See, for example, Aurelian Craiutu, "Tocqueville and the Political Thought of the Doctrinaires," *History of Political Thought* 20, 3 (1999), or the special issue on "French Liberalism and the Question of Society," *History of European Ideas* 30, 1 (2004), esp. the article by Melvin Richter, "Tocqueville and Guizot on Democracy: From a Type of Society to a Political Regime," pp. 64–67. In reality, however, the notion was a commonplace.

[11]*DA* I.1.3, p. 107; AG, p. 52.

[12]Cf. what Le Play calls the "social constitution," as discussed in part 1.

more on what Montesquieu baptized the "principle" of a regime, as distinct from its "nature": "There is a difference between the nature of a government and its principle: its nature is what makes it what it is, while its principle is what makes it act. One is its particular structure, while the other consists of the *human passions* that cause it to move."[13] For example, the nature of republican government is that sovereignty belongs either to certain families (in an aristocratic republic) or to the entire people (democracy). The principle is *virtue*, that is, the conscious preference given to the general interest over the particular interest (which could ultimately rise to the level of heroism). What is interesting about Montesquieu's concept is that the principle establishes a precise correspondence between political power and society, including society's psychological characteristics and passions: "the human passions that move" the government are *analogous* to the dominant passions in society. If this is correct, then Montesquieu's view was quite close to Tocqueville's treatment of local communities as the concrete embodiment of democracy. If "the people reign" in both state and society, it is because, by analogy, the authority of the collectivity is accepted, just as majority rule determines which decisions are legitimate in the representative system. Thus what might correspond to Montesquieu's "principle" in Tocqueville would be either equality or popular sovereignty. And Tocqueville does present both in these terms. For instance, he says that the "fundamental principle" (*principe générateur*) of the state is popular sovereignty, while in society this principle figures as the right of the individual to judge for himself and govern himself.[14] Popular sovereignty corresponds to social and moral individualism, and this gives rise to two complementary definitions of democracy (see part 1).

In fact, it is rather *equality* that plays in "democracy" (Tocqueville's ideal type) the role of "principle" in Montesquieu's sense *because equality is at once a norm and a passion*. It is translated into legal rules, and it also engenders a mechanism of competition, envy, and imitation. It feeds the democratic imagination.

It is also fair to say that equality is in the law (the Code Civil in France) only because it is in people's minds, and vice versa. The problem that France faced after the Revolution was how to stabilize a demand for "equality of conditions" that ran far ahead of what the law allowed under the July Monarchy. Paraphrasing Montesquieu, we might say that this does not prove that everything was equal in Louis-Philippe's France (far from it); rather,

---

[13] *De l'esprit des lois*, III, 1, p. 536 (emphasis added).

[14] I will come back to this because Tocqueville is responding to Joseph de Maistre's notion of a "fundamental principle of constitutions."

equality was "that without which the government would be imperfect." Perfect democracy—which Tocqueville thought both impossible and lethal—would nevertheless be democracy in which the demand for equality was fully satisfied.[15]

Here, then, we see the gap between Montesquieu and Tocqueville as well as the filiation. Tocqueville is describing a dynamic rather than a structure or "perfect" type, as Montesquieu is doing. Modernity amplifies the appetite for equality, and socialism is itself a historic phase of modernity. This leads to the provocative formula in the introduction to the first *Democracy*: "The gradual development of the equality of conditions is therefore a providential fact. . . . Does anyone think that democracy, having destroyed feudalism and vanquished kings, will be daunted by the bourgeois and the rich?"[16] What Montesquieu taught Tocqueville was faith in the unity of the social (power and civil society) and the perception of a "principle" through which the political and the civil nurtured each other (and perhaps intoxicated each other). There is a democratic "social state," which can be distinguished from its political superstructure, as in the July Monarchy, in which the state was parasitic on society but in which analogies and affinities between state and civil society could also exist (as in America, where the federal system was a "state of states" that Tocqueville described as decentralized).[17] Of course the social state could also be associated with a pathological government: both Napoleon and Napoleon III *despotically cultivated equality* in continuity with absolutism.

---

[15] As we will see in part 3, Tocqueville, citing Pascal, said that this was impossibility itself, even from a metaphysical point of view (the human condition). He wrote that "no equality instituted by men will ever be enough for them." *DA* II.2.13, p. 173; AG, p. 627.

[16] *DA* I, Introduction, p. 61; AG, p. 6.

[17] Tocqueville describes the July Monarchy in these terms: "It strikes me that we have destroyed the status positions that once gave certain individuals the wherewithal to battle tyranny on their own. Privileges once vested in families, corporations, and individuals are now bequeathed to the government alone." Ibid.; AG, p. 11. Montlosier said the same thing during the Restoration (before rallying to the July Monarchy); this, too, was a theme common in Ultra circles.

Counterrevolutionary Traditionalism

A MUFFLED POLEMIC

A SOCIETY OF INDIVIDUALS?

In the counterrevolutionary school, it remained an article of faith from the time of the Directory to the end of the nineteenth century that individualism is destructive of the social bond, that it is impossible to create a society from individual atoms. The Code Civil chopped society into little pieces, creating social fragmentation.[1] On this last point, Tocqueville was in total agreement: the "law of inheritance," he said, should be placed "at the head of all political institutions" in both ancient and modern treatises on politics.[2] It explained everything about the democratic structure: in France, the Code Civil was a *machine* that "crushes or shatters anything in its way, it rises up from the earth only to hammer down again and again until nothing remains but a shifting, impalpable dust, on which democracy rests."[3] This lyrical description (which I have abridged) was repeated hundreds of times in the nineteenth century, especially by traditionalists.[4] For Tocqueville, in this instance the sociologist rather than the jurist, this was the basis of American society as "democratic social state," and it was this basis that made it possible to understand American mores and political customs. There was no American

---

[1] See, for example, the jurist J.-B. Coquille, *La France et le Code Napoléon* (Paris: Victor Lecoffre, n.d. [1882?]).

[2] Furthermore, political laws "are merely the expression" of this, that is, of the social state. On this point, Tocqueville was the heir of Montlosier, whose central idea Saint-Simon praised: "One must first be civil power in order to exercise a political power." See *De la monarchie française depuis son établissement jusqu'à nos jours*, 1814, 3:273. For Montlosier, it was the "civil" or "social constitution" that counted and not the constitutional charter: "Without a written constitution, a civil power, simply because it is civil, can in fact exercise political power." See Paola Cella, " 'Pouvoir civil' et 'pouvoir politique' nel pensiero di Montlosier," *Il pensiero politico* 2 (1983): 189–214.

[3] *DA* I.1.3, p. 109; AG, p. 54.

[4] See the 1826 debate on the proposed Peyronnet law in my *L'Individu effacé*, pp. 297ff., and my "Terminer la Révolution par le Code civil?" in *Les Penseurs du Code civil*.

aristocracy[5] because "the families of the great landowners have nearly all been absorbed in the common mass."[6]

Nevertheless, Tocqueville did not believe that one could simply say that individualism destroys the social bond. To a certain extent he conceded the point,[7] but he was also impressed by the way in which individualistic Americans joined together to form associations, linking their particular interests to the general interest and ultimately creating a society with sovereignty of the people. In contrast to Bonald (who argued that democratic republics are not "constituted") and de Maistre (who held that a democratic republic is a society without sovereignty and therefore without solidity), Tocqueville thus recognized that *society could be constituted in new ways*: associations linking public and private, forms of life created by decentralization, avowed or implicit religions, and so forth.[8] But he aimed his criticism primarily at an idea that de Maistre had made famous: "the generative principle (*principe générateur*) of political constitutions."[9]

When a contemporary reader of Tocqueville read that "the generative principle of the republic is the same principle that governs most human actions,"[10] he had to sit up and take notice because for de Maistre the equally general generative principle was necessarily in God: indeed, the great error of the Moderns, de Maistre argued, was the belief that man is master of himself and of society (in keeping with what Kant called the autonomy of practical reason). Heteronomy is the fundamental principle. Man "begins to believe that he is really the direct author of everything that is accomplished through him. He is, in a sense, the trowel that thinks he is an architect" but is in fact "a tool of God."[11]

That this whole passage in Tocqueville is aimed directly at de Maistre is indicated by any number of *signs*: references to God, the reference to the

---

[5]In contrast to what Guizot argued in his public polemic, *De la démocratie en France*, 1849, or his private polemic (letter to Tocqueville in 1846): see part 5 below.

[6]*DA* I, p. 112; AG, p. 57. In a letter to Kergorlay (*OC* XIII-1, p. 232), Tocqueville explained that there was an aristocracy of landowners owing to the primogeniture laws carried over from England, but the reform of inheritance laws destroyed this group, or nearly so. Tocqueville had little to say about the role of important slaveholding families in the South.

[7]See his celebrated distinction between "reflective and tranquil" individualism and selfishness or egoism, *DA* II, p. 125; AG, p. 585.

[8]Here I differ with the conclusions of Gérard Gengembre, who wrote in a very informative paper that Tocqueville "ratified the desocialization of social man and the deconstitution of the social order." See Gérard Gengembre, "Tocqueville ou le dialogue imaginaire avec la pensée contre-révolutionnaire," *Tocqueville Review* 27, 2 (2006): 299.

[9]Joseph de Maistre, *Essai sur le principe générateur des constitutions politiques et des autres institutions humaines* (Paris: Société Typographique, 1814).

[10]*DA* I, p. 520; AG, p. 459.

[11]De Maistre, *Essai sur le principe générateur*, p. 14.

"generative principle," the reference to "individual reason," which is ubiquitous in the writings of de Maistre, Bonald, Lamennais, and their entire school.[12] The God that Tocqueville invokes here is not the one who used man as his "trowel" but rather the creator who gave man his intellectual and moral autonomy, the source of political self-government:

> Providence equipped each individual, whoever he might be, with the degree of reason necessary to guide his conduct in matters of exclusive interest to himself alone. This is the great maxim on which civil and political society in the United States is based: fathers apply it to their children, masters to their servants, towns to the people they administer, provinces to towns, states to provinces, the Union to the states. Extended to the whole nation, it becomes the dogma of popular sovereignty.
>
> Thus, in the United States, *the generative principle of the republic* is the same principle that governs most human actions. Hence the republic penetrates, if I may put it that way, into the ideas, opinions, and general habits of the Americans at the same time that it establishes itself in their laws.[13]

In other words, for Tocqueville, it was not God who penetrated the private and public, social and political, individual and collective life of the people as the "generative principle" of a republic; it was rather the sovereignty of the people, the republican idea. And in accordance with the Tocquevillean distinction between two spheres of democracy, there is an *isomorphism* between the two spheres owing to "individual reason." In family, town, and state, each individual becomes the judge of his or her own interest and of the relationship of that interest to the interest of the community.[14] That is why "individual reason" appears in this passage. It is aimed squarely at counterrevolutionary

---

[12] In comparing Tocqueville and Guizot, Pierre Manent argued that "the Tocquevillean notion" of *generative principle* is "far more enigmatic" than Guizot's "civilization." See Pierre Manent, "Guizot et Tocqueville devant l'ancien et le nouveau," in *François Guizot et la culture politique de son temps*, ed. M. Valensise (Paris: Le Seuil, 1991), p. 151. Ironically, Manent later became de Maistre's editor. When placed back in its original context, the notion does indeed play on both enigma and transparency, but the Maistrian source settles the matter. In his magisterial work *Tocqueville et la nature de la démocratie* (1982; reprinted Paris: Fayard, 1993), Manent showed the subtle and polymorphous nature of the Tocquevillean notion, pp. 16–23.

[13] *DA* I.2.10, p. 520; AG, p. 458. Emphasis added.

[14] Think of the celebrated pages of Saint John Crèvecœur, who in 1795 propagated the myth of an "agrarian" America: the yeoman farmer is the typical American, the happiest man in the world. "We are a people of cultivators scattered over an immense territory.... We are all animated with the spirit of industry, which is unfettered and unrestrained because each person works for himself." The quote is from the letter to Raynal that served as preface to *Lettres d'un cultivateur américain*, according to Manuela Albertone, "The French Moment of the American National Identity: St. John de Crèvecœur's Agrarian Myth," *History of European Ideas* 32, 1 (March 2006): 57.

thinkers and is part of another hidden dialogue between Tocqueville and the school of Joseph de Maistre: "In the United States, the religion of the majority is itself republican. That religion subjects the truths of the other world to individual reason, just as politics leaves the interests of this world to the good sense of all, and it allows each man free choice of the path that is to lead him to heaven, just as the law grants each citizen the right to choose his government."

Tocqueville here reaffirms the argument that democracy has become the new form of the religious because, and to the extent that, "individual reason" created the authority to which it subjected itself at a time when dogmatic religions were in decline, as I showed in part 1.[15] An individual who believed in his independence of mind did not shed all his other beliefs.[16] On the contrary, he adhered to collective authority, whose first dogma is equality of all minds. Thus Tocqueville begins his passage with "the dogma of popular sovereignty," a phrase that he uses several times.[17] Democratic man's reason has a *credo*, which associates the collective with the individual, in the sense that what corresponds to popular sovereignty (political sphere) is the individual conceived as (1) apt to guide himself, (2) capable of seeking his own interest, and (3) equipped for that purpose with reason. And if "the republic is everywhere"[18] in America, if it "penetrates" everywhere, it therefore becomes the "spiritual place" of which Malebranche and later Lamennais spoke. What is individual is also social, and what is social is or becomes individual. It would be difficult to challenge the rudimentary sociology of the traditionalists more effectively.

Another way of stating the "principle" of the republic as Montesquieu saw it would be as follows: "Judge for yourself what your interests are, and their relation to the collectivity."[19] For Tocqueville, equality was the *principle* of

---

[15] True, Tocqueville liked to believe that Catholic influence was expanding in America. As René Rémond, *Les États-Unis devant l'opinion française, 1815–1852*, points out (see esp. pp. 121–62), this argument figured prominently in the French debate about the United States.

[16] Both Lamennais and Bonald argued that a Protestant cannot say "I believe" because he begins by questioning.

[17] "In the United States, the dogma of popular sovereignty is not an isolated doctrine unrelated to either habits or the whole range of dominant ideas."

[18] See the epigraph of part 1.

[19] As a people with a utilitarian spirit, Americans were not "virtuous," Tocqueville noted in his travel notebooks. He was at that time in the process of replacing the content of the republican principle as Montesquieu saw it with what would become "self-interest properly understood" in *Democracy in America*. See *Œuvres*, La Pléiade, 1:230: "The principle of the ancient republics was the sacrifice of the private interest to the general good, and in this sense one can say that they were *virtuous*. The principle of this republic seems to me to be to bring private interest back into the general interest. A sort of refined and intelligent egoism seems to me to be the shaft around which the whole machine revolves." Sing Sing, May 29, 1831.

democracy, the place where the political converged with the passions of the people: what he called "the philosophy of the Americans" postulated equality of intellect at both the individual and collective levels.

Three years after the publication of the first *Democracy*, Tocqueville once again discussed modernity's great innovation in individual law and self-identity: "According to the modern, democratic, and I daresay correct notion of liberty, each individual, because he is presumed to have received from nature the intelligence (*lumières*) needed to regulate his own behavior, derives from birth an equal and imprescriptible right to live independently of his fellow men in all respects bearing on himself alone, and to pursue his own destiny as he sees fit."[20]

In terms of practical results, he registered his astonishment at the political education of the American people: "No other people is more advanced in its political education."[21] And he confessed that this was the source of "the only hope I have for the future happiness of Europe."

Joseph de Maistre had often written that "the people are always mad, always childish, always minors." Tocqueville could not approve of this simplistic judgment, although it undoubtedly contained a grain of truth: "When the enemies of democracy argue that one person alone can do what he sets out to do better than the government of all, it seems to me that they are right."[22] But detractors such as de Maistre failed to understand the type of unintentional effect that the cynicism of those in power can have in democracy, for it is by showing contempt for the people that one arouses them. What must be understood is that democracy is always a *dynamic* and not simply a regime, a constitution, or a system of institutions. "When a man of the people is called to government, his self-esteem increases. Because he now has power, some very enlightened minds are ready to advise him. People look to him constantly for support and, by trying to deceive him in a thousand ways, manage only to enlighten him."[23]

An Investigation into the Phrase "Generative Principle"

A possible objection to this line of argument is the following: Is it possible to prove that Tocqueville was thinking of the counterrevolutionaries, and in

[20] Tocqueville, *État social et politique de la France avant et depuis 1789*, written at the behest of John Stuart Mill and published in 1838. Quoted in *OC* II-1, p. 62, and in *ARR*, p. 80.

[21] Travel notebooks, *Œuvres*, La Pléiade, p. 254.

[22] *DA* I.2.6, p. 341; AG, p. 280.

[23] Ibid., p. 340; AG, pp. 279–80. This passage would be worthy of the new Machiavelli of the democratic age whom we need to update the argument of *The Prince* or *The Discourses on Livy*.

COUNTERREVOLUTIONARY TRADITIONALISM ⊗ III

particular of Joseph de Maistre, as targets of his critique? Electronic index-ing of *Democracy in America* helps to confirm this interpretation, bearing in mind that the keys that were available to the 1835 reader of the work are no longer available to us. If Tocqueville used the phrase "generative principle" frequently in various contexts, that would mean that for him, given his sen-sibility as a writer, it was a neutral, commonplace notion. But in fact he did not: the phrase never appears in either the second *Democracy* or *The Ancien Régime and the Revolution*. It occurs only three times in the first *Democracy*, and in a very specific context. Let us examine these points in greater detail.

Apart from the passage we just examined, the concept appears twice in the first part of the first volume of *Democracy in America*. The first instance is in the chapter devoted to "the principle of popular sovereignty in America."[24] In the second instance, the response to de Maistre is even more direct: "the generative principle of the laws, by nature essentially republican,"[25] namely, public opinion, truly "the dominant power," is the same in America as in the *monarchy* of Louis-Philippe.[26] Indeed, this is one of the rare passages in which Tocqueville treats France in 1835 not as an example of a monarchy en-joying an administrative state that has been in place for centuries but rather as a "quasi-republic," as Lafayette had baptized it from the balcony of the Hôtel de Ville.

"A monarchy amidst republican institutions": this celebrated formula is here marshaled polemically against de Maistre, in the sense that public opin-ion becomes the generative principle,[27] and the king himself is supposed to become the neutral power as conceived by Benjamin Constant, following the evolution of public opinion.

The text goes on to make an important point about the difference be-tween the Orleanist king and the American president Andrew Jackson: royal power "penetrates in a thousand ways the administration of individual inter-ests" because the king appoints thousands of officials, far more, proportion-ately, than does the president of the United States.

In the end, de Maistre's thought is "extenuated" (in the etymological sense) after being called to the bar via the phrase suggestive of the theocratic vision.

---

[24] *DA* I.1.4, p. 118; AG, p. 62. "The principle of the sovereignty of the people was the generative prin-ciple of most of the English colonies in America."

[25] *DA* I, p. 197; AG, p. 140.

[26] Ibid., p. 196; AG, p. 139.

[27] Tocqueville is driving home the point against the prophets of the Right, who predicted that the United States would inevitably turn toward centralized sovereignty and monarchy: "Therefore I believe that France, with its king, more closely resembles a republic than the Union, with its president, resembles a monarchy." Ibid., p. 197; AG, p. 140. The syncopated style signals the polemical irony.

For de Maistre, man can neither create nor reform a constitution because "every constitution is divine in its principle."[28] Furthermore, his argument is based largely on supposed experience: "Look at history, which is experimental politics."[29] Tocqueville responded that the American laboratory was the perfect place for a political experiment in which the "generative principle" of the constitution and law lay in the creative activity of human beings. Democracy in Tocqueville's sense "spreads throughout society a restless activity, a superabundant strength, an energy that never exists without it." And, in turn, these effects of individual activity "can accomplish miracles."[30]

Miracles in a modern democracy? If Tocqueville, too, had a vision of Providence, it was one that countered the pessimism of the great Savoyard theocrat. The opposite position can be found in Bonald, for whom artificial human constructs were a dead end: "The republic has begun in the United States, and the form of government that it has adopted is entirely the work of man. Nature has had nothing to do with it. Hence it is rapidly progressing toward disorganization."[31]

In Tocqueville, what I will call (in part 3) the "Jansenizing position" consists in identifying positive aspects of the Fall, the remedy in the disease, as it were, whereas for de Maistre, the future is irrevocably condemned: "Man in relation with his Creator is sublime, and his action is creative. By contrast, once he separates from God and acts on his own, he does not cease to be powerful, because power is a privilege of his nature, but his action is negative and culminates only in destruction."[32]

For Tocqueville, man separated from God is *capable*[33] of rules and authority—authority susceptible at times of wisdom (common sense) but at other times prey to monstrous avatars. At the end of the second *Democracy*, he wrote:

> I am doing my best to enter into this point of view, which is that of the Lord [i.e., favoring human equality], and trying to consider and judge human affairs from this perspective.... Providence did not create mankind entirely independent or altogether enslaved. Around each man is traced, to be sure, a fatal circle beyond which he may not venture, but within the ample thus defined man is powerful and free, and so are peoples.[34]

[28] De Maistre, *Essai sur le principe générateur*, p. 46.
[29] Ibid., p. 47.
[30] *DA* I, p. 341; AG, p. 281. This is the passage on "the enemies of democracy."
[31] Bonald, *Théorie du pouvoir*, pp. 376–77.
[32] De Maistre, *Essai sur le principe générateur*, p. 73.
[33] Cf. the formula of the Church fathers, borrowed by Pascal: man is "capable of God" (*capax Dei*).
[34] *DA* II.4.8, pp. 401, 402; AG, pp. 833, 834.

An Investigation into the Phrase "Individual Reason"

The notion of "individual reason"[35] counterbalances what Tocqueville borrowed from and polemically attacked in the traditionalist repertoire. Like de Maistre, Tocqueville used this idea to evoke independence of judgment as it had been conceived since the days of Luther and Descartes. For Tocqueville, it stood for a "philosopical method." The first chapter of the second *Democracy*, "On the Philosophical Method of the Americans," directly echoes this ideological register. As we have seen, de Maistre's "Study of Sovereignty" contained a number of formulas strikingly similar to Tocqueville's. For instance, de Maistre wrote: "Philosophy, that is, individual reason, becomes harmful and therefore culpable if it dares to contradict or question the sacred laws of this sovereign [general reason]."[36]

Tocqueville, for his part, developed a thesis about "philosophy [as] the natural antagonist of authority" in the margins of the published chapter.[37] In shorthand style, he noted: "Revolt against all authority. Attempt to appeal to individual reason in all matters. General and salient character of philosophy in the eighteenth century, essentially democratic character."[38]

From a lexicological point of view, is it true that "individual reason" is yet another phrase that Tocqueville used rarely owing to its traditionalist connotations? Indeed, we find only one occurrence in the first volume of *Democracy* and six in the second (but none in parts 3 and 4 of the latter). Can we explain this very selective distribution in terms of specific, emotionally significant contexts? Indeed, in the first *Democracy*, the phrase occurs toward the end of the final chapter, the part that deals, as we saw earlier, with "the generative principle of the republic" as well as with the religion of the

---

[35] The phrase itself is contestable in purely philosophical terms: from Plato to Descartes and Descartes to Kant, reason was neither individual nor collective (in the sense of addition); it was rather the faculty of thought, but in the element of the universal. What was individual was, strictly speaking, *judgment*, not reason. For example, when Descartes wrote in the *Discourse on Method* that "those who use only *their pure natural reason* will judge my opinions better than those who believe only in old books," it would be absurd to read "their pure natural reason" as an individual property. Such formulas show, as in the work of Victor Cousin, the political and sociological use that was made of philosophical thought in the nineteenth century; see my *L'Individu effacé*, pp. 459–72, 491–506.

[36] De Maistre, *Étude sur la souveraineté*, p. 285.

[37] Nolla II, p. 18, n. u.

[38] Ibid., n. t. The same formula is found in the manuscripts of *ARR*: Tocqueville speaks of revolutionaries who reject historical experience and prefer to rely on "their individual reason." *OC* II-2, p. 167, also pp. 165–66. In the published text the terms appears twice (*OC* II-1, chaps.1 and 2 of book 3) in opposition to "authority" and "historical experience." This is indeed the traditionalist sense. The text states first that the philosophical theorists of the Ancien Régime "wielded sole authority" owing to the use they made of "their individual reason," pp. 194 and 195, and that the Church then "recognized an authority superior to individual reason," p. 204.

majority, which "subjects the truths of the other world to individual reason, just as politics leaves the interests of this world to the good sense of all."[39]

In the second *Democracy*, the idea is found in two chapters, "On the Philosophical Method of the Americans" and "On the Principal Source of Beliefs among Democratic Peoples," which are crucial for the question of intellectual and moral freedom.[40] The final occurrence is somewhat later in the first part of the second volume, and again the theoretical and semantic context is of course religious: the chapter is entitled "How Religion Uses Democratic Instincts in the United States." Here Tocqueville explains in a confessional mode that of all dogmatic beliefs, "dogmatic beliefs in regard to religion seem to me most desirable of all."[41] And here we also find a passage with a prominent anacoluthon that draws the eye: "If he has no faith, he must serve, and if free, believe." That is why we also find the previously cited passage, which harks back to both Lamennais and Pascal's wager:[42] "General ideas about God and human nature are therefore ... the ones most appropriately shielded from the usual action of individual reason, and in which there is most to gain and least to lose in recognizing an authority."

General reason and individual reason: this is Lamennais.[43] The comparison of what is gained and what is lost by believing in God is Pascal's wager. In parts 3 and 4 of volume 2 of *Democracy in America*, Tocqueville did not use the phrase "individual reason." Nevertheless, chapters 6 and 7 of part 4 *have to do with the independence of the individual* and the institutions that can save individuality from the rise of the new despotism. The issue is no longer independence from traditional authority or from God.

Indeed, a writer like Tocqueville, always concerned to *distinguish* different domains of reference, objects of discussion, and phases of his argument, was always careful when using terms outside of what one might call their vital context. From his master Pascal he learned that there are places where one must write "the capital of France" and other places where one must write "Paris."[44]

---

[39] *DA* I.2.10, sec. 5; AG, p. 458.

[40] *DA* II.1.1 and 2, pp. 11, 14, 17, 18, and 19; AG, pp. 485, 487, 491, and 492–93.

[41] *DA* II.1.5, p. 29; AG, p. 501.

[42] My coupling of this passage with the name of Pascal is not gratuitous because Tocqueville explicitly evokes the wager elsewhere (*DA* II, p. 158).

[43] Lamennais was himself a disciple of de Maistre. It suffices to open the *Mémorial catholique*, controlled by Lamennais, to find repeated instances of the idea that true authority is beyond the grasp of "individual reason."

[44] In Pascal's *Pensées*, ed. Lafuma, p. 575.

6

The Discovery of the Collective

In *Democracy in America*, what is properly called Tocqueville's sociology stems from his conviction that the collective is a specific object of study because it obeys distinctive laws of its own. Here again, the initial impetus came from traditionalists such as Bonald, who opposed "man" and "society." Bonald forcefully expressed what his adversary Maine de Biran would call his social metaphysics in the Chamber of Deputies on January 28, 1817, in a debate about freedom of the press:

> People knew then because they believed. They knew in religion, in morals, in politics, in the sciences of law and mores, and in the science of society. They walked securely in the bright daylight of authority and experience, and they were careful not to ask man for enlightenment that was to be found exclusively in society. Other times, other ideas. Man has ceased to know anything since he began to doubt everything.... People began to see enlightenment in man because they no longer recognized it in society.[1]

The knowledge in question was thus a form of social wisdom backed by "authority and experience"—in other words, the château and the presbytery: it was a knowledge that was in no way critical of *tradition*.[2] Indeed, it was tradition. Thus according to Bonald, to know was to believe. And what did one believe in? Basically, in Society, as a sort of "repository"[3] or memory of experience. With Protestantism and Cartesianism people wanted to believe in man, that is, in the critical spirit. Society therefore dissolved, and nothing but individuals remained—individuals who, for example, demanded freedom of the press. They no longer wished to believe, and therefore they no longer knew anything.

---

[1] Bonald, "Opinion sur le projet de loi relatif aux journaux," in *Œuvres*, vol. *Discours* (1847), p. 478.
[2] In the etymological sense: the act and art of transmission. Here, tradition meant not a state of affairs located in the distant past but a present enriched by an unbroken chain of memory.
[3] Just as we saw earlier that for Tocqueville the Public was the repository of authority.

The link between this traditionalist conception and the Catholic world-view is clear. It suffices to recall that for Bossuet, innovators "had no offspring in the Church." *Non nova sed nove*, as the bishop of Meaux liked to say: the Church never creates anything new but may eventually amend its teachings. From the standpoint of the Protestant Awakening, Alexandre Vinet set himself against this political and theological position. In 1836, writing in *Le Semeur* (a Protestant newspaper published in France), he indignantly attacked the alliance between Catholicism as a spiritual attitude, the Church as institution, and political traditionalism:

> Those who conceived of the Christian religion as one may conceive of the state, namely, as an involuntary society . . . , those who enveloped religious obligations in the obligations of a blind faith, in the manner of a body that takes it upon itself to believe for everyone, a body that knows what each of its members may not know and lives a life of which each of its members may be unaware; those who have forbidden direct contact between each individual and the Word of God—those people have built a powerful, carefully calculated system based on certain tendencies of human nature.[4]

Maine de Biran also combated this traditionalist sociologism, anticipating the conflict that would erupt seventy years later between Durkheim and Gabriel Tarde.[5] "As if society were a mysterious being," he wrote, "existing by itself independent of individuals and as something other than their combination; as if society without individuals possessed a system of truths given at the beginning and received passively by individuals."[6] Tocqueville refuted this simplistic conception, although it clearly obsessed the spirit of the age.[7] He also profited from it, however. He, too, believed that "society knows," but for him this did not mean that faith no longer existed in an age of individuals armed with the tools of criticism. What is original about his analysis is that he showed how individuals in society can achieve a result *opposite* to that embodied in their image of themselves and their expectations; to "deconstitute," to borrow Bonald's term, is to create a different constitution: the power of

[4] Alexandre Vinet, "De l'individualité et de l'individualisme," April 13, 1836, in *Le Semeur*, reproduced in Alexandre Vinet, *Philosophie morale et sociale*, ed. Bridel (Lausanne: Payot, 1913), 1:334.

[5] P. Macherey makes the same observation in "Bonald et la philosophie," *Revue de synthèse*, no. 1 (January–March 1987).

[6] Maine de Biran, *Œuvres* (Paris: Vrin, 1987), X–1:98: manuscript concerning Degérando (history of philosophy) and mainly attacking Bonald. Biran's understanding of philosophy (metaphysics) was far superior to that of his adversaries.

[7] Even Proudhon, a theorist of the contract, mutualism, and individual autonomy, occasionally lapsed into hypostases of the collective, for example, in *La Pornocratie* and *Justice dans la Révolution et dans l'Église*.

the collective. The originality of Tocqueville's sociology resides entirely in the analysis of this inversion, which makes it impossible to classify him as a "methodological individualist," as is too often alleged.

It is interesting to note that Tocqueville wanted to be elected to the seat in the Académie Française that had once been held by Bonald. As Gabriel de Broglie wrote with amusement, it would have been curious to see how "Tocqueville praised Bonald,"[8] but it never happened: defeated by Ancelot in the election of February 25, 1841, Tocqueville was not elected to the Académie until December, when he filled the seat formerly held by M. de Cessac, who had been a minister under Napoleon.

We might thus say that Tocqueville's relation to the traditionalists on this point was one of "dissenting agreement," which he might have formulated by saying "democratic society knows." For instance, in the chapters devoted to the family and to the status of women in America, Tocqueville, though careful to stress the conscious and deliberate thoughts of individuals, also analyzed the pursuit of a distinctive goal by the social order as such.

A REVEALING TERRAIN: WOMAN AND THE FAMILY

"Democracy [like aristocracy] also attaches brothers to one another, but it goes about it in a different way."[9] The personification of democracy in this passage ("democracy" is a conscious being) is not a metaphor, for Tocqueville repeatedly stresses the aptitude of the democratic social state to maintain its coherence. In this instance, where women are concerned, the coherence stems from "the influence of democracy on the family" (the title of *Democracy* II.3.8) and, more precisely, from "the philosophical method" that the Americans have adopted.[10] Young American girls learn very early, while still under paternal authority, to "think for themselves," so that in marriage they

---

[8] Gabriel de Broglie, interacademic speech of June 13, 2005, "Tocqueville et l'histoire," p. 3 (site of the Académie des Sciences Morales et Politiques). Tocqueville's candidacy was opportunistic, "no doubt to put himself in line," as André Jardin remarked: see the Tocqueville-Ampère correspondence, *OC* XI, p. 146, n. 11. Still, Tocqueville accepted the possibility that he might have to compare *Democracy in America* to the writings and speeches of Bonald. Jardin gives a detailed account of this episode in his biography of Tocqueville, p. 220. Benoît, *Tocqueville: Un destin paradoxal*, p. 283, confuses the elections of January 28, 1841 (in which Ancelot confronted Ballanche and Tocqueville withdrew in favor of Ballanche), and February 25 (in which Tocqueville was a candidate and was beaten by Ancelot).

[9] *DA* II.3.8, p. 243; AG, p. 689.

[10] On this point, see the manuscript (Nolla II, p. 165, n. c) and the long fragment that was supposed to conclude chapter 9 concerning the relation between philosophy and ... the flirtatiousness of young women in society (Nolla II, p. 172).

retain a sort of equality of judgment, even though they are supposed to admire their husbands[11] and devote themselves to household chores.

At the end of chapter 9, moreover, Tocqueville does not shrink from offering advice to future reformers in France. American education, he observes, "tends to develop judgment at the expense of imagination and to make women respectable and cold rather than tender wives and amiable companions of men." Men might accordingly have grounds for complaint. What counts, however, are society's superior purposes: "Although [American] society is more tranquil and better regulated, private life often has fewer charms. But these are secondary ills, which ought to be braved for the sake of a greater interest." So much for the French notion of the romantic woman, a residue of aristocratic influence. For Tocqueville, French society, in which marital difficulties were frequent[12] and fleeting passion was valued, was not viable. Here he is speaking as an expert sociologist, in his own eyes at any rate, because one might call him rather a typical conservative: "At this point no choice remains: a democratic upbringing is necessary to protect women from the perils with which the institutions and mores of democracy surround them."[13]

A democratic upbringing will improve a woman's mind, but only to keep her confined to the home. In the French original, Tocqueville uses the professorial *we*: "At the point we have reached, we are left with no choice." He takes the reader by the hand—something he rarely does in *Democracy in America*. Note, too, his assertion of the need to "protect women" (*garantir la femme*): authority commands the shaping of mores. This view of the matter contrasts with American practice as Tocqueville describes it: women are allowed to "think for themselves" in order *to teach* them to "contemplate with a calm and steady eye . . . the vast panorama of the world."[14] When the reformist sociologist speaks and raises his voice, it is to ask that women be protected from a danger that besets them in democracy: Was he thinking of the gender's weaknesses?

---

[11] See Tocqueville's very ironic letters on this point to his sister-in-law, the wife of his brother Hippolyte: June 9, 1831 (*OC* XIV, p. 103), and November 29 (p. 148).

[12] Consider the case of Tocqueville himself, who married Mary Mottley against the wishes of those close to him as a consequence of a "judgment" based on rather curious criteria. He then loved her tenderly despite frequent infidelities (so frequent that Kergorlay intervened), for which he reproached himself. For the criteria that Tocqueville himself expressed twelve days before his marriage, see his rather incredible letter to Camille d'Orglandes, *Lettres choisies. Souvenirs*, p. 343. He had broken off his relationship with Rosalie Malye in 1828, when she resigned herself to marrying a wealthy rentier, and it seems that the wound had not yet completely healed.

[13] *DA* II.3.9, p. 249; AG, p. 694.

[14] There is a hint here of Descartes and his "method": the "great book of the world" is the phrase used in the *Discourse on Method*. It is the continuation of the philosophical method of the Americans within the family that awakens this echo of Descartes.

But to be fair to Tocqueville, before adopting the professorial "we," he pointed out that the Americans hoped that "individual independence would regulate itself" and that religion would figure only as a last resort. This was of course quite different from the threat of the convent in Catholic Europe. Furthermore, his comparison was based on the aristocratic education of women in France, where young women were fragile creatures because they were kept isolated from reality, which then burst in upon them all at once. He then developed this idea.

Can individuals know the social purpose to which they contribute? The answer, according to Tocqueville, seems to be yes when the contradiction between "society" and other factors that create the "social state" is not too great. When it comes to the education of women, the "Americans are more consistent" than the French. In France, "opinions and tastes are still a strange mix combining vestiges of all the ages of the past," so that the advent of the bourgeoisie did not abolish the "timid, sheltered, almost cloistered upbringing" of the aristocratic age, after which young women are suddenly abandoned at age twenty-eight or so, "without guidance or assistance, to the disorders that are inseparable from democratic society."

Thus the French and American cases differ with respect to the consistency of democracy's ends with the means employed by individuals. The Americans know how to develop the *principle* of their fully democratic society: equality of minds (*esprits*), as envisioned by Protestantism and Cartesianism. Tocqueville begins chapter 8 with some remarks about *Protestant* nations, and in his manuscript he wrote a note to himself that it was best not to say too much about this.[15] The French, for their part, were unfaithful to their national philosopher Descartes: they were ambivalent libertines, sometimes liking their libertinage and other times loathing it. "The constitution of moral man" had yet to find its unity, and it *needed* to do so: this accounts for the sociologist-professor's somewhat inflated tone at the end of chapter 9.[16]

The argument that Tocqueville develops in chapters 8–12 of *Democracy* II.3 is interesting for the way in which it reveals the suppleness of his sociology. On the one hand, "society knows." Democratic society inevitably achieves its social purposes by way of its individualistic principle: "Judge for yourself what your interests are and how they relate to the community." Yet

---

[15] As we saw earlier, he considered this to be dangerous terrain. In this passage, Protestantism becomes the modern source of the democratic idea: it "directed democracy to heaven before establishing it on earth." Cf. *Œuvres*, La Pléiade, 2:1141, and Nolla II, p. 169, n. c.

[16] Think of Durkheim and the astonishing posthumous collection of his lectures entitled *L'Éducation morale*. Durkheim instituted a highly authoritarian scholarly discipline around the themes of society, the republic, and collective consciousness.

to a great extent individuals also cooperate: they become aware of collective *rules*, and this makes it easier to meet society's requirements. These are "sociological rules" in Durkheim's sense rather than laws drafted by lawmakers. In these chapters, Tocqueville several times describes laws as mere reinforcements of intrinsic social dynamics.

Consider, in particular, the last page of chapter 12, where Tocqueville writes that the Americans "seem to me to have shown an admirable grasp of the notion of democratic progress."[17] He summarizes the way in which their vision deliberately and prudently shapes reality and shrewdly and accurately judges the effects they wish to achieve. In the following passage, the italicized phrases are signs of volition:

> Thus, Americans *do not believe* that man and woman have the duty or right to do the same things, but they *hold them in the same esteem* and *regard them* as beings of equal value but different destinies.[18] Although they *do not ascribe* the same form or use to a woman's courage as to a man's, they *never doubt* her courage; and while *they hold* that a man and his helpmate should not always use their intelligence and their reason in the same way, at least *they believe* that a woman's reason is as secure as a man and her intelligence just as clear.

One can therefore say literally that the Americans know what they are doing, where "Americans" denotes both a unified collectivity and a group of individuals obedient to the rules of society.

Note, too, however, that if the Americans have understood "the true notion of democracy," it is because they have understood Tocqueville. Woman *must* remain socially inferior to man but intellectually and morally his equal. Should Tocqueville be forgiven? When one is a sociologist *avant la lettre*, one is in possession of what society "knows." But the relation can be turned around: society is invested with the ideology of the observer. As Tocqueville proudly remarks:

> Americans have thus allowed woman's social inferiority to persist but have done all they could to raise her intellectual and moral level to parity with man, and in this respect they seem to me to have shown an admirable grasp of the notion of democratic progress. I, for one, do not hesitate to say that although women in

---

[17] But see also pp. 248–49, which contains the following phrases: "They judged . . . they wished . . . they sought . . . they preferred." The conscious designs of individuals are strongly emphasized.

[18] "The Americans" are therefore in a position of exteriority in relation to man and woman: they are, on the one hand, the collective itself and, on the other, in each instance a singular man or singular woman. The relation of whole to parts is subtly presented.

the United States seldom venture outside the domestic sphere, where in some respect they remain quite dependent, nowhere has their position seemed to me to be higher.

I refer anyone who may still be smiling to Tocqueville's manuscript, on which he wrote that no one would imagine "transforming" a woman into a lawyer, judge, or soldier.[19] To do so would be incompatible not only with the basic principle of political economy (the division of labor) but also with Pascal's distinction between *orders*.[20] Here Tocqueville invoked his highest intellectual authority.

Was woman's "function" thus of a different "order" from man's? Clearly, on this point, Tocqueville as sociologist did not go beyond what was commonplace for his time. Yet he believed that he had found an unanswerable argument against traditionalism and against the bourgeois spirit of the July Monarchy. The sociologist Tocqueville offered himself this piece of advice: "Say clearly somewhere that the women of America strike me as markedly superior to the men."[21] Feminists owe him a debt of gratitude.

THE CONSTRAINING ESSENCE OF THE SOCIAL BOND

Tocqueville thus took a middle-of-the-road position: individuals living in a given social state are not free to will or practice whatever they like, but if they *understand* the social state, they can work toward consistency, order, and ultimately tranquility in their social and moral lives. Tocqueville remained close to Montesquieu, who wrote that "in a well-regulated monarchy, subjects are like fish in a large net: they think they are free, yet they are trapped."[22] Their freedom is not totally illusory, but it is partly based on a misapprehension: it is a conditioned belief. If the whole is to be "well-regulated," the conditions must not be visible to the actors. In a similar vein, Tocqueville observed that when "the social bond . . . seeks to be loosened everywhere," and men can no longer "all be forced to do the same things," then "a way must be found to persuade them to will those things for themselves."[23] This is the role of the "new political science" that Tocqueville announced in the introduction to *Democracy in America*, about which so much ink has been spilled. To cleanse the blemishes

---

[19] Nolla II, p. 179, n. d.

[20] Ibid., p. 180, n. k.

[21] Ibid., p. 181, n. m.

[22] See commentary in Lucien Jaume, *La Liberté et la loi*, pp. 100ff.

[23] Manuscript, Nolla II, p. 183, n. c. This lengthy passage (on "manners") concerns the unity of "moral man" and the model that Cuvier represents; see the passage discussed earlier.

from the new social order, this social science must suggest a "way" to induce all men to will for themselves what a well-regulated democracy requires.

Although this is a serious question of great magnitude, it can be discussed in connection with less important things, which Tocqueville, following Montesquieu, calls *manners*. "These things," Tocqueville says in the manuscript, "are insignificant, but the cause that produces them is serious. *What you have before your eyes are the slight symptoms of a great malady*."[24] Symptoms of a major social crisis can be read in small details: "You can be certain that when every man thinks he can decide on his own what clothes to wear or what linguistic usage is correct, he will not hesitate to make his own judgments about everything."

To judge for oneself is therefore the sign of the revolution that will unleash the democratic torrent.[25] As we have seen, however, democracy also tends to drive toward uniformity; hence in Tocqueville's view a profound duality shapes this social form. We will encounter this idea of duality frequently in what follows. It is at the heart of his thought as a moralist and reader of Pascal (and we find the same Jansenist reference in a celebrated text of Durkheim's on *homo duplex*[26]). Under the name "democracy," society itself participates in this duality, according to Tocqueville. In the chapter entitled "Some Reflections on American Manners," Tocqueville distinguished between the phase in which the aristocracy has just fallen, when "men have lost the common law of manners," and the phase in which democracy has developed a dynamic of its own. In the latter (that is, the American case, not the French), individual liberty is more apparent yet individuals have limited ability to differentiate themselves from one another:

> When equality is complete and long-standing, men having roughly the same ideas and doing roughly the same things do not need to agree with or copy one another in order to act and speak in the same way. You constantly see a host of minor variations in their manners but no major differences. They are never perfectly alike, because they do not share the same model; they are never highly dissimilar, because they do share the same condition.[27]

---

[24] Ibid.

[25] This is the central theme of my *L'Individu effacé*. There I saw Tocqueville not as the first to see things this way but as the most important follower of Benjamin Constant. (There is no chapter devoted to Tocqueville, but he is the second most cited author in the index.)

[26] Durkheim offered a lengthy Pascalian portrait of man as a "monster of contradictions" in his 1913 article "Le problème religieux et la dualité de la nature humaine." The reference is to fragment 130 of Pascal's *Pensées*, Lafuma ed., p. 514.

[27] *DA* II.3.14, p. 270; AG, p. 712.

Tocqueville, determined not to be led astray by a rigid and abstract thesis, added numerous refinements to his portrait of democratic uniformization. In his manuscripts, for example, he noted that in aristocratic nations like England, "eccentricity ultimately becomes a national habit, which one then finds among individuals of all ranks." But he then asked himself if there might not be something paradoxical in this formula: "Can one say that eccentricity is a habit?"[28] In general, however, he associated the logic of the social (beliefs, mores, and manners) with social *constraint*: even when an individual comes up with a way to stand out, his invention is not purely arbitrary, because there are historical conditions and *sociological* motifs that transcend the sphere of the individual and his inwardness.

Still the "constraint of the social" is the not the same thing as the *authority* of the social, in that the former achieves its effects without being noticed, whereas authority is recognized and acknowledged.[29] Furthermore the collective constraint can be exercised from within, by way of motivations consistent with the fact that men, as Tocqueville puts it in the cited passage, have "the same condition." The constraint arises from an identity of situation, as Tocqueville's incisive remarks about American patriotism attest: "The inhabitants of the United States talk a great deal about their love of country. I confess that I do not trust this calculated patriotism, which is based on interest and which interest, by attaching to another object, may destroy."[30] This is a rather serious contention since it calls into question not only the self-consciousness of individual actors (but that is a sociologist's point of view) but also a very important aspect of the American "civic spectacle" (saluting the flag and reciting the pledge of allegiance in the schools, the doctrine of *e pluribus unum*, etc.). But Tocqueville continues as follows:

> Nor do I attach much importance to what Americans say when they daily proclaim their intention to preserve the federal system adopted by their forefathers.
>
> What keeps large numbers of citizens subject to the same government is much less the rational determination to remain united than the instinctive and in some sense involuntary accord that results from similarity of feeling and likeness of opinion.

This de facto similarity, in which personal feelings surprisingly lead many individuals to converge on the same action, is in some ways reminiscent of

---

[28] Nolla II, p. 191, n. d, text of April 20, 1838.

[29] Raymond Boudon does not make this distinction when he speaks of "social power" in Tocqueville; see *Tocqueville aujourd'hui*, pp. 167ff., 175, 187–88.

[30] *DA* I.2.10, p. 492; AG, p. 430.

what Locke called the "law of opinion" (which he set alongside "natural law" and "civil laws") or a "secret and tacit consent,"[31] which ensures adherence to customs, fashions, and beliefs that maintain the social order. The difficulty is the same as with Tocqueville: How can consent be tacit? What has to be understood is that the individual does not reason or deliberate but feels himself to be in harmony with what is being done around him as well as *in his name*. This is American patriotism according to Tocqueville: before institutions come into play, the fact that individuals find themselves in a similar situation (equality of conditions) *conditions the adherence* that the collective actually expects and demands. Durkheim held a similar view: "Owing to my birth, I am necessarily part of a particular nation. When I become an adult, I am supposed to acquiesce in this obligation merely because I continue to live in my country. But what difference does this make? My acquiescence does not make my obligation any less imperative."[32]

Tocqueville was as interested as Durkheim in the invisible constraint of the collective: the social bond is in essence constraining, even, and perhaps especially, when it demands signs of adherence (as in the flag ceremony). It follows that law (the federal system and political institutions) is not a direct agent of the social bond but rather its expression and reinforcement. Tocqueville clearly ascribed priority to the social bond, however: "I cannot accept the proposition that men constitute a society simply because they recognize the same leader and obey the same laws. Society exists only when men see many things in the same way and have the same opinions about many subjects and, finally, when the same facts give rise to the same impressions and the same thoughts."[33] These are fairly restrictive conditions, and Tocqueville observes with irony that the United States is probably more of a "society" than many contemporary European countries, even though America contains "twenty-four distinct sovereignties," diverse religions, three "races," and major economic differences between its northern, southern, and western regions.

What matters for us is the originality of Tocqueville's conception of society. Society, he believed, cannot exist without the constraint that the

---

[31] See Locke, *Essay on Human Understanding*, II.28.10, and the analysis in *La Liberté et la loi* (chapters on Locke).

[32] Émile Durkheim, *Les Règles de la méthode sociologique* (Paris: Presses Universitaires de France, 1973), p. 104. Bonald, one of the fathers of sociology, put it more bluntly: "Society is a veritable state of war between virtue and error . . . [between] nature, which wants the society of all, and man, who tends to isolate himself from society or, rather, to make himself a society of one; and the name *God of the armies* . . . means only the God of societies." See *Essai analytique sur les lois de l'ordre social*, in *Œuvres*, p. 14.

[33] *DA* I.2.10, p. 492; AG, p. 430.

collective imposes on each individual,[34] but in a democracy society can *be represented* in the eyes of its members only by their supposed adherence to it—or at any rate tacit adherence. Democracy presents itself to its agents as an entirely deliberate and freely chosen way of life, the opposite of despotism. And the political sphere (the election of leaders) serves as a mirror for the interpretation of the social sphere. To the outside observer, this indispensable illusion seems false; he cannot accept the thesis of deliberate, fundamental, and contractual adherence. If the democratic accord is "instinctive and in a sense involuntary," as Tocqueville says, it follows that while adherence is certainly real, it is not the *foundation* of society.[35] It does not create the social bond out of nothing but rather develops it through *individual interactions.*

Thus we see that ultimately the idea of collective authority combines with and complements the idea of adherence to society: internal adherence and external authority mutually reinforce each other. We have already encountered this logic, in which the part creates the whole which then subjugates it in return, with the consent of the individual as a "free slave."

For Tocqueville, this appears to be the true logic of the social, and we will see it at work again in the relation between master and servant.

The Master and the Servant Are Both Servants of Opinion

Social constraint supported by voluntary adherence is a mechanism that Tocqueville analyzed numerous times. It is at the heart of an admirable chapter of the second *Democracy* entitled "How Democracy Modifies Relations between Servant and Master."[36] Tocqueville shows us what follows from the individual initiative of master and servant and how they are in effect obedient to a social rule that exists independent of their will: "Within the society of servants, as in the society of masters, men exert substantial influence on one another. They acknowledge fixed rules and in the absence of law are

[34] This is worth pointing out at a time when many people speak rather abstractly about Tocqueville's "liberalism."

[35] Note the ambivalence of the Pilgrims: rupture on the one hand, transfer of previous (English and Dutch) customs on the other, compact, etc. As Denis Lacorne has shown, Tocqueville embellished the influence of the Mayflower pact: "Tocqueville et la thèse du 'point de départ' de la démocratie américaine," Tokyo colloquium, "La France et les États-Unis, deux modèles de démocratie?" June 10–12, 2005, proceedings in Japanese: R. Matsumoto, N. Miura, and S. Uno, eds., *Tocqueville et le présent de la démocratie* (Tokyo: Tokyo University Press, 2009). See also Denis Lacorne, *Religion in America: A Political History* (New York: Columbia University Press, 2011), pp. 22–39.

[36] *DA* II.3.5, pp. 221ff.; AG, pp. 669ff. For Philippe Raynaud's analysis, see the article "Tocqueville" in P. Raynaud and S. Rials, eds., *Dictionnaire de philosophie politique* (Paris: Presses Universitaires de France, 1996).

guided by what they encounter as public opinion. Orderly habits and a kind of discipline prevail." Thus, if we consider first aristocratic society, the master "comes to look upon his servants" through selfish eyes, while the servant "in a sense deserts himself, or, rather, he invests himself entirely in his master. There he forges an imaginary personality." Aristocratic society "wills" this *exis*, this role that each individual plays in a free but constrained manner (a *habitus*, to borrow a term from Pierre Bourdieu).

In democracy, by contrast, the servant "is not a different man from the master." The only tie between the two is the wage contract, and "public opinion . . . creates a sort of imaginary equality between them despite the actual inequality of their conditions." It is essential, however, to understand that neither man is free to reject what Tocqueville calls "public opinion."[37] They must accept it because, as members of a democratic society (possibly with equal voting rights), they have both contributed to creating the social order. "Imaginary equality" is a constraint they cannot reject: the individual sanctions the social because the social is also an individual product. In this case, Tocqueville is not simply talking about a convergence of sensibilities (in which everyone does the same thing at the same time in the same situation). Rather, he is speaking of *external* pressure (as we saw in part 1): "Ultimately, this omnipotent opinion pervades the souls even of those whose interest might inspire them to resist it. It alters their judgment even as it subjugates their will. In the depths of their souls, master and servant no longer see any profound dissimilarity between them."

Tocqueville the sociologist, observing the actors, plumbs "the depths of their souls" and finds a collective pressure, which creates an "authority." This is not perceived as such, however. It is the observer who calls it public opinion. What the actors feel is rather a pressure present *within* the social bond itself.

This can be put another way: instead of an identifiable incarnate power (the despot) or a codified juridical and institutional system (the state, the law), the democratic bond causes both master and servant to defer to the spirit of the times, each in his own way. Although the spirit of the times is intangible, they would quickly feel its effects if they were to attempt to violate its rules. Public opinion rules here. We are close to what Durkheim would call a "social fact" in his *Règles de la méthode sociologique*: "A social fact can be recognized by the external coercive power that it exerts or is capable of exerting on individuals. And the presence of this power can be recognized by

---

[37] Durkheim would say "collective consciousness," which exists solely through individual interaction but feeds back onto each of its involuntary authors.

the existence of some definite sanction, or else by the resistance that the fact opposes to any individual enterprise that tends to go against it."[38]

Just as Tocqueville demonstrates how each member of the master-servant pair can sincerely have feelings that are in reality prescribed by his function, so Durkheim has this to say about the sentiments of a mob: "No doubt it can happen that if I unreservedly abandon myself to the crowd, I will not feel the pressure exerted on me by [the collective enthusiasms]. But the pressure is felt the moment I try to fight against it. If an individual tries to oppose any of its collective manifestations, the feelings that he denies will turn against him."[39]

Note, moreover, that when Tocqueville describes his own experience of painful love (in rather neutral language), his description resembles Durkheim's.[40] He observes that in aristocratic circles there are "large numbers of fleeting and clandestine attachments,"[41] and that in case of mismarriage, conflicts soon emerge:

> When a man and a woman seek to meet despite the inequalities of the aristocratic social state, they have immense obstacles to overcome. After stretching or breaking the bonds of filial obedience, they must make one final effort to escape the dominion of custom and the tyranny of opinion, and when at length they come to the end of this arduous undertaking,[42] they find themselves as strangers among their natural friends and close relatives: the prejudice they have braved separates them. This situation soon breaks their courage and embitters their hearts.

Collective constraints also impinge on aristocratic society. Such constraints are more formalized owing to the importance of *manners*. They are articulated in terms of honor[43] and are often personalized (as in paternal authority). It is presumably not the "majority" that guides the young aristocrat

[38] Durkheim, *Les Règles de la méthode sociologique*, p. 11. See also p. 14 for a general definition of a social fact as an external constraint on consciousness.

[39] Ibid., p. 6.

[40] Tocqueville's relationship with Rosalie Malye was cut short by pressure from his family and his friend Louis de Kergorlay. The importance of this experience is discussed by Reiji Matsumoto, "Tocqueville on the Family," *La Revue Tocqueville* 8 (1986–87): 142–46.

[41] *DA* II.3.11, p. 256; AG, p. 699.

[42] This was the case with Tocqueville, who, after seven years, decided to marry Marie Mottley and was thereafter greeted with hostility within his milieu to the end of his life. These lines were written some years after the marriage (which took place in October 1835). In announcing Tocqueville's death, his family refused to mention his wife. See Manzini, *Qui êtes-vous M. de Tocqueville?* p. 155, and Benoît, *Tocqueville moraliste*, p. 551.

[43] Tocqueville devoted a good deal of thought to honor, relying for help on his friend Kergorlay and his father, Hervé de Tocqueville. See the notes and letters in Nolla II, pp. 200–202.

but rather honor and custom (as in the reminder that "such and such is not done in our world"). As a magistrate, Tocqueville himself wrote a treatise on honor and dueling[44] and fought a duel (probably in connection with Rosalie) in which he was seriously wounded.

In any case, underlying filial obedience in the aristocracy we find the same forces of social constraint, which Tocqueville described as the "empire of custom and the tyranny of opinion." The discourse of honor was simply the form that *opinion* took in the aristocracy, where *esprit de corps* occupied the place of the democratic public.

Thus we see why "democracy [as well as aristocracy] binds brother to brother" and how "it does so in a different way." This was the formula with which we began our examination of Tocqueville's sociology, which was based in part on "discordant accord" with counterrevolutionary thought. Counterrevolutionary thinkers were already familiar with *esprit de corps*, but Tocqueville tried to point out what they had completely underestimated in the democracy they rejected, namely, the importance of everyday constraints and instances of authority.[45]

---

[44] In *Mélanges*, see the treatise on dueling, probably written in 1828: *OC*-XVI, pp. 49ff. See also the analysis of this text by Mario Tesini, "Onore e pubblica opinione. Il discorso sul duello di Tocqueville," in *Il teatro della politica. Tocqueville tra democrazia e rivoluzione*, ed. Federico Mioni (Reggio Emilia: Edizioni Diabasis, 1990), pp. 159–82.

[45] In a well-known essay of 1828, Bonald managed only to contrast *esprit de corps* with "party spirit." See Bonald, *Mélanges littéraires, politiques et philosophiques* (Paris: Adrien Le Clère, 1854), pp. 217ff.

∾ 7

Tocqueville and the Protestantism of His Time

THE INSISTENT REALITY OF THE COLLECTIVE

We have already seen how much importance Tocqueville attached to Protestantism. He saw it as the historical and cultural source of modern political democracy and believed that, in social terms, it contributed to the exercise of individual judgment that is political democracy's indispensable complement. Yet his (embarrassed and anxious) recognition of Protestantism's due did not lead him to accept the sociological axioms or epistemology of such leading Protestant writers as Alexandre Vinet and Benjamin Constant.[1] Indeed, Vinet saw what I have called the logic of the collective but vehemently refused to grant it legitimacy or, in the end, to analyze it.[2] In many respects Tocqueville was close to Vinet, for him a major figure of the period 1825–48, but their views of religion in democracy reflected different methodological and philosophical choices. As for Benjamin Constant, his book on religion, on which he worked throughout his life, was deemed almost scandalous by liberals, many of whom could not understand how a theorist of "liberty in everything" (as he wrote in 1829) and therefore an advocate of critical judgment and control of authority could argue that religion was a necessary part of any free society. We have already encountered his statement that "some religious peoples may have been enslaved, but no irreligious people has remained free."[3]

Tocqueville made this thesis his own, drawing on the American example,[4] but he developed a view opposite to that of Constant: whereas the latter insisted on the disinterested character of religious sentiment, Tocqueville

---

[1] In *De la religion*, 5 vols. (Paris: Bossange-Treuttel and Wurtz, 1824–31), Constant declared his Protestant sensibility.

[2] Vinet allowed himself to label "socialist" all of the following: the Catholic Church, certain behavioral patterns of antiquity, and political writers of his own time such as Saint-Simon and Buchez.

[3] Constant, *De la religion*, 1:89.

[4] About which Constant had very little to say. Note, however, that Constant cited Alexandre Vinet in *De la religion*.

sought to prove in various ways that it was the (anthropological and socio-logical) *utility* of religion that counted. Here, too, democracy pursued its own ends, and the Christian religion became the expression of a quest for moral happiness and satisfaction through which the collective discovered a unified image of itself.

Furthermore, from the external standpoint of a social observer, religion is "useful" in the sense that it teaches people to limit their boundless ambitions and pretension to satisfy all their desires—both passions that democracy has a tendency to exacerbate.

Hence we can say that the Protestant individualism in Constant and Vinet has direct implications for thinking about the nature of the social. Tocque-ville rejects this view. Once again, he is close to Durkheim and not far from regarding the religious as the unconscious self-image of a group.

Let us consider examples of texts from the two Swiss authors, who, despite being Swiss, influenced the way in which *Democracy in America* was read be-cause all cultivated French readers were familiar with them. In 1828 Vinet received a French award for an essay on freedom of religion from the Société de la Morale Chrétienne.[5] By contrast, Constant rattled his audience and seemed to confirm that "Coppet liberalism" was a foreign import.[6]

TOCQUEVILLE DISAGREES WITH CONSTANT: SELF-INTEREST PROPERLY UNDERSTOOD

Tocqueville was not without personal beliefs when he began to investigate religion. Although he was looking for its social utility, he did not hesitate to affirm his own convictions. For instance, he wrote that (1) "there is no better illustration" than America "of the usefulness and naturalness of religion," and (2) "in the United States . . . the sovereign is religious, hence hypocrisy must

[5] See Vinet, *Mémoire en faveur de la liberté des cultes* (Lausanne: Payot, 1944 [1826]), on which Guizot prepared a report for the Société de la Morale Chrétienne and Barante presented his observations. *Le Globe* published a review (4:227), and *Mémorial catholique* featured a long polemical essay (6:338–52). In 1842 Vinet completely revised his book and published an interesting *Essai sur la manifestation des convictions religieuses*. I quote from the second revised edition (Paris, Chez les Éditeurs, rue de Rivoli, 1858). Sainte-Beuve praised Vinet's work as a literary critic in the *Revue des deux mondes*, 11:641–58, September 15, 1837. At the time Sainte-Beuve was preparing his Lausanne lectures, which would become *Port-Royal*, the first volume of which appeared in 1840. No one in France was unaware of Vinet's impor-tance as a moralist, theologian, and literary critic.

[6] In a series of articles on Constant, Laboulaye, *Revue nationale et étrangère*, no. 21, pp. 5–27, took an original approach to his writings on religion: "For the past twenty years, Benjamin Constant has devoted himself to the defense of religious ideas. . . . Constant, who belonged to no church, had arrayed against him liberal incredulity, Catholic dogmatism, and public indifference." See p. 25.

be common."[7] These two passages occur in the same paragraph. In social life there is nothing deplorable about the prevalence of hypocrisy (including strict respect of the sabbath, public preaching on morality, etc.) because what matters is that the community sees itself as obeying a common rule and believes in a transcendent reality. Anthropologically, man is "naturally religious." Tocqueville often stated this belief (which he shared with Constant) as an incontestable axiom. In the following section he wonders about the power of religion in the only country that had separated church and state at that time. He concludes that the human heart possesses both "a natural disgust for existence and an overwhelming desire to exist." Here he offers a glimpse of his Jansenism (the duality of man), which suited the Romantic era quite well. This leads him to a profession of faith that might have been written by the mature Constant: "Religion is therefore nothing other than a particular form of hope, as natural to the human heart as hope itself. Men stray from religious belief through a kind of aberration of the intelligence, and with the aid of a type of moral violence against their own nature: an invincible inclination brings them back. Unbelief is an accident; faith alone is the permanent condition of humankind."[8]

But if man is religious by both vocation and historical tradition, why try to show that religion is also *useful*, as Tocqueville does in several places in *Democracy in America*? There are two answers to this question. First, he makes no secret of his wish for an end to the dreadful war between church and state that the Revolution bequeathed to France. Like any number of his contemporaries, from Royer-Collard to Laboulaye and from Constant to Jules Ferry, Tocqueville was convinced that there was no fundamental reason why the Catholic Church could not reconcile with modern society. In fact, liberal Catholics who tried to do so paid a price because the *Syllabus* and Vatican Council of 1870 ended all hope of reconciliation.

Tocqueville also had theoretical reasons for writing as he did: the needs of human nature and the "religious sentiment" (as Constant called it[9]) are

---

[7] *DA* I.2.9, p. 396; AG, p. 336.

[8] Ibid., p. 403; AG, p. 342. In the same passage, p. 402, AG, p. 341, Tocqueville also wrote that "the religion I profess brought me into contact with the Catholic clergy." But in his correspondence (especially with Mme Swetchine and Corcelle) he discusses the pain of losing his faith in an adolescent crisis in which he discovered eighteenth-century writers in the library of his father, a prefect in Metz, as well as the pleasures of love and sex: he fathered a child with a servant. Like Constant, who affirmed his affinity with the Reformation, Tocqueville wished to show his approval of his upbringing. In this way they are strangely similar: both men wished to praise something from which they felt inwardly alienated and even excluded.

[9] In *De la religion*, Constant opposed sentiment and "forms." This is the leitmotif of the book, and it enabled Constant to criticize the hold of the "sacerdotal castes" on ordinary believers (in Egypt as well as in the Catholic Church of the Restoration).

not enough to explain the increasing influence of religion on the democratic spirit. In this respect, Islam (which Tocqueville studied) and Christianity have very different effects. Furthermore, as we have seen, religion haunts "democracy" in two respects: as tradition (Christianity) and as a novel phenomenon ("democratic faith"). Hence all of Tocqueville's effort went to demonstrating the *utility* of Christianity in the United States by linking it to the "philosophical method" of Americans, which stressed the following precept: "Judge for yourself your own interests and their relation to the community."

Looking at things in this way once again brings up the question of *the authority of the group* over its members: the authority of the priest (in any church or denomination) depends on what the believers or citizens think is useful. Tocqueville's idea is that "self-interest properly understood" is the optimal instrument of collective authority, which priests manage intelligently. This accounts for the importance of this concept in *Democracy in America*, despite the fact that Constant indignantly rejected it in *De la religion*.[10]

For Constant, if Protestantism accepted this moral utilitarianism or social pragmatism, it would betray its own central tenets. Tocqueville believed the opposite: acceptance was the way for Christianity to save itself politically, even though it meant becoming a mere *opinion*. We earlier encountered what seemed like an offhand remark in the chapter on "the principal source of beliefs among democratic peoples": "If one looks into the matter closely, it becomes apparent that religion itself reigns [in the United States] far less as revealed doctrine than as common opinion."[11] Ultimately, owing to the new "repository" of belief, an extraordinary permutation would take place: "Faith in common opinion will become a sort of religion, with the majority as its prophet." This should be understood as saying that Christianity, having become extremely *useful*, will inevitably mutate into something quite different but with the same power of attraction: "a sort of religion."

A few sentences later, Tocqueville concluded that "intellectual authority will be different, but it will be no less potent." To a friend of Protestantism like Benjamin Constant (who died in December 1830), such a statement would presumably have seemed odious. Tocqueville's contemporary Alexandre Vinet would have felt the same way. To Tocqueville's readers, therefore, his view would have seemed different from theirs in two ways: with Constant

---

[10] "Self-interest properly understood" is a notion whose paternity can probably be ascribed mainly to Helvétius, as Constant stated in *De la religion* (preface, p. xxxi, note). Tocqueville knew Helvétius's work well. His books were considered indispensable in château libraries in the eighteenth and nineteenth centuries.

[11] *DA* II.1.2, p. 18; AG, p. 492.

he differed on the question of self-interest properly understood, and with Vinet he differed on the question of authority.[12]

❧

To be clear, on the question of self-interest, Tocqueville did not advocate a vulgar utilitarianism. He looked to the collective, social finality, which in this world uses individual self-interest as its instrument. His thesis is set forth in the brief chapter entitled "How Americans Apply the Doctrine of Self-Interest Properly Understood in the Matter of Religion." The gap between what society "knows" and what individuals say appears here as well. Tocqueville concedes that among the people he met, certain "zealous Christians . . . regularly forgot themselves so as to work more ardently for the happiness of all." But he then adds that he "cannot help thinking that they are deluding themselves,"[13] which almost completely negates his concession.

For the sociologist, there are two levels to distinguish: believers believe that their belief has nothing to do with self-interest of any kind, but unwittingly, and without wanting to know, they cause the group to take a decisive step. In a passage that might have been written by Montesquieu, Tocqueville describes the situation: "I do not believe, therefore, that self-interest is the sole motive of religious men,[14] but I do think that self-interest is the principal means[15] whereby religions themselves guide men's conduct, and I have no doubt[16] that it is from this angle that they appeal to the crowd and become popular."

This is fairly close to the thinking of Helvétius but expressed in a style of veiling and unveiling that derives from Montesquieu. The passage is followed by the response to an interlocutor, whom readers of Tocqueville might well have taken to be the author of *De la religion*: "Hence I see no clear reason why the doctrine of self-interest properly understood should turn men away from religious beliefs."

Tocqueville thus attacked the main theme of the preface and even of book 1 of Constant's work. We will come back to this point, but note for now how Tocqueville cleverly contrives to move from "religious men" and their "motives" to "religions themselves" and their "means." In this way the social

---

[12] Vinet also attacked individualist utilitarianism, however. See *Philosophie morale et sociale* (Lausanne: Bridel, n.d.), vol. 1, "Critique de l'utilitarisme," published in *Le Semeur* in October and November 1831.

[13] *DA* II.2.9, p. 157; AG, p. 614.

[14] The preterition is very much in the style of Montesquieu: we must anticipate other motives, not an absence of motives.

[15] Hence one must assume other means (such as praise of sacrifice).

[16] The litotes softens the shock to come: read as "I assert."

institution binds individuals ("guiding men" and "appealing to the crowd"), and the group is organized as a collective of faith. The decisive blow (a true dagger thrust for a disciple of Constant) comes at the end of the chapter:

> Not only do Americans adhere to their religion out of self-interest, but they often locate the kind of self-interest that might cause a person to adhere to religion in this world rather than the next.... American preachers refer to this world constantly and, indeed, can avert their eyes from it only with the greatest of difficulty. Seeking to touch their listeners all the more effectively, they are forever pointing out how religious beliefs foster liberty and public order, and in listening to them it is often difficult to tell whether the chief object of religion is to procure eternal happiness in the other world or well-being in this one.[17]

The actors play the role that "democracy" (in Tocqueville's sense) assigns them: their interest in believing exactly coincides with their interest in society. Preachers,[18] who play an important role in carrying off this well-tempered illusion, complete the identification of salvation with well-being, which is just the name given to interest in society. Tocqueville zeroes in on this term to denote what individual actors find important.

This was how man's "natural religious condition" was translated into social terms in the United States, where, as Tocqueville saw it, the spirit of religion and the spirit of liberty supported each other. It would surely also be reflected in the democracy of the future, in the public's quest for well-being. The message of these chapters was a moderate one, delivered in a tone marked by distance and irony, which, as in Montesquieu, encouraged the reader to look for something beyond the text. In the chapter on religion, for example, it is worth trying to understand what becomes of the good that one does for others out of love of God. Tocqueville allows a calculated doubt to hover over this "magnificent expression."[19]

Was Tocqueville suggesting that Americans were to be admired? Or was he warning against the confusions that had become inevitable in the United States? Today, with the spectacle of creationism, televangelism, megachurches, and the mixture of fundamentalism with politics common among Christian conservatives, it is tempting to believe that he was issuing a warning.

---

[17] *DA* II.2.9, p. 159; AG, p. 616.

[18] Tocqueville uses the word here to refer to Catholic priests, Protestant pastors, and other faith leaders.

[19] *DA* II.2.9, p. 158; AG, p. 615.

Although Constant often expressed himself in similar terms, his critique of the eighteenth century led him to the opposite conclusion. It was then, Constant argued, that self-interest properly understood had been valued to the point where it became a *substitute* for religious sentiment.[20] Any assessment must take into account the results achieved by the brilliant, cynical, libertine minds who were the ornaments of a society that Constant described as "a collection of artfully catalogued skeletons and cleverly arranged petrifactions." A series of revolutionary crises culminating in Napoleon's dictatorship delivered a de facto verdict on all this. This system of well-matched egotisms had proved irresistible because it removed all motives for sacrificing immediate self-interest: "[This society's] natural effect was to make each individual his own center. But when each man is his own center, everyone is isolated. When everyone is isolated, there is nothing but dust. When the storm arrives, the dust turns to mud."[21]

Here the style is not Montesquieu's but rather Seneca's: Constant the moralist condemns what he himself knew and practiced, including the lure of position when religion ceases to bridle appetites.[22] For Constant, utilitarianism, abetted by individualism, is inevitably isolating. It cannot create a social bond but leaves the atomized masses vulnerable to a despot.[23] But the force of religious sentiment runs counter to the search for pleasure and the acceptance of injustice: "Liberty can establish and maintain itself only through disinterestedness, and any moral system based on something other than religious sentiment must rest on calculation. In order to defend liberty, one must be capable of immolating one's life, and what is greater than life for a person who sees beyond life only nothingness?"[24]

The religious sentiment, which in the Christian case might be called disinterested individualism,[25] should not be viewed as the cement that holds a

[20] See the preface to *De la religion*, pp. xxxiii–xxxvi.

[21] Ibid., p. xxxviii.

[22] We find the same idea in Tocqueville: ambition for position in France is one of his themes. It is one of the ways in which the state and administration acquire influence.

[23] "No people was ever more independent, and we might even say moe democratic, than the Arabs while Islam was most fervent. Protestantism preserved Germany under Charles V from universal monarchy. England today owes its constitution to Protestantism. By contrast, the absence of religious sentiment favors the designs of tyranny." Ibid., pp. 87–88.

[24] Ibid., p. 89.

[25] To avoid ambiguity, Vinet contrasted *individuality* with individualism: "Because I stressed individuality, some cried individualism. Was this fair? Wasn't it clear that individualism is nowhere more effective than where individuality is lacking, and that no politics is more atomistic than the politics of despotism?" See the preface to the 1845 German translation in *Essai sur la manifestation des convictions religieuses*, p. xi.

group together. For Constant, religion is the source of the ability to stand up to power. Hence it has social effects, but that is no reason to call it "useful," either objectively (sociologically) or subjectively. It is as foolish and inappropriate to see religious sentiment as a social power as it is to treat beauty as a utilitarian means. Even Chateaubriand fell into this trap in the *Génie du christianisme*:

> Just as the search for an immediate use for all the beauties of nature . . . withers the charm of the splendid ensemble, so, too, by never losing sight of the fact that religion must be useful, one degrades religion. Secondly, because pragmatic utility implies nothing about the truth of a theory,[26] man is not more religious because he is told that religion is useful, because no one believes in pursuing a certain purpose. Finally, the utility of religion serves as a pretext for those who govern to do violence to the consciences of the governed, so that with the stroke of a pen, one places persecuting masters over unbelieving peoples.[27]

If we assume that Tocqueville read these pages of Constant or was a participant in the debate, it is clear that the disagreement between the two writers could not have been greater. For Constant, it is purely and simply wrong to speak of the utility of religion. Voltaire had already made this mistake in the Enlightenment, and nineteenth-century conservatives repeated the error. It was foolish to seek to restore a declining religion by vaunting its beneficial effects on public morality: "No one believes in pursuing a certain purpose." Tocqueville's entire sociology of religion was discredited in advance. As for the social power that the religion of the moderns would supposedly make acceptable, it would come in the guise of "persecuting masters."

Or else a religious group might constitute itself within society, but this would involve the "sacerdotal religions," which Constant attacked and which he saw as perversely capturing the religious sentiment, when historically that sentiment had been advancing toward ever greater individual liberty and responsibility.

❧

Hence there is disagreement. To be clear, Tocqueville himself had no appetite whatsoever for religion as a camouflage for social interest. Although his

---

[26] Tocqueville agrees. I call this his sociological cynicism. He read Plato with emotion, as his correspondence makes clear: "One will tell them beautiful lies," reads a famous passage in Plato. Cf. also his nostalgia for feudal aristocracy: "The manners of aristocracy draped human nature in beautiful illusions, and though the portrait was often deceptive, there was noble pleasure in looking at it." *DA*, II.3.14, p. 272; AG, p. 714.

[27] *De la religion*, 1:114. The passage that follows this text is devoted to Chateaubriand, Fénelon, Rousseau, and Montesquieu, all of whom fail to appreciate the dignity or grandeur of religion according to Constant. Fénelon is nevertheless credited with disinterested love of God (for which Rome condemned him).

work contributed to the rise of sociology in the nineteenth century,[28] a better understanding of his own opinion requires understanding his Jansenist leanings, which will be discussed in part 3. For now it is worth noting that in 1838, that is, in the time between the publication of the two volumes of *Democracy in America*, he wrote a long letter to Royer-Collard in which he confessed his deep melancholy upon discovering that "his" Norman peasants were hardly disinterested. The following passage is worth quoting at length:

> These people are honest, intelligent, fairly religious, passably moral, and very well behaved. But they are by no means disinterested. To be sure, selfishness in these parts is not like selfishness in Paris, which is so violent and often so cruel. It is a gentle, tranquil love, tenacious in its particular interests, and little by little it absorbs all other feelings and dries up nearly all sources of enthusiasm. They combine this selfishness with a certain number of private virtues and domestic qualities, which, taken together, make them decent people but poor citizens. I would nevertheless forgive them for not being disinterested, if on occasion they made an effort to believe in disinterestedness. But they do not care for it, so that despite the many tokens they offer of their good will, I feel oppressed.[29]

This is quite a confession for someone who did so much to justify the fusion of religion and pragmatism among America's Puritans: "I feel oppressed." The irony is that with his lament for the loss of enthusiasm and disinterestedness, Tocqueville belongs in the company of Mme de Staël and Benjamin Constant.[30] But his politically motivated pedagogy and his conception of "democracy" as the irresistible shape of Europe's future led him to express a different view in public. Once again, his strategy as a writer (in this case as a sociologist) was at odds with his personal convictions as a man.

THE ANTISOCIOLOGICAL SPIRIT OF ALEXANDRE VINET

The comparison of Tocqueville with Vinet could be pursued in several directions. Both admired the way in which church and state had been separated in America, yet both also noted how the early New England communities reproduced the forms of intolerance from which they had themselves previously suffered.[31] Both were able to distinguish between individualism,

---

[28] On this point see Robert Nisbet, *The Sociological Tradition* (New York: Transaction, 1994). Nisbet ties Tocqueville too closely to conservative thinkers, however.

[29] Tocqueville, *OC* XI, p. 64.

[30] See my *L'Individu effacé* on de Staël's analysis of "enthusiasm" in *De l'Allemagne*. Tocqueville frequently quoted Mme de Staël, whose work he apparently knew well.

[31] See, for example, Vinet, *Mémoire en faveur de la liberté des cultes*, part 1, chap. 21.

which isolates, and "individuality," which affirms personal responsibility.[32] But Vinet could not accept the forms of collective authority over individual minds that Tocqueville saw as ultimately inevitable. In one of his more impassioned articles, Vinet wrote that it is a mistake to conceive of the relation between society and the individual consciousness as one of direct confrontation.[33] Vinet may have believed that Tocqueville was guilty of this error. Nevertheless, when he cited Tocqueville in his *Essai sur la manifestation des convictions religieuses* in 1842, he was careful to note the ways in which *Democracy in America* criticized the tyranny of the public. As a close reading of the following passage shows, however, he was also critical of Tocqueville's failure to distinguish between religion and opinion:

> [T]his multiplicity of sects is an important [factor]. All readers of M. de Tocqueville will recall the rather stunning chapter in which he reproaches democracy for having dematerialized despotism by creating a moral tyranny of the majority. This malady seems to have developed to the utmost degree in America. Clearly, however, it has not affected religion. On the contrary, religion is obviously the last refuge of the disgraced principle. True Christianity is the most potent reactant against factitious unity. It is by turns a cement and a solvent. Shall we pity America for having found this counterweight and perhaps remedy to the shortcomings of democracy?[34]

In other words, what saves Christianity from unity by coercion is the multiplicity of denominations. Tocqueville, who was able to grasp the tyranny of the majority, should have been able to understand the positive role played by that multiplicity.

It is worth asking whether Vinet, who did not hesitate to comment on the work of a wide range of his contemporaries, ever published a review of *Democracy in America*. We know that the review that appeared in *Le Semeur* in February-March 1835 was written by Henri Lutteroth, the pastor of the church on rue Taitbout, who personally assigned reviews for this important Protestant periodical.[35] The journal also published an anonymous review of the second volume of *Democracy*, and there is good reason to think that

---

[32] Both men shared the idea, but Tocqueville almost never uses the term "individuality," contrary to what E. Nolla writes: *DA* II, p. 97, n. b; see *DA* II, p. 232, Tocqueville's note, in which he twice uses the phrase "spirit of individuality."

[33] Alexandre Vinet, "De l'individualité et de l'individualisme," in *Le Semeur*, April 13, 1836, reprinted in Alexandre Vinet, *Philosophie morale et sociale*, ed. P. Bridel (Lausanne, Payot, 1913), vol. 1.

[34] Alexandre Vinet, *Essai sur la manifestation des convictions religieuses*, 2nd ed. (1858), p. 477.

[35] Françoise Mélonio, doctoral thesis, 3:16.

this second review was written by Vinet.[36] Whereas the first review limited itself to a series of quotes and a very general compliment, the second developed Vinet's habitual themes. The author states explicitly that Tocqueville "was mistaken about the principle of the Reformation" in presenting "individual reason" "in Luther, Descartes, and Voltaire [as] making use of the same method." Whereas the eighteenth century "denied authority," the sixteenth century "restored its loftiest meaning" through the reign of the Good Book. Furthermore, Tocqueville believed that in America there was belief without struggle and that believers were purely passive. He therefore tended to see religion as a mirror of collective consciousness, which was to mistake its nature entirely: "In religion, man is not called upon to believe his fellow man, who is no less ignorant about it than he is himself. He must believe God alone" (p. 138).

Vinet's thinking is most obvious when the author praises Tocqueville on the tyranny of the public[37] but explains that with that notion he is describing bad Protestants. People who merely *believe the majority* "imagine themselves to be Christians but in reality are not."

Like Vinet, the author of the review adds that, in Tocqueville, the utilitarian doctrine of "self-interest properly understood" cannot "combat individualism" or "ennoble the human race," much less "underpin or support religious beliefs" (p. 163). In sum, Tocqueville is a good critic of individualism but fails to understand how Christian (and Protestant) liberty *rescues* the individual from the "immaterial" form of despotism that he so perspicaciously observed.[38]

Vinet did not hesitate to claim that "society does not exist apart from the individual. It is in the individual himself, as an inclination, a need, an attribute. Society is man in search of his fellow man." Accordingly, there is no need for the sociological perspective: "Because society is in us, why set it up as a separate being, a fantastic rival?"[39] In theological terms, what existed before the Fall was not society but *communion*. Above all Vinet sought to prevent "society" from staking a claim to authority, which it could then exercise either gently or violently. The result would be what he called "social

[36] Mme Doris Jakubec (University of Lausanne) was kind enough to search the Vinet archives for a manuscript but did not find one. I wish to thank Prof. Jakubec for this and other research assistance in Lausanne. The review in question appeared in *Le Semeur* of April 29, vol. 9, no. 18; May 20, no. 21; and July 29, 1840, no. 31. Citations follow the pagination of vol. 9 (1840).

[37] "Faith in common opinion, the author wittily observes, then becomes a sort of religion, of which the majority is the prophet" (p. 138).

[38] He also failed to see two types of *imitation*: that of individual shepherds and that corresponding to the Gospel precept to "be imitators of Jesus Christ" (p. 253).

[39] Vinet, *Philosophie morale et sociale*, 1:360, 361.

pantheism," which he believed to be on the rise in all modern states. Tocqueville of course developed a similar idea in the chapter of the second *Democracy* entitled "What Makes the Mind of Democratic Peoples Receptive to Pantheism?"[40] The following passage by Tocqueville might have been written by Vinet because it attacks democratic ideology, or, as Vinet preferred to call it, socialism:[41] "Even though such a system destroys human individuality—or, rather, because it does—it will hold a secret charm for men who live in democracy. All their intellectual habits prepare their minds for it and pave the way for them to adopt it."[42]

In the same spirit, Vinet wrote the following in his 1836 article: "In [today's] society, one cannot help but notice that individualism is enthroned and individuality proscribed!" It follows that society is supposed to know, and know better than the individual. We have seen how important this idea was to Bonald and how Tocqueville borrowed it to analyze the animating spirit of democracy. We have also seen how Vinet attacked those who tried to imagine the state and civil society on this model, based on the conception of the Church in Catholic dogma. This "body that takes it upon itself to believe for all," which knows more than its members, especially in its lower ranks—that is, "the faithful"—must not become a model of society legitimated by a defective sociology.[43]

Vinet's target was the Catholic ecclesial model, which placed a hierarchy between those who know and read the Text and those who are obliged *to receive* the Word. This model was capable of assuming many guises. For Vinet, the unity of Protestantism lay in the *protest* against the principle of authority and not in any kind of dogma, which in any case varied considerably from denomination to denomination.[44]

---

[40] See Vinet, "De l'individualité et de l'individualisme," in ibid., 1:330; and *DA* II.1.7, pp. 41ff.; AG, pp. 512–13.

[41] See Alexandre Vinet, "Du socialisme considéré dans son principe," in *Réformation au XIXe siècle*, 1846, then in a brochure of the same title, and finally reprinted in *Philosophie morale et sociale*, vol. 2.

[42] *DA* II.1.7, p. 42; AG, pp. 512–13.

[43] Raymond Aron observes that historically, sociology and socialism were intimately intertwined, as Durkheim's thought proves. See the excellent book by J. C. Filloux, *Durkheim et le socialisme* (Geneva: Droz, 1977). In his inaugural lecture at Bordeaux in 1888, Durkheim argued that "the individual must be aware of the social mass, which envelops and penetrates him, whose active presence he feels constantly, and this feeling governs all his conduct," because this is what teaches him "to be in solidarity with others." See Emile Durkheim, *La Science sociale et l'action*, ed. J. C. Filloux (Paris: Presses Universitaires de France, 1987), pp. 109–10. Although some recent interpreters try to paint Durkheim as more of a methodological individualist, this interpretation is far-fetched.

[44] "The name 'Protestant' is indeed appropriate. The formation and existence of this communion constitute nothing other than a *protest* against the principle of authority." *Essai sur la manifestation des convictions religieuses*, p. 173.

He therefore criticized any and all efforts to imitate the Catholic Church and recast religion as a form of "social authority." The following passage is reminiscent of Tocqueville: man "seeks the priest or creates him. He also seeks another kind of priest, the multitude or the nation. The only use he makes of his freedom is to place himself at the service of a master, and that master is not God."[45]

Whereas Tocqueville seemed to resign himself to the "repository of authority," Vinet, obedient to his theological premises, refused. He also regarded nationalism as a prime example of what we would today call a "holistic" construct, which required individuality to abdicate. Party spirit was yet another way to confuse a form of devotion to others with the only "true" form of such devotion, which is charity. Here again Vinet was close to Tocqueville's way of thinking: a person might believe, in a great effusion of militant spirit, that he was giving himself to the collectivity yet in fact be fooling himself by actually serving some hidden personal aspiration: the individual "creates for himself a second, more expansive personality out of this corporatist or associative instinct, whereupon his ego derives the utmost satisfaction from the very sacrifices that seem most thoroughgoing and devotion that seems most absolute."[46] When someone says "my party," what counts is the possessive pronoun *my*.

Thus the social and political spirit leads to great confusion by combining what ought to be kept separate. Whereas the Gospel "creates charity without obliterating individuality," the party spirit requires the individual to disguise his instincts and defer to an outside authority while seeking the recognition of the group. The search for a secure identity leads to the loss of one's true *self*.

In the end, belief originating in the state, the society, or the nation should not exist. Vinet radically rejected what Tocqueville called common (or public) opinion because in his eyes it always meant loss of individuality.[47] On this point, his 1826 and 1842 essays both contain striking and celebrated formulas: "If society has a consciousness, this implies that the individual has none, and since consciousness is the seat of religion, if society is religious, the individual is not."[48] Which leads to the counterformulation: "But all this

[45] Vinet, "Du socialisme considéré dans son principe," in *Philosophie morale et sociale*, 2:153.

[46] Vinet, "Sur l'individualité," ms., reproduced in ibid., 2:424.

[47] Individuality in the sense of an intimate relation between the soul and God. In the first instance religion involves a direct relationship with God, not a relationship among men. See Alexandre Vinet, *Questions ecclésiastiques,* 2 vols. (Paris: Payot, 1946). Here he echoes the thinking of Pierre Bayle in his remarkable discussion of *Compelle intrare*: see my analysis "Bayle: la conscience, juge et législateur," in *La Liberté et la loi*, pp. 79–89).

[48] *Essai sur la manifestation des convictions religieuses*, p. 204.

falls before one fact: society is not a being."[49] Hypostases are dangerous because there is no end to them: "If society is a man, it is the only man; if society has a consciousness, there is no other; if society has a religion, there is only its religion."

Clearly, Vinet was in complete disagreement with Tocqueville, with respect not to their personal convictions but to their analytic methods. He and Tocqueville disagreed no less than Tocqueville and Constant. The source of the disagreement was the same: the problem that social institutions posed for Protestantism when they claimed primacy in regard to individual choice and examination. Characteristically, Vinet, in his theory of institutional action and its influence on individuals, expressed objections that Tocqueville undoubtedly shared but saw as defeated by the rise of democracy:

> Institutions, which exercise equal and uniform pressure on all members of the social body, create a range of mores and establish a national character and national physiognomy. Each member of the association feels this influence. In this sense, moreover, we can say that institutions act on individuals. But it must also be said that the individual they have created is factitious and exists only in the spirit and interest of the whole.... Unless some moderating force intervenes, the more individual the people, the less individual the men and women who make up that people.[50]

This 1836 text figured in a critique of the preface of Lamartine's *Jocelyn*, which Tocqueville regarded as a symbol of his times. The author of *Democracy in America* might well have replied that "what you say is true, M. Vinet, but your objection is aristocratic." On that subject he could speak with confidence.

ON THE AMERICAN SIDE: PROTESTANT CRITIQUES
OF SOCIAL CONFORMISM

Did Tocqueville have any Protestant interlocutors in America comparable to Vinet? Although I have deliberately chosen not to explore American intellectual life in this book, I must nevertheless discuss several encounters that deeply influenced Tocqueville's thinking. He met, argued with, and read the sermons of the great Unitarian pastor William Ellery Channing, whom Laboulaye would later popularize in France. In his discussions with

---

[49] Ibid., p. 208.
[50] Vinet, "Du rôle de l'individualité dans l'œuvre d'une réforme sociale," in *Philosophie morale et sociale*, 1:333–39.

Channing, Tocqueville objected that not every individual in society has the leisure, taste, or fortitude to form his own opinions. Hence *dogmas* are necessary, and dogmas need institutions to inculcate them and establish their authority. He also mentioned to Channing his rather surprising admiration of the political consequences of Protestantism: "It seems to me that Catholicism had established that ability should govern in religion—religious aristocracy if you will—whereas you introduced democracy. I confess that the possibility of governing religious as well as political society by means of democracy does not seem to me to have been proven yet by experience."[51]

Channing replied that in religion the individual can be free because direct dialogue with God is possible. In politics, by contrast, the masses are "comparatively ignorant" in relation to experts such as economists and therefore must not be taken as competent authorities. The difference with Vinet is fairly clear, although Channing, like Vinet, believed that the claim of the Catholic Church to know better than the individual deserved criticism: the dogma of infallibility, he argued, had to be subject to appeals to reason to gain acceptance. Bayle had already made the same objection.

Tocqueville might have pressed his investigation of the Protestant mind further and learned more about the opposition of some to granting institutions primacy over individual judgment. The philosophical movement known as Transcendentalism began in Boston and nearby Concord. It was led by Ralph Waldo Emerson, who published his essay "Self-Reliance" in 1837. Emerson was critical of American conformism in all its forms. The son, grandson, and great-grandson of Protestant pastors who himself served in that capacity for three years (1829–32), Emerson broke with the Unitarians to become the father of American Romanticism. He quickly gained fame in Europe as well.[52] Another resident of Concord, Henry David Thoreau, became famous for his refusal to pay taxes in protest against the war with Mexico and the continuation of slavery in the South. His essay "Resistance to Civil Government," a mix of anarchism and liberalism, gained worldwide renown as the inspiration of movements of "civil disobedience."

---

[51] Tocqueville, *Œuvres*, La Pléiade, 1:77–79. In English, see GZ, p. 246. The entire conversation can be found in Tocqueville's notebooks under the entry for October 2, 1831.

[52] Emerson became known in France somewhat later thanks mainly to Émile Montégut, who published a well-informed study entitled "Un penseur et poète américain, Ralph Waldo Emerson," *Revue des deux mondes*, August 1, 1847, pp. 462–93. In 1850 Montégut followed this with another article on Emerson and his friend Thomas Carlyle: *Revue des deux mondes*, August 15, 1850, pp. 722–37. One of Emerson's formulas was "Insist on yourself; never imitate." See Sandra Laugier, "La confiance en soi contre le conformisme" in *Une autre pensée politique américaine* (Paris: Michel Houdiard, 2004). Laugier also translated Emerson's essays into French.

Tocqueville was apparently unaware of the "Transcendentalist Club," which might have confirmed his views on the tyranny of public opinion, American conformism, and the Protestant origins of the refusal to submit to the putatively greater wisdom of collective authority. By contrast, we can assume that he was aware of the work of another major critic of American conformism, James Fenimore Cooper, who was free of Protestant influence. Tocqueville read Cooper's novels (which, along with those of Washington Irving, were well-known in France), and in 1828 he ordered the *Notions of the Americans Picked Up by a Travelling Bachelor*, in which Cooper, then living in Europe, looked at America through the eyes of an outsider.[53] While serving as American consul, the novelist lived in France from 1826 to 1828 and again from 1830 to 1833. Through Lafayette he supplied Tocqueville with letters of recommendation to various Americans.[54] Cooper's *The American Democrat*, published in 1838, contains a theory of public opinion as "the particular form in which, under a popular government, tyranny exhibits itself."[55]

But wasn't it rather Cooper who took his inspiration from the first volume of *Democracy in America*? Further research is needed to answer the question. In any case, when Cooper published his study, he hoped that the state of New York would adopt it as a textbook, but Tocqueville's volume was chosen instead. The two writers were competitors. At a time when the election of Andrew Jackson to the presidency had increased the influence of the lower classes, some intellectuals had grown wary of the power of the collective. This new climate stimulated Tocqueville's sociological intuition and allowed him to formulate a theory that responded to these concerns.

[53] On this work, see the letter to Beaumont, March 14, 1831, *OC* VIII-1, p. 105 and n. 7. We also know from Tocqueville's manuscripts that he carefully read Cooper's letters on Switzerland (1836).

[54] I am grateful to Hugh MacDougall, secretary of the Société James Fenimore Cooper, for this information.

[55] James Fenimore Cooper, *The American Democrat*, 1838 (Indianapolis: Liberty Fund, 1981), p. 103. See also p. 84.

PART THREE

Tocqueville as Moralist

May they at least be respectable people (*honnêtes gens*) if they cannot be Christians.

—Pascal, *Pensées*

Hence it is not useless for men to shun vice not only out of charity but also out of that sort of amour-propre that is called *honnêteté*.

—Nicole, *De la charité et de l'amour-propre*

[W]ould not people, even without loving democratic government, be prepared to adopt it as the most useful and honorable (*honnête*) remedy for society's present ills.

—Tocqueville, *Democracy in America*

There is today general agreement that Tocqueville's view of America was that of a moralist. But what does the term "moralist" mean? According to the dictionary of the French Academy, a moralist is a writer who deals with mores. La Bruyère, a writer Tocqueville admired from the time he was a schoolboy (according to his friend Louis de Kergorlay[1]), is a prime example of the type. By studying "characters" he was able to portray a concrete situation while at the same time capturing general truths about the human race. *Les Caractères ou les mœurs de ce siècle* (Characters, or the mores of the present age): the subtitle indicates that La Bruyère, like Molière, sought to induce his contemporaries to look at themselves, to make them laugh at their own foibles. *Castigat ridendo mores.* Was Tocqueville a moralist in this sense? At times he made notes to himself to insert in his text a portrait in the manner of *Les Caractères* or *Les Lettres persanes*, and occasionally he followed through.[2] When he explained to Mme Swetchine why he did not wish to take the title

---

[1] See *OC* XIII-2, p. 360: article by Kergorlay in *Le Correspondant*, "Étude littéraire sur Alexis de Tocqueville."

[2] He also scolded himself for being too slavish a follower of the classics: "All this rather mannered ... imitation of La Bruyère." See Nolla II, p. 149, n. c; see also p. 150, n. b: "mannered and precious."

"comte de Tocqueville," he spontaneously recalled a passage in which La Bru-yère recounts the parable of the philosopher and his tailor.[3]

To be sure, Tocqueville absorbed the style of the seventeenth- and eighteenth-century moralists (along with that of Montaigne), as his every sentence reveals, but because his *political* purpose was to draw lessons from the American example, he became a moralist of a different kind. By tempera-ment and tragic philosophical outlook he was closer in spirit to the Jansenist moralists Pascal and Nicole.[4]

It is therefore worth clarifying the sense in which Tocqueville can be con-sidered a moralist and how the moralist vein in his work related to his private life. We come closer to the inner man in the passages written by the moralist than in those attributable to the political scientist or sociologist. So let us begin by considering the definition of a moralist before turning to the ques-tion of Tocqueville's Jansenist sympathies, which have often been evoked but to date little studied. In so doing we will come to see the personality of the author in a new light.

[3] The philosopher, La Bruyère wrote, "allows his tailor to dress him. There is as much weakness in shunning fashion as in affecting it." Similarly, Tocqueville claims that he neither assumed nor rejected the noble title, and in the same letter to Mme Swetchine, he replaces the philosopher by the *honnête homme*. In fact, we know from Jean-Louis Benoît that Hervé de Tocqueville established an entail to ensure that his château in Tocqueville (Normandy) would pass to Alexis. It was a decision of his father to pass the title of count to Alexis, which in practice the son rejected. He nevertheless sincerely wanted the château, so in a sense he was given the suit but chose not to wear it.

[4] When his book on the Revolution appeared, he noted that "I am alone" and added that, because he was not obedient to any party, he was concerned "solely with the truth." *Œuvres*, La Pléiade, 3:1018. To Mme Swetchine he complained at length about his isolation. When *Democracy in America* appeared, he wrote to several correspondents that the book would not please anyone because it defied the thinking of all existing parties.

The Moralist and the Question of *l'Honnête*

WHAT IS A MORALIST?

Tocqueville the moralist addressed himself to legislators and reformers. Helvétius's definition applies: "Moralists devote themselves to the study of the use that can be made of rewards [and punishments], and of how these can help to couple individual interest to the general interest. To achieve such a union is the ultimate goal that the moralist should set for himself."[1]

This definition nicely captures the heart of Tocqueville's concern with what he called democracy. He was not concerned simply with mores, or with the corruption of ancient or Christian virtue. He envisioned his subject in terms of *reconstituting the general interest*. Although Helvétius was widely read in his own day as well as in Tocqueville's, his work was sometimes attacked for its alleged materialism.[2] Nevertheless, it directly inspired Beccaria (a writer whom Tocqueville appreciated) and Bentham. Helvétius's chief concern was to find a morality adapted to the needs of the new commercial society, in which private interests played a central role. Although these were seen as potentially corrosive, they were also impossible to eliminate. The problem was therefore to *redirect* private interests to serve the collectivity. As we saw previously in studying Tocqueville's relation to the traditionalists, this was a concern he shared. A "moralist" was therefore someone who judged the immanent tendencies of existing mores in order to steer them cleverly in new directions. Helvétius wrote that "virtue can be achieved only by uniting the individual interest and the general interest."[3] Tocqueville agreed and made this observation the basis of his theory of self-interest properly understood.

To be a moralist in this sense implied that one did not believe that older forms of morality, or even moral philosophy as such, were well adapted to

---

[1] Helvétius, *De l'esprit*, discourse 2, chap. 22 (Paris: Éditions Marabout, 1973), p. 183.

[2] Note, however, that in Maigrot's anthology for students, *Illustrations littéraires de la France*, 1st ed. (1837), a chapter is devoted to Helvétius.

[3] Helvétius, *De l'esprit*, p. 139.

modern society. Tocqueville made just this point in one of his manuscripts: "If morality were powerful enough in itself, I would not attach so much importance to utility. If the idea of the just were more powerful, I would not speak so much about the idea of the useful."[4]

This thought was the basis of a series of reflections that run throughout the two volumes of *Democracy in America*, comparing the just and the useful, or, more commonly, *l'honnête*[5] and the useful. Tocqueville was therefore a moralist in the same sense that he was a political thinker: he imagines not only an adversary whom he must defeat but also an interlocutor whom he must convince. In characterizing his thought, it is best to avoid contrasting the moralist with the man of action, as is so often done, because the former wrote only at the behest of the latter and often in obedience to his dictation, even if he kept certain more personal thoughts to himself. This is especially true in the section entitled "On the Idea of Rights in the United States," to which the manuscript cited above referred. Half of this text is a lawyer's brief on behalf of political rights and, more generally, individual rights. The moralist (who seeks to link rights to self-interest) adopts the style of a lawyer as well as the authority of a legislator or governor. Note the textual signs (italicized) that the writer has an interlocutor in mind:[6]

> Democratic government causes the idea of political rights to filter down to the humblest of citizens, much as the division of property brings the idea of property rights in general within everyone's reach. This, *in my view*, is one of its greatest merits.
>
> *I do not say* that teaching everyone to make use of political rights is an easy thing to do: that is not my point. *All I mean to say* is that, when it can be done, the effect is great.
>
> And *I would add* that, if ever there were a century in which an attempt to do so ought to be made, it is this one.
>
> *Do you not see* that religions are on the wane and that the divine notion of rights is disappearing? *Does it not strike you* that mores are crumbling and that, along with them, the moral notion of rights is fading away?
>
> *Is it not obvious to you* that belief is everywhere giving way to reasoning and sentiment to calculation? If, in the midst of this universal upheaval, *you do not succeed* in linking the idea of rights to the personal interest that stands out as the

[4]Nolla I, p. 188, n. u.

[5]*L'honnête* is best left untranslated because, as will emerge from the subsequent discussion, its meaning is complex and not adequately conveyed by any single word in English.

[6]I/you references are italicized. I also retain the short paragraphs of the text as published, which give a sense of the "respiration" of the lawyer/orator.

only fixed point in the human heart, what means of governing the world *will be left to you* other than fear?[7]

In this hortatory style, the moralist is the one who *knows*, the expert. He bases his knowledge, moreover, on his experience of foreign mores: to a doubting French interlocutor[8] he teaches a lesson about the possibility of a democratic society in which rights confront the state. In this connection, it is worth recalling that La Bruyère forbade himself to exhort or advise: "It was not maxims that I truly wished to write, moreover: maxims are like laws in morals, and I admit that I have neither authority enough nor genius enough to play the lawgiver."[9] By contrast, Tocqueville stood with Helvétius: he wanted "to play the lawgiver."

Furthermore, as the above quote from *Democracy in America* shows, the issue was "the human heart." Sociology and political theory were not enough by themselves. The moralist or philosopher of the passions had a specific competence of his own. Self-interest, we are told, is "the only fixed point in the human heart" in a society characterized by perpetual change ("change-ism," to borrow a term from Pierre-André Taguieff). Tocqueville shared the Jansenist view of "amour-propre," which he interpreted in a distinctive way of his own.[10] The crucial point is that self-interest is cleverly expanded to become an interest in reciprocity. Through a "sort of tacit and almost involuntary agreement,"[11] Americans were able to institute a reciprocal exchange of services, which was based neither on love of one's neighbor (the Christian precept) nor on sincere interest in others but rather on an elementary calculation: "Each one owes the others temporary support and may in turn claim the same for himself."[12] Note, moreover, that tacit agreement on reciprocity is the middle way—the way of disabused wisdom—that one finds in La Rochefoucauld, more in *Les Réflexions diverses* than in *Les Maximes*.[13]

---

[7] *DA* I.2.6, p. 334; AG, pp. 273–74 (translation modified).

[8] A little further on, he responds: "when I am told ... I respond that." See ibid., p. 335; AG, p. 274.

[9] La Bruyère, preface to *Les Caractères*, in *Les Moralistes du XVIIe siècle*, ed. J. Lafond, "Bouquins," Robert Laffont (1992), p. 695.

[10] As we will see, Jansenism, as represented by Domat and Nicole, recognized the social consequences of amour-propre, which in itself is asocial.

[11] *DA* II.3.4, p. 220; AG, p. 668.

[12] Ibid.

[13] On this point, Paul Bénichou wrote that "the *implicit* [my italics] avowal of the law of interest governs the society of *honnêtes gens*; order is established on this basis, provided that each person knows how to attenuate in the eyes of others what everyone knows." See Paul Bénichou, "L'intention des *Maximes*," in *L'Écrivain et ses travaux* (Paris: Corti, 1967), p. 32.

If we take things a step further, however, we see that the need for others also implies a need for their esteem, for otherwise confidence in the future would disappear. On this point, too, Helvétius showed the way.[14] He explained how raw self-interest is ultimately refined or sublimated. "There is a happy conformity between our self-interest and the public interest, a conformity ordinarily produced by the desire for esteem, which leads us to feel toward others tender feelings that earn their affection as recompense."[15] In other words, the need for social recognition (in a utilitarian spirit) gives rise to new affections: "tender feelings."

ख०

How did Tocqueville's contemporaries read these arguments? There were two schools of thought, which influenced each other despite mutual loathing: one devoted to the Jansenist theory of amour-propre (that is, love of self and love of all things for oneself[16]), the other to Helvétius's theory of self-interest properly understood.[17] Somewhat paradoxically, those who read Tocqueville's analysis of American mores discovered a vivid version of what he had absorbed in France of a culture labeled aristocratic. The farmer-general Helvétius and the noble lord François de La Rochefoucauld had almost identical views on the general theme of refined self-interest. When Tocqueville wrote that Americans' "enlightened love of themselves" led them "to help one another out,"[18] that the strategy of self-interest properly understood "turns personal interest against itself,"[19] and that a man "may find it in his own interest to forget himself, as it were,"[20] he, too, was discussing the question of disinterested interest, or the social education of primitive egoism.

La Rochefoucauld's maxim 236 summarized the subtleties and ruses of such socialization: "It seems that amour-propre is the dupe of goodness, and that it *forgets itself* [my italics] when we work for the benefit of others." But, La Rochefoucauld adds, "it does so in order to reach its destination by the

[14] Along with the thinkers of the Scottish Enlightenment, especially Adam Smith in his *Theory of Moral Sentiments*: "the impartial spectator."

[15] Helvétius, *De l'esprit*, third discourse, chap. 16, p. 297.

[16] This is the definition given by both Pascal and La Rochefoucauld. To be sure, the Augustinian theme of *amor sui* transcended Jansenism.

[17] According to Benjamin Constant, *De la religion*, the concept of "self-interest properly understood" originated with Helvétius. In fact, it was a commonplace in the seventeenth century and then the Enlightenment. See, e.g., Anna-Maria Battista, *Politica e morale nella Francia dell'età moderna*, ed. A. M. Lazzarino Del Grosso (Genoa: Name, 1998), and Giuseppe Zarone, *Etica e politica nell'utilitarismo di Cesare Beccaria* (Naples: Istituto Italiano per gli Studi Storici, 1971).

[18] *DA* II.2.8, p. 154; AG, p. 611.

[19] Ibid., p. 155; AG, p. 612.

[20] *DA* II.2.4, p. 132; AG, p. 591.

safest route. It lends at interest on the pretext of giving. Ultimately, it buys everyone in the most subtle and delicate way."[21]

Tocqueville owned an anthology of French moralists,[22] which contained a passage from a letter to Mme de Sablé: "Interest is the soul of amour-propre.... Amour-propre divorced from its interest—if I must put it that way—can neither see nor hear nor feel and ceases to live."[23]

THE MEANING OF *L'HONNÊTE*

America's social philosophy was thus self-interest reoriented (or "refined," in the sense in which one refines a crude substance). This accounts for the importance of another idea in Tocqueville's work, that of *l'honnête*. The term, which has a long history, acquired particular importance in the seventeenth century's portrait of *l'honnête homme*. It is interesting to note, however, that Cicero already set *honestum* in opposition to *utile*.[24] Cicero defended the thesis that "everything that is honorable is useful,"[25] which became a celebrated axiom. In *De finibus* he wrote that "the only good is honor"[26] but placed it on the third degree of a scale. The first degree is primal, animal utility (that is, self-preservation). The second is reasoned choice. The third is to aim steadily and repeatedly for the good: honorability becomes the objective of the wise man. Note, moreover, that *honestum* involves a "common pooling of interests."[27] For that reason, *honestum* "is either virtue itself or an act

---

[21] La Rochefoucauld, *Œuvres complètes* (Paris: La Pléiade, 1964), p. 435.

[22] Aimé-Martin, ed., *Moralistes français* (Paris: Didot, 1836), containing Pascal, La Bruyère, La Rochefoucauld, Duclos, and Vauvenargues. The library of the château de Tocqueville contained the 1847 edition, but the first edition seems to date from 1836, and there were numerous subsequent editions. Aimé-Martin, well-known in his day, published a revised edition of La Rochefoucauld in 1822. Elsewhere he challenged La Rochefoucauld's theory of amour-propre.

[23] *Moralistes français*, p. 186 of the 1878 edition, or see La Rochefoucauld, *Œuvres complètes*, p. 623. This would become maxim 510 in the posthumous edition.

[24] Montaigne, whom Tocqueville quoted directly on this point, entitled a chapter of his *Essais* "De l'utile et de l'honnête," referring primarily to Cicero, *De officiis*, book 3.

[25] See "Le Traité des devoirs" (*De Officiis*), in *Les Stoïciens* (Paris: La Pléiade, 1962), p. 555. See also Cicero's discussion based on the Platonic myth of Gyges: "The gentleman (*honnête homme*) is one who is as useful to others as possible and who harms no one." Cicero, *Des termes extrêmes des biens et des maux* (*De finibus*), trans. J. Martha, rev. ed. (Paris: Belles Lettres, 1999), pp. 596ff. See also *De finibus*, p. 271, which contains the statement that "the only good is decency (*l'honnête*)."

[26] Cicero, *De finibus*, 2:23.

[27] As a commentator on the Greek philosophers, Cicero notes that *honestum* belongs entirely to the *politikos*. It expresses man's nature and is deployed through association of interests. Ibid., 2:150. What Aristotle regarded as a human aptitude for rational exchange, Cicero developed primarily as "social interest." Hence Testard's (French) translation of *De officiis*, in which he renders *honestas* as "moral beauty" and *honestum* as "beauty," is open to question.

governed by virtue."²⁸ In fact, Cicero's reinterpretation made virtue an eminently social quality: "honorable men" lived together in a way that combined justice in Plato's sense with prudence in Aristotle's sense. Furthermore, the Greek *arete*, usually translated as virtue, has the root *ar*, which means that which is appropriate or opportune.

Unlike justice, *honestum* was a matter of education, manners, and politeness in the classical sense. Cicero maintained the classic distinction between *rectum* (that which conforms to a rule) and *honestum* (good as an object of praise in society). In the eighteenth century Voltaire insisted that virtue must be seen in social terms. In the *Dictionnaire philosophique* he wrote:

> What is virtue? Kindness to one's neighbor.... We live in society. For us, therefore, nothing is truly good but that which is good for society. A solitary man may be sober and pious. He may wear a hair shirt. He may well be a saint. But I will not call him virtuous until he performs some act of virtue that benefits others. As long as he remains alone, he is neither beneficent nor maleficent. For us, he is nothing.²⁹

Tocqueville broadly shared this utilitarian view, at least in his public pronouncements (which should be carefully distinguished from his personal preferences). He took to heart the Ciceronian axiom that "everything honorable is useful," deploring the fact that the French understood it less well than the Americans: "All around me I see people who by word and deed appear to want to teach their contemporaries that what is useful is never dishonorable. Will I never find anyone willing to make other people understand how what is honorable can also be useful?"³⁰

Indeed, in Tocqueville's text, as in Cicero, "honorable" refers to both a moral good and a social relation. In contrast to "virtue," which is abstract, universal, and disinterested,³¹ honor is associated with a social form, with

---

²⁸ Ibid.

²⁹ Voltaire, "Vertu," in *Dictionnaire philosophique*, p. 373. Tocqueville read Voltaire often and owned several editions of his work. To his friend Nassau Senior he said that Voltaire was the best prose writer of the eighteenth century, just ahead of Buffon.

³⁰ *DA* II.2.8, p. 156; AG, p. 613.

³¹ According to Tocqueville's travel notebooks, Americans are not "virtuous," but they are helpful. This observation comes when the traveler compares what he sees with what he read in Montesquieu about "the principle of ancient republics." The American republic stems from a different source: "A sort of refined and intelligent egoism seems to be the pivot around which the whole machine turns" (May 29, 1831, *Œuvres*, La Pléiade, 1:230). Tocqueville also contrasts virtue (or duty) with honor in similar terms: the former relates to an abstract norm, whereas the latter is a quality that one seeks to have in order to win the approval of others (see documents reproduced in Nolla II, pp. 200–201). Montesquieu's celebrated remarks on honor in a monarchy inform this discussion.

collective utility, which is understood to include personal utility. Ultimately, a person who behaves honorably makes himself agreeable to others and reaps the reward for doing so:

> In the United States people rarely say that virtue is beautiful. They maintain that it is useful and give proof of this daily. American moralists do not hold that a man should sacrifice himself for his fellow man because it is a great thing to do; they boldly assert, rather, that such sacrifices are as necessary to the man who makes them as to the man who profits from them.... They do not deny, therefore, that each man may pursue his own self-interest, but they do their utmost to prove that it is in every man's interest to behave honorably.[32]

Virtuous interest (that is, entirely utilitarian virtue) could thus hardly avoid being opposed to *grandeur*. If moralists were to say that there was greatness in doing something, they would refer to a morality that was no longer available under democracy. Indeed, this question was the subject of an exchange of letters between Tocqueville and Royer-Collard between 1838 and 1843. When one wrote that "the feeling of greatness is lacking, and one might say that the imagination of greatness is dying," the other responded several years later that "I need grandeur, *even if no longer in this world*. I am of course not asking to have the privileges of nobility back, but I would like to see *gentlemen* again."[33]

In this opposition between *le grand* and *l'honnête*, it is worth pointing out that among the meanings of the second term is *moyen*, meaning "average" or "decent": *une honnête rétribution* (a decent salary), *une honnête retraite* (a decent pension), and so on. *Honnêteté*, decency, respectability is the virtue of average people, the people who, in Tocqueville's eyes, constitute democratic society. Think of the politician Édouard Herriot's use of the phrase *Français moyen*, typical Frenchman. American Christianity therefore spoke not of man's grandeur but of his well-being: Clergymen, "even as they hold out the other world to the faithful as the great object of their hopes and fears, ... do not forbid the honest (*honnête*) pursuit of prosperity in this one."[34]

Finally, *l'honnête* is diametrically opposed to heroism. Writing to Corcelle in 1838, Tocqueville spoke of his reading of Plutarch and the image of the

---

[32] *DA* II.2.8, pp. 153–54; AG, pp. 610–11. Recall that the following maxim is attributed to Helvétius: "The art of politics is to ensure that it is in everyone's interest to be virtuous." See *Notes, maximes et pensées* (Paris: Mercure de France, 1906).

[33] Tocqueville, *OC* XI, pp. 64, 117.

[34] *DA* II.1.5, p. 37; AG, p. 509.

hero that he found there: "I have a very different conception of virtue. But they are great."[35]

In any case, *l'honnête*, semantically related to honor, possessed one essential quality in Tocqueville's eyes: it slowed the headlong search for material satisfactions, which he believed to be a fundamental feature of modern democracy. To slow was not to abolish: because *l'honnête* was linked to *both* collective interest *and* self-interest, it could also serve the materialistic appetites, as Tocqueville explained in his chapter on "the love of material pleasures." With this we come to the heart of Tocqueville's thinking as moralist as well as the relation between the man and the writer, both of whom speak in the first person as a sign of sincerity and emotion: "I reproach equality not for leading men into the pursuit of forbidden pleasures but for absorbing them entirely in the search for permitted ones. In this way the world might well come to see the establishment of a kind of respectable (*honnête*) materialism, which rather than corrupt souls would soften them and in the end silently loosen the tension in their springs."[36]

This "respectable materialism" is an oxymoron because materialism in Tocqueville's sense is entirely selfish.[37] But the oxymoron can also be seen as related to a complementarity that Tocqueville consistently denounced and believed to have been realized in the coup d'état of 1851:[38] depoliticization and acceptance of despotism in exchange for material comfort. Tocqueville had discussed the greatest danger of "democracy"—material attachment to the despot[39]—in a series of exchanges with his cousin and confidant Louis de Kergorlay. In 1836 Kergorlay wrote that "the number of people who unconsciously cultivate matter [that is, who are unwitting materialists] is immense," while "those who aspire as we do to the pleasures of the mind" are rare. He hoped to make "men with beautiful horses, beautiful furniture, etc." ashamed of their materialism. Tocqueville replied that he was working along similar

[35] Tocqueville, *OC* XV-1, p. 97. Tocqueville had three editions of Plutarch in his library, which was not unusual at the time. He expressed the same sentiment to Gustave de Beaumont after reading Plutarch: "I fall prostrate when I emerge from these dreams and find myself face-to-face with reality." *OC* VIII-1, p. 284, letter of 1838. Similar, in a letter to Royer-Collard, Plutarch again provided the occasion for an expression of regret at the loss of "greatness." *OC* XI, p. 61. The Greek and Latin notebooks that Tocqueville kept as a young *collégien* are in the Saint-Lô archives.

[36] *DA* II.2.11, p. 167; AG, p. 622.

[37] Here Tocqueville's target is not the materialism of the philosophers, of which he was also critical, but the common meaning of the term, aimed at those who lived for "consumer society" at the expense of any form of spirituality or idealism.

[38] See the preface to *ARR*.

[39] Tocqueville was ambivalent: was the despot a man (Napoleon) or was it the democratic state, which ruled anonymously? Remember that the danger was in "the democratic social state" itself, with its religion of the Public (see parts 1 and 2).

lines, especially since he was just then reading Plato. Democratic society was obsessed with physical pleasures and needed a morality, he maintained. How to choose between soul and body? Tocqueville stated his opinion, which would in short order influence the second volume of *Democracy in America*:

> I am constantly wracking my brains to find out whether there might be some middle way between these two extremes, which would lead neither to Heliogabalus nor to Saint Jerome. Because I take it for granted that you will never get most men to embrace either one, and fewer will embrace the latter than the former. I am therefore not as shocked as you are by *respectable materialism* [Tocqueville's emphasis], of which you complain so bitterly. Not that it doesn't arouse my contempt as much as it does yours. But I look at it pragmatically, and I ask myself if something if not similar then at least analogous might not still be the best that can be expected not of some particular individual but of our poor species in general.[40]

The analog of materialism that Tocqueville had in mind would become the utilitarianism of self-interest properly understood, or *l'honnête*, on which he had touched briefly in volume 1 but would develop more fully in volume 2. This made his job that of a teacher, a moralist who hoped to *transform mores*:

> No power on earth[41] can prevent growing equality of conditions from prompting the human mind to investigate what is useful or from disposing individual citizens to turn inward on themselves.
>
> It is to be expected, therefore, that individual interest will become more than ever the principal if not the sole motive of human action; but it remains to be seen how each person will interpret his individual interest.[42]

Tocqueville hoped that his book would influence opinion in favor of a certain view of individual interest.[43] He was calling for another form of individuality, a specifically *social individuality* adapted to democracy. Here again, his plan was to appropriate and then demolish the traditionalist argument (see part 2). Immediately after the chapter from which I just quoted, he therefore turned to the question of reconciling religion with the principle of

---

[40] Tocqueville, *OC* XIII-1, p. 389.

[41] A discreet reminder of the "other life," in which virtue and disinterestedness—*charity* in Jansenist terms—is supposed to be the only motive of man's behavior.

[42] *DA* II.2.8, p. 156; AG, p. 613.

[43] He was apparently ignored on this point: from the time of Mme de Staël, the French rejected utilitarian ideas in favor of the ideas of Victor Cousin and his school. See my remarks in *L'Individu effacé*, pp. 40ff and 114ff.

utility. To readers of Bossuet and Fénelon, who had clashed over this issue,[44] Tocqueville argued that the Americans had managed to reconcile the two and that Pascal, in his celebrated wager, would have agreed with them.[45]

Tocqueville was like the Sophist Protagoras, who, according to Plato, proposed to teach not what was true but what was most advantageous to his fellow citizens.[46] His notion of *l'honnête* was intended to awaken what was best in selfish democratic man (his desire for nobility, his ability to admire) in order to lead him toward the things that religion consecrated: "How religious beliefs sometimes divert the American soul toward immaterial gratifications" is the title of one of his chapters (II.2.15), which is a stinging attack on materialism, both philosophical and practical, as well as a plea on behalf of what Tocqueville calls "spiritualism."[47] His prescription of the legislator's task is unambiguous:

> Hence lawmakers in democracies and all decent (*honnêtes*) and enlightened men who live in them must apply themselves unstintingly to the task of uplifting souls and keeping them intent on heaven. All who are interested in the future of democratic societies must unite and together make constant efforts to spread a taste for the infinite, a sense of greatness, and a love of immaterial pleasures.

L'honnête, that is, the sense of collective utility and of the personal benefits to be derived from it (confidence, esteem and various forms of retribution), must therefore include the religious: "decent and enlightened men" cannot be atheists. If we include the diatribe against materialism, we might almost attribute this passage to Robespierre in his war on the *philosophes* and his defense of Rousseau against Helvétius, whose bust at the Jacobin club he ordered to be smashed.[48]

---

[44] On the dispute over pure disinterested love of God and its political consequences, see Lucien Jaume, "Fénelon critique de la déraison d'État," in *Raison et déraison d'État*, ed. Y.-C. Zarka (Paris: Presses Universitaires de France, 1994), pp. 395–422. Constant and Tocqueville often cited Fénelon as an observer of absolutist culture.

[45] *DA* II.2.9, p. 158; AG, p. 615: Tocqueville makes a strange comparison between Pascal's wager and American preachers who "refer to this world constantly" (ibid., p. 159; AG, p. 616). In fact, Tocqueville probably incorporated the "pragmatic Jansenism" of Nicole, who made clever use of the concept of "concupiscence." See below.

[46] See Plato, *Theaetetus*. According to the relativist Protagoras, man is the measure of all things, so that "all things that appear to be just and beautiful in each city are so as long as the city decrees they are." What is advantageous is therefore a purely subjective utility, an opinion. "Some people are wiser than others, but no one has false opinions." Plato demolishes this view, but his critique reveals the dexterity of the sophist, the friend of democracy.

[47] He read Plato in Victor Cousin's edition and conceived "spiritualism" in light of these two philosophers.

[48] *DA* II.2.15, p. 181; AG, pp. 634–35. Read the entire passage and compare it with Robespierre's major speeches on virtue.

Thus the moralist Tocqueville was well aware of what society (all too often) ignored. The paradox is that his methods as a moralist were the opposite of his methods as a sociologist (which we explored in the previous part of the book). Tocqueville the moralist wanted schools to teach the existence of God and the immortality of the soul, which gave a surprising tinge to his "liberalism." Like Rousseau, but also like Robespierre, he believed that a civic religion was necessary and that those who refused to accept it were enemies: "If you encounter among the opinions of a democratic people any of those wicked theories that intimate that everything perishes with the body, you must regard those who profess such theories as natural enemies of the people." Tocqueville does not hide the fact that he is expressing his own innermost feelings or that he sees the need for a *law*:

> There are many things about the materialists that offend me. Their doctrines seem to me pernicious, and their pride revolts me. If their system were of any possible use to man, it would seem to be in giving him a modest idea of himself. But the materialists do just the opposite. When they have done enough in their estimation to prove that they are mere brutes, they strut about as proudly as if they had proven they were gods.

Plato proscribed the poets. Tocqueville contemptuously called for repression of materialist ideas:

> Materialism in any nation is a dangerous malady of the human spirit, but it is particularly to be feared in a democratic people, because it weds with marvelous ease the defect of the heart most commonly found in democratic peoples. Democracy encourages the taste for material pleasures. If this taste becomes excessive, it soon leads men to believe that everything is mere matter, and materialism in turn adds to the forces that propel pursuit of those same pleasures with wild ardor. Such is the fatal circle into which democratic nations are driven. It is good for them to see the danger and pull back.

In other words, democracy cannot perceive its own good. In practice it is fatally drawn toward materialism. Hence actually existing democracies ("democratic nations") must constantly be reminded of the danger. "It is good for them to see" really means that they must be shown: the moralist must instruct them, and instruct them well, that there is a higher utility in religion. Robespierre put this bluntly: "If God did not exist, we would have to invent him."[49] Tocqueville, for his part, explained the "benefits" of God for

---

[49] Robespierre used these words in a speech to the Jacobins on November 21, 1793 (1 Frimaire, Year II). On the formula and the practical (political) utility of God, see Lucien Jaume, "Robespierre:

democracy: "Most religions are merely general, simple, and practical means of teaching men the immortality of the soul. This is the greatest benefit that a democratic people can derive from its beliefs, and it is what makes beliefs more necessary to such a people than to all others."[50]

L'honnête, which we interpreted as a sort of refined hypocrisy, an elegant lie about human nature in modernity, can in the end only be sustained by a "supplement of soul," an injection of immortality. Instead of "respectable materialism" we end up with "respectable spiritualism," the kind preached by American ministers who, without ever losing sight of the realities of this world, infuse them with hope and set them off with a judicious chiaroscuro.

By adopting the position of the public moralist, the man Tocqueville was able to strike a compromise between his negative emotions (horror of mediocrity, chronic depression and anxiety) and his reasons for hope (democracy was accomplishing miracles and would accomplish more in the future). For the sake of comparison, note that La Rochefoucauld, the dogged theorist of amour-propre, later arrived at a different analysis, in which he presented life in society as "true" (in the posthumous *Réflexions diverses*). He may then have written with an eye to reforming mores (although there is still dispute about this).[51]

The time has come to say in what respects it is correct to speak of Jansenism in connection with Tocqueville. Any number of commentators have asserted without proof that he was a Jansenist.[52] The question can be rephrased: Did the idea that *honnêteté*, or socialized self-interest, could be used to reform and perfect "democracy" have Jansenist roots, and, if so, how can one prove it?

des principes révolutionnaires à l'Être suprême," in *Robespierre, Figure-Réputation*, ed. A. Jourdan, Yearbook of European Studies (Amsterdam: Rodopi, 1996), pp. 37–52. I also discuss a surprising similarity between Robespierre and Necker, who in 1788 published a work entitled *De l'importance des opinions religieuses*. Indeed, Robespierre paid homage to Necker on this issue in 1788.

[50] All the quoted passages are from *DA* II.2.15, p. 181; AG, p. 635.

[51] This is the interpretation of Jean Lafond and Paul Bénichou. See the chapter "Du vrai" in *Réflexions diverses (Moralistes du XVIIe siècle)*, pp. 196–97. This chapter was not included in the Aimé-Martin edition of *Moralistes français* in Tocqueville's library.

[52] At a session of the Académie des Sciences Morales et Politiques, Raymond Aron criticized L. Diez del Corral for lack of rigor and credibility in discussing Pascal's influence. See *Revue des travaux de l'Académie des Sciences Morales et Politiques* (1965, 2nd trimester): 70–83.

Tocqueville's Relation to Jansenism

For generations now, scholars have been arguing that Tocqueville had deep sympathy for Pascal and perhaps for Jansenism. It should be noted, however, that when he wrote to Kergorlay that he lived "a little every day" with Pascal, Rousseau, and Montesquieu—in a passage that has been cited a hundred times over—he was simply repeating, literally, advice offered to him by his confidant two years earlier, in 1834.[1]

Still, the point is not to deny that Tocqueville had a personal interest in Pascal, even if it is impossible to say which edition he read.[2] It remains to be seen what effects meditation on Pascal had on Tocqueville's writing. Furthermore, we cannot speak of "Jansenism" without examining what the public image of Jansenism (one of the most controversial schools of thought in French intellectual history) was in the 1830s and 1840s. And finally, we will need to say something about Tocqueville's stance with respect to that image. To approach Tocqueville's supposed "philo-Jansenism" in any other way would run the risk of substituting our own subjective interpretation for the reality, as if we, in the twenty-first century, were capable of direct communication with (1) the gentlemen of Port-Royal, (2) their hidden or avowed disciples in the eighteenth century, and (3) the inevitably complex emotions of Tocqueville, the former pupil of Abbé Lesueur, who by the late 1830s knew full well that Jansenism had been all but demonized by any number of contemporary thinkers.

An Effective Meditation on Pascal

Was Tocqueville then a Jansenist sympathizer who, in Pascalian terms, kept a "thought in the back of his mind" while describing the spectacle of the world?

---

[1] See Tocqueville, *OC*, XIII-1, pp. 418, 366. In an essay on Tocqueville for *Le Correspondant*, moreover, Kergorlay wrote that Tocqueville had forged his style by reading both Pascal "for the substance of the language" and Voltaire "for ease and lightness of touch." This article is interesting chiefly as confirmation of his reading of Pascale "as he approached maturity." *OC* XIII-2, p. 360.

[2] As Françoise Mélonio observes in a note in *Mélanges* (*OC* XVI, p. 551, n. 1), Tocqueville's manuscript is a series of notes and comments on Pascal's *Pensées*.

Is this crypto-Jansenist the "hidden Tocqueville" for whom we are searching in this third part of our book? This hidden Tocqueville is always present, behind the curtain, as it were, but he reveals his presence only through discreet signs. One reader intuited what he was trying to suggest: Villemain, in his review of volume 1 of *Democracy in America*.

Tocqueville's innermost thoughts emerge with particularly clarity in two places: a subsection of chapter I.2.5 entitled "Concerning the People's Choices and the Instinctive Preferences of American Democracy," in which he considers the effects of the spirit of equality on electoral choices, and chapter II.2.13, entitled "Why Americans Seem So Restless in the Midst of Their Well-Being," which also deals with equality and competition between individuals.[3] Both passages deal with dissatisfaction in the midst of satisfaction, or, to put it in Pascal's terms, with "distraction" (*divertissement*). Equality, both as desired result and as ardently sought objective, is an elusive quarry. Pascal believes that it is an objective that dispenses individuals from the need to think about death, and Tocqueville, who quotes Pascal in the first passage, speaks of the "eternal flight" of satisfaction. He is not clear, however, about what is dissimulated (or "veiled"—the importance of the term will become clear) in and through this flight.

Here is the first passage, in which Tocqueville does something that he does only rarely, which is to identify the source of his reflection, in this case Pascal:

> We must not blind ourselves to the fact that democratic institutions develop the sentiment of envy in the human heart to a very high degree. This is not so much because such institutions give everyone the means to equal everyone else as because those means continually prove unavailing to those who employ them. Democratic institutions awaken and flatter the passion for equality without ever being able to satisfy it to the full. No sooner does full equality seem within the people's reach than it flies from their grasp, and its flight, as Pascal said, is eternal. The people passionately seek a good that is all the more precious because it is close enough to be familiar yet far enough away that it cannot be savored. The chance of success spurs them on; the uncertainty of success vexes them. They struggle, they tire, they grow bitter. Anything that is beyond them in any quarter then seems an obstacle to their desires, and no form of superiority is so legitimate that the sight of it is not wearisome to their eyes.[4]

---

[3] *DA* I.2.5, pp. 284ff.; AG, pp. 225 ff.; and *DA* II.2.13, pp. 171ff; AG, pp. 625ff.
[4] *DA* I.2.5, pp. 285–86; AG, p. 226.

"The people" (a term that appears more frequently in Pascal than in Tocqueville) is here used in a sociological rather than a political sense to refer to "the lower classes," as mentioned elsewhere in this chapter. For Tocqueville, it is precisely at this level of society that one sees most clearly the elemental human passion to have what one's neighbor already possesses. But this desire is universal (affecting all strata of society), and its object is equally universal: "complete equality."[5] Anyone who experiences this desire for complete equality comes to feel that it should be easy to attain, for instance by not electing distinguished individuals to high office. But the belief that equality is within easy reach is an illusion and leads to repeated disappointment. Pascal agreed. Here is the passage that Tocqueville recommends we consult:

> Such is our true condition. It is what renders us incapable of either knowing with certainty or wallowing in absolute ignorance. We are adrift on a vast sea, always uncertain and directionless, driven this way and that. If we try to moor ourselves to some fixed point, it shakes us loose and abandons us, and if we seek to follow, it eludes our grasp, slips away, and flees in *eternal flight* [my emphasis]. Nothing stops it for us. This is our natural state, yet nothing could be more contrary to our inclination. We burn with desire to find a firm footing and steady foundation upon which to raise a tower unto the heavens, but cracks appear throughout our foundation, and the earth opens until we find ourselves gaping into the abyss.[6]

Tocqueville retained the general spirit of the text: democratic society is in permanent agitation, uncertain of its bearings and vexed by anxiety.[7] But what Pascal described as characteristic of the human condition in general, Tocqueville transposed to the democratic situation, and this is why he cannot follow Pascal when the author of the *Pensées* adds, in the same passage on man's "disproportion," the following: "This being the case, I believe that each man should remain at rest, in the estate in which nature placed him." In democracy, fewer and fewer people would remain at rest ("in a room," as

---

[5] Tocqueville was of course familiar with Montesquieu's remarks on the desire for equality in everything, to which the Republic ultimately succumbs.

[6] Pascal, *Œuvres complètes*, Lafuma ed. (Paris: Le Seuil, 1963), *pensée* 199 (and not fragment 390 as given in Nolla I, p. 152, n. f). Or sec. 72 of the Brunschvicg edition: "Disproportion de l'homme," Pascal, *Pensées et opuscules* (Paris: Hachette, n.d.). One can also consult the edition of Sellier, who uses a third numbering (1976, then 1991, reprinted in *Moralistes du XVIIe siècle*, ed. Lafond). I use the Lafuma numbering throughout, followed by the page, followed by the section in Brunschvicg.

[7] One thinks of Locke's "uneasiness," which his French translator Pierre Coste rendered with the old French word "*mésaise*." Locke was both a reader of the Jansenists and Pierre Nicole's English translator.

Pascal said), and a man's "social condition" was no longer an "*état*" given, as Pascal believed, by nature: *competition had begun.*[8]

In a democracy, everyone is impatient with his condition. In the second passage we will consider, Tocqueville said this: "Having destroyed the obstructing privileges enjoyed by some of their fellow men, they run up against universal competition."[9] We saw earlier that equality was for Tocqueville the sociologist what Montesquieu called the *principle* of democratic society. Now we see that for Tocqueville the moralist it became "democracy's distraction," if I may put it that way. He develops this idea, once again in a Pascalian vein:

> In democratic nations men easily achieve a certain equality but not the equality they desire. That equality recedes a bit further every day, yet it never disappears from view, and as it recedes, it entices them to chase after it. Although they always think they are about to catch up with it, invariably it eludes their grasp. They get close enough to know equality's charms but not close enough to enjoy them, and they die before having fully savored its delights.[10]

Again, the theme is elusiveness, the torture of Tantalus to which the democratic mentality is subjected. The promise of a better future always looms in the distance. In this instance Tocqueville did not cite Pascal but left no doubt that he had in mind the long fragment on distraction (*divertissement*) in which Pascal says that men "choose an attractive object that charms them and arouses their ardor."[11] Like men in general according to Pascal, the citizens of "democracy" do not know themselves, and unfortunately they turn their drive for equality, in which they believe as a source of ultimate joy, against their own lives:

> To these causes we must attribute the strange melancholy that the inhabitants of democratic countries often exhibit in the midst of plenty, and the disgust with

[8] "Such is our condition (*état*)": the word is common in Pascal. It refers sometimes to a social characteristic but often to a metaphysical condition. In context it sometimes refers to "man's condition after the Fall."

[9] *DA* II.2.13, p. 173; AG, p. 627.

[10] Ibid., p. 174; AG, p. 628.

[11] Pascal, fragment 136, p. 517, Br. 139. There is disagreement about the text. We follow Brunschvicg: "And so, when one reminds them that what they so ardently seek cannot satisfy them, if they replied as they ought to do if they thought about it properly, that in so doing their aim was solely to find a violent and impetuous occupation to distract them from thinking about themselves, which is why they choose an attractive object that charms them and arouses their ardor, they would leave their adversaries with no room to reply. But they do not answer in this way, because they do not know themselves. They do not know that what they are after is the pursuit and not the capture."

life that sometimes grips them as they go about their comfortable and tranquil existences.

People in France complain that the number of suicides is increasing. In America, suicide is rare, but I have been assured that insanity is more common there than it is elsewhere.

These are different symptoms of the same malady.

For Pascal, men, living in dissatisfaction, do not wish to think of death, even though they have a certain experience of it. For Tocqueville, it is to escape from poignant dissatisfaction that they turn toward death. Of the insistent desire for equality he wrote that "in satisfying it, one sharpens it."[12]

Thus we see that Tocqueville's text in places reveals his heartfelt attraction to Pascal, which contemporary readers would have recognized as a gesture toward the Christian culture of the old regime and to the preaching of Bossuet, Bourdaloue, and Massillon (authors to whom Tocqueville referred often in his manuscripts and letters). So we are for now in the proximity of Jansenism, but we must now ask what this appellation might have signified toward the end of the Restoration and in the first fifteen years of the July Monarchy.

REPRESENTATIONS OF JANSENISM IN TOCQUEVILLE'S TIME

Among the cultivated readers of Tocqueville's time a certain image of Jansenism held sway. This image may seem surprising today. It was marked by the struggles around Jansenism in the parlements of the eighteenth century and the Civil Constitution of the Clergy during the Revolution. There is lively historiographic debate about these issues at the moment owing to a revival of interest in eighteenth-century Jansenism.[13]

One can gauge what the average cultivated individual thought about Jansenism by looking at the work of leading literary critics such as Abel Villemain and Charles de Sainte-Beuve, the author of the monumental *Port-Royal*. As Sainte-Beuve himself noted with astonishment, in the period 1835–40 most people had a rather distorted idea of early Jansenism, which they "regarded as representing nothing other than the advent of *reason* and *philosophy* in

---

[12] *DA* II, p. 361. See also *DA* II.2.13, p. 174; AG, p. 627: "The desire for equality becomes ever more insatiable as the degree of equality increases."

[13] See Catherine Maire, *De la cause de Dieu à la cause de la Nation* (Paris: Gallimard, 1998) and the controversy in the journal *Commentaire* concerning the work of Dale K. Van Kley, *The Religious Origins of the French Revolution: From Calvin to the Civil Constitution, 1560–1791* (New Haven: Yale University Press, 1996).

religion. In many respects, however, Port-Royal was just the opposite."[14] Indeed, if we think of Pascal's critiques of the pride of reason and philosophy, there are grounds for surprise.[15] To be sure, Port-Royal could boast of one important philosopher, Antoine Arnauld, who engaged in controversy with Descartes, Leibniz, and Malebranche. But what earned the friends of Port-Royal their image as champions of the individual, the inner life, and the right to judge for oneself was their *attitude* toward religious and political authority in the wake of the celebrated controversy over "respectful silence," the condemnation by Rome in 1705, and the papal bull *Unigenitus* of 1713. One can also point to their appeal to public opinion (against the Jesuits), which was initiated by Pascal's *Lettres provinciales*.

Villemain, in a celebrated essay on Pascal, was therefore able to claim that Port-Royal had embraced survivors of the Fronde and that it represented the side of rebellion in a permanent clash "between arbitrary authority and independent thought."[16] In the dispute about the "five propositions" attributed to Jansenius, Villemain claimed that the Jansenists had insisted on "the free and natural exercise of reason." This interpretation, which one might call secularist, had a bright future ahead of it. In Alain's *Entretiens au bord de la mer* we find a definition of Jansenism as a self-justifying intellectual attitude derived straight from Villemain: "What is Jansenism? It is resignation to an order without respect. It is rejection of submission to an alleged divine order of things and profound suspicion of so-called divine justice. This did not change the religion but did eventually purge it of idolatry."[17]

To obey without respecting, to keep one's "thought in the back of one's mind" (Pascal), was a constant theme in Alain, who held Descartes and Pascal in equal esteem. A century earlier Villemain wrote that "in this eternal struggle, the solitary men of Port-Royal, who seemed to debate only scholastic subtleties, stood for freedom of conscience, free examination, and love of justice and truth."[18]

---

[14]Charles Augustin Sainte-Beuve, *Port-Royal*, book 4, sec. 3, ed. Maxime Leroy (Paris: La Pléiade, 1954), 2:477, note.

[15]For a compendium of paradoxical uses of Jansenism in the nineteenth century, see H.-F. Imbert, *Stendhal et la tentation janséniste* (Geneva: Droz, 1970). Imbert rightly stresses the confusion that existed around the term "Jansenism" in Stendhal's time and shows nicely how it was often a condition of success (especially in politics). The classic work of Léon Séché, *Les Derniers jansénistes (. . .) depuis la ruine de Port-Royal jusqu'à nos jours, 1710–1870*, 3 vols. (Paris: Perrin, 1890–91), is too quick to draw a parallel between liberal Catholicism and Jansenism.

[16]Abel-François Villemain, "De Pascal considéré comme moraliste et comme écrivain," 1827, reprinted in Villemain, *Discours et mélanges littéraires, rev. ed.* (Paris: Didier, 1873), p. 143.

[17]Alain (Émile-Auguste Chartier), *Entretiens au bord de la mer*, in *Les Passions et la sagesse* (Paris: La Pléiade, 1960), p. 1369.

[18]Villemain, *Discours et mélanges littéraires*, p. 144. See also his report on the 1842 Académie competition, p. 137.

Similarly, Ernest Havet wrote in his study of Pascal's *Pensées* that *Les Provinciales* offered an "eternal model of oppositional rhetoric."[19] The modern historian René Taveneaux has continued the tradition that runs from Villemain to Alain. In his authoritative work, he writes: "Owing to its fundamental individualism, Jansenism threatened the authority of the state as conceived by Louis XIV. Against unconditional obedience it proposed autonomy of conscience and thus undermined the principle of *raison d'État*. The distinction between rightfulness and fact (*le droit et le fait*)[20] . . . would thus justify free examination."[21]

One might ask (but this is not the place to do so) whether this way of presenting the issue was not, in the first place, only too well suited to one very special judge, Louis XIV; and, in the second place, whether it did not owe a great deal to the teleological interpretation of the Enlightenment as a "sequel to Jansenism," at the risk of overlooking the reality of a religious conception that it would be rather audacious to call "individualism." Catherine Maire's subtle and complex reinterpretation suggests the need for a more cautious approach.[22]

The implication is that the public associated this image of early Jansensim as a "school for critical thinking" with a political stance. Along with Fénelon and the Huguenots, the friends of Port-Royal were cast as victims of "arbitrariness" and absolutism.[23] They would later be painted as allies not only of Protestantism but also of Gallicanism, especially thanks to Joseph de Maistre's pamphlet *De l'Église gallicane* (1820). Although contemporary readers such as Sainte-Beuve agreed that de Maistre's treatment of Pascal and his friends was superficial and crude, it seems to have exerted real influence on public opinion. Here is a sample of de Maistre's rhetoric:

> How, then, could such a sect have attracted so many supporters, and even fanatical supporters? How could it have created such a stir? How could it have beleaguered both state and church? Several causes conspired to these ends. I have already touched on the chief among them. The human heart is naturally

[19] Quoted in Sainte-Beuve, *Port-Royal*, 3:1089 (note to p. 199). In 1851 Havet published a celebrated edition of the *Pensées*, with copious commentary.

[20] Recall the terms: Were the five condemned propositions really in Jansénius's book *Augustinus*? While accepting the "rightfulness" (*le droit*) of their condemnation, did one not reserve the right to question the proof (*le fait*) of their presence?

[21] R. Taveneaux, *Jansénisme et politique* (Paris: Armand Colin, 1965), p. 33. Same formulas in Taveneaux, "Jansénisme," in *Dictionnaire du Grand Siècle*, ed. F. Bluche (Paris: Fayard, 1990).

[22] On the image of Port-Royal in the nineteenth century, especially among republicans, see also Catherine Maire's essay in *Les Lieux de mémoire*, ed. Pierre Nora (Paris: Éditions Gallimard, 1992), 3:110–18. There, Maire still seems to share's Taveneaux's view of Port-Royal's "individualism."

[23] Recall that Louis XIV ordered Port-Royal des Champs to be leveled in 1710. Gravestones were to be knocked down, and the bodies of nuns buried there were to be thrown into a common pit.

rebellious. Raise a banner against authority and you will never want for recruits: *Non serviam*. This is the eternal crime of our wretched nature.[24]

It had become commonplace to draw a parallel between Jansenism and Protestantism. Followers of de Maistre credited Jansenism with a certain vitality stemming from its successful introduction of Protestant ideas into the Catholic Church itself. Indeed, according to *Le Mémorial catholique*, Jansenism "consists essentially in granting to each individual church . . . and each individual the right to set limits to spiritual sovereignty on questions of faith, morality, and discipline."[25] To the extent that Jansenism was seen as favorable to freedom of the individual and the critical spirit, it was, we are told, politically drawn toward popular sovereignty. Hence the charge of "republicanism" launched by Saint-Simon and echoed today by some scholars in regard to authors such as Jérôme Besoigne and Nicolas Le Gros.[26]

There is no need here to examine the rather surprising influence attributed to Jansenism or to enter into debate with other historians. As far as Tocqueville is concerned, two observations will suffice. First, one finds in Sainte-Beuve a remarkable passage on "the morality of *honnêtes gens*," which Sainte-Beuve derived from *Les Provinciales*. The conciliatory approach to morality found there supposedly developed into the morality of the middle class, said to be particularly impatient with pious affectation. In this view, Molière's *Tartuffe* perfectly embodied the morality of *honnêtes gens*. Sainte-Beuve concluded this lengthy development with an imaginary conversation between Pascal and Molière. It is interesting to note that this new concept of the *honnête* was oriented primarily toward practical life and moral moderation:

> Since the downfall of the old society and the old class system and the rise of the middle class, this morality is above all embraced by the leading strata in modern society. It incorporates the results of philosophical meditation along with Christian habits and maxims. It is a compromise, which for that very reason suits the needs of the day. Its finest aspects are what I would call rationalized or, rather, *utilitarianized* [Sainte-Beuve's italics], Christianity, which has achieved the status of useful social practice.[27]

---

[24] Joseph de Maistre, *De l'Église gallicane dans son rapport avec le souverain pontife* (Lyon: Pelargaud, 1863), pp. 32–33. The author had just placed Calvinism among the historic representatives of the "eternal crime."

[25] *Le Mémorial catholique*, quoted in H.-F. Imbert, *Stendhal et la tentation janséniste*, p. 73.

[26] See Taveneaux, *Jansénisme et politique*, pp. 212–15, which reproduces Besoigne, *Catéchisme sur l'Église pour les temps de troubles*, and pp. 208–9 for Le Gros and Maultrot on the nation as repository of authority.

[27] Sainte-Beuve, *Port-Royal*, 2:248.

Tocqueville in his correspondence also speaks of applying Christianity to the education of citizens while reproaching clergymen for being obsessed with the past and making sarcastic observations about overzealous believers, who were among his reasons for rejecting liberal Catholicism.[28]

Christianity as a "useful social practice" appealed to both Tocqueville and his contemporaries. During the July Monarchy the bourgeoisie presumably approved of a religion that promoted social peace and good manners after the "follies" of the Restoration (the union of throne and altar, the law on sacrilege, etc.). It is worth noting that Sainte-Beuve, who was invited to Lausanne by the Vinet circle to lecture on Port-Royal,[29] met Tocqueville at Mme de Récamier's, where he had the opportunity to read excerpts of *Port-Royal*.[30]

The second observation is that during the Restoration, Jansenism and its martyrology formed an integral part of a child's upbringing in certain families. Among people close to Tocqueville, this was true of Duvergier de Hauranne[31] and his friend Lanjuinais,[32] and of course Royer-Collard. Léon Séché has written that Royer-Collard's library "contained 700–800 volumes, 30 of which were by Port-Royalistes and according to him sufficient for obtaining knowledge of human nature."[33] Royer's remark to Sainte-Beuve has often been repeated: "He who does not know Port-Royal does not know humanity."[34]

Royer-Collard absorbed the image of Port-Royal he received from his mother, and this in turn enhanced his political stature: "The fact that in my public life I gave no thought to myself came from them," he said.[35] Pierre-Paul Royer-Collard would never forget his upbringing. Raised in Sompuis (near Vitry-le-François), a village steeped in the Jansenist spirit, notably under the

---

[28] Tocqueville openly mocked Montalembert, Lacordaire, and Louis de Carné. He was far more diplomatic in his correspondence with the very Catholic Francisque de Corcelle.

[29] René Bray's learned and charming book *Sainte-Beuve à l'Académie de Lausanne* (Paris: Droz, 1937) is still worth reading. It sheds light on the links between the "Vaudois Awakening" and French thought, also exemplified by *Le Semeur*, in which Vinet took part (see part 2 above).

[30] According to Tocqueville's good friend Ampère, the author of *Democracy in America* began to frequent the Abbaye-aux-Bois just after the publication of the first volume.

[31] For this family the illustrious ancestor was Saint-Cyran, the inspirer of *Augustinus*, whom Richelieu imprisoned for five years. See "Saint-Cyran," in *Dictionnaire du Grand Siècle*, and *Dictionnaire de Port-Royal*, ed. Jean Lesaulnier and Antony Mc Kena (Paris: Honoré Champion, 2004). Jean-Ambroise Duvergier de Hauranne was given the abbey of Saint-Cyran as a temporary benefice, from which he took his religious name.

[32] Tocqueville's correspondence with Victor Lanjuinais will soon appear in the Gallimard *Œuvres complètes*.

[33] Séché, *Les Derniers Jansénistes*, 2:216. Having visited the library, which has been preserved as it was, I can confirm this.

[34] Sainte-Beuve, *Port-Royal*, 1:105.

[35] Quoted in ibid., 2:602.

influence of his great-uncle Paul Collard, he was the son of Angélique Collard, who was both a pious woman and a strong personality.[36]

Royer-Collard was a proud, uncompromising man who spoke his mind even at the risk of wounding his allies and who displayed a flair for parliamentary oratory. In his day he was regarded as an heir of the most august Jansenist tradition. Tocqueville was clearly very impressed by this elder statesman, to whom he turned for advice. Later he wrote a long portrait of him, which included the following description: "A singular mixture of a few petty passions and some very great sentiments, of unwitting vanity, loftiness of soul, and imposing pride: all in all, an impressive and noble figure."[37] But his admiration comes out most clearly in notes that he took on Royer's courses and speeches in 1841: "The last vestige of the great political figures, the grand political passions, the great political characters. Nothing is left of all that."[38]

TOCQUEVILLE'S JANSENIST LEANINGS

What was Tocqueville's attitude toward these images of Jansenism? What influence did they have on his thought and writing?

One surprising fact stands out: in *The Ancien Régime and the Revolution* Tocqueville did not see Jansenism as an important factor in the development of eighteenth-century public opinion or in the early stages of the Revolution, even through its influence on the Civil Constitution of the Clergy. Yet if Alexis de Tocqueville was silent on the subject of Jansenism, his father Hervé was loquacious.[39]

Tocqueville's silence might seem astonishing, particularly in someone reputed to be steeped in "Jansenist culture." He was fairly critical of the

---

[36] See R. Langeron, *Un conseiller secret de Louis XVIII. Royer-Collard* (Paris: Hachette, 1951), chap. 1. See also Villemain, *La Tribune moderne en France et en Angleterre* (Paris: Calmann-Lévy, 1882), 2:247–80, essay on Royer-Collard.

[37] Letter to Freslon, 1858, in Tocqueville, *OC* XI, introduction by André Jardin, p. x, or Tocqueville, *Lettres choisies, Souvenirs*, p. 1310. Tocqueville was dumbfounded to find in Royer-Collard a "natural republican" in the service of the elder branch of the Bourbons. Royer was truly a man of internal conflict.

[38] Tocqueville, *OC* XI, p. 103. There was also criticism: Tocqueville compiled a whole "dossier" on Royer-Collard, which is included in this volume of *OC*.

[39] Hervé de Tocqueville, *Histoire philosophique du règne de Louis XV* (Paris: Librairie d'Amyot, 1847), 2 vols. In the preface Tocqueville's father wrote that "Jansenism opened the breach through which eighteenth-century philosophy intruded," p. 2. Chapter 4 is largely devoted to Jansenism, which "clumsily provided philosophism with its arms." Therefore, "upon the death of Louis XIV, France was Jansenist, not because of its doctrines, which most Frenchmen were incapable of judging, but because of hatred for the Jesuits and a predilection for their adversaries," p. 54. Sainte-Beuve also saw Jansenism as a "breach" that made way for the eighteenth century: preface to vol. 1 of *Port-Royal*, 1840. See La Pléiade edition, 1:102. Tocqueville was of course familiar with this thesis.

important role that the parlements claimed for themselves in the eighteenth century, but he never mentioned the influence of Jansenism among the parlementaires, even though this was well-known at the time (though to be sure historians have only recently rediscovered as important a figure as Adrien Le Paige[40]). His silence was certainly tactical, perhaps even embarrassed. It is nevertheless important to note that the appellation "Jansenism" covered any number of not very consistent traits. Take the case of Tocqueville's tutor, Abbé Lesueur. It is hard to say precisely what his attitude toward Jansenism was, since he both admired and cited Joseph de Maistre[41] while also revering the Jansenists, whom de Maistre detested. In theory, it should not have been possible to be both a Maistrian and a Jansenist, just as it should not have been possible to be both a communist and a liberal, though to be sure de Maistre was far more hostile to political Jansenism than to the movement's theology or spirituality. Thus we see that the label "Jansenist" no longer had a very specific meaning in Tocqueville's time.[42]

Even if we presume that readers of *Democracy in America* were inevitably influenced by ambient opinion on these issues, we should not expect to find evidence of that opinion in Tocqueville, who did not take a position on political Jansenism even when he could easily have done so in *The Ancien Régime and the Revolution*. In any case, with an author like Tocqueville, it is never wise to assume that he was subject to some supposedly widespread cultural influence (such as Jansenism); we must always look at what he actually wrote, often recasting common topics in his own terms. Jansenism was indeed an element of Tocqueville's thinking, but not in open dialogue with the reader. The question of what type of Jansenism he praised remains.

Just as he did not simply "apply" themes borrowed from Montesquieu, Tocqueville did not simply transcribe the common opinions about Jansenism that we have just rehearsed. What did Jansenism mean to him? He rarely broached the subject in his published correspondence. His personal view seems to have been most clearly expressed in a letter to Corcelle from 1856.

---

[40] In Maire, *De la cause de Dieu à la cause de la Nation*, Le Paige occupies a central place. Furthermore, Francesco di Donato has described Le Paige's conception of Parlement as the "hidden sovereign" of the absolutist state. See "La puissance cachée de la robe," in *L'Office du juge: part de souveraineté ou puissance nulle?*, ed. O. Cayla and M.-F. Renoux-Zagamé (Paris: LGDJ, 2001).

[41] For the most recent study of this question, see Jean-Louis Benoît, *Tocqueville moraliste*, as well as his biography, *Tocqueville. Un destin paradoxal*.

[42] Always precise, Jardin, *Alexis de Tocqueville*, pp. 44–45, listed the overtly Jansenist works that Tocqueville had in his library but that may have come from his father (who was also tutored by Abbé Lesueur). These include the Latin commentary on the four Gospels by Jansénius (1649), Hersan's *Idée de la religion chrétienne* (1723), and a catechism approved by Colbert, the Jansenist bishop of Montpellier (new ed., 1782).

In it he is quite skeptical about the seventeenth-century Jansenist theology of grace, which he regarded as too close "to the fatalism of the Ancients or the Muslims' belief in predestination." What he did admire was the moral grandeur (a term we have encountered before) of some Jansenists: "No one can deny that most of the great men of their time were of their persuasion, or that most of them were themselves very great men, or that they and those around them exhibited the highest, most virile, solid, and proud virtues of the day."[43]

To judge by *Democracy in America*, however, we cannot say that this image of Jansenism, which Tocqueville obviously respected, had much influence on either the form or the substance of the book. To be sure, when he compares (in his manuscripts) Pascal and other writers of "the age of aristocracy" to writers of the democratic era, the image comes up, but the essence of the matter lies elsewhere, and it is very important to an understanding of Tocqueville, as we shall see: it quietly shapes the analyses of the sociologist and the political scientist, which we examined in previous chapters. To probe Tocqueville's "Jansenist leanings" more deeply and to explore his recasting of common themes, we must take up six questions, in order of increasing importance. We will then be able to look at what we have just learned about Tocqueville the moralist in a new light.

Human Finitude

There is one theme that Tocqueville presents as self-evident in *Democracy in America* and with pathos in his correspondence: human beings easily forget their limits, of which they must therefore be reminded if a disciplined democracy is to exist. These limits are twofold. First, man's knowledge is limited: the study of society may yield probable knowledge but not certainty.[44] Investigation, comparison, and "philosophical" hypotheses are indispensable for explaining history and social forms. Tocqueville wanted to write a book about India, and his study of Islam later informed his interest in Algeria, which he visited twice.[45] Second, man's strength is also limited, and this is a source of great danger to democracy, because egalitarian competition

---

[43] Tocqueville, *OC* XV-2, p. 193. Tocqueville was criticizing a recently published essay by Louis de Carné.

[44] In a letter to Charles Stöffels dated November 19, 1831, Tocqueville wrote: "For the vast majority of points that we need to know, we have only plausibilities and approximations. To despair that this is the way it is is to despair of being human, for this is one of the most inflexible laws of our nature." *Œuvres*, Beaumont ed., 7:83, or Tocqueville, *Lettres choisies. Souvenirs*, p. 240.

[45] Not only did Tocqueville consider becoming a colonist in Mitidja, but his interest in the future of colonization and its effects on French domestic politics led him to engage in study and research and become active in the legislature on these issues.

TOCQUEVILLE'S RELATION TO JANSENISM ເຂ 171

compels him to ignore or even deny his limits. For Tocqueville, the finitude that is man's lot is not a minor consideration but a major criterion.

He says this quite clearly in one of the manuscripts for the second volume: "A man ... gifted with intelligence superior to that of the vulgar. He has beautiful thoughts, grand sentiments, and carries out extraordinary actions." This raises a question in Tocqueville's mind: "Where does he place the limit of his knowledge and his judgment of things?"[46] He then issues a revealing warning: "If he sets no limit, there is no need for further discussion, and I take it for granted that he is wrong."[47] Tocqueville's perception of society was thus informed by an unshakable awareness of human frailty and, even more, by disapproval of frailty that goes unrecognized. In an almost Pascalian turn of phrase, he wrote that "the surest sign of the frailty of the human spirit" is ignorance of its own frailty.[48]

This perception of society and human self-understanding was not simply characteristic of Tocqueville the man. He applied it, as moralist and author, to the subject of his study. In the chapter on "the infinite perfectibility of man,"[49] he notes that democratic man can become intoxicated with this idea. Although Tocqueville took up the idea of "perfectibility" from Mme de Staël (who engaged in polemic about it with Chateaubriand's entourage[50]), he nevertheless pointed out to his readers the danger it posed owing to its propensity to invade the imagination. Democratic man becomes caught up in a breakneck race reminiscent of the Pascalian theme of distraction: "Thus, always searching, falling, picking himself up again, often disappointed, never discouraged, he marches indefatigably on toward the immense grandeur that he can but dimly make out at the end of the long road that mankind has yet to travel."[51]

[46] This is Socrates's criterion of wisdom (*sophia*) in the *Apology*: to know what one knows and where one's knowledge ends. For Socrates, self-knowledge defines the limit of man's wisdom or at any rate of his own wisdom, after the Delphic oracle calls him "the wisest of men."

[47] Nolla II, p. 41, n. d. Tocqueville, who claimed to be exasperated by personalities such as Guizot and Montalembert, probably meant this judgment to apply to them.

[48] Ibid.

[49] *DA* II.1.8. The manuscripts quoted in the previous paragraph pertain to this chapter.

[50] Tocqueville associated *equality* with the idea that "man in general is endowed with the infinite faculty of perfecting himself." Think of what Constant wrote in *Mélanges* (1829): "The perfectibility of the human race is nothing other than the tendency toward equality." See also Constant, *Œuvres complètes* (Tübingen: Max Niemeyer), vol. 3-1, *Écrits littéraires (1800–1813)*, ed. P. Delbouille and Martine de Rougemont, esp. pp. 370–89 (manuscript of Constant, among four others dealing with the connection between perfectibility and equality). Compare Tocqueville: "Equality suggests a number of ideas that would not otherwise occur to the human mind and modifies most of the ideas that it already holds. As an example I will take the idea of human perfectibility. ... Equality did not bring it into being but did give it a new character." *DA* II.1.8, p. 43; AG, p. 514.

[51] *DA* II.1.8, p. 44; AG, p. 515.

Tocqueville was so taken with the idea of the disproportion between man and his hopes that he referred in his first draft to the relation between the individual and the mass, the singularity and the totality, but later eliminated this reference. The digression was not in keeping with the theme of the chapter, but it tells us something significant about the way Tocqueville thought: democracy is not a machine for creating gods.[52] One of its serious perversions was to mistake itself for such a machine.

The Enigma of Man

At various points in his life Tocqueville insisted on yet another limitation of man, the third in our series, namely, that man can neither understand himself nor know himself. "What a chimera is man?" Pascal's formula recurs in various forms. In 1843 Tocqueville wrote to his friend Eugène Stöffels: "What misery is the lot of man, plunged as he is into irremediable ignorance of all things that he knows himself no better than the most remote of objects and sees the depths of his soul no more clearly than the center of the earth!"[53]

Man's inability to understand himself led Tocqueville to indulge in a truly Pascalian reflection in his chapter on poetry in democracy and related manuscripts. These are worth reading closely because they provide the key to the "esoteric" side of Tocqueville the moralist (using "esoteric" in Leo Strauss's sense).

In the manuscripts Tocqueville twice broaches the subject of human impotence. In his first formulation he touches on the idea of human misery, which later found its way into the letter to Stöffels quoted above: "Thus, man ignores even the main motives of his own actions, and when, tired of searching throughout the universe for the truth, he turns inward, the darkness thickens as he looks within and seeks to know himself."[54]

His second draft is more pathetic in tone and style. This time, the main point is delayed until the end of the first sentence and, in a style that "sounds Pascalian," is set forth in a cascade of three clauses with the same subject, "he," which heightens the contrast between the finitude of man and the

[52] I am alluding to Bergson, who wrote that "the universe is a machine for creating gods." See Henri Bergson, *Les Deux sources de la morale et de la religion* (Paris: PUF, 1998), chap. 4.

[53] Tocqueville, *Lettres choisies. Souvenirs*, p. 524. Compare Pascal on the union of soul and body: "Man is in his own eyes the most prodigious object of nature" (*pensée* 199, p. 528, Br. 72). Note that Eugène and Charles Stöffels were brothers and both friends of Tocqueville. The unpublished correspondence shows that Charles was the recipient of advice and criticism of all sorts owing to his lifestyle and philosophy, of which Tocqueville strongly disapproved. Tocqueville's friendship with both proved lasting: Eugène died in 1852, while Charles outlived Tocqueville by twenty-seven years, dying in 1886.

[54] Nolla II, p. 77, n. v.

immensity of the questions he faces: "And when, tired of looking for what causes his fellow men to act, he seeks instead to discern what drives himself, he still has no idea what to think. He searches the world over, and still he doubts. Ultimately he turns inward, and the darkness thickens as he seeks to know himself." This is reminiscent of Pascal's fragment on man's distraction, in which he wrote: "They do not know . . . they imagine . . . they think they are searching. . . . They have a secret instinct."[55] The anxious actions of human beings are juxtaposed to drive home the criticism. In the published text, however, Tocqueville opted for a different presentation. Although still fully Pascalian—it speaks of the "hidden God" and of veiled spiritual realities—it is directly applicable to language (to the arts and poetry).[56] What is man? His nature is irremediably hidden from himself, yet he can glimpse certain glimmers from within: "If man knew absolutely nothing about himself, he would not be poetic. . . . Man is sufficiently exposed, however, to see something of himself, yet sufficiently veiled that the rest remains shrouded in impenetrable darkness, into which he makes repeated forays in the vain hope of understanding himself fully."[57]

From the end of the passage we see that Tocqueville retained the idea of self-knowledge, but he has now replaced the original presentation with the dialectic of the visible and the hidden, which Pascal developed at several points in the *Pensées*. Once again, Tocqueville has rearranged Pascal's text, transposing to the situation of man what Pascal understood in terms of man's knowledge of God: "There is enough light for those whose only desire is to see, and enough obscurity for those who are of the opposite disposition."[58] According to Tocqueville, man is "sufficiently exposed" to have some idea of himself and to represent himself in plastic or verbal art, but he is also "sufficiently veiled" that his real being eludes him. This vision of the world leads Tocqueville to the concept of "figurations," which was central to Jansenism: here we have the "figures" of human history and of democracy itself, which can *signify* more than the world of material pleasures in which it is mired. We thus encounter the Tocquevillean idea of a duality that cannot be transcended.

---

[55] *Pensée* 136, p. 517, Br. 139.

[56] I will return later to the question of "Deus absconditus," the phrase engraved on the seal of Port-Royal. This refers to a hidden God and not a remote or absent one, as some have claimed. According to this interpretation, which is not universally accepted, God is actually close.

[57] *DA* II.1.17, pp. 96–97; AG, p. 559. In 1840 Tocqueville described himself in the following terms: "This anxious and unstable soul, which despises all the goods of this world yet strives constantly to have them," in order to flee a "painful numbness" that emerges whenever he stops. *OC* XIV, p. 214.

[58] Pascal, *pensée* 149, p. 521, Br. 430.

Tocqueville as Thinker of Duality

As we have seen, Tocqueville consistently maintained the duality of soul and body, which for him represented two very different sources of satisfaction. "Democracy" takes pleasure in material goods, which feed or comfort the body: "There, the desire for wealth at any price, the taste for business, the love of profit, the pursuit of well-being and material pleasures are ... the most common passions." As noted previously, Tocqueville repeated this point twenty years later under Bonapartist rule because "it is the essence of despotism to encourage and extend" material gratifications.[59] Despotism is a natural product of democracy because it knows how to make use of material pleasures. In *The Ancien Régime* Tocqueville discusses "the sort of passion for well-being that is the mother of servitude, as it were, that allows proper manners (*honnêteté*) and prohibits heroism, and that excels at making well-behaved men and cowardly citizens."[60] We find the same tone in certain passages of *Democracy in America*: the "cowardly love of present pleasures" makes *l'honnête* morally intolerable in Tocqueville's eyes.

The duality of body and soul gives rise to a form of *l'honnête* that ultimately results in a compromise with moral corruption. Once again, the theme is Pascalian.[61] In offering advice to a young aristocrat (possibly the duc de Chevreuse), Pascal explained that a person in this "estate" could in any case give satisfaction to those around him, but that satisfaction remained sinful: "These people are full of concupiscence. What they want from you are the goods of concupiscence. It is concupiscence that ties them to you. You are therefore strictly speaking a king of concupiscence." A king of concupiscence can moderate the demands made on him and justly discharge his social obligations: "The path I am showing you is no doubt more honorable (*honnête*), but in truth it is always a great folly to damn oneself."[62]

We can now see how Tocqueville used the dualism of spiritual and material goods (corresponding to the dualism of soul and body) once again to transpose the issues: servitude, "disciplined men" versus "cowardly citizens," *l'honnête* versus heroism—these were realities of the world of concupiscence in the Christian sense.[63] To put it another way, in the spirit of Saint Paul,

---

[59] Preface to *ARR*, *OC* II-1, p. 74.

[60] Ibid., p. 175.

[61] Pascalian rather than Jansenist, because Domat and Nicole to a large extent rehabilitate calculations of *l'honnête*.

[62] Pascal, *Trois discours sur la condition des grands*, in Pascal, *Œuvres complètes*, Lafuma ed., p. 368.

[63] There can be no doubt that the Christian heritage itself reassimilated the Socratic conception of the value of the just and wise life. The same is true for the preference accorded to moral values over material goods. Tocqueville thus contributed to the formulation of a modern humanism that combined

this was to be both in the world and "of" the world. After the passage cited above, Tocqueville described the mixture of motives that one is likely to find in a society of well-being: the taste for material pleasures "often combines with a kind of religious morality. People want to be as well off as possible in this world without renouncing their chances in the next."[64] Here we sense the disapproving, mocking tone of the moralist.

As aware as he was of man's duality, Tocqueville was himself divided on the best advice to give to democracy. His attitude toward the economy was typical. Like Villeneuve-Bargemont, whom he knew and read, he favored a Christian political economy but had difficulty defining exactly what this meant.[65] Here I will confine myself to mentioning what he wrote to Kergorlay in 1834, when there was discussion of the possibility of founding a journal (along with Beaumont): "Although political economy today strikes me as materialistic in all its efforts, I would like the journal to emphasize the more immaterial aspects of this science; I would like it to bring in ideas and feelings of morality as elements of prosperity and happiness; and I would like it to try to rehabilitate spiritualism in politics and to make spiritualism popular by driving home its utility."[66]

"Spiritualism in politics" was an idea that Tocqueville might have found in the works of any number of his contemporaries,[67] but in his eyes it constituted a response to the fundamental dualism of the human condition. In democracy it acquired an essential role because "the passion for material well-being is essentially a middle-class passion."[68] Here we see how working in the moralist vein allowed Tocqueville the man to hold on to "the thought in the back of his mind." The observations of the sociologist, political scientist, and writer were inspired by his *spiritualist need*, which he sought to propagate in various ways, some transparent, others less so. The term "spiritualism" recurs throughout the chapters concerned with "material pleasures." For instance, Tocqueville wrote that "it is particularly important to make sure that

---

Socraticism, Stoicism, and Christianity. See, for example, E. Burty, *Littérature et politesse. L'invention de l'honnête homme, 1580–1750* (Paris: Presses Universitaires de France, 1996), chaps. 4 and 5. In any case, it is clear why Tocqueville often said that he enjoyed reading Plato.

[64] *DA* II.2.11, p. 166; AG, p. 621.

[65] In 1848 Tocqueville was critical of the socialists for considering only material satisfactions. Of course the work of writers such as Pierre Leroux and Pecqueur refutes this idea because their political ideas were steeped in religiosity.

[66] Tocqueville, *OC* XIII-1, pp. 361–62.

[67] Including, among others, the liberal Catholics, Lamartine's "social party," a good many legitimists, and Victor Cousin and economists who embraced his philosophy.

[68] *DA* II.1.10, p. 162; AG, p. 618. See part 1.

spiritualist opinions prevail in democratic times."[69] Yet in these same chapters he prefers to quote Socrates and Plato, and it is easy to see why: he did not wish to tie himself too closely to Christianity or to appear to lend his support to the Catholics of *L'Avenir*.[70] He also wished to "uplift souls" and "keep them intent on heaven." Earlier I compared this passage to Robespierre.[71] A democratic lawmaker, Tocqueville argued, ought to be a spiritualist: "Lawmakers in democracies and all decent and enlightened men" should devote themselves to the task of uplifting souls.

Thus the moralist ceded to democracy but sought to lead it to the heights, to satisfy the body while thinking of the soul. This abiding passion tells us something about the inner tensions of Tocqueville's politics, ever mindful of dualism yet for that very reason uneasy about achieving a synthesis, a reconciliation of body and soul. Between Saint Jerome and Heliogabalus Tocqueville therefore envisioned self-interest properly understood. We turn next to a reexamination of this concept in the light of Jansenism.

A Poison as Antidote: The Society of Amours-Propres, or, from Domat to Tocqueville

The whole issue of man's dual nature spurred Tocqueville's interest in the thinking of certain Jansenists who saw society as a device for reconciling the amour-propre of different individuals. Although Pascal explored this issue to some extent, Pierre Nicole and Jean Domat went further. Paradoxically, this idea of society served to legitimate the capitalist market economy. Pascal admired the way in which corrupted human nature could still attest to the possibility of grandeur, or to the memory of grandeur: men make laws and establish a *social code* of reciprocal services. Even if this is merely a "tableau of charity"—a mere image of true love of one's neighbor—it nevertheless possesses a certain force: "Grandeur of man in his very concupiscence, to have been able to derive an admirable regulation from this and to have created a tableau of charity."[72]

---

[69] *DA* II.1.15, p. 183; AG, p. 637.

[70] It is interesting to read the letter of 1832, in which Kergorlay explained to Tocqueville his view of the young liberal Catholics of *Le Correspondant*, such as Louis de Carné, who were much more moderate than those of *L'Avenir*, while at the same time arguing that there should be no alliance with them, despite the esteem they deserved. Tocqueville seems to have agreed with this. See Tocqueville, *OC* XIII-1, p. 257.

[71] *DA* II.1.15, p. 181; AG, p. 635.

[72] Pascal, *pensée* 118, p. 513, Br. 402. See Gérard Ferreyrolles, *Pascal et la raison du politique* (Paris: Presses Universitaires de France, 1984), pp. 131–45, and "Politique et dialectique dans les *Pensées* de Pascal," *Le Nouveau Commerce*, no. 79–80 (Spring 1991); see also "Pascal," in *Dictionnaire des œuvres politiques* (Paris: Presses Universitaires de France, 1986), p. 866.

In Pascal's terms, this is the "reason of effects": human duality is used to explain the admirable social order that one observes. Pascal's friend, the jurist Domat, developed this point brilliantly in his *Traité des lois*: "From amour-propre, which is society's poison, God has made a remedy, which helps to maintain it."[73] Tocqueville also employed this image of using the poison of amour-propre as its own antidote: a blessing in disguise. Had he read Domat? Perhaps, because prospective magistrates often studied Domat's work. Yet when Tocqueville told Corcelle of his immense admiration for *Le Traité*, he said that he was reading it for the first time rather late in life.[74] Nevertheless, in Tocqueville's text *equality* occupies the place of amour-propre in Domat's. This will come as no surprise since we have already seen that in democratic man's breakneck race, equality is both a subjective passion (the hunt) and an elusive object (the quarry). Toward the end of the second volume, Tocqueville returns to this inherent duality in equality and offers his most profound interpretation: equality leads in two directions, toward either anarchy or servitude. Yet equality can also ennoble man through his "taste for free institutions." This section of the book ends, however, with the threat of "mild despotism," which endangers all democracy. Thus the antidote in the poison exists but offers only a relative protection or cure: "I admire equality when I see it deposit an obscure notion of, and instinctive penchant for, political independence in every man's heart and mind, thereby preparing the remedy for the ill that it provokes. It is this aspect of equality that I hold dear."[75]

This is the same point that Domat made, and which I quoted above: "From amour-propre, which is society's poison, rather than mutual love, God has made a remedy, which helps to maintain it." What Domat called the "principle of division" becomes an instrument of union and organization (especially in the law) as well as exchange. Tocqueville was in fact *a theorist of the society of amours-propres*. We are now in a position to grasp his concept of democracy, with all the inner resonances it had for him: democracy meant society after the Fall, but expressed in secular terms.

There are even more striking parallels between Tocqueville and Nicole's treatise *De la charité et de l'amour-propre*.[76] From the outset Nicole proposes

---

[73] Domat, *Les Lois civiles dans leur ordre naturel*, 2nd ed. (Paris: Jean-Baptiste Coignard, 1685), containing in vol. 1 *Le Traité des lois*, p. xxxix: marginal title. Here I quote from chap. 9 of *Le Traité*: "On the state of society after the fall of man, and how God maintains it."

[74] Tocqueville, *OC* XV-2, p. 72. In 1843 Victor Cousin drew attention to Domat's work as a moralist in "Documents inédits sur Domat," which appeared in *La Revue des deux mondes* and was included in his *Jacqueline Pascal* (1845).

[75] *DA* II.4.1, p. 354; AG, p. 788.

[76] I use the term "parallels" advisedly: I have no evidence that Tocqueville ever referred to Nicole's work. When his contemporaries referred to Nicole, moreover, they did not call attention to the fact. For

to show the good effect of "enlightened amour-propre" and to reinterpret the crucial notion of *honnêteté*.[77] Nicole's characterization of amour-propre was in fact shared by all Jansenist-influenced writers: amour-propre lurks in the depths of the human heart ("Such is the monster that lurks within our bosom"), where one can analyze its intrinsic "properties" before studying its various guises in civility and *honnêteté*:

> These intrinsic properties are that corrupt man not only loves himself but loves himself without limit or measure, that he loves only himself, and that he relates everything to himself. He desires all sorts of goods, honors, and pleasures for himself, and he desires them only for himself or in relation to himself. He makes himself the center of everything. He would like to dominate everything and would like it if all creatures were occupied solely with making him happy, praising him, and admiring him. Since this tyrannical disposition is stamped on every man's heart, it makes man violent, unjust, cruel, ambitious, obsequious, envious, insolent, and quarrelsome.[78]

Yet the same brutal amour-propre becomes marvelously supple through intelligent calculation, or, as Helvétius and later Tocqueville would put it, through self-interest properly understood: "One gives in order to get. This is the source and foundation of all human commerce, which takes a thousand diverse forms. Because man does not simply trade merchandise for other merchandise or cash; he also trades works, services, attention, and civilities. . . . Thus through commerce all of life's needs are somehow met without the involvement of charity."[79]

The remedy is therefore appropriate to the reality of the disease: society as it is shows how to *convert* the primordial violence of desire into patience, self-interested prudence, and embellishments. Tocqueville wrote that the doctrine of self-interest properly understood was "marvelously tolerant of human weakness" and that "it turns personal interest against itself and uses the spurs that excite the passions as a means of guiding them."[80] This could hardly be closer to Nicole's thinking and to the Jansenist conception of

example, Jean-Denis Lanjuinais, the father of Tocqueville's friend, wrote a note on Nicole, published in J.-D. Lanjuinais, *Œuvres* (Paris: Dudey-Dupré, 1832), 3:639–50. It is striking that even Sainte-Beuve, in the chapter of *Port-Royal* devoted to Nicole (chap. 7 of book 5), avoided talking about the essays on sociable and cunning amour-propre. He called Nicole "a Christian Bayle, a Jansenist Bayle." See La Pléiade, 2:879.

[77] See Nicole, *Essais de morale*, ed. Laurent Thirouin (Paris: Presses Universitaires de France, 1999), p. 381.

[78] Nicole, *De la charité et de l'amour-propre*, p. 382.

[79] Ibid., p. 384.

[80] *DA* II.2.8, p. 155; AG, p. 612.

l'honnête. At the very least it is a reinvention of Nicole by Tocqueville based on his Pascalian reflections on the "tableau of charity" of which "concupiscence" is capable. It is also possible that the Jansenist source was reinforced by the inspiration that Hume, who was widely read in Tocqueville's time, drew from it. The remark about "turning personal interest against itself" is explicit in Hume.[81]

Tocqueville wrote that "when the public governs," everyone courts the esteem and goodwill of others. When "pride dissimulates, contempt does not rear its head. Egoism is afraid of itself."[82]

At times Tocqueville follows the path that Nicole recommends at the beginning of his treatise on charity and amour-propre, to plumb the depths of the human heart, "to consider in its lair and basic inclinations" the monster we bear within us.[83] What this yielded for Tocqueville was the following: "And if we plumb the depths of our hearts, won't we all be frightened to discover what envy makes us feel about our neighbors, friends, and relatives? We are not jealous of these people because they are neighbors, friends, and relatives but because they are our likes and equals."[84]

Thus it is envy, as the passion for equality with one's "likes" (*semblables*), that moves the human heart. This is obvious in "democracy," but Tocqueville adds that it is in fact "a truth in all ages and applicable to all men." "Likeness" is here understood not as it ought to be in the Christian sense (identity and fraternity of the children of God, members of the same body in Christ, all descendants of Adam) but rather in the sense of the society of amours-propres.[85] The "like" is a person who must respond to the tyrannical demand that the egoistic individual addresses to him and who is interesting only in that respect. He is of interest to the extent that he can *resemble* his interlocutor, not in spirit or truth but by virtue of what he possesses.

In regard to this very self-interested concern in the "like," witness the marvelous duality and duplicity of the vocabulary: Tocqueville plays on the

---

[81] For example, see David Hume, *A Treatise of Human Nature*, sec. 2: "There is no passion, therefore, capable of controlling the interested affection, but the very affection itself, by an alteration of its direction." Tocqueville owned several of Hume's philosophical essays.

[82] *DA* II.2.4, p. 132; AG, p. 590.

[83] Nicole, *De la charité*, p. 381. Like Nicole, Tocqueville recommends scrutinizing the human heart, yet he also agrees with Nicole that knowledge of oneself and one's motives is inaccessible. Indeed, this tension is characteristic of Jansenist Augustinianism. La Rochefoucauld, Domat, and Nicole all describe the heart as omnipotent and alien to reason. See below the letter to Charles Stöffels from the unpublished correspondence.

[84] Nolla II, p. 244, n. d.

[85] For further analysis of this question (the "like" and its equivocal uses in *Democracy in America*), see Lucien Jaume, "Le 'cœur démocratique' selon Tocqueville," *La Revue Tocqueville*, bicentennial of Tocqueville's birth, 27, 2 (2006): 35–44.

notion of likeness (my spiritual brother and/or my narcissistic reflection), much as interest—etymologically, "that which is between us"—can be either a gift of attention devoted to others or the profit in view of which I consider the other. Such are the linguistic resources of amour-propre.

Tocqueville is therefore Jansenist in the specific sense that "if we plumb the depths of our heart," we will find evil. The same personal vision led him to write this Pascalian fragment: "Egoism, vice of the heart. Individualism, of the mind."[86] Yet we know that there are two kinds of individualism: one that is subsumed by egoism, and another that is open to friendship, affection, and a collective existence. "Drawing from concupiscence, we have established admirable rules of order, morality, and justice."[87] In Tocqueville's mind, this Pascalian aphorism perfectly captured what he had witnessed in America, including the generalized hypocrisy in religion of which he wrote to correspondents early in his journey.[88] Similarly, Tocqueville *projected* onto his idea of self-interest properly understood what he took from Pascal's three orders, or, to put it another way, the difference between the people, the quasi-clever, and the wise:

> A little learning reveals to men how their personal interest differs from that of their fellow men. A great deal of learning shows them how the two interests frequently coincide. Three successive states:
>
> 1. Ignorance—instinctive self-sacrifice
> 2. Semi-science. Egoism.
> 3. Complete enlightenment. Reflective sacrifice.[89]

It was undoubtedly in this sense—Christian moralism as propadeutic to the journey, as it were—that Tocqueville was able to say upon landing in America that *it was man's metaphysical condition that interested him*. In a letter to Ernest de Chabrol, written in November 1831, he said this: "The more I study this country and everything else, and the longer I live, the more terrified I am to discover how little certainty man is in a position to acquire in this world."[90] The comparison might seem incongruous, but it isn't, because

---

[86] Quoted in Nolla I, p. lxxi, n. 257.

[87] Pascal, *pensée* 211, p. 529, Br. 453.

[88] To Kergorlay he preferred to say that it was a sort of insurance against all risks: "People adhere to a religion here as our fathers took medicine in the month of May: 'Even if it does no good,' they seem to say, 'at least it does no harm.'" See *OC* XIII-1, p. 228.

[89] Nolla II, p. 114. See also Mélonio, *Tocqueville et les Français*, p. 93. Pascal also wrote that there are three categories of human beings: according to the flesh, the spirit, or the will. The "carnal are the rich, the kings; their object is the body." The "curious and learned" have the spirit for their object. The wise men have "justice for their object." *Pensée* 933, p. 624, Br. 460. Here, the rich take the place of the people.

[90] Quoted in Nolla II, p. 77, n. v.

the questions that Tocqueville had been asking for ten years[91] were questions that had disturbed him as a young man and that he wished to reconsider by exploring the mores of a foreign country. Ultimately, for Tocqueville, the question of *l'honnête* was complementary to the question of authority, whose importance to the political thinker we saw in part 1 and to the sociologist in part 2. His personal uncertainty stemmed from wondering how much of his upbringing he could continue to accept in the wake of his adolescent crisis and continued anxiety about religion. Both questions—that of *l'honnête* and that of authority—were embodied in a single figure, that of Tocqueville's father Count Hervé. After writing to Corcelle about his recently deceased father,[92] Tocqueville said that all his qualities as a writer stemmed from his education: *The Ancien Régime and the Revolution* appeared ten days after his father's death, and this coincidence made the confession easier.[93] The dialogue with his father through the book and now impossible—a dialogue about a subject that preoccupied them both, namely, the history of their class—led Tocqueville to pour his heart out to his friend. When Corcelle congratulated him on his book, Tocqueville replied that the credit should be bestowed elsewhere: "If I am worth anything at all, I am indebted above all to my upbringing, to those examples of honesty, simplicity, and honor that I found around me upon coming into to the world and as I progressed through life. To my parents I owe far more than my existence."[94]

Spiritual Authority and the Double Aspiration

We are now in a position to examine the extent to which Tocqueville's goal of spiritualizing what he called "democracy" was related to the previous

[91] Another famous statement, which François Furet called credible but enigmatic, can be found in an 1834 letter from Tocqueville to his cousin Camille d'Orglandes: "It was ten years ago that I conceived most of the ideas that I have just expressed to you." That would mean that Tocqueville asked himself many questions when he was nineteen, well before his journey to America in 1831. For a long time this letter was incorrectly attributed to the correspondence with Kergorlay, where one finds it in *OC* XIII-1, pp. 373–75. The correction is due to the editors of *Lettres choisies. Souvenirs*, p. 309. I will return to the question of "ten years" in part 5, when I discuss family relations.

[92] Letter dated June 18, 1856. Tocqueville explained that his father was the living image of a wise attitude toward religion.

[93] Recall that Hervé de Tocqueville was also a historian of the Ancien Régime. The unpublished correspondence shows that Tocqueville tried to delay the publication of his book because he was worried about his father's health.

[94] Tocqueville, *OC*, XV-2, p. 164. Note that, to judge by what he says to his correspondents, Tocqueville, while writing his book, was engaged in criticism of the Ancien Régime that he had not anticipated. This only heightened the relation/distance he felt with respect to his father, which forms the basis of another, equally powerful duality (see part 5 below).

question about new forms of authority. To ennoble democracy, "to raise souls up toward heaven," was to attempt to breathe another kind of aspiration into a society based on majority rule and immediate material gratification. This brought democracy's fundamental duality into focus: was it a *fact* or an *end* (*telos*)? As fact, it had a tendency to end in despotism in one form or another, collective or personified. As a moral end, leaders were obliged constantly to measure it against the competing ideals of liberty and grandeur. Once again we turn to Pascal: "The nature of man can be considered in two ways: according to its end, and then man is grand and incomparable; or according to the multitude . . . and then man is abject and vile."[95] By virtue of the "thought in the back of his mind," Tocqueville the moralist rejected the naïve utilitarianism of modern society because he could not stop himself from hoping that leaders, at least, would aspire to greatness. What Pascal called "contrarieties"[96] informed Tocqueville's thinking about man, democracy, and himself. The theme of man as enigma and "chimera" touched him because it was for him a matter of lived experience. It is enough to read his description of himself to Mary Mottley at the time of their marriage to understand how personally he took the idea of dualism that he shared with Pascal:

> Who can understand the many trivialities that fill my soul and yet the vast, boundless taste that ever draws it toward greatness? A thousand times I have wished that God had not allowed me to see the wretchedness and limitations of our nature, or that he had shown them to me from on high. But no, I belong to humanity, to the most common and vulgar humanity, and yet I glimpse something above and beyond humanity. In all things I pursue an ideal that recedes constantly. I must have all or nothing, and I struggle daily between the feebleness of my means and the immensity of my desires. There you have the whole of me, the most incomplete and incoherent of all the members of a species that is itself the most incoherent and incomplete of all that have ever been created. . . . The various parts of my being are ill-matched and ill-joined, and I am constitutionally incapable of ever achieving the happiness to which I aspire.[97]

---

[95] Pascal, *pensée* 127, p. 514, Br. 415.

[96] In the Lafuma edition, under "Papiers classés," *contrariétés* are treated in chap. 7, pp. 513ff.

[97] Excerpt from the letter of December 26, 1837, which should be read in its entirety in Tocqueville, *Lettres choisies. Souvenirs*, p. 400, or *OC* XIV, p. 410. He also wrote to Mary in a similar vein in August 1834: "Nothing in me fits together. . . . My strengths and mind put me in the center, my passions and weakness on the extremes." *Lettres choisies. Souvenirs*, p. 305. Among those passions was his attraction to women, which Tocqueville claimed was invincible and from which his wife suffered. To Mme Swetchine, twenty-two years later, he confessed to a "sort of sick sadness that has tormented me from time to time throughout my life." *OC* XV-2, p. 268.

This is one of the moments in which Tocqueville confesses his melancholic and depressive tendencies. There are many others. The experience of writing, the practical business of making texts, had the effect of distancing Tocqueville from these depressive tendencies (which he calls his "spleen"), not only to cultivate abstract thought in order to find (temporary) peace and the pleasure of understanding, but also to shape a vision that was derived from both his reading of the moralists and his observation of America. All in all, he is indeed a romantic figure, who also conducts an analysis of the Romanticism of his time (see part 4 below).[98]

It is remarkable, is it not, that while in America, and barely twenty-six years old, Tocqueville described himself in much the same terms as Saint Paul in a celebrated epistle: "I see the good very clearly yet do wrong every day."[99] What he says here to his friend he would say later to his fiancée, and what he is describing is the experience of a morally and psychologically divided self: "In my own eyes I am a forever insoluble problem. I have a very cool head and a rational, even calculating, mind. Yet at the same time I experience ardent passions that overwhelm but do not convince me, taming my will yet leaving my reason free."

So, while there is a Jansenist basis in Tocqueville's work, though perhaps less apparent than the writing suggests, it began with a very personal experience that Tocqueville nevertheless wanted to see as illuminating the nature of man in general. Rather than follow in the footsteps of René, Lord Byron, or Jocelyn, he chose for his medicine what Raymond Aron called "the limpid, sad prose of *Democracy in America*."[100] Though evocative in many ways, this prose is not as limpid as it might have seemed to a twentieth-century reader.

It is remarkable to discover the degree to which Tocqueville believed that his "existential" situation justified and confirmed his Jansenist-tinged view of humanity. In an unpublished letter to Charles Stöffels, he forcefully insisted that Stöffels's work in philosophy would lead nowhere because man cannot

---

[98] His romantic propensities are clear in a letter written upon his return to Metz, where he revisits the scenes of the passion for Rosalie that he was obliged to repress thirteen years earlier: "I experienced many singular emotions upon visiting places that had once been witnesses to so many passions now spent, so many agitations now calmed. . . . My feeling was not regret for the past but rather an overwhelming sense of the weakness of the human heart, which so quickly lets go of what it believed it held so fast, of the fleeting course of time, of the mutability of man, of his lack of steadfastness, of the void and nothingness of life." Letter to Kergorlay, *OC* XIII-1, pp. 380–81.

[99] Tocqueville to Eugène Stöffels, October 18, 1831, *Lettres choisies. Souvenirs*, p. 238. Saint Paul said: "For what I want to do I do not, but what I hate I do." Romans 7:15. One knows the importance that Ovid's remark acquired: "I see the best and approve of it, I do the worst." See *Metamorphoses*.

[100] Raymond Aron, *Les Étapes de la pensée sociologique* (Paris: Gallimard, 1967), introduction, p. 21. As Raymond Boudon recently pointed out to me, Tocqueville's prose is sometimes also exuberant and gay (on the "wonders of democracy").

know himself: "No matter what you do, you will never penetrate the obscurity of the human heart, and you will never see its depths clearly enough to classify systematically what lurks within. . . . Perhaps no other human being has sought as tenaciously as I have to observe the workings of his own mind and follow all the movements of his own heart."[101] Note the fidelity to the Jansenist vocabulary. "Heart" is used here in the Augustinian sense: "The mind is always the dupe of the heart" (La Rochefoucauld). Or "It is not the mind that acts but the heart that governs" (Domat).

Tocqueville concluded as follows: "I am so totally ignorant of myself that I still cannot clearly make out the secret motives for most of my actions." The problem was not just the burning passions of Tocqueville the man. What he rejected was rational and philosophical analysis of the mind: "I am a fortiori incapable of appreciating with rigorous exactitude the various faculties that make up my soul."[102]

The Key to a Style: Meaning through Images

To ennoble democracy, purify its passions, spiritualize the political profession: clearly Tocqueville had in mind something other than the present "social state," just as, in studying America, he had in mind something other than America.[103]

Ultimately, we are led to ask whether this whole discourse is not in fact an *image* of something else. We must once again ask the question "What did Tocqueville actually mean by 'democracy'?"

One contemporary managed to lift the veil, if I may put it that way. The perspicacity and deep knowledge of Villemain[104] enabled him to propose a

---

[101] Letter dated September 13, 1832, Château de Beaumont-lès-Chartres (the home of Beaumont's father).

[102] To be sure, he conceded thirteen years later to his friend Bouchitté, a noted philosopher, that "the faculty you have to, as you put it, look within yourself and observe the most intimate operations of your mind is one of the rarest and most precious gifts that a man can possess." Letter of October 21, 1855, unpublished.

[103] "I confess that in America I saw more than America. I sought there an image of democracy itself." *DA* I, Intro., p. 69; AG, p. 15.

[104] See esp. his *Cours de littérature française* and his portraits of several Church Fathers in *Nouveaux Mélanges historiques et littéraires*. During the Restoration, along with Guizot and Cousin, Abel Villemain was one of the "princes of youth," and in 1820 reactionaries sought to shut down his courses at the Sorbonne. See the ironic portrait in P. Moreau, *Le Romantisme* (Paris: Del Duca, 1957), pp. 98–100. Tocqueville went easy on Villemain but called him a "pedant twice over" in a letter to a friend. For a fierce portrait of Villemain ("the spirit of a clerk and bureaucrat, the morals of a domestic servant"), see Baudelaire, "L'esprit et le style de M. Villemain," posthumously published in *L'Art romantique*, Baudelaire, *Œuvres complètes*, ed. Y. G. Le Dantec (Paris: La Pléiade, 1951), pp. 1142–59.

hermeneutic reading of *Democracy in America* shortly after its publication. Because of its figurative construction, the text contains several layers of meaning, Villemain argued:

North America is here both a portrait and a symbol. The author uses it, as it were, much as the Church uses sacred history when it treats each narrative of the past as a *figure* [Villemain's italics], an image of the present or future. Applied to political history, this method is ingenious and brilliant. In the end, however, it dazzles and fatigues much as the eyes are fatigued when they try to look at two things at once.[105]

Commenting on this article, Françoise Mélonio wrote that "Tocqueville's discourse, like Pascal's, is figurative. Just as the Old Testament was for Pascal the figure (or type) of the New Testament, America is the figure of our future."[106] In fact, the "figurative" in Pascal has two aspects. The first is the so-called figurist[107] current of Jansenism, which was mainly elaborated at the seminary of Saint-Magloire. The argument was that the future can in fact be deciphered by careful reading of old texts such as the Bible. The second and in this case more important aspect was Pascal's own notion of *a hidden spiritual sense* expressed in perceptible "figures." In Pascal's own lapidary formulation, "Figure implies absence and presence."[108] In fact, the whole argument about "the hidden God" can be understood as a discussion about signs and Pascalian hermeneutics. This reading of Pascal seems lately to have fallen into disfavor, however, although it was approved by the early twentieth-century scholar Jacques Chevalier.[109] Pascal borrows extensively from the doctrine of Saint Paul: invisible things are represented to us via visible things until we can see them directly.[110] Pascal summarizes this idea in a fine passage from the *Pensées*:

[105] Villemain, "De la démocratie en Amérique par Alexis de Tocqueville," *Journal des savants* (May 1840): 263. Reproduced in Françoise Mélonio's doctoral thesis.

[106] Mélonio, *Tocqueville et les Français*, p. 109.

[107] The figurist current is central to Catherine Maire's book, *De la cause de Dieu à la cause de la Nation*. The *parlementaire* Le Paige was its principal animator.

[108] Pascal, *pensée* 265, p. 534, Br. 677. In the Lafuma edition, see chap. 19, "Loi figurative."

[109] See Jacques Chevalier, *Pascal* (Paris: Plon, 1922), pp. 246ff., on "*figuratifs*," which includes references to key texts. Chevalier, whose authority was discredited by his having served as a minister under Pétain, made an important contribution. See also his edition of Pascal, *Œuvres* (Paris: La Pléiade, 1939). Louis Marin's brilliant variations, *Pascal et Port Royal* (Paris: Presses Universitaires de France, 1997), do not convince me, especially when compared with Chevalier's plainspoken sincerity.

[110] Romans 1:20. See letter from Pascal and Jacqueline Pascal to Mme Périer: Lafuma ed., p. 273. Tocqueville admired Bourdaloue for his skill in relating "material images to invisible truths." See his letter to Corcelle of 1854, *OC* XV-2, p. 130. Similarly, his friend the philosopher Bouchitté's book on Poussin enabled him to understand "the immaterial aspect of painting." See Tocqueville's report to the Académie

After the death [of Christ], Saint Paul came to teach men that all things become known through figures, that the kingdom of God consists not in the flesh but in the spirit, that the enemies of men are not the Babylonians but their passions . . . and so on. But because God did not want to reveal these things to this people, who were unworthy of them, yet did want to make them manifest so that they might be believed, foretold the time clearly and sometimes expressed things clearly but in figures, so that those who loved figuring things might dwell on them and those who loved what was figured might see them.[111]

The hidden God is not a remote God[112] but a God who veils a part of his presence: "He hid himself even more by wrapping himself in humanity," that is, by sending Christ.[113] In the same vein, Scripture "has two perfect meanings, the literal and the mystical." And finally, the whole sensible world is matter for interpretation for those who know how to read it: "All things conceal some mystery. All things are veils that conceal God."[114] It is therefore possible, in the pessimistic Pascalian view, to rise somewhat above the pettiness, for the other postulation is in our *capacity*, in the Pascalian sense of man as "capable of God."[115] The condition of man is such that there is "darkness enough" for some to sleep and "light enough" for others to perceive the presence of God. As Pascal wrote to Mme Périer, "We must make use of the place into which we have fallen to recover from our fall."

Tocqueville in many ways shared this idea: given democracy as it was, with its materialistic tendencies, he looked to the telos of democracy and the dignity of man, for "while it is true that a part of the human mind is drawn toward that which is limited, material, and useful, another part is naturally

---

Française, April 13, 1858, for the Prix Bordin, *OC* XVI, p. 310, *Mélanges*. See the letter to Bouchitté, January 8, 1858, in *Lettres choisies. Souvenirs*, p. 1279, in which Tocqueville enumerates a series of theist-type beliefs and expounds on "the destiny of this singular creature that we call man, to whom just enough intelligence is granted to see the wretchedness of his condition and not enough to change it."

[111] Pascal, *pensée* 270, p. 535, Br. 670.

[112] As Catherine Maire wrote of Etemare: "God is not 'hidden,' that is to say, remote, but a flagrant presence, as in the theology of Port Royal, which defined itself in terms of this gap: he is 'veiled,' or immanent but impossible to grasp, even uncertain." See *De la cause de Dieu à la cause de la Nation*, p. 188. Among the eighteenth-century figurists, however, "the distance between figure and meaning evaporated," leaving room for different figures of the people of God, including the Gentlemen of Port-Royal. This was the "historical mystery" that interested Etemare and also had political consequences.

[113] Pascal, fourth letter to Mlle de Roannez, Lafuma ed., p. 267.

[114] Ibid., p. 288. Letter to Mme Périer: "As we have often said to each other, corporeal things are but an image of spiritual things, and God has represented invisible things in visible ones." Lafuma ed., p. 261.

[115] "It is not true that everything reveals God, and it is not true that everything hides God, but it is true that he hides himself from those who try him and reveals himself to those who seek him, because all men are both unworthy of God and *capable of God*." *Pensée* 444, p. 557, Br. 557.

drawn upward to the infinite, the immaterial, and the beautiful."[116] This "democracy" (as Tocqueville conceived it) is an image of the fall but also of the possibility of recovery.[117] It was in this sense that "God led the world through ever greater equality" toward a wholly mysterious end, as Tocqueville wrote in several letters and repeated in his introduction to *Democracy in America*.

How seriously did Tocqueville intend this statement? The question has often been asked. Many readers have taken it to be a mere rhetorical flourish in a writer known for attacking historical fatalism. The key to understanding Tocqueville's thesis (repeated several times elsewhere in his work) is Pascal's thinking about "figures." Democracy carries with it a hidden *meaning*, which few people will be able to decipher, but Tocqueville's reader is expected to be among them.[118]

∞

Yes, North America is both a portrait and a symbol, as Villemain said, and Villemain was a good observer of the Christian culture of his time. For the moralist, North America was a portrait or scenario that gave insight into the problem of the human condition, not least because it had embarked on the adventure of modernity. But as we have seen, the human problem was not really soluble in Tocqueville's eyes: man cannot know himself; he eludes his own grasp in every respect. *Democracy in America* is therefore also an oracle: what the Pythia said at Delphi could be interpreted in many ways, none of which was definitively true.

In private Tocqueville disclosed how he really felt about this point; for instance, to his friend Chabrol in a letter I cited previously from November 1831. Chabrol was a childhood friend, a magistrate and aristocrat like Tocqueville himself, with whom he shared an apartment from 1829 to 1831. Tocqueville confided in him on philosophical matters. On the question of "the misery of man" and the *veils* of this world he struck a deliberately

---

[116]*DA* II.1.9, pp. 50–51; AG, p. 520.

[117]Yet it did not enable Tocqueville the man to regain his faith. He complained bitterly of this in a longer letter to Corcelle in 1850: "If you know any recipe for belief, for God's sake, give it to me. But what can the will do in the face of the mind's freedom? If will could command belief, I would long since have been devout." *OC* XV-2, p. 29.

[118]Compare Rousseau. The device of stating a position while at the same time proposing it as the key to something else has its equivalent in Rousseau in the advent of the "wise legislator," the veritable "scandal" of *The Social Contract*. This exceptional person, this Calvin of the temporal city, seems to call into question the theory of the general will and the sovereignty of the people. If such a guide is necessary, what becomes of the systematic *equality* of all the parties to the social contract and of all the citizens whose opinions are supposed to count in the making of law? The whole perspective and tone of Rousseau's political philosophy changes abruptly. Interpretation becomes necessary. Sovereign people or sublime leader?

Pascalian tone: "The deeper one goes into any subject, the vaster it becomes, and behind every fact and observation lurks a doubt. Everything we possess in this life is like the backdrop at the opera, which prevents you from making out the precise contours of what lies behind it. There are people who are content to live in such perpetual semiobscurity. I find it tiresome and dispiriting."[119]

The image of the opera backdrop, that is, of a veil that suggests what one is supposed to see (especially in the baroque period),[120] is a good one for Tocqueville's own writing. It can apply to both the *subject* of the text ("What is democracy?") and to the artist or artisan who does the writing ("Who is he to say what he says?"). The perspicacious reader must look beyond the letter of the text—as Abel Villemain did. Sainte-Beuve also understood the message (see the appendix to this chapter).

⊙

Let us summarize: the reflection on the misery and grandeur of man is the work of the moralist, which also inspired the political scientist and the sociologist. There is a Tocquevillean "art of writing," as various scholars have recognized.[121] We can now be more precise, however: *this art of writing was Jansenist in spirit.*

It is curious that Louis de Kergorlay, who confirmed for posterity that Tocqueville was a reader of Pascal, maintained that Pascal was not the key to his friend's thought and style. Shortly after saying this, however, he added that Tocqueville "excelled in these beautiful sad touches all the more because of a secret affinity between them and the state of his soul."[122] A chiaroscuro judgment!

---

[119] Quoted in Nolla II, p. 77, note v; GZ, p. 168. The editor is quite right to compare this letter with the text on poetry in democracy (in which Tocqueville was thinking of *Jocelyn ou la chute d'un ange*), which is the passage concerning man as both "sufficiently exposed" and "sufficiently veiled" to remain enigmatic.

[120] See the reflections of Philippe Sellier, *Essais sur l'imaginaire classique* (Paris: Honoré Champion, 2005), p. 299, on baroque writing and its effects of anamorphosis. The spectator sees an aspects of something that assumes a different profile if seen from another point of view.

[121] Cf. Claude Lefort, *Écrire à l'épreuve du politique* (Paris: Calmann-Lévy, 1992), pp. 61–62: Tocqueville "has an extremely distinctive art of writing, which keeps the reader constantly alert, obliges him to maintain a fluid gaze or stream of ideas, and prevents him from clinging to any certain position." This notion comes from Leo Strauss, whose works on the matter, such as *Persecution and the Art of Writing* (1952), deserve close attention. Did Tocqueville write under persecution? No, certainly not. But he did proceed behind a veil, not to say a mask: his message is plurivocal. In his correspondence we see him protest vigorously when his critics reduce his thought to a single thesis, for or against democracy.

[122] Kergorlay, in *OC* XIII-2, p. 361.

CONCLUSION: TOCQUEVILLE AGAINST THEOLOGICAL POLITICS

The time has come to dispel a misunderstanding: Tocqueville was neither devout nor militant. He had no intention of publicly advocating a religious dogma, although he was, as we have seen, in favor of publicly censuring materialism. For those who would like to enlist Tocqueville in the cause of religious revival, a beautiful letter to Kergorlay will set things straight. In it he explains that, from the standpoint of civic virtue, a book like *L'Imitation de Jésus-Christ* is useless and even dangerous:

> I have always believed that there is danger even in the best passions when they become ardent and exclusive. I do not except the religious passion. I would even rank it first, because when pushed to a certain point, it eliminates, more than other passions, everything other than itself and creates, in the name of morality and duty, the most useless and dangerous citizens. I confess that I have always (*in petto*) regarded a book such as *L'Imitation de Jésus-Christ* as supremely immoral if considered as anything other than instruction for a cloistered life.[123]

There is without a doubt a public, civic morality that must not be confused with religious morality: Christianity distinguished the spiritual power from the temporal power, and Tocqueville believed that there was no reason to challenge this settled view. The question of *l'honnête* coincides with the question of civility, that is, with the civic spirit and the values that govern social life. Although Christianity can *accompany* and reinforce *l'honnête*, it cannot replace it. The term occurs later in the same letter:

> It is not *healthy* [Tocqueville's italics] to detach oneself from the earth and from one's interests, affairs, and even pleasures, provided they are *honnêtes* [my italics], as the author [of *L'Imitation*] teaches, and those who live by the light of such a book can scarcely avoid sacrificing the sources of public virtue in exchange for certain private virtues. A certain concern with religious truths short of total absorption in the other world has therefore always seemed to me to be the condition most compatible with human morality in all its forms.

Tocqueville wrote these lines in 1857, toward the end of his life, which only underscores the importance he attached to a worldview that would not create "useless" or "dangerous" citizens. He did not share the sectarian side of Port-Royal, and in this respect he was closer to Nicole than to Pascal. In fact

---

[123] Tocqueville, *OC* XIII-2, p. 328.

he was in a different place altogether, which is why it is better to say that he had "Jansenist leanings" than to call him a Jansenist. In the same period he revealed what he expected of a Christian education in two well-known letters to Mme Swetchine.[124] In his view, it was the job of priests not to support a regime but to teach Christians that they "belong to one of the great human associations, which God surely institutes to make the bonds that attach individuals to one another more visible and palpable, associations that are called peoples and whose territory is called the Fatherland."

These "great human associations" are themselves an *image* of the fraternity of the human race, an image that could not be replaced and materialized by a religious *body*, which, on the pretext of "truth," would negate the specific political character of the nation. To Tocqueville, religious democracy seemed as unpleasant as socialist democracy: he rejected theological politics.

The Jansenist leanings of Tocqueville the man also fostered another idea: namely, that neither God nor democracy can be taken as an idol without sacrificing the dignity of man.

APPENDIX TO CHAPTER NINE: TOCQUEVILLE AND SAINTE-BEUVE, A JANSENIST ENCOUNTER?

The relationship between Tocqueville and Sainte-Beuve has been little studied to date, perhaps because Sainte-Beuve remarked that he had been intrigued by the young aristocrat enthusiastically defending 1789 at Mme Récamier's, in a tone that brooked no reply. As Sainte-Beuve put it: "This type of mind impressed me, I confess, more than it attracted me, and despite friendly overtures, my attitude remained more one of respect than of friendship."[125] It is easy to imagine Ballanche, Chateaubriand, and other habitués of Mme Récamier's salon raising questions about the Revolution that Tocqueville refused to let pass since his own self-image was at stake.

The day after Sainte-Beuve published a review of the first volume of *Democracy in America* in *Le Temps*, Tocqueville offered his friendship. He proposed that the two men meet frequently because "I cannot help thinking that we have many points in common and that a sort of intellectual and moral intimacy might soon come to exist between us if we found the occasion to get to know each other better."[126]

---

[124] See *OC* XV-2, p. 292: the clergy should concern itself with preparing the young, especially young women, for public life. For the meaning of nation and fatherland, see p. 296.

[125] Letter from Sainte-Beuve to Gustave de Beaumont in 1865, quoted in Nolla II, p. lxxvii.

[126] Letter of April 8, 1835, ibid., p. xlii, n. 113. Reproduced in Sainte-Beuve, *Les Nouveaux Lundis* (vol. 10) and *Les Premiers Lundis* (vol. 2). The review is noteworthy for its intelligent synthesis. Sainte-Beuve

What had Tocqueville sensed about Sainte-Beuve? Probably a certain spiritualist interest that both men shared, which included their interest in Pascal, Vinet, and the Augustinian moralists. It is amusing to note that when Sainte-Beuve wrote about the chevalier de Méré in the *Revue des deux mondes* in 1848, he said that it was "ill-mannered" to compare the notion of *l'honnête homme* with self-interest properly understood. In a word, this was "an American way" of going about things because in America a man could be affable at dinner in the evening yet fail to greet you the next day because there was no profit to be had from the encounter.[127]

The most important point, however, is that Sainte-Beuve published the introductory lecture of his Lausanne course on the Jansenists in the *Revue des deux mondes*. It ends with a discussion of the theme of the veil: Sainte-Beuve evoked for his listeners the idea of "veiled poetry," the art form most closely associated with the Jansenists, that is, poetry that leaves "a veiled impression, tacit but profound." He compared this to a "veiled sun" that he had observed over Lake Leman, "an area of reflected light, of authentic but not dazzling light that made its way across the lake, reassuring and consoling my gaze."[128]

There is no need to insist on the evident sympathy, in the primary sense of the term, with the spirit of Tocqueville's writing. As we have seen, Tocqueville saw man as a poetic creature "veiled" from his own gaze by the same veil that hides spiritual realities from view.

Tocqueville read the *Revue des deux mondes*, and he met Sainte-Beuve many times at Mme Récamier's, where passages from *Port-Royal* were often read aloud, along with excerpts from Chateaubriand's *Mémoires d'outre-tombe*.[129] Hence it is possible that there was a certain chemistry between the two. For personal reasons, probably, Sainte-Beuve preferred not to speak of this and contented himself with a few choice observations about Tocqueville, sometimes acidulous, often perspicacious.[130]

---

immediately grasped the importance of the town as the key to Tocqueville's thought and distinguished his work from that of writers he knew well, such as Fiévée, Montlosier, and Bonald.

[127] Sainte-Beuve, "Le chevalier de Méré ou De l'honnête homme au dix-septième siècle," reprinted in *Portraits littéraires*, ed. G. Antoine (Paris: Robert Laffont, 1993), pp. 1173ff. Mitton was the one who confused the *honnête* and the useful, to which Pascal replied that "you hide the Self, but it is always there." See, in *Moralistes du XVIIe siècle*, Damien Mitton, *Pensées sur l'honnêteté*. Sainte-Beuve, in comparing Méré's notion of the *honnête homme* with American mores, remembered his reading of Tocqueville, but it was also a commonplace at the time to say that American manners lacked refinement.

[128] Sainte-Beuve, "Discours préliminaire," delivered November 6, 1837, and published December 15, 1837, *Revue des deux mondes*, 12:689–715, later included in *Port-Royal*, 1:110 of La Pléiade edition.

[129] See above. In part 5 we will look at Tocqueville's relations with Chateaubriand.

[130] Françoise Mélonio gives several savory quotes from Sainte-Beuvre in *Tocqueville et les Français*, pp. 184–85. She concludes, for reasons other than those examined here, that "between the two men, there were differences of doctrine, but both adopted the 'Jansenist' posture and style."

PART FOUR

Tocqueville in Literature

DEMOCRATIC LANGUAGE WITHOUT DECLARED AUTHORITY

> I have studied and meditated upon the style of other writers for quite some time.
>
> —to Charles Stöffels, 1834

> I do not know when people will tire of comparing the democracy of our time with that which bore the same name in Antiquity. . . . For me, it is enough to contemplate the statues that those ancient civilizations left us. I cannot believe that the sculptor who delivered the Apollo Belvedere from marble worked in a democracy.
>
> —Manuscripts of *Democracy in America*, volume 2

TOCQUEVILLE AS ANALYST OF THE POLITICS OF LANGUAGE

There is a real *question* about Tocqueville's style and attitude toward literature. The question concerns both the author's approach to his subject and his stance toward it.

To begin with, he chose an ostensibly simple and transparent style of writing based on "natural" rules allegedly derived from the work of seventeenth- and eighteenth-century authors—authors whom Tocqueville regarded as representatives of an aristocratic society, or, in the case of the eighteenth century, as examples of the best possible confluence of aristocracy and democracy. In his eyes Voltaire was the greatest French writer, followed by Buffon. Applying this canon, which we might call "classical," to the "democracies" of his time, Tocqueville made up his mind to express his views on democracy in a style derived from a different source.[1]

---

[1] His choice was of course consistent with the rule he adopted throughout the work: to consider democracy from the vantage point of that which it had lost and rejected, namely, the world of aristocracy.

In the study of society, moreover, Tocqueville attended closely *to the life of language*. In the first part of volume 2 of *Democracy in America*, he looked at American literature, poetry, theater, historiography, and political oratory.[2] What is noteworthy, if ultimately predictable, about this reflection on democratic language is that it brings us back to the problem of authority. Tocqueville gives us yet another variation on the basic theme around which his entire work was organized: *What authority over language exists in democratic societies?*

One of his recommendations, moreover, was to seek as much inspiration as possible from the works of Antiquity to offset the defects of democratic language, and especially the inability of democratic society to acknowledge a permanent—or, as we might say today, an "authorized"—arbiter or judge. "Everyone who aspires to excel in literature in a democratic nation should feast often on the works of Antiquity. There is no more salutary hygiene," because such works "prop us up where we are most likely to fall," owing to our penchant for turning literature into a pure "industry," a competition for literary prizes and financial enrichment.[3]

Thus Tocqueville's two engagements with the written and oratorical language of democracy—through its ancient sources, on the one hand, and its contemporary uses, on the other—converged. His own style, which he regarded as derived from aristocratic sources,[4] allowed him to critique "democratic" authors and propose possible improvements. I hasten to add that his approach yielded another benefit: it allowed him to call attention to a new form of grandeur, that of man, of human nature at its most abstract, most general, and most worthy of respect. Democratic literature might lack patience, refinement, and elevation, but it was alive to the destiny and universality of mankind, "which is the same everywhere."[5]

Tocqueville adopted the standpoint of "aristocratic" language to judge both France and the United States, and in this same perspective he also

[2] *DA* II.1.9-21. As we shall see, there are a few very important comparative remarks about painting but nothing about music. Tocqueville was exasperated by the music he heard in the United States.

[3] *DA* II.1.15, p. 80; AG, p. 546. Tocqueville is clear that he is referring here to elites. Literature is indispensable to society's "head," but the majority can be satisfied with the study of science, technology, and commerce.

[4] Aristocratic here refers both to ancient authors (Tocqueville regarded Athens and Rome as *aristocratic* republics) and to French writers of the seventeenth and eighteenth centuries.

[5] This formulation—which one also finds in Montesquieu—reflects Tocqueville's belief in the continuity of Stoicism, Christianity, and modern democracy. It occurs frequently in *Democracy in America*, in particular in a number of passages that I comment on: see p. 115, and also p. 282 ("the constitution of man, which is everywhere the same"), as well as the conclusion of *DA* II, concerning "the great bond of humanity, [which] is growing tighter" (p. 400). In the *Traité des devoirs*, Montesquieu wrote: "Man, everywhere reasonable, is neither Roman nor barbarian." See *Œuvres complètes* (Paris: Le Seuil, 1964), p. 182.

suggested that it might be useful to incorporate certain aspects of the ancient world into the modern one. Of course he was far from the only writer at the time to take his inspiration from seventeenth-century and ancient models. The Romantics rejected these classical influences, precipitating the battle of Romanticism. As we saw earlier, however, Tocqueville favored *metanoia*, or the transfer of the aristocratic soul to the new world as a source of discipline and wisdom.[6] Like Hermes "psychopomp," Tocqueville served as a conductor of souls for those who shared his background, to whom he conscientiously submitted his manuscripts for review and for whom he organized readings. He nevertheless believed that democratic literature had suffered from the loss of aesthetic authorities. This was the harsh aspect of his critique. Aristocrats had the habit of command, especially in the *theater*, which was crucial for the understanding of society. "An aristocracy deliberately imposes on dramatic authors certain ways of saying things. It wants to set the tone for how everything is said."[7] It transmits its values, imposes its subjects (princes, heroes, and demigods), and influences staging. By contrast, democracy cannot impose such a social model of good taste because the confused diversity of a nonhierarchical society is reflected on stage by the same "confused mixture of conditions, sentiments, and ideas" that theatergoers are pleased to encounter in everyday life. Hence the "theater becomes more striking, more vulgar, and more true."

As a result, however, judgment is subject to the "whim of each author and each audience," and "no agreement is possible" among the "large number of judges, who, because they have no way of meeting, render their verdicts independently." The formula retains the image of the judges in the parlements of the Ancien Régime. The phrase "because they have no way of meeting" conveys the idea that the locus of literary authority is nonexistent or at best empty.

Tocqueville applied his analysis of the theater to literature as well, but with certain differences. This is interesting because it reveals *the authority of the social* as a collective force upon the languages (i.e., the literary activities) of democracy. But since the public's authority over authors is neither explicit (and therefore responsible) nor identifiable, it is not an authentic authority. Ranging from the simple power to influence to complete despotism, literary authority in democracy does not possess the *visibility* that the aristocracy embraced. As Lémontey put it, "despotism is everywhere and the

---

[6] In the Greek religious vocabulary, *metanoia* meant the regeneration of the soul by way of introspection and reflection on the past.

[7] *DA* II.1.19, p. 103; AG, p. 505. The aristocracy imposes its manner and tone on society as a whole, Tocqueville insisted, because nonaristocrats go to plays shaped by aristocratic tastes.

despot nowhere."[8] Hence literature in a democratic society suffers from both innumerable constraints and a dearth of rules. Society is less protected from the opportunism of authors in search of easy success because there are fewer rules and forms that such authors must respect.

The future member of the Académie Française, who clearly no longer believed in the power of what had once been called "rhetoric,"[9] or in the Académie itself, wrote that "in a democratic people one does not find men who, by virtue of their education, enlightenment, and leisure, are permanently disposed to study the natural laws of language and to enforce respect for those laws by observing them themselves."[10] There can be no doubt that Tocqueville—author, but also sociologist, moralist, and political scientist—at times operated under the illusion that he had revived this vanished function. He believed in "natural laws" of language and as an author tried to respect them, to set an example for others. Yet no *permanent* authority in the matter was likely to survive.

For us, today, one of the most interesting things about Tocqueville is that he believed in this *politics of language,* to which he devoted some of his most brilliant passages. In substance, the ideas he develops were commonplaces of the time, but Tocqueville puts them to work in support of one of his central themes, namely, that the state cannot be the only authority in a democracy; it is quite incapable of any such thing.

In *Democracy in America* Tocqueville poses as a sort of Plato of a "republic of language" aware of the dangers of democracy. This duality—the author's choice of his own style and of democratic language as his subject—is what I wish to focus on for now. To understand what was at stake, it is best to proceed by examining the chapters of volume 2 of *Democracy in America* in the light of contemporary conflicts. To be sure, Tocqueville did not so much re-create the period's debate (including the "battle of *Hernani*" in April 1830 and its aftermath) as he reflected it. Our task will be to examine the *meaning* of his analytic strategy, which at first glance seems quite conservative.

What did Tocqueville the literary stylist aim to achieve? What accounts for the relationship between his material and his treatment of it? Between the profuse and lawless languages of democracy and Tocqueville's disciplined

---

[8]Lémontey was a liberal historian whose *Essai sur l'établissement monarchique de Louis XIV,* which came out in 1818, anticipated a number of the arguments in *The Ancien Régime and the Revolution.* At the end of his essay he explains that jurists and others who served Louis XIV established an authority that was in fact fragile, so that eventually "one found in France despotism everywhere and the despot nowhere." See *Œuvres* de P. E. Lémontey (Paris: Sautelet, 1829), 5:169.

[9]This is a concept that needs defining because its historical meaning has been forgotten.

[10]*DA* II.1.16, p. 87; AG, pp. 551–52.

adherence to classical standards? Was he not proposing himself for the position of expert *authority*? Like Mme de Staël more than thirty years earlier,[11] might not Tocqueville have been seeking to institute or institutionalize literature not as a purely recreational activity but as a form of politics (touching on mores, morality, and social instruction)? In some respects, like Germaine de Staël herself, whose book showed him the way, Tocqueville refused to accept the unruliness of written and spoken language in the democratic era. Yet he also warned against unrealistic optimism in regard to "intellectual power."

Mme de Staël had written that "good taste exerts a genuine political influence"[12] and had hoped to win "enlightened men" over to the republican cause: "This class, once reunited, would form a tribunal of opinion that would distribute blame and praise with some semblance of justice."[13]

Tocqueville always cited Mme de Staël, along with Chateaubriand and a few others, as the principal linguistic reformer of the early nineteenth century. But she was also the person who coined and gave currency to the term "vulgarity" as the antithesis of "enlightened" taste.[14]

Like Tocqueville, moreover, Mme de Staël assumed that adapting to the future (which in her mind meant the republic) depended on continuity with humanist teaching: "It is impossible to be a good student of letters without studying the ancient authors and without acquiring perfect knowledge of the classic works of the Age of Louis XIV."[15] Tocqueville's *metanoia* was quite compatible with what we might call the "modernization of tradition" attempted by Mme de Staël, Fontanes, and Chateaubriand within the republic of letters prior to the Romantic crisis of 1828–30. Tocqueville, standing on the other side of the revolution of 1830, witnessed the triumph of the modernizing party, but he also saw that party splinter into several factions: Romanticism had freed audacious writers to pursue their individual ambitions. In the preface to *Hernani* (January–March 1830), Victor Hugo wrote that "Romanticism ..., all things considered, is ... just *liberalism* in literature.... And before long ... literary liberalism will be no less popular than political liberalism. Liberty in art, liberty in society—those are the twin goals."[16] This was certainly not Tocqueville's view. He defended a much more

---

[11] Germaine de Staël, *De la littérature considérée dans ses rapports avec les institutions sociales*, 1800 (two editions, with important variants and corrections).

[12] Germaine de Staël, *De la littérature*, ed. G. Gengembre and J. Goldzink (Paris: Garnier-Flammarion, 1991), chap. 2: "Du goût, de l'urbanité des mœurs et de leur influence littéraire et politique" (p. 307).

[13] Ibid., p. 319.

[14] Ibid., p. 281, note on vulgarity as a new term, and preface to the second edition, p. 57.

[15] Ibid., p. 57.

[16] Victor Hugo, *Théâtre complet* (Paris: La Pléiade, 1963), 1:1147.

conservative understanding of literature,[17] even though he did not have an answer to the question of how to ensure a "novelty of the traditional." Mme de Staël failed in her attempt, while the second wave of Romanticism, led by Hugo and Lamartine, overreached. Interestingly, Tocqueville refused even to regard them as leaders, as authorities for the new age. His view was that there were no more individual authorities, or at any rate that there would be none in the future age of democracy. The question of *power* in language and literature therefore had to be approached from a different angle, in terms of sociology—but a sociology different from that which we explored in part 2.

This question is not without current interest, because in France, at any rate, the issue of language is an eminently political one. Think, for example, of the debate about the modernization of certain spellings (which figured in a decree issued by Prime Minister Michel Rocard and published in the *Journal officiel*, though never really enforced), or the debate about the feminine form of words such as *auteur* or *professeur* or *sapeur-pompier*. In an amusing article published in *Le Figaro*,[18] Maurice Druon discussed the various names given to the Commissariat Général à la Langue Française created by Georges Pompidou. He expressed astonishment at the title of the "Délégation à la langue française et *aux* langues de France," the new name of the commissariat, and at the fact that its head, one B. Cerquiligni, had identified fifteen languages spoken in metropolitan France. In 1992 France called a halt to a certain evolution in the direction of linguistic coexistence that could be seen in other parts of Europe: Article 2 of the 1958 Constitution stated in no uncertain terms that "the language of the Republic is French." Apparently, in the land of Boileau, Vaugelas, and Grévisse's classic grammar manual *Le Bon usage*, language is a matter of national identity.

---

[17] In private, he called Hugo an "unruly genius" when Hugo was a candidate for the Académie Française in 1839, at the same time as Tocqueville: see letter to Beaumont, *OC* VIII-1, p. 435. Note that Hugo, born in 1802, was of the same generation as Tocqueville, came from the legitimist camp, entered the Académie in the same year (1841), and, compared to Tocqueville, moved more rapidly and markedly to the left. There may have been a certain rivalry between the two men.

[18] "Which language are we using in fact?" *Le Figaro*, November 4, 2002.

Resisting the Democratic Tendencies of Language

TOCQUEVILLE'S ASPIRATION: TO BE A "WRITER"

Tocqueville commented frequently on his own practice of writing, mostly in his correspondence or in conversation with close friends such as Ampère, Kergorlay, Nassau Senior, and, late in life, Charles de Grandmaison. In a long letter to Charles Stöffels dated July 31, 1834, thus shortly before the appearance of the first volume of *Democracy in America*, he developed this theme; Marc Fumaroli has commented on it.[1] Tocqueville praised his friend for wanting "to work on his style," an encouragement that he would have occasion to repeat often, because Stöffels' vague, wordy letters irritated him. In the 1834 letter he recommended the use of "figures" as appropriate as Pascal's comparison of the universe to an "infinite sphere whose circumference is everywhere and center nowhere."[2] Toward the end of his life, when Tocqueville was deeply involved in the writing of *The Ancien Régime and the Revolution* and reading classical authors such as Bourdaloue, Bossuet, and Massillon, he sometimes excused himself, or pretended to excuse himself, for taking such a scrupulous interest in questions of style. If we believe him, one reason for the friendship and respect he felt for Victor Cousin was Cousin's fine style—an appropriate instrument for dealing with the authors about whom Cousin wrote during the Second Empire (including the great female letter writers, the *précieuses*, and the Jansenists). On May 5, 1854, Tocqueville addressed Cousin as "everyone's master in the art of writing."[3] Later he amused himself by sending Cousin an invitation that was a parody of pretentiousness.[4]

---

[1] Marc Fumaroli, *Chateaubriand. Poésie et Terreur* (Paris: De Fallois, 2003).

[2] Fumaroli charitably corrects the inaccurate quote from Pascal: ibid., p. 730. It is amusing that Tocqueville's example of a perfect, clear, and appropriate image is in fact a misquote. Laurence Guellec calls attention to this "strange lapse" in *Tocqueville et les langages de la démocratie* (Paris: Honoré Champion, 2004), p. 313.

[3] Unpublished letter. Cousin had just published in the *Revue des deux mondes* an article on Mme de Sablé, which became the basis of a book.

[4] Unpublished letter dated July 15, 1856: "For God's sake, my dear colleague, do not deceive me this time [about your visit to Tocqueville], because we have invested great hopes in the thought of seeing you received in our home." And earlier: "Since you are a philosopher who travels little and is a master of all

Tocqueville often employed humorous turns of phrase, moreover, and imitated the style of other writers. Two posthumously published texts, *Journey to Lake Oneida* and *Two Weeks in the Wilderness*,[5] should be read as essays in the spirit of Romanticism and romance (i.e., combining the influence of Rousseau and Chateaubriand).[6] Tocqueville made the journey to Lake Oneida in upstate New York in part to *find* the French couple about whom he and his friend Beaumont had dreamed in France since reading the book entitled *Voyage au lac Onéida*, which was in fact plagiarized for various anthologies.[7] Tocqueville thus took a literary exercise as his starting point in the search for a foreign reality, which ultimately sent him back to his own emotional past. Life became literature because this literature had poetically embellished his youthful life: "Behold the strange power of the imagination over the mind of man! To us these wild places, this still and silent lake, these verdant islands did not seem new. On the contrary, we felt that we had returned to a place where we had spent a part of our youth."[8]

Similarly, *Two Weeks in the Wilderness* (meaning, in the forests of America) is a text punctuated by digressions about the human mind in the grip of melancholy turned to joy by the sight of the virgin American forest.[9] Mme de Staël, Victor Hugo, and many other Romantics had of course lauded melancholy as the modern sentiment par excellence.

So much for Tocqueville's desires as a writer.[10] There can be no doubt that for him, literature had to be an occasion for a *meditation* on the fragility of

---

forms of language, I was a little afraid that you might be fobbing me off with words while withholding your person from view."

[5] For English translations of these, see *GZ*.

[6] On the *Voyage au lac Onéida*, see *Œuvres*, La Pléiade, vol. 1, notes for p. 355 given on p. 1359. Evoking the young Frenchman who is the hero of the tale, who flees France after the revolution but is forced to abandon his island in Lake Oneida after the death of his wife, Tocqueville compared him to a dead tree: "He was still standing but no longer alive" (p. 359). This passage paints a sort of picture of the noble save in reverse: the hero leaves civilization, finds happiness in nature, and then returns in wretchedness to society.

[7] As revealed by Françoise Mélonio in La Pléiade edition.

[8] *Œuvres*, La Pléiade, p. 356; GZ, p. 399.

[9] See *Quinze jours dans le désert*, in *Œuvres*, La Pléiade, 1: esp. 392–93. One passage, on pp. 407–8, can be compared with "a night in the wilderness of the New World" in one of the seven versions of Chateaubriand's *Génie du christianisme*. This piece also draws on Rousseau's reverie on the lac de Bienne. Tocqueville also described his impressions of Sicily, which he visited in 1826–27, a highly stylized version of which was published by Beaumont (and can be found in La Pléiade edition, 1:3–28). The style is reminiscent of Chateaubriand (esp. pp 16–17), with the Greek and Latin references that Chateaubriand favored. There is even a political passage describing a proud Sicilian reproaching Naples for its tyranny. Cf. Chateaubriand, *Voyage en Italie*, in *Itinéraire de Paris à Jérusalem* (Paris: Firmin-Didot, 1859), 2:354–55.

[10] Other documents attest to these desires, such as the letter to his wife in which he discusses Walter Scott and Kenilworth Castle, visited by moonlight: see *Lettres choisies. Souvenirs*, p. 293. Or the Persian tale he wrote in his youth, in about 1828, "Conte écrit pour la fête de ma mère," entitled *Fatmé*,

the human condition,[11] or on civilization as a source of material upheaval and pain. For instance, he gives a vivid portrait of the destruction and decadence of the American Indian in *Two Weeks in the Wilderness*. Characteristically, in the *Voyage*, he described the wilderness as doomed and living only by reprieve: "By what peculiar caprice of fate, we wondered, had we ... been brought to witness scenes from the primitive world and discover the still-empty cradle of a great nation? ... In a few years these impenetrable forests will have fallen. The rumble of civilization and industry will disrupt the silence of the Saginaw. The whisper of its waters will no longer be heard echoing in the woods."[12]

He had just heard, and described for his reader, that rumble of civilization in the form of a rifle shot: "It was as if civilization in its advance had let loose a long and terrifying war cry."[13] Before long, "civilization" would prevail along the entire length of the Saginaw River, and the shot echoing in the forest—the sign of two worlds in confrontation—would cease to be a possibility. What is interesting about this passage, which is reminiscent of Chateaubriand's *Mémoires d'outre-tombe*, is Tocqueville's extended reflection on the special beauty of the doomed forest, which leads to a melancholy lament for what was even then passing out of existence.[14]

Tocqueville even offered his own interpretation of American beauty, a beauty compounded of the traveler's ideal and dream. The following important passage will help us to understand what he says about the literature of democratic peoples inclined to favor "the useful" over "the ideal": "It is, I think, this idea of destruction, this nagging thought of imminent and inevitable change, that makes the American wilderness such a unique and touchingly beautiful sight to behold. One takes it in with a pleasure tinged with melancholy. One must admire it, as it were, in haste."[15]

Thus, for the traveler versed in history and sociology, the American wilderness was a *landscape for the soul*. It conveyed a specific meaning to the dreamy

---

ou le bonheur est ici, Archives Saint-Lô, AT 2709. Many pages of the *Souvenirs* fulfill these writerly desires through descriptions of situations and portraits of individuals, often carried off with the verve of a Daumier. For example, Tocqueville gives us the Assembly of 1848, in the spirit of "The Representatives Represented" by Daumier.

[11] The Persian tale cited in the previous note, written when Tocqueville was twenty-three, is a meditation on the illusions of youth.

[12] *Œuvres*, La Pléiade, pp. 408–9; GZ, p. 437.

[13] Civilization? Tocqueville was given to personification of "general ideas" described in abstract terms, as we will see in a moment. In his eyes, this type of figure was characteristic of democratic literature, and he accused himself of giving in to this penchant.

[14] Think of Poe's "Nevermore!" in *The Raven*.

[15] *Œuvres*, La Pléiade, p. 409; GZ, p. 437.

spectator (as suggested by the title of Albert Béguin's book, *The Romantic Soul and Dreams*). "One feels proud to be human, yet at the same time one somehow feels bitter regret that God has granted man so much power over nature. The mind is assailed by contradictory ideas and sentiments, yet no impression is without grandeur, and all leave an indelible trace."

Melancholy, "bitter regret," "ideas" that grip the mind: this, for Tocqueville, was the essence of literature, whose function was to move, to instruct, to elevate—in a word, to disquiet. The reader from an industrial society is thus forewarned of his future by way of this encounter with the world's past (as Chateaubriand might have put it).

But while Chateaubriand in his (real or imagined) peregrinations rediscovered the primitive freedom of natural man,[16] Tocqueville became all the more anxious about *future threats*, as he put it in correspondence from the end of this travels in America, especially in letters to Charles Stöffels and Ernest Chabrol. To the latter he wrote this on November 19, 1831: "I am tormented by a thousand worries about the future."[17]

Tocqueville remarked that American "savagery" was a spectacle not for American writers but for his European contemporaries. This was only partly true, but it shows that even in terms of "style" he looked at the United States not for itself but for Europe. Like Lévi-Strauss, he left Europe to find himself in the "*tristes tropiques*" (*mutatis mutandis*) of the American wilderness and its native inhabitants.

But the choice of a style appropriate to the "landscape of the soul" does not mean that every sort of effusion was permissible.[18] Tocqueville was critical of Chateaubriand on several occasions, especially in private.[19] In several

---

[16] While traveling downstream by canoe, Chateaubriand produced the following commentary: "Primitive freedom, I find you again at last! . . . Here I am as the Lord created me, sovereign over nature, carried in triumph by the waters, with the inhabitants of the rivers for company and the population of the air singing hymns to me, the animals of the land saluting me, and the forests bowing their heads as I pass. Is the immortal seal of our origin engraved on my brow or that of social man?" See "Journal sans date," in *Voyage en Amérique*, book of 1827; from Chateaubriand, *Œuvres choisies* by C. Florisoone, 8th ed. (Paris, Hatier, 1936), p. 260, or from *Œuvres romanesques et voyages* (Paris: La Pléiade, 1969), 1:704. On the relation to the American "wilderness," Chateaubriand wrote: "The soul is glad to plunge in and lose itself in an ocean of eternal forests" (version of *Essai sur les révolutions*, part 2, chap. 57). For Tocqueville, the forests were not "eternal": this was his own stylistic intervention.

[17] As Marc Fumaroli has shown, the *Mémoires d'outre-tombe* would later incorporate the Tocquevillean feeling of anxiety about the future. For a discussion of the relations between the two writers, see part 5 below. The nephew learned from his uncle by marriage (an unpublished 1835 letter confirms this), but later the reverse was true, as Fumaroli shows.

[18] Indeed, Tocqueville's most highly stylized "literary" texts were not published until after his death by his traveling companion Beaumont.

[19] As Antoine Rédier was the first to reveal (before others copied him with errors), Tocqueville at the age of twenty wrote a critique of Chateaubriand in which he reproached him for treating America as a

letters he mocked Chateaubriand's "rage to embellish the truth rather than simply describe it accurately.... M. de Chateaubriand himself described the real wilderness, or at any rate the one with which I am familiar, with false colors" because he neglected "the immensity of nature and ... the ridiculous smallness of man."[20] In this, Tocqueville is quite unfair.

We turn next to the question of what "writing well" meant to Tocqueville, who recommended it to Charles Stöffels but who was nevertheless vexed by the whole question, to judge by his manuscripts.[21]

DEMOCRATIC LANGUAGE AS THE SPUME OF A "PERPETUAL MOTION"

After modestly confessing that his style did not satisfy him, Tocqueville explained in his letter to Stöffels that a writer's style consists in "a certain way of grabbing the reader's attention." Characteristically, he begins by emphasizing his interest in the *reception* of the text. To explain the truth of the writing—a truth to which we have just seen he was attached—Tocqueville emphasized the writer's relation to his audience: an author is a person who writes for others. In his eyes this point was crucial: "There is a quality common to all great writers, which in a sense forms the basis of their style, on which each one then plants his own colors. That quality is quite simply common sense."[22]

What was at stake in this appeal to common sense (which inevitably recalled Descartes)? It was political, in the broad sense of the word, as well as ethical: common sense evoked both the liberal *community* that Tocqueville was searching for and the faculty that each member of that community can consult individually in order to express himself and make judgments of taste.[23] Marc Fumaroli detects the mark of Pascal in *L'Esprit de géométrie*: the natural is what anyone resolved to demonstrate his humility must be able to see. This leads to a proposition that aptly describes Tocqueville's

model for France. This was his response to a paper that his uncle published in the *Journal des débats* on October 24, 1825. Tocqueville spoke of a "misleading resemblance" between the American republic and France, which is amusing if nothing else. As we shall see, Silvestre de Sacy, a literary liberal, writing in the same newspaper fifteen years later, makes the same criticism. Tocqueville was unable to get his article published, and he later marked it "very mediocre." Indeed it was, but it is nevertheless an early sign of the rivalry between the two men. See Rédier, *Comme disait M. de Tocqueville*, pp. 92–93.

[20] Letter to Mme de Circourt, *OC* XVIII, 1983, p. 25, February 14, 1851. Of course Beaumont and Tocqueville, who had absorbed several tics of style from the master of the period, continually corrected their manuscripts to erase any trace of his influence, which was considerable (and in this case, if we take it to mean "attraction exerted against the will of the writer concerned," the term "influence" is truly applicable, even if I try to avoid using it in this book).

[21] Unless expressly indicated otherwise, all references are to *DA* II.1, chaps. 9–21.

[22] Tocqueville, *Lettres choisies. Souvenirs*, p. 302.

[23] Here we see the "individual reason" that the traditionalists feared, as I showed in part 2.

concern with the reader: "The best books are those whose readers believe they could have written them. Nature, which alone is good, is quite familiar and common."[24] The counterpart of this in Tocqueville is always to adopt the reader's point of view. The reader sets the rules. But what is the meaning of this imperative? The voluntarist ethic is intended to manage a powerful tension: on the one hand, Tocqueville urges writers to resist the laxity of democratic standards, to shun the temptation of a bizarre or purple prose in order to escape from the commonness of equality, while on the other hand he insists that the (democratic) reader deserves the closest attention. At bottom, it is a question of the *universality* of language—because Tocqueville believes that words have a true meaning—and the universality of man, whose *reason*, whether crude or cultivated, hesitant or confident, must be respected.[25]

Indeed, it was in speaking of the public in the Age of Louis XIV and what it expected of writers that Tocqueville revealed in passing his own literary ethic: "One is surprised to discover that audiences set great store by plausibility and attach considerable importance to consistency of characterization, so that no character in a play ever does anything that cannot be easily explained and understood."[26] Furthermore, people *read* the plays of Corneille, Racine, and Molière after seeing them, which, according to Tocqueville, was no longer the case in the democratic theater.[27]

The writer who remained consistent and who could always explain what he had written set himself up as his own *examiner* because the right to examine had been invested in the audience. There was an ethic implicit in this view. One is reminded of Adam Smith's idea of the "impartial spectator": one should do nothing that could not be justified to another, whether a physically distinct individual or what Smith called the "inner man." Indeed, the Scottish Enlightenment championed the idea of common sense. In his

---

[24] Pascal, quoted in Fumaroli, *Chateaubriand*, p. 730. The same idea can be found in Fénelon's famous *Lettre à l'Académie*. Fénelon argues that the author should efface himself and should devote all his effort to clarity so that the reader need not work to understand his meaning. "I want a sublime so familiar, so mild, and so simple that anyone might at first be tempted to believe he could have discovered it easily." See Fénelon, *Œuvres*, Jacques Le Brun (Paris: La Pléiade, 1997), 2:1161.

[25] Tocqueville's remarks on Indians are worth considering. The "savage" (cf. *Two Weeks in the Wilderness*) may seem barbaric, base, and repulsive, yet he remains fully human. The idea of a superior race is nowhere to be found in Tocqueville's writing. Compare Alcide d'Orbigny, a great scholar in his day and also an Americanist (who spent eight years in South America), who distinguished himself as both ethnographer and zoologist. See, for example, the brochure published by the Muséum d'Histoire Naturelle, *Alcide d'Orbigny. Du Nouveau Monde . . . au passé du monde* (Paris: Nathan, 2002). Wilhelm von Humboldt, another great traveler in the Andes, also rejected the hierarchy of races.

[26] *DA* II.1.19, pp. 103–4; AG, p. 566.

[27] To be sure, the plays of Anouilh, Giraudoux, Ionesco, and other modern playwrights are read, but Tocqueville was thinking of the Romantic theater of Hugo, Dumas, and others.

celebrated treatise on *The Theory of Moral Sentiments*, Smith wrote: "Whatever judgment we can form . . . must always bear some secret reference, either to what are, or to what, upon a certain condition, would be, or to what, we imagine, ought to be the judgment of others. We endeavor to examine our own conduct as we imagine any other fair and impartial spectator would examine it."[28]

It is easy to understand why Tocqueville spoke of "common sense" in his letter to Stöffels: individual style, *l'homme même* according to Buffon, is not an incommunicable singularity[29] but rather something that enriches the universal through diversity.[30] The letter to Stöffels continued thus: "Study all the writers bequeathed to us by the Age of Louis XIV and Louis XV and the great writers from the beginning of our own era such as Mme de Staël and Chateaubriand, and you will find common sense as the basis of them all."

Indeed, in *De la littérature*, Mme de Staël insisted on common sense as the rule of all written expression. Tocqueville insisted that common sense was difficult to define but suggested that it was a disciplined order of thoughts together with a reduction of the complex to the simple, taking "care to use words in their true sense." "Insofar as possible," he added, one should limit expression to "the narrowest and most certain meaning."[31] On this last point, Tocqueville attacked his contemporaries in biting terms that he would use again in *Democracy in America*. Certain authors were unscrupulous enough to seek facile advantages (of reputation and wealth) with the democratic public: "I know men so clever that if one disputes the meaning of a phrase, they will substitute another on the spot without changing a single word, each word being more or less appropriate to the subject." Such writers—laxists rather than liberals—were not interested in either common sense or the ethics of responsibility: "They may be good diplomats, but they will never be good writers." They were not afraid of insincerity because they were not interested in truth.

---

[28] Adam Smith, *Theory of Moral Sentiments* (London: A. Millar, 1790 [1759]), III.1.2. In later editions, Smith would increasingly insist on the feelings "within a man's own heart."

[29] Most commentators on Buffon's celebrated formula—*le style, c'est l'homme même*—including Tocqueville in this letter understood it to mean not that style expresses the singular individual but rather that it conveys the major features of *human nature*, a point that is often misunderstood today.

[30] "Diversity," a term frequently used by both Chateaubriand and Tocqueville, was a subject that interested them greatly (as it did John Stuart Mill). The question common to all three men was the following: would democracy tolerate the flourishing of diversity, a quality characteristic of the democratic social state at its inception?

[31] This understanding of "common sense" in writing coincides with Fénelon's in his *Lettre à l'Académie*. See the comments by Jacques Le Brun on the notion of common sense in Art, which supposedly come from Father Rapin: Fénelon: *Œuvres*, 2:1727.

For Tocqueville, this summed up much of the problem of democratic literature: by blurring the issue of responsibility (of the author and thus of the
reader), it *encouraged intellectual fraud*.

In chapter II.1.16 ("How American Democracy Has Changed the English
Language"), theoretically devoted to America, Tocqueville strongly attacked
those who "allow the meaning of words to become uncertain" in *French*.[32]
This, he maintained, was a deliberate tactic of writers in search of illicit gain:

> An author begins by slightly bending the original meaning of a known expres-
> sion, and, having altered it in this way, he does his best to adapt it to his sub-
> ject. Another author comes along and bends the meaning in another direction.
> A third takes it down yet another path, and since there is no common arbiter,
> no permanent tribunal that can fix the meaning of the word once and for all, the
> situation remains fluid.

In this remarkable passage, Tocqueville takes the writer to be a sort of
sparrow stealing from the common hoard while lamenting the absence of any
authority capable of *fixing* the meaning of words. I will come back to these
two points—literary authority and the longing for a final state of language—
because they were issues in an important debate in the first half of the nineteenth century.

End of a Sacred Function?

It will be clear by now that Tocqueville regarded writing as a sacred function and the writer as a sort of social magistrate. The antithesis of this was
the literary industry, or the search for the greatest profit at the lowest cost.[33]
The industrial writer is willing to go without *esteem* (we are a long way from
Adam Smith) as long as people buy his books and talk about him: "He does
not need to be admired . . . ; it is enough if people have a taste for his work."
In aristocratic ages, a writer works for *glory*, which means that he looks well
beyond the audience of his own time. In fact, the princely court or at any rate
the noble caste acts as a censor, forcing the writer to work toward an image of
the beautiful that transcends the real, the prosaic, and—to use an image that
Tocqueville had in mind—the bourgeois potboiler.

It is interesting, moreover, to see how Tocqueville thought of himself as
a student of the artisans and master craftsmen who worked for kings and

---

[32] *DA* II.1.16, p. 86; AG, p. 550.

[33] "On the Literary Industry," *DA* II.1.14, p. 77: Democracy "introduces the industrial spirit into the
heart of literature." See also Sainte-Beuve, "De la littérature industrielle," in *Portraits contemporains*, new
ed., vol. 2 (Paris: Michel Lévy, 1869), originally published in the *Revue des deux mondes*, 1839.

aristocratic families.[34] Seeking to produce artifacts of rare quality, these workmen of the past "worked for a limited number of very hard-to-satisfy customers. Their hope of profit depended primarily on the perfection of their workmanship." With the destruction of privileges and guilds, however, the descendants of these talented craftsmen are rarely "given the opportunity to show what they can do. . . . They carefully husband their efforts, settling for shrewd, self-critical mediocrity."[35] This observation reveals the perceptiveness of the Norman squire who was obliged from time to time to restore the chateau.

Just as the modern worker is not called on to do his best,[36] because there is no authority, no arbiter of taste to demand it, and no "repository" of the ideal, so, too, is the democratic writer not called on to transcend himself or to ennoble common sense. On the contrary, he will behave like the thieving sparrow.[37] He will claim his share of singularity, his astonishing or scandalous effects, from the common sense that Tocqueville thought all writers should respect. He will advertise his "variations" on the general theme, which is all his style is capable of achieving. And to do that he will ignore "the true meaning of words" and aim instead for the average reader, just as a hunter will aim at the middle of a flock of birds. The image is Tocqueville's: "As a result, it seems as if writers almost never stick to a single thought but always aim at a group of ideas, leaving it to the reader to judge which one has been hit."[38]

The Unstable World

Since "common sense" in writing is both a community and a faculty, moreover, the author who aims at a group of ideas is also aiming at a public—the real target. What Tocqueville had in mind was the penny press (which began with Émile de Girardin) and popular novels (such as those written by Alexandre Dumas and Victor Hugo). To put the point in the most extreme terms, in democracy the content of what you say does not matter. The important

---

[34] "In What Spirit Americans Cultivate the Arts," *DA* II.1.11. The manuscripts show that Tocqueville was also thinking of other hierarchical societies such as that of India, about which he wrote.

[35] *DA* II.1.11, p. 63; AG, pp. 531–32.

[36] For instance, speaking of watchmakers, Tocqueville says: "Virtually all the watches made nowadays are mediocre, but everybody has one."

[37] Sainte-Beuve spoke of piracy in an amusing article about the writer Töpffer: "Where is the elite public? Where is the enlightened circle? I see only scattered individuals, a boiling foam on waves that can be quite brilliant as they crash against the shore, which is called *language*, and pirates called *men of letters* who haunt the rocks. Sauve-qui-peut in the chaos, and the plunder goes to the daring." *Revue des deux mondes*, March 1841, p. 858, reprinted in *Portraits contemporains*.

[38] *DA* II.1.16, p. 86; AG, p. 550.

thing is to express your point of view, which will soon be followed, as a matter of equality, by someone else's point of view.[39] Furthermore, in democracy everyone wants to do what everyone else does: why would anyone believe in the existence of competence, unequal abilities, or a hierarchy of functions if an ignorant public unjustly rewards those who merely pretend to possess superior skills? To believe Tocqueville, language expresses the mimetic confusion that prevails in society: "When men, no longer bound to their place in society, see and communicate with one another constantly, when castes are abolished and classes are replenished with new recruits and become indistinguishable, all the words of the language get mixed together." Society itself collectively embodies and exacerbates this amour-propre, which Tocqueville, as we have seen, took from the seventeenth-century moralists. Instead of common sense, one has "the hypocrisy of virtue, [which] is common to all ages," but one has even more the "hypocrisy of luxury," which "belongs more particularly to democratic centuries."[40] This is because craftsmen cheat, just as writers do: they strive to endow useful things "with outstanding qualities they do not really possess." Tocqueville mentions fake jewelry, copied paintings, and sham architecture. Literary conduct will follow the same logic: a slapdash copy of some great work of the past will be passed off as an "œuvre." Here we see yet another sign of our author's Jansenist attitude: "In the confusion of classes everyone hopes to appear to be something he is not and goes to great lengths to succeed at this." Today, at the risk of being taken for a hidebound conservative, one might say that the journalist plays at being a professor and the professor at being a journalist, or that an actor plays at being a politician, a philosopher at being a newspaper columnist or sociologist, and so on. Tocqueville could have quoted Beaumarchais: for him, democratic society, like other societies, is a game of masks,[41] but with the added factor that *equality* forbids recourse to a judge external to society. Hence democratic society is particularly fraudulent in the realm of art. It is a

[39] There is an obvious temptation to transpose Tocqueville's fierce portrait, inspired by La Bruyère, to our own times. In this connection, one should reread the chapter of the *Caractères* entitled "On the Court," as well as the end of La Bruyère's acceptance speech at the Académie française, in which he pretends that he did not ask to be a member and therefore claims that he has been recognized for his meditations alone. In today's media society, the tired audience listens with one ear to academics (like the author of these lines) who are invited to say what everyone already knows but which needs to be *signed* by a recognized authority. The content of the message is as thin as the time allowed for the interview is short. Research ceases to mean anything and becomes confirmation, ratification of an "ambulatory" opinion (to borrow Tocqueville's word).

[40] *DA* II.1.11, p. 64; AG, p. 533.

[41] "Democracy is not the source of this sentiment, which is all too natural a product of the human heart." Ibid.

society of petty plagiarism and approximation, and its language is in constant flux: "The perpetual fluidity that is so prominent a feature of democracy is forever reshaping the face of language as well as business."[42]

TOWARD A PLATONISM IN ART

We thus come back to a question that others asked but Tocqueville made specially his own: Did democracy lack an authoritative institution in intellectual matters?[43] If commerce could proceed on its own thanks to the market, could literature develop on its own and correct its errors by way of competition and interaction? Yet we can also ask whether Tocqueville was right in thinking that modern society, for all its liberty and equality, lacked a literary authority.

Tocqueville's anxiety stemmed primarily from his moral and ideological stance: his idea of literature transcended the principle of common sense. What he longed for was the satisfaction of the ideal: in *Democracy in America* he therefore alluded to Raphael. Later he would mention Poussin, in an 1858 letter to Bouchitté about his book on that artist (and Philippe de Champaigne). As we saw earlier, Tocqueville appreciated the fact that "the immaterial aspect of painting [was] superbly represented in the book." In it, he added, "one senses the philosopher as much as the artist, and I have never understood more completely how qualities of mind can produce masterpieces that seem destined to excite our senses alone."[44]

The chapters of volume 2 concerning the arts make it clear that Tocqueville was keenly aware of the absence of a spiritual authority, or even a *spiritualist* authority. He believed that art must show us not simply what is but what ought to be, or what cannot be seen with the body's eyes alone. That is why he later congratulated Cousin on his philosophy of the beautiful, a sort

---

[42] *DA* II.1.16, p. 84; AG, p. 548.

[43] Later we will see that, during the Restoration, this question was explicitly dealt with on the right by the Bonald-Lamennais school at the *Mémorial catholique*.

[44] Letter dated February 14, 1858, unpublished correspondence, passage quoted in Tocqueville, *Mélanges, OC* XVI, p. 310, n. 3. Victor Cousin, in *Du vrai, du beau et du bien* (1853), p. 239, also argued that Poussin "is in a sense the philosopher of painting." This debate continues today. Recall, too, that Bouchitté, a Catholic philosopher and the author of works on Lamennais, theology, and art, had been engaged in dialogue with Tocqueville since youth and that he "heroically" listened to four complete readings of the first volume of *Democracy in America* (see letter of Tocqueville dated January 15, 1835, which accompanied a copy of the book). Their conversations about Poussin and painting are confirmed by other letters, albeit from nearly twenty years after the publication of volume 2. It is nevertheless likely that Tocqueville consulted his friend about the passages on painting.

of modern version of Platonism.[45] In volume 2 he argues that art should not limit itself to description and imitation because there is something immaterial in man that can be made to speak and move only by rejecting empiricism and realism. In a remarkable passage in chapter II.1.11 he asserts a strong belief in the Platonic ideal.

Of course, for Tocqueville, as we have seen, *man is naturally poetic*: this is a consequence of the veil over human existence, to put it in Pascalian terms.[46] He follows the alternation of the *Pensées*, in which the obscurity of sin is compared to the light of grace, but transposes this antithesis into the realm of poetry. Pascal wrote: "If there were no obscurity, man would not be aware of his corruption. If there were no light, man would have no hope of a remedy." Being in-between allowed for progress (Pascal's "thou shalt not search for me," supposedly addressed to man by God), and Tocqueville made this the very condition of art: "If man knew absolutely nothing about himself, he would not be poetic, for no one can portray a thing of which he has no idea. If he saw himself clearly, his imagination would remain idle, having nothing to add to the picture." This is the reason for the earlier reference to Raphael: "I doubt that Raphael produced as elaborate a study of the intricate workings of the human body as do the draftsmen of today." And to David and his school, "as good anatomists as they were painters." But Raphael "aspired to surpass nature. He sought to make of man something superior to man. He undertook to embellish beauty itself."[47]

For Tocqueville, Raphael's mystical character, his ability to work in the in-between realm in which the spirit registers awareness of its incarnation, represented the very essence of the beautiful,[48] but democracy tended not to see

---

[45] Letter dated November 1, 1856, in response to receiving a copy of *Du vrai, du beau et du bien* (6th ed.). Tocqueville, admiring "the second part, which deals with art," indicated that he had read the first edition of the book (1853) as well as previously published studies. Indeed, in 1845 Cousin reread with Janet his celebrated course of 1818 "On absolute ideas of the true, the beautiful, and the good," and he published an article in the *Revue des deux mondes* entitled "Du beau et de l'art" (1845, pp. 773–811). It is possible that Tocqueville was aware of the 1818 lectures when he wrote volume 2, especially since the text was published in 1836 and Cousin, who had become the official philosopher of the July Monarchy, was a celebrity of the day.

[46] "Man is sufficiently exposed, however, to see something of himself, yet sufficiently veiled that the rest remains shrouded in impenetrable darkness." *DA* II.1.17, p. 96; AG, p. 559; Nolla II, p. 77.

[47] *DA* II.1.11, p. 65; AG, p. 534.

[48] The reference to Raphael was commonplace in the nineteenth century and even before. See, for example, Voltaire, "Goût," in *Dictionnaire philosophique*, which refers to Poussin, Claude "Le Lorrain," and Raphael. The idea that Raphael transcended the human was also commonplace. Although Charles Perrault defended the Moderns against Boileau in the famous quarrel of the Ancients and Moderns, he wrote this about Raphael: "Et tout ce que forma l'adresse de sa main / Porte un air noble et grand, qui semble plus qu'humain" (Everything shaped by his talented hand / Bears an air of nobility and grandeur that seems more than human." See *Le Siècle de Louis le Grand* (1687).

this. Democratic institutions (such as schools) and social conditions (mores) influenced what Tocqueville called the "imitative arts" and "commonly discourage portraits of the soul and encourage portraits of the body." These arts, which are useful to democracy, substitute the study of sensations and movements for that of sentiments and ideas. "Finally, in place of the ideal, they put the real." Here a contemporary reader would have heard echoes of a debate about ideal beauty that had been going on since the beginning of the century, in which the ideal was opposed not only to the "real" as an object of imitation but also to "composite beauty" (based on observed reality).[49]

The name of Poussin was often invoked in this debate by way of two dialogues by Fénélon, which placed him in opposition to Parrhasius and Leonardo da Vinci.[50] It seems likely that Tocqueville was simply repeating of Raphael what Fénelon had reportedly said about Poussin: "The arts bring us closer to divinity. They enable us to glimpse a perfection beyond nature, which exists only in our minds."[51] Indeed, in comparing Raphael to David, Tocqueville wrote that only the former "showed us glimpses of divinity." The truth is that all this was fairly conventional at the time; the quotes were expected *topoi*.

◎

All in all, the quoted paragraphs of chapter II.1.11 tell us a great deal about the (conventional) aesthetic that guided Tocqueville in his critical approach to "democracy." "To make of man something superior to man": we are in the orbit of a classical, Christian, and aristocratic aesthetic, which makes the comparison with Chateaubriand inevitable. The superiority of Christian over ancient art, especially in painting, is one of the major themes of *Le Génie du Christianisme*. An admirer of Poussin, Claude, and Raphael, Chateaubriand, who was Tocqueville's uncle by marriage, wrote that "the Christian

[49]See Annie Becq, "Esthétique et politique sous le Consulat et l'Empire: la notion de beau idéal," *Romantisme* 51 (1986): 23–39. One faction defended the idea that beauty resides within the soul and is not derived from sensory experience. Important writers such as Mme de Staël and Chateaubriand (in *Le Génie du christianisme*) took this side of the argument. The "pope of philosophy," Victor Cousin, following Hegel, argued that art was the *expression* of the idea and the ideal. Provocatively, Cousin asserted that "only what is inward is beautiful; there is no beauty but that which is not visible." He pointed to Socrates and to the Apollo Belvedere on which Winckelmann commented maladroitly. See *Des idées absolues de vrai, de beau et de bien* (Paris: Hachette, 1836), p. 257.

[50]See Fénelon, *Dialogues des morts*, for the two texts, as well as the learned commentary by Anne-Marie Lecocq, *La Leçon de peinture du duc de Bourgogne. Fénelon, Poussin et l'enfance perdue* (Paris: Le Passage et New York Editions, 2003).

[51]This apocryphal dictum was attributed to Fénelon, but Tocqueville, as a reader of *Les Natchez*, had surely encountered it. In that book Chateaubriand put these words in Fénelon's mouth. See Fumaroli, *Chateaubriand*, p. 375.

religion, being of a spiritual and mystical nature, provided painting with an *ideal beauty* more perfect and more divine than that to which a material cult gave rise." It was also Chateaubriand who devalued the recourse to anatomy: Christianity "gives more sublime tones to the human figure and makes us more fully aware of the soul in the muscles and ligaments of matter."[52]

THE CONVENTIONS OF "THE NATURAL" ARE NO LONGER GUARANTEED BY AN AUTHORITY

The Question of the Natural Christian from Chateaubriand to Tocqueville

From another point of view, one might say that Tocqueville's aesthetic appealed to a certain idea of "the natural" that exists only thanks to the guardians of taste. This conception of art has been influential in France since Boileau, "the legislator of Parnassus." For Tocqueville, it served to highlight the American difference.[53] Above all, it was useful for diagnosing a specific problem of democracy: "The author and the public corrupt each other." In this way they come to cultivate what Tocqueville called "the bombastic" (*le boursouflé*). He was thinking of French Romantic poets in particular, perhaps anticipating the arrival of Baudelaire's *Fleurs du Mal* or recalling Hugo's praise of the "grotesque" (in the preface to *Cromwell*). "Finding no more material for the ideal in what is real and true, poets give up on truth and reality altogether and create monsters."[54]

But what "natural" did Tocqueville have in mind? Nothing is more protean or harder to grasp than the idea of the natural in art. Rabelais's idea of the natural, typical of the awakening due to the Renaissance, was not the same as Racine's, who portrayed the passions in the sense of Port-Royal. Rousseau's idea of the natural had little to do with that of the so-called naturalist school.

---

[52] Chateaubriand, *Le Génie du christianisme*, part 3, book 1, chap. 3 (Paris: Hachette, 1863), pp. 338–39; or, in La Pléiade edition, *Essai sur les révolutions. Génie du christianisme*, ed. Maurice Regard (Paris: Gallimard, 1978), p. 793.

[53] Tocqueville believed, however, that American literature was still in its infancy, insofar as writers like James Fenimore Cooper and Washington Irving were imitators of Walter Scott, and American poetry had yet to be born. This opinion was quite common at the time. The most influential critic was Philarète Chasles, as René Rémond showed in *Les États-Unis devant l'opinion française*, pp. 302–8. Chasles's views evolved, as evidenced by the various articles he published in the *Revue des deux mondes*. Late in his life, in May 1857, Tocqueville wrote to Mignet that the Americans had overcome "their contempt for letters," leaving room for hope: "It is impossible to imagine anything as petty, as lackluster, as filled with miserable interests, or, in a word, as antipoetic as life in the United States, but among the philosophies that guide it, there has always been one that is full of poetry, and that one is like the hidden fiber that gives strength to all the rest."

[54] *DA* II.1.18, p. 100; AG, p. 562.

And so on. The natural in Tocqueville's sense was applicable in two areas: to the "natural laws" of language and in the realm of spiritualized human nature according to the Christian ideal. Tocqueville, like Chateaubriand, moved constantly from one to the other because, in accordance with seventeenth-century canons of taste, he believed that form and substance are inseparable.[55] The natural that Tocqueville recommended consisted of the union of "common sense," ideal, and form, carefully chiseled but not overly ornate.[56]

Inevitably Tocqueville experienced the tension between nature and the ideal to which Chateaubriand had called attention and explained as an effect of Christianity. Chateaubriand wrote that "only man is capable of being represented as more perfect than nature and as approaching divinity. No one would think of painting the *ideal beauty* of a horse, an eagle, or a lion. Doing so serves as a marvelous proof of the grandeur of our ends and the immortality of the soul."[57]

This, Chateaubriand argued, explained the high aesthetic of knighthood, which combined crude customs with a noble ideal and produced individuals "savage in body and civilized in soul."[58] Knighthood joined the material to the spiritual, creating a "beautiful mixture of *truth* and *fiction*," which Homer was unable to do because polytheism did not incorporate the Christian mystery of immortality and incarnation, the duality of man. For Chateaubriand, it followed that *Jerusalem Delivered* was superior to the *Iliad*: "Although Tasso was in nature in regard to physical objects, he was above nature in regard to moral objects."[59] This comparison was so frequently copied that it, too, became a commonplace.

It is easy to see what united the image of knighthood with that of the age of Louis XIV in the aesthetics of both Chateaubriand and Tocqueville:

[55] E. Tabet, *Chateaubriand et le XVIIe siècle* (Paris: Champion, 2002), pp. 138–43, shows that Chateaubriand rejected the idea that the language of "the classics" (such as Bossuet, for him the preeminent writer) was admirable but that they lacked profundity of substance. Chateaubriand was reacting in particular to Voltaire, whose thesis Mme de Staël would follow in *De la littérature*, part 1, chap. 19.

[56] Tocqueville's conception seems to have been fairly close to Fénelon's. The latter, in his reception speech to the Académie Française, advocated "a disciplined and correct genius, which turns everything into sentiment, which follows nature step by step, always simple and gracious, which brings all thoughts back to the principles of reason and which finds truth only in that which is true." Fénelon rejected the "florid style" of his day, just as Tocqueville would reject the "bombastic" style of his. For a commentary on Fénelon's speech, see Lecocq, *La Leçon de peinture du duc de Bourgogne*, pp. 152ff.

[57] Chateaubriand, *Génie du christianisme*, 2.2.11, p. 226.

[58] Note that the aristocracy of which Tocqueville speaks when he evokes the Ancien Régime or his ancestors (battle of Hastings) is portrayed by Chateaubriand in the nostalgic form that his nephew appreciated. Somewhat later, in an article entitled "La chevalerie" and published in the *Revue des deux mondes* (1838), 13:265–304 and 423–57, Tocqueville's friend Ampère would describe the mores and values of knighthood.

[59] Chateaubriand, *Génie du christianisme*, 2.2.11, p. 226.

Christian virtues were at work in society. Chateaubriand listed them in his discussion of knighthood: loyalty, sincerity, service to the community, honor, and bravery. These were the very terms that Tocqueville used when he spoke of the uneasiness he felt in the world of politics.

⊘⊘

Inevitably Tocqueville felt the tensions that Christianity produced when it invested the world. Inevitably, too, he discovered the tensions that animated the world of letters in the seventeenth and eighteenth centuries. To assign art the mission of rising above nature and of "making of man something superior to man," and to glorify the painter who "embellished beauty itself," implied the existence of *norms*, and that meant conflicts with those who resisted those norms. Tocqueville knew about the dispute concerning *Le Cid* and the debate about taste that was still raging when he was born; he knew about the quarrel of the Ancients and Moderns, the reflections on the sublime, the controversies about the relation between nature and grace, and so forth. In his own time there erupted yet another dispute, about Romanticism, a movement that Tocqueville observed but never explicitly mentioned.[60] How can one possibly understand the question of language and writing in Tocqueville without studying the debates about Romanticism? Few commentators have observed this methodological prerequisite. As André Jardin remarks, "what [Tocqueville] contrasted as aristocratic and democratic literature was, broadly speaking, classicism and romanticism."

Romanticism and the "Dispersion" of Power

Pierre-Simon Ballanche, whom Tocqueville met at Mme Récamier's and who became his friend and colleague at the Académie, caused a stir with his celebrated *Essai sur les institutions sociales*, first published in 1818 and reprinted in 1830 with an important new preface.[61] He argued that the literature of the classic period—which he defined as both a tradition and a normative model—"will soon be nothing but an archeological artifact."[62]

---

[60] Jardin, *Tocqueville*, pp. 246–47, denies that Tocqueville was indifferent to the art of his time, even though he says little about it in his correspondence. Indeed, the chapters on art in vol. 2 of *Democracy in America* contain a sustained if veiled polemic against Romanticism that most commentators have failed to notice.

[61] Citations are to the edition of the "Corpus des œuvres de philosophie en langue française" (Paris: Fayard, 1991). Tocqueville, speaking for the Académie at Ballanche's funeral in 1847, expressed great admiration for him. See Tocqueville, *OC* XVI, pp. 285–87.

[62] Ballanche, p. 74.

To those who still admired Bossuet, he added that "this generation will die without posterity."[63] Although Ballanche had little liking for early Romantic literature, he predicted "the imminent end of the reign" of his idol Chateaubriand, who was also the idol of Mme Récamier's salon.[64] He also predicted the triumph of the new world: "We are just now fighting with all our might against the invasion of Romantic literature, but our very exertions prove how powerful this literature is."[65] The foreign invasion was coming at this point mainly from Germany in the form of poets such as Novalis and Schelling and theorists such as the brothers Schlegel. Mme de Staël helped to legitimate this "foreign" Romanticism in *De l'Allemagne* (1810), despite numerous reservations. The imperial minister Savary, also known as the duc de Rovigo, told her as much: "Your book is not French."[66]

Ballanche's definition of Romanticism was broadly compatible with Tocqueville's later critique of Romanticism in France:

> The name "Romantic literature" has been applied to works whose authors profess greater independence with respect to the rules of composition, who combine words in new ways, and who above all invent new styles. Their texts tamper with the laws of analogy and extend the range of imitation, and the intellect undermines the fixed canons of written language. Their subjects are drawn from modern traditions.[67]

For instance, the "tampering" with the "laws of analogy" of which Ballanche complained was responsible for much of the impropriety, ambiguity, and bombast that Tocqueville ascribed to democratic literature.

[63] Ibid., p. 82. The preceding pages (79–80) are notable for their sparkling irony.

[64] "M. de Chateaubriand, who is still at the height of his talent . . . culminating so admirably [along with Delille] all the traditions of our double classical language, whose reign is about to end," etc. Ibid., p. 73.

[65] Ibid., p. 74. At the time, Romanticism seemed to be essentially a foreign product, stemming from Germany, England, and Italy. In 1813 Mme Necker de Saussure translated Wilhelm Schlegel's *Course of Dramatic Literature*. This work, which Benjamin Constant criticized and Stendhal rejected, had a major impact on French opinion. See R. Bray, *Chronologie du romantisme* (Paris: Boivin, 1932), pp. 8–18.

[66] See the letter reproduced in Mme de Staël, *De l'Allemagne* (Paris: Garnier, n.d.), p. 3: "General Police. Cabinet of the Minister. Paris, October 3, 1810. Your most recent book is not French. I am responsible for halting the presses. I regret the loss that booksellers will incur, but it is not possible for me to allow the book to appear. [signed] Duc de Rovigo." On the conflict with Napoleon and the moral and political ideas set forth in *De l'Allemagne* that were at the origin of this conflict, see Jaume, *L'Individu effacé*, pp. 40ff.

[67] Ballanche, ibid., p. 74. A remarkable but little-cited overview of French Romanticism in all its diversity and stylistic innovation is that of Charles Bruneau in vol. 12 of F. Brunot, ed., *Histoire de la langue française* (Paris: Armand Colin, 1948). I am deeply indebted to this very valuable work. According to Bruneau (pp. 120–31), it was Mme de Staël who introduced the Romantic genre created by August Schlegel in France. This would have been in the period 1804–10.

Who, then, would safeguard the natural and common sense? For an answer we must turn to chapter II.1.16, where Tocqueville concludes that rules that "derive . . . from the very nature of things" will probably command less and less respect.[68] These rules stipulate that there are turns of phrase and expressions that are "vulgar because the sentiments they are supposed to express are *really* low" and others that are "lofty because the objects they seek to depict are *naturally* quite high" (my italics in both). Democracy neither can nor will respect the natural in refined language: someone will always dare to say everything, to show everything, or even claim that the distinction between high and low is meaningless. Tocqueville no doubt had in mind a manifesto like the one that Hugo included as a preface to *Cromwell*. That splendid text, which appeared in 1827—the year in which the Cénacle married Romanticism with liberalism—defended the legitimacy of *the grotesque* in modern drama. For Hugo, the modern muse "will be aware that not everything in creation is humanly *beautiful*, that the ugly *exists* alongside the beautiful, the deformed alongside the graceful, the grotesque back-to-back with the sublime, good with evil, darkness with light." And had not Christianity demonstrated the duality of man? (Clearly Christianity could be invoked in justification of very different aesthetic positions.) So the sublime would become the expression of the soul, while the grotesque would be the expression of "the beast in man," that is, of "every kind of ridiculousness, infirmity, or ugliness."

If we examine Hugo's colorful history of France and Europe, we see that the grotesque allowed for *democratic participation* in the arts, in civilization, and in culture: think, for example, of the hunchback Scarron "on the very edge of Louis XIV's bed," on which the king's wife, still called Mme de Maintenon, was about to lie down.[69]

For Tocqueville, the source of this democratic disrespect was the structure of social power. "In a democratic people one does not find men who, by virtue of their education, enlightenment, and leisure, are permanently disposed to study the natural laws of language and to enforce respect for those laws . . ." Satisfying these prerequisites requires a different social state characterized by education, leisure, and enlightenment: in other words, aristocratic *otium*. In

---

[68] *DA* II.1.16, p. 87; AG, p. 550.

[69] The quotes in this paragraph are from Victor Hugo, *Théâtre complet* (Paris: La Pléiade, 1963), preface to *Cromwell*, 1:416, 420, 421. It would have been interesting if Senior or Ampère had questioned Tocqueville about this text. In fact, in a conversation with Senior in 1850, Tocqueville was critical of the modern taste for "the grotesque," his term for the style of authors who sought to go beyond tradition no matter what the cost, and he also chastised Hugo as a descendant of Chateaubriand "tempted by the Devil." See *OC* VI-2, pp. 303–4.

Tocqueville's time, impatience with what Guizot might have called "superiorities" made such educated men of leisure anomalies.[70] Furthermore, it was of the essence of democratic language to be unstable and to make short shrift of traditions and norms: democratic language, like democratic society, was constantly on the move. In any case, who creates the language? It is never authority: "With [democratic] peoples, the majority makes the law in regard to language as in regard to everything else."[71] Thus it is the "needs of industry," the "passions of the parties," and the necessities of everyday life that influence the way people speak. Language must seduce by virtue of being "chic," new, and flashy: "Democratic nations love change for its own sake. This can be seen in language as well as in politics. They sometimes feel a desire to change words even when there is no need."

The democratic idea of language is thus the polar opposite of the idea of a linguistic conservator or arbiter. Debate would continue throughout the Romantic era about whether it was possible to "fix" language—the formula was a veritable obsession. Voltaire had insisted on stability,[72] but Hugo laughed at it, even though he repeated Voltaire's demand. "A language cannot be fixed," he declared in the preface to *Cromwell*.[73]

Clearly Tocqueville did not regard the Académie Française as a source or reference for literary writing. Although he assiduously and at times happily played a role within the Institut and the Académie and was proud to have been awarded the Prix Montyon,[74] he said nothing in the second volume of *Democracy in America* about the role of these institutions. In his manuscripts he described them as an aristocratic legacy.[75] He might have given a more nuanced analysis of the French case, but he obviously did not share

[70] I compare Tocqueville and Guizot in the next chapter.

[71] *DA* II.1.16, p. 93; AG, p. 548–49.

[72] See Voltaire's letter to Pinot Duclos, cited by Tabet, *Chateaubriand et le XVIIe siècle*, p. 139, n. 98: classical writers should be published "with notes that will fix language and taste." In the article on "languages" in the *Dictionnaire philosophique*, Voltaire wrote that "one must absolutely respect the way in which good authors spoke, and when one has a sufficient number of proven authors, the language is fixed. Thus nothing can now be changed in Italian, Spanish, English, or French without corrupting them." Quoted in Bruneau, in *Histoire de la langue française*, pp. 114–15.

[73] Cf. C. Bruneau, in *Histoire de la langue française*, pp. 210–11. We find a different idea in the 1826 preface to *Odes et balades*: "One must dethrone Aristotle so that Vaugelas may reign alone." Bruneau, p. 193.

[74] The Prix Montyon was awarded to books deemed to be "the most useful for morals," and it was Villemain who, though to a certain extent dubious about the book's audacity, prepared the report on the first volume of *Democracy in America* that earned it the prize. See Villemain, *Discours et Mélanges littéraires*, report of 1836: this "apparently quite critical work" does not present only ideas "useful to morals and applicable by us" [*sic*]. Nevertheless, the book "sets one to thinking" and "inspires generous sentiments." See p. 278.

[75] "An academy whose purpose is to channel thinking in a certain direction and impose a method is contrary to the genius of democracy; it is an aristocratic institution." Nolla II, p. 90, n. h.

Ballanche's view that "opinions" had become democratic in France before the Revolution, while mores had remained aristocratic.[76] Nevertheless, he was an eyewitness to the conflict that had pitted the Académie Française against Romanticism, which Charles Bruneau followed in detail. This controversy raged from the time that Auger delivered his manifesto against Romanticism[77] until Lamartine's acceptance by the Académie in April 1830.[78] Averting his eyes from the French case but recognizing the victories of Hugo and of the representatives of Jeunes France at *Le Globe*, Tocqueville alluded to the battle of *Hernani*: "Aristocratic literary canons will be amended little by little, by gradual and so to speak legal means. In the theater, they will be overturned by riot."[79]

Tocqueville's characterization of the vitality of democratic literature is important. He uses the term that he used in volume 1 to characterize sovereignty in the American republic: *éparpillement*, or dispersion. Alluding to France and other democracies with long-standing traditions, he notes that "ranks ... have mingled and combined. Knowledge, like power, is infinitely divided and I daresay *widely dispersed*."[80] If everyone is empowered to make law with respect to language, then no one actually makes the law.[81] Dispersion means that there is no central authority to sort through the wide variety of creative output from many different sources. But since every writer depends on a bit of fraud, "altering somewhat the meaning of an expression from its original definition," *everyone* (in the community of readers) is at the mercy of a few. And since "there is no common arbiter, no permanent tribunal," the public cannot be warned or protected or disabused of these acts of fraud. The "pirates" of whom Sainte-Beuve spoke in 1841 thrive on this

---

[76] This is the central theme of Ballanche's *Essai sur les institutions*, which allowed him to be the "progressive conservative" that Paul Bénichou described in *Le Temps des prophètes* and Mona Ozouf described in "Ballanche," in *Dictionnaire des œuvres politiques*.

[77] A virulent attack: "Must we wait until the cult of *Romanticism*... insults our masterpieces and, through illegitimate successes, perverts the floating mass of opinions that are always at the mercy of fortune?" April 24, 1824, in Bruneau, in *Histoire de la langue française*, p. 181.

[78] At the same time, however, the Académie opened a competition for the Poetry Prize: "The point is to oppose this invasion, which has something barbarous about it, to fight for our altars and our homes. The Académie invites our poets to treat a subject that calls upon their patriotism and talent, that is at once national and literary." *Journal des savants*, August 1830: note the date! Reproduced by Bruneau, in *Histoire de la langue française*, p. 227. Romanticism is described as a barbaric invasion that threatens French, "the universal language of Europe."

[79] *DA* II.1.19, p. 102; AG, p. 564.

[80] *DA* II.1.13, p. 72; AG, p. 541. My italics.

[81] The text actually reads: "the majority makes the law." I have modified it because Tocqueville insists elsewhere on the *diversity* of audiences and performances, especially in the theater.

dispersion of "power." The writer is as much the reflection of his audience[82] as the audience becomes the echo of what it reads and hears.

Art has power in a democracy, but Tocqueville did not believe that that power was visible or institutionalized. In his eyes, this was the whole difference between aristocracy and democracy as both social structure (or social state) and political organization (popular sovereignty). Strictly speaking, the *law* of language cannot be defined. It varies from one linguistic production or work to another. If everyone makes the law, then in fact there is no law. Thus Tocqueville offered no analogy with the New England town as a deliberative body, nor did he believe in enduring personal power.[83] Or, for that matter, in the incentive or repressive power of academic institutions. In a democracy, therefore, no one can preserve *the conventions of the natural*, which in Tocqueville's eyes were the conventions most appropriate to the simplicity and clarity of human nature.

The "Sociological Rules" of Democracy Supplant Visible Authority

Tocqueville's investigation of the sources of authority in literature thus seems to reach no conclusion, at least not in the terms in which the question was posed before Tocqueville and which framed his approach. Indeed, if our interpretation of these chapters of volume 2 is correct, it seems that Tocqueville did not believe that the majority exercised the cohesive and at times coercive force over written language that it exercised over public opinion.

A Sociologist of Democratic Art

In fact, the observer of democracy sensed (rather than explicitly described) yet another difference between the aristocratic and democratic types. The chapter on poetry (II.1.17) is the best example of this. It is best to read this chapter in the edition of Nolla (pp. 73–74) because the passages from the manuscripts included in this edition confirm a certain propensity of Tocqueville's that may help to explain his sometimes puzzling choices.

---

[82] To borrow a phrase from Bonald (1802), which was frequently commented on but which Mme de Staël had in fact already dealt with: "Literature is the expression of society." See Louis de Bonald, "Du style et de la littérature," in Bonald, *Œuvres complètes*, Migne ed., vol. 3, part 5, "Mélanges," p. 988.

[83] This point of view may seem unreasonable. The salons he frequented set fashion. For a contemporary account, see Mme Ancelot, *Les Salons de Paris* (Paris: Tardieu, 1858). There were also circles and currents, beginning with the famous Cénacle. Hugo exercised a veritable pontificate, Béranger's fame was immense, etc.

In this chapter, Tocqueville does not contrast aristocracy with democracy. Rather, he compares a *class* that is individualized by its actions to what Durkheim might call a "social rule," namely, the condition of *equality*. It is worth noting that it is equality that becomes a personified entity,[84] not democracy.[85] Here the source of authority is not a dominant class or aesthetic norm (although the "painting of the ideal" is examined in this chapter); it is rather a rule that operates in silence, the social condition of equals, or what Tocqueville calls the "democratic social state." The aristocracy, a ruling class conscious of the values it defends and *capable* of "ideal beauty" (as Pascal says man is "capable of God"), is contrasted to the impersonality of competitive equality.[86]

What democracy requires, then, is a *sociology of art* rather than a specific aesthetic: this is the point that Tocqueville seems to be making to the reader or appears to adopt as his own. Are ideal beauty and poetics therefore exclusively limited to aristocratic times? In fact, the second half of the chapter takes a very different tack: the "poems of democracy" do exist. They are the poems of human destiny, of men who take humanity as their subject. Tocqueville refers to Childe Harold, René, and Jocelyn. These are not so much individual characters as symbols of the human condition and "certain still obscure aspects of the human heart."[87] But this aesthetic of democracy, humanitarianism (a term that people were beginning to associate with Lamartine), was strictly dependent on sociology.[88] To put it another way, equality makes individuals and ultimately nations more alike, leading to the broadest possible generalization and abstraction: "Nations themselves grow more similar until they seem, in the eye of the beholder, to merge into one vast democracy, each citizen of which is a people. For the first time in history, the features of the human race become clearly visible."[89]

[84] Tocqueville notes this in connection with democratic tics: "I have personified equality in several places," which would have been inconceivable in the age of Louis XIV. *DA* II.1.16, p. 88; AG, p. 552.

[85] A term that appears only once and which is contested in an intercalated passage in the Nolla edition.

[86] The reader can confirm this by following the text, which I abridge here: "Equality not only discourages portrayal of the ideal but also reduces the number of objects to be portrayed.... Aristocracy keeps society immobile.... In this respect, aristocracy is quite favorable to poetry. Even when equality does not undermine religions.... Aristocracy leads the human spirit naturally.... Having deprived poetry of the past, equality then strips away part of the present." Nolla II, p. 74; AG, p. 555.

[87] Ibid., p. 78; AG, p. 560.

[88] Tocqueville, who was familiar with Bonald's literary determinism, moderated this in II.1.13: "I would say more than I mean to if I were to state that a nation's literature is always subordinate to its social state and political constitution." Along with "several other" causes, however, these were "primary." Bonald had written: "In Germany, the literary state is the faithful expression of the social state." He added: "*Society* here means the form of political and religious constitution." See "Du style et de la littérature," pp. 1046, 976. Once again Tocqueville was reinterpreting Bonald's vision, even to the point of using his terminology. It was not Guizot who invented the idea of the "democratic social state," which Bonald had formulated at the turn of the century.

[89] Nolla II, p. 76; AG, p. 558.

If, then, man takes himself as his own subject—while remaining "sufficiently failed" to be an enigma to himself—it is because equality is constantly pushing him in that direction. This is the historical consequence of equality in the realm of language and art: it *depersonalizes* social power, which continues to exist in the aesthetic dimension but is no longer exercised in a visible manner.

Aristocracies (in Antiquity, India, or at the courts of Louis XIV and Louis XV) institutionalize authority so that it is perceptible, but the rule of equality (and competition) operates invisibly rather than as the rule of a definite "subject." There is no "repository" of the rule, to continue the parallel with the Tocquevillean theory of public opinion as the source of beliefs. In the republic of letters, authority is the province of all, but also of none, because each poet feels its effects through the pressure of his competitors. In fact, the word "authority" is not appropriate; *constraint* would be better.

This historical fact should be compared with Durkheim's definition of a "social fact": a coercive phenomenon, externally produced, resulting from the interaction of groups of people independent of any *psychological* motives that the constraint may stimulate but which are not responsible for its existence.[90]

❧

The Tocquevillean vision ultimately turns out to be quite profound. Although he may at times have been inaccurate or even unjust about contemporary phenomena such as salons, circles, and the Académie, he fleshed out and reinforced his analysis of the democratic logic. He tells us that this logic will become increasingly hostile to the idea that any one person or group of persons may dictate criteria of propriety, manners, or taste—what Pierre Bourdieu called "distinction." The public sets itself up as king: it claims the right to apply to its own tastes the royal formula, "It pleases the king."

The formula "everyone makes the law" (in everyday language or aesthetic styles) thus mischievously conveys a hidden message: "Everyone is subject to the law of everyone else." For a democratic writer, the constraint is real: the rule is other people. The key lies in a passage from Lémontey that I quoted earlier: effective despotism everywhere, but a despot who resides nowhere. A free society.

This despotism can be human, compassionate, and quite mild (in the image of heroes such as René or Jocelyn), but its reality is that of a power—democratic social power, which has replaced the authority of aristocracy.

[90] See Émile Durkheim, *Les Règles de la méthode sociologique* (Paris: PUF, 1973), p. 5: social facts "consist in ways of acting, thinking, and feeling, external to the individual, which are endowed with a coercive power by virtue of which they impose themselves on the person." These "ways of acting" thus become rules (see part 2 above). With this definition Durkheim sought to establish the discipline of sociology as independent of psychology with its own criteria of "scientificity."

This is a long way from the viewpoint of Voltaire, who still believed in a literature guided by the aristocratic spirit and who claimed to rule minds and shape opinion.[91] The magus Hugo and King Voltaire—these were precisely the phenomena that Tocqueville believed could be dispensed with in imagining the future of democratic society.

Voltaire's idea of the "connoisseur" (which was destined for a bright future in art criticism) was typical of eighteenth-century social hierarchy and specialization. By contrast, Tocqueville saw in the literature of modern times the realization of a great myth of liberalism: society without government, but not without social power. In his chapter on historians, he once again contrasts "august personages standing in the limelight" to the world he sees ahead: "By contrast, when all citizens are independent of one another and each of them is weak, none exerts a very great, much less a very durable, power over the masses. At first sight, individuals seem to have absolutely no power over the masses, and society seems to proceed on its own owing to the free and spontaneous cooperation of all its members."[92]

Such is the "dispersion" of social power, which ensures that it is not globally visible, while another actor, called "the state," is. When Tocqueville visited America in 1831, we know that he was struck by the sight of a society that seemed to work all by itself: "Things seem to be in motion all around you, yet the force that drives them is not apparent. The hand that guides the social machinery constantly evades detection."[93]

Tocqueville as Academician: Another Attitude

In his practice as an academician, however, as well as in his various candidacies and solicitations of reviews,[94] Tocqueville showed that he believed in a very real institutional power. This required any number of concessions, as, for example, when he delivered the traditional speech on the Prix de Vertu

[91] His article on taste in the *Dictionnaire philosophique* is admirably assured: "In the long run, only connoisseurs can lead the public, and this is the only difference between enlightened nations and the crudest of the crude. . . . There are enough cultivated minds in Paris to lead the crowd. That crowd can momentarily be swayed by popular movements, but it takes several years to settle its taste in the arts." This passage is omitted from certain editions but is found in the text published at http://www.voltaire-integral.com.

[92] *DA* II.1.20, pp. 107–8; AG, p. 569.

[93] *DA* I.1.5, p. 134; AG, p. 79. In a letter to Kergorlay dated June 29, 1831, Tocqueville wrote that he had discovered a people who "do without government," insofar as "each person here sees himself as interested in the public welfare and the application of the law. Instead of relying on the police, they rely only on themselves. The result is that public force is everywhere, even though it is never apparent."

[94] As recorded in his correspondence; I omit the details. Tocqueville was quite attentive to his relations with critics and newspapers. I will say more later about the case of Silvestre de Sacy, whom Tocqueville severely reprimanded.

in 1847, which was built around the usual academic *topoi*. At times he suffered from the effort of diplomacy, as he confided to Beaumont: "I owe it to the Académie not to deliver a speech that would damage it."[95] Montyon had endowed two prizes in his will, one for the literary work "most useful to morals" (which was awarded to Tocqueville and Beaumont for their work on the penitentiary system and then to Tocqueville for *Democracy in America*), the other to honor the most virtuous actions. Tocqueville was therefore obliged to intone long lists of honorable actions in this or that village under such and such circumstances. The classical peroration surely cost its author, even though he placed his personal stamp on it: "This [award] ceremony is grand, and it is also useful. Indeed, this is the way to encourage and spur virtue, not by distributing cash or even laurels to a few laureates but by inspiring in minds a taste for the beautiful, which leads so naturally to a taste for *l'honnête;* and by inspiring in souls love of pure and healthy pleasures, which fortify rather than dissipate."[96]

Tocqueville's personal touch is clearest perhaps in the final lines of the peroration, where he argues that the Prix Montyon pays homage to equality: "the equality that a similar virtue among all good men must create." Although Tocqueville awards himself this personal satisfaction—constraint through equality is his theme—he also speaks of actions that inspire a taste for the beautiful. The editor tells us that it was customary to distribute to the popular classes each year eight thousand pamphlets praising virtuous acts.[97] Thus even the most naïve, didactic literature was seen as having potential social consequences. The Académie also recognized the potential social consequences of the many surveys it sponsored to improve the economy, morality, social bonds between classes, and so on.[98]

Clearly Tocqueville the academician and social reformer attributed genuine importance to the propagation of new ideas in the France of his time.

---

[95] *Mélanges, OC* XVI, p. 288, n. 2.

[96] Ibid., p. 303.

[97] Measure adopted in 1829 at the behest of the poet Andrieux. Ibid., n. 10.

[98] For instance, Tocqueville wrote two texts on pauperism for the Société Académique of Cherbourg. These are reproduced in the Gallimard edition of the *Mélanges*. See Eric Keslassy, *Le Libéralisme de Tocqueville à l'épreuve du paupérisme* (Paris: L'Harmattan, 2000). See also the critical anthology Tocqueville, *Textes économiques*, ed. J.-L. Benoît and E. Keslassy (Paris: Pocket, 2005). Tocqueville was much concerned with questions of poverty, about which he wrote a great deal. From the time of his trip to America (during which he began a "plan for a free association for the elimination of begging") to the end of his term as a member of the Conseil Général of La Manche (from which he resigned in April 1852), he wrote and edited numerous texts on these issues in the spirit of the social Catholics, whom he read attentively.

LITERATURE CONTINUES TO HAVE A MISSION

The picture changes if we turn back to *Democracy in America*: there are no more leaders, no "romantic magi" (as Paul Bénichou might have said). But what, then, could literature do?

Ultimately, in Tocqueville's view, literature continued to have a mission, and its freedom of action was to be encouraged. In fact, despite the democratic penchant for pantheism (in Tocqueville's sense, meaning the antithesis of individual responsibility) and historical fatalism (Thiers, Mignet), he believed in free will. In the introduction to *Democracy in America*, he had argued that a "new science" was needed as a preparation for action in a new society. Tocqueville's sociology was intended as an argument against fatalism.

He believed, for example, that "lofty scientific vocations" should be encouraged as a counter to the utilitarian spirit that tended to permeate learning and turn it toward applied science. Henceforth "the social power should direct all its efforts to supporting advanced studies and fostering great scientific passions."[99] And of course "the social power" is distinct from the state. In passages such as this, Tocqueville's tone is clearly different.

Furthermore, because democracy was threatened with "Chinese-style" immobility (as John Stuart Mill also argued), this, too, was something to be combated: a fundamental contradiction of the society of perpetual mobility was that it might paralyze itself, arresting the spirit of research, just as a society based on belief in individual judgment could engender a tyranny of the majority.[100]

Barbarism is a possibility in democracy but not an inevitability: "If there are peoples who allow the torch of enlightenment to be snatched from their grasp, there are others who use their own feet to stamp out its flames."[101]

Another mission for literature is studied in chapter II.1.20, which concerns historians. If the "doctrine of fatality ... is so attractive to those who write history in democratic times," writers need to defend the doctrine of free will.[102] And since "our contemporaries" believe in the collective ("they are still quite prepared to recognize the strength and independence of men joined together in a social body"), one must show that men associated in this way will enjoy the new freedom. Tocqueville added a sentence that clarified the point of his sociology: "One should be careful not to obscure this idea,

---

[99] *DA* II.1.10, p. 59; AG, p. 528.

[100] Marcel Gauchet has popularized the Tocquevillean idea of "democracy [in the workplace] against itself."

[101] *DA* II.1.10, p. 60; AG, p. 529.

[102] *DA* II.1.20, p. 110; AG, p. 572.

because the goal is to exalt men's souls, not to complete the task of laying them low." This was no doubt the advice that he gave himself, to judge by the scope of his critique of modern literature.

To reinforce human dignity is, or ought to be, the goal of democratic literature. Although there is no recognized authority, each author retains an individual responsibility. This was Tocqueville's view of "literature," a term that for him covered a domain and a dynamic that are scarcely comprehensible to us today. We must turn next to uncovering that lost meaning, which has been supplanted by our equation of literature with fiction and activity without any specific social purpose. "What is literature?" an heir of the nineteenth century asked some time ago. His answer: "To write is both to reveal the world and to propose it as a task to the reader's generosity."[103]

---

[103] Jean-Paul Sartre, *Qu'est-ce que la littérature?* (Paris: Gallimard, 1948), p. 76. The text, very antibourgeois in tenor, frequently invokes Baudelaire and General Aupick. Frankly it is today chiefly of archaeological interest (as Ballanche would have said). If I may offer a personal reminiscence, during a meeting at La Mutualité, which must have been around 1965, Sartre lectured on the question "What can literature do?" before an audience of well-known writers, whom he scolded in a manner that was at once "committed" and professorial, and therefore rather tiresome.

Tocqueville in the Debate about
Literature and Society

Mme de Staël wrote that "progress in literature [signifies] the perfection of the arts of thinking and expression." From this we divine that we are no longer living in her world, which was also the world of Tocqueville. The word "literature" was then applied to all expressions of the life of the mind—with some hesitation in regard to natural science. Indeed, it was Mme de Staël's *De la littérature considérée dans ses rapports avec les institutions* that helped to stabilize this idea in France. It was a book that attempted to institutionalize literature as an activity that would bear its ultimate fruit in the republic to come.[1] In a "preliminary discourse" of the same work, she discusses literature "in the broadest sense," meaning "philosophical texts and works of imagination, as well as anything to do with the exercise of thought in writing, except for the physical sciences."[2]

That is why, when Tocqueville treats language in general, he can move easily across the realm of "science, literature, and the arts" (to borrow from the title of chapter II.1.9). At the time, the essayist, the moralist, and the political writer were as much a part of "literature" as the poet and novelist, and so was the philosopher. Mme de Staël insisted on the latter point, arguing that the age of philosophical literature had arrived. This is one reason why it is plausible to believe that Tocqueville read her book.[3] Note, too, that the chapters of

---

[1] See the introduction to *De la littérature* (Paris: Garnier-Flammarion, 1991) by G. Gengembre and J. Goldzink. Axel Blaeschke published an important scholarly edition with Classiques Garnier in 1998. Citations here are to the Garnier-Flammarion edition unless otherwise indicated.

[2] De Staël, *De la littérature*, p. 66.

[3] As André Jardin hypothesized. Certain references in the manuscripts seem to refer to *De la littérature*. For instance, concerning the place of women, see La Pléiade edition, 2:1145 (note concerning p. 725, citation of a manuscript). Ampère, an ardent admirer of Mme de Staël, talked to Tocqueville about her constantly, but we learn from an article published after Tocqueville's death that his friend was astonished by his underestimation of the importance of *L'Allemagne* for the youth of 1810. As noted previously, Tocqueville never hesitated to say in his writing and correspondence that the author of *Corinne* was, along with Chateaubriand, one of the best writers of the century and that she had modernized literary language..

Democracy in America that we have been examining end with a consideration of parliamentary eloquence, as does Mme de Staël's book.

Broadly speaking, it is impossible to understand Tocqueville's argument without considering a debate that had been raging since the early days of the empire about the relation between literature and society and the meaning of rhetoric. "What did they read between the neatly ruled lines?" to borrow Lucien Febvre's question about Rabelais's readers.[4] This is necessary because if we accept today's categories, what was at stake for Tocqueville is scarcely perceptible.

DEMOCRACY IN AMERICA FIGURED IN A "LITERARY" DEBATE

During the Restoration, the idea of modernization, of adaptation to the new society born of the Revolution, was central to every discussion of literary practice. Bonald's formula—"Literature is the expression of society"—aptly captures the tenor of this postrevolutionary debate.[5] Tocqueville was influenced by these discussions, which his theory of democratic literature would transform.

Bonald sought to acknowledge the upheaval caused by the Revolution without legitimating it. Taking the reformist program of the Ideologues as his target, he argued that literature can be understood only in terms of its social "causes." It is therefore always a *product*, never a free and active agent. He wrote that "style is the expression of the intellectual man—his thought, his spirit, and his character. Literature is therefore the expression of the moral part of society, that is, of its constitution, which is its soul, its spirit, and its character."[6] In view of Bonald's sociological project,[7] he had to argue for strict determinism: "literary progress" does exist, there is a history of literary invention, but such invention is "a necessary result of the constitution" (in the Bonaldian sense). For the counterrevolutionary Bonald, progress was "a

---

[4] Lucien Febvre, *Le Problème de l'incroyance au XVIe siècle. La religion de Rabelais*, rev. ed. (Paris: Albin Michel, 1942), p. 7.

[5] The date of Bonald's formula is generally given as 1802. It appears in both *Législation primitive* and the article in the *Mercure* in that year (concerning the quarrel between the Ancients and Moderns), which figures in a note at the end of the text, whereas the formula occurs in the first paragraph. But as Gengembre and Goldzink point out on p. 42 of their introduction to *De la littérature*, it was in 1796 that Bonald, in *Théorie du pouvoir politique et religieux*, announced his plan to "compare" what he called "the state of the arts in various peoples" with their institutions. Mme de Staël meanwhile published *De la littérature* in 1800.

[6] Bonald, "Du style et de la littérature," quoted in A. Blaeschke, introduction to *De la littérature*, p. cii. Bonald also equates "constitution" with "social state."

[7] See part 2.

result and not a *means.*" Bonald's theory was thus a precursor of Taine's, for whom the explanatory variables were milieu, race, and moment. For instance, it was scarcely conceivable to think of the epic style without considering the characteristic *unity* of monarchical government, which thus forms the basis for the stylistic rule requiring "unity of action."

> If the poet wished to recount events in a society of common people, he would have to tie the action to a single character, whose virtues and exploits would make him the hero of the poem, if he were not the head of the nation. And in order to compose the poem, it would be necessary in some way to constitute the society.[8]

This remarkable passage reveals the rather native obstinacy of the "reactionary" obsessed with his king, as well as Bonald's characteristic concern with the idea of "constituting" and "constituent power." He intends his argument to be complete and rigorous and offers the following example, which Hugo and other Romantics may well have taken to heart: "This lack of unity is the principal vice of the disappointing works of Silius Italicus, Statius, and even Lucan, who wrote only about wars of republics against republics or citizens against citizens and therefore failed to see that the profusion of characters in a world of equality excluded the unity of action that epic poetry so rigorously requires and that a heroic poem cannot be an epic poem."

The society of equality cannot sustain great epic characters: clearly the lesson was not lost on Tocqueville. As one might expect, *revolutionary* literature becomes, later in the text, the "worthy expression of a revolutionary society" once France has shed "its natural constitution of religion and state" and seen "its morals denatured."[9]

Somewhat paradoxically, however, Bonald ends his essay with lavish praise for the art of oratory under the Constituent Assembly: "Never before had eloquence dealt with such lofty issues with such force, knowledge, and gravity."[10] The paradox is only apparent, however. It illustrates Bonald's problem: despite the social decadence, literature has progressed. The Revolution was not a great black hole and had to be conceptualized as a historical phenomenon. This led Bonald to a lengthy discussion of the factors influencing oratory in Athens and Rome compared with France in 1791, when all of Europe was listening as France developed publishing of books and newspapers for the masses. To be sure, the explanation is not altogether convincing,

---

[8] Bonald, "Du style et de la littérature," in *Œuvres complètes*, Migne ed., 3:995.
[9] Ibid., pp. 1003–4.
[10] Ibid., p. 1014.

and the determinism is not as clear as Bonald thinks (did great orators really "express" a society of madness, immorality, and crime?), but, broadly speaking, he makes his point that the Revolution was an era of "public" eloquence, that is, of "generalized reason," as opposed to the literature of private life and private interests. The Constituent Assembly was a "prodigy of talent and errors": this fine oxymoron indicates that, for Bonald, the Revolution was anything but *un bloc*, a unified whole.[11]

THE RESTORATION AS TURNING POINT: RHETORIC, LITERATURE, AND MORALITY

Rhetoric and the Baccalaureate

According to Françoise Douay-Sublin, the preeminent authority on the subject, a new rhetorical model appeared in France during the Restoration. Competing with the age of Louis XIV, of which Voltaire had created a powerful image, and with imperial Rome, which had been so important under Napoleon, was "the English parliamentary model, which led to a 'revival' in France of the ideals of ancient Athens and republican Rome."[12] It was in this context that questions about rhetoric were included in the baccalaureate exam in 1820 and that Villemain, in celebrated lectures that drew a passionate following among Parisian youth, discussed the eloquence of the British Parliament.[13] Today it is difficult to appreciate the importance of rhetoric, which Douay-Sublin described as "the cornerstone of the humanist edifice." If Mme de Staël and Tocqueville ascribed so much importance to eloquence in a regime of liberty,[14] it was because they believed that in democratic society persuasion was a constant necessity: consent had to be obtained. Both

---

[11] As Mona Ozouf points out in "Ballanche," in *Dictionnaire des œuvres politiques*, the formula "the Revolution is *un bloc*" (as Clemenceau put it) was a favorite of the extreme Right during the nineteenth century until it passed to the other side of the political spectrum. Bonald, who was less simple than is sometimes said, also wrote that France would become "more powerful as a result of the Revolution" if the Revolution succeeded in establishing political and administrative unity. See Bonald, "Du traité de Westphalie et de celui de Campo-Formio," in *Œuvres* (1847), p. 558. Cf. the article on Bonald by Bernard Manin in *Dictionnaire des œuvres politiques*.

[12] Françoise Douay-Sublin, "La rhétorique en France au dix-neuvième siècle à travers ses pratiques et ses institutions," in *Histoire de la rhétorique dans l'Europe modern, 1450–1950*, ed. Marc Fumaroli (Paris: Presses Universitaires de France, 1999), p. 1115.

[13] See Villemain, *Tableau de la littérature au XVIIIe siècle*, vol. 4. The lectures were given in 1828, and the professor clearly drew his references from Westminster, not Paris.

[14] Tocqueville's manuscripts show that he considered including a section on American religious oratory. The Restoration also saw a renaissance of religious oratory in France. Tocqueville read the Church fathers as well as the great religious orators of the seventeenth century, and he studied the sermons of

praised "common sense" for the same reason, as did Alexandre Vinet, a preacher of the Swiss awakening.[15] Mme de Staël maintained that "reasoning and eloquence are natural bonds in a republican association. What can you do with man's free will if you do not possess the force and truth of language, which penetrates souls and inspires them with what it expresses?"[16]

For our two authors, and according to an idea shared by many people at the time, to think well was also to speak well, but speaking well implied paying attention to the community for which one spoke (or wrote). Speaking well and writing well were not distinguished. Both were necessary in order to make oneself properly understood. As we have seen, Tocqueville made a point of placing himself in the position of his presumed reader. *Democracy in America* was in fact addressed to several different readers, and from this we can make out the features of the readers Tocqueville had in mind. One could almost apply to Tocqueville's work Barthes's description of Arcimboldo's painting: "It dictates to the reader, in its very design, the obligation to approach or withdraw, assuring him that he will lose none of the meaning with this movement and will always remain in a vital relationship with the image."[17] In the case of Tocqueville's text, with its multiple registers of meaning, several possible readers exist, and several vital relationships to the picture of the human and political condition.

To return to the art of oratory, the instruction that Tocqueville received (whether from his tutor or from his preparatory school in Metz) bears the mark of a society that had begun to rediscover public speaking after the lugubrious silence of the imperial years. At the time it was usually "a single individual, the professor of rhetoric, who taught French, Latin, Greek, morality by way of religion, and of course history."[18] As Douay-Sublin shows, the publication of textbooks in rhetoric reached a peak in 1820 owing to the inclusion of the discipline in the baccalaureate exam, or *bac*. History gradually achieved autonomy, while philosophy fought to have its own separate

---

Channing and other American preachers. He also attended, along with thousands of others, Lacordaire's lecture series at Notre-Dame.

[15] Mme de Staël, *De la littérature*, pp. 69–70, wrote: "True intelligence is nothing but the ability to see clearly. . . . Genius is common sense applied to new ideas. The genius adds to the treasure of common sense; he conquers for reason." What struck her commentator Vinet was the way she combined common sense with sensibility. He wrote that "sensibility is far more an element or condition of common sense than an enemy. *Common sense . . . is a sense*, a just sentiment of reality." See Vinet, *Études sur la littérature française au XIXe siècle* (Lausanne: Georges Bridel, 1908), 1:181.

[16] Mme de Staël, *De la littérature*, p. 77 and the entire section on "literature in relation to liberty," pp. 76–82.

[17] Roland Barthes, *L'obvie et l'obtus* (1982), passage reproduced in *Arcimboldo*, catalog *Beaux-Arts Magazine*, TTM ed. (2007), p. 63.

[18] Douay-Sublin, "La rhétorique en France," p. 1115.

examination for the *agrégation*. Philosophers clashed with "rhetors" in a conflict whose aftereffects are still felt today. Victor Cousin, philosopher, professor, and minister of education, who served for more than twenty-five years as the chairman of the jury for the *agrégation* in philosophy, played an important role, first during the Restoration (as a member of the liberal opposition) and then in government under the July Monarchy. At the turn of the century, when Mme de Staël published *De la littérature*, she argued that the art of speaking required the art of thinking, that is, philosophy, to show it the way.[19] Hence there was a hierarchical order but also a vital link between Plato and Cicero and John Locke and Lord Stanhope or George Washington.

Later in her book, Mme de Staël insisted on a new meaning for the term "philosophy," making it synonymous with opposition to established power of any kind: "I call 'philosophy' the investigation of the principle of all political and religious institutions, the analysis of historical character and events, and finally the study of the human heart and of the natural rights of man."[20]

She concludes that "a philosophy of this kind presupposes liberty, or must lead to it." The link between philosophy and politics was thus tight and direct. In England, as opposed to the France of Louis XIV and Napoleon, parliamentary government encouraged critical thinking and reasoned opposition: "The mind cannot fully develop its strength without attacking power. It was through opposition that the English developed the talents necessary to become ministers."[21] Here, in the love of speaking well associated with thinking well, we find the source of the liberalism of the subject, of individual judgment, which the Coppet group spread and Tocqueville adopted after them. He was an heir with a difference, however, because he devoted all his effort to showing that the same "democracy" that requires every man to judge for himself risks allowing individual judgment to be stifled by collective judgment. But Mme de Staël herself (more than Benjamin Constant) perceived the danger that threatened "a democratic state" in which "people might persuade themselves that it is pointless and almost harmful to have any unduly visible superiority to the multitude whom one

---

[19] When asked to define philosophy, she described it as "general knowledge of causes and effects," independence of reason, an "exercise in reflection," and finally, "in literature, works that have to do with reflection and analysis." See *De la littérature*, p. 80, note.

[20] Ibid., p. 187.

[21] Ibid., p. 323. On this idea, see my comparison of Mme de Staël with the philosopher Alain: "La fonction de juger dans le Groupe de Coppet et chez Alain," *Alain dans ses œuvres et son journalisme politique* (Paris: Institut Alain/La Menuiserie, 2004), pp. 205–14.

wants to captivate. The people might become accustomed to choosing crude and ignorant officials."[22]

The Rise of Anthologies

In addition to the teaching of rhetoric during the Restoration and the link between eloquence and representative government, it is important to notice the way in which literary *topoi* were held up as examples to students by way of anthologies of selected pieces. Tocqueville, like his contemporaries, often read "the classics" in anthologies that were commonly found in château libraries. Historians of literature have shown that the most widely read of these anthologies was a work by Noël and Delaplace, *Leçons de littérature et de morale ou Recueil en prose et en vers des plus beaux morceaux de notre langue dans la littérature des deux derniers siècles* [Lessons on Literature and Morality, or Anthology in Prose and Verse of the Finest Examples of Our Language in the Literature of the Last Two Centuries], which went through twenty-nine editions between 1804 and 1862.[23] This two-volume work (one for poetry, the other for prose) was often imitated owing to its success and official recognition when it first appeared. One imitator was Le Brun de Charmettes, who published *Le Muséum littéraire* in 1822 and explicitly acknowledged drawing his inspiration from the pioneering work of Noël and Delaplace. He, too, published two volumes and organized his selections by topic, but with a somewhat different set of choices.[24] A conservative monarchist with a sarcastic wit, Le Brun de Charmette is notable for his apt account of the period's ideological conflict between liberals and traditionalists, most notably in his *Épître au comte Edmond de V... sur le libéralisme*.[25] Well-known in his day for reviving the national myth of Joan of Arc (with two works, one in prose, the other in verse), he also captured the spirit of the time by calling his anthology a "museum": one visited the great authors (including contemporaries such as Chateaubriand and related figures such as La Harpe and Fontanes) as one might visit a museum, and at the same time one tried to model one's "style" on their examples. Tocqueville's readers would not have been surprised by the "literary precepts" that conclude the volume devoted to prose writers: there they would have found an excerpt from Pascal, a short piece by Buffon, and

---

[22] *De la littérature*, p. 77. Tocqueville would later argue that the elite would shun power and electoral battles in the United States. On parliamentary eloquence in America, his opinion was mixed, as we shall see.

[23] Douay-Sublin, "La rhétorique en France," pp. 1129, 1150.

[24] The full title was *Études françaises de littérature et de morale* (Paris: Audin, 1822), with *Muséum littéraire* as "faux-titre." Douay-Sublin does not include this book in her listing of the most popular titles.

[25] The text is reproduced in appendix 4 to the French edition of the present volume. It was part of a collection that Le Brun de Charmette published in 1831, *Épîtres politiques sur nos extravagances*.

a text by Fontanes. Note this passage from Pascal: "We must put ourselves in the place of those who are to hear us and test on our own hearts the turn we give to our language in order to see if one is made for the other, and to assure ourselves that the listener will be forced, as it were, to yield." As we saw earlier, Tocqueville adopted this very precept for *Democracy in America*.

As for Buffon, a passage in *Le Muséum littéraire* succinctly expresses what Mme de Staël would argue later in *De la littérature*: "To write well is at once to think well, feel well, and describe well: it is to possess intelligence, soul, and taste at the same time."

Clearly Tocqueville was working familiar terrain and was in tune with elite tastes as expressed at the time by Germaine de Staël. Listen to one more of her comments: "Half-baked reflections and insights trouble man without enlightening him." And after describing genius as the birth of new ideas from common sense, she adds that "sophisms, insights called ingenious even though they lack accuracy, and indeed whatever does not fit must be regarded as flaws and nothing else."[26] It is enough to read Tocqueville's notes on the manuscripts of *Democracy in America* to see that he took these recommendations to heart: one of the most frequently recurring questions is whether he ought to move some passage to another place in order to have a more powerful and precise effect on the reader.

Respect the reader was the main tenet of this school of "literature," which came under harsh attack from the second and third generation of Romantics. It was to these attacks that the "sage" Tocqueville was responding, and it is impossible to understand his response apart from its historical context. From the standpoint of the twenty-first century, all of this is of merely archeological interest, to borrow a word from Ballanche. As Charles Bruneau pointed out, the *bousingots*, or young Romantics, followers of Jeunes France in the mold of Théophile Gautier and above all Pétrus Borel, took pleasure in the improper and dissonant use of language. The idea of *épater le bourgeois* became the very raison d'être of literature, and in an important sense it has remained so ever since.[27]

Literature and Moral Training

During the years when Tocqueville was studying (and writing two theses in Latin), Restoration culture was influenced by a third important factor, namely, the revival of *the humanist idea*. Humanist education rested in part

---

[26] *De la littérature*, p. 70.
[27] See Bruneau, in *Histoire de la langue française*, pp. 440–50, on Hugo's playful use of adjectives such as *vermeil* and *fauve*.

on the belief that the way for a student to find himself was to study works of high quality. In Italy this belief gave rise to an important polemic on imitation. Politian (1454–94) answered a critic thus: "You tell me that after studying Cicero for so many years, I still do not express myself as he did. But I am not Cicero, and it was indeed from him that I learned to be myself."[28]

The elites of the Restoration believed that a man not only formed himself by imitating others but also familiarized himself with the *moral principles* illustrated by selected excerpts from "great authors." This type of literary education was therefore closely linked with morality, not to say moralism. To see this, it is enough to quote the introduction to the leading textbook, that of Noël and Delaplace: "Each selection in this anthology is not only an exercise in careful reading . . . but also a lesson in virtue, humanity, justice, religion, devotion to king and country, disinterestedness, and love of the public good."[29]

Tocqueville mocked French education to a certain extent because its reliance on the classics risked cutting young students off from the realities of their own time. It was something of an obsession of the day, particularly among legitimists such as Villeneuve-Bargemont, that educated young people were likely to become radicals. Tocqueville echoed this view: if education was focused exclusively on literature, there was a danger of turning out embittered graduates because "on account of their social and political state they would daily experience needs that their education never taught them how to satisfy, and they would therefore invoke the Greeks and Romans to sow trouble in the state rather than cause it to bear fruit through their industry."[30] Boileau's quip—"Who will deliver us from the Greeks and Romans?"—had become proverbial. Yet the same Tocqueville also maintained that it was indispensable for students to be steeped in Greek and Roman literature, as the title of chapter II.1.15 of *Democracy in America* indicates: "Why the Study of Greek and Latin Is Particularly Useful in Democratic Societies." The reader of Plutarch, the man who had been charmed by Villemain's edition of Cicero's *De Republica*, was here expressing his personal predilections.

By the time he finished his law studies, Tocqueville had formulated an educational policy of his own: teaching at different levels should be sharply differentiated, the elite required a classical culture, there should be adaptation as well as continuity in the teaching of ancient and modern "classics,"

---

[28] Quoted in Eugenio Garin, *L'Éducation de l'homme moderne* (Paris: Fayard, 1968), p. 96. I draw on this work in the following account of this aspect of humanism.

[29] *Leçons françaises de littérature et de morale*, 7th ed. (1816): 1:xi, quoted in J.-P. de Saint-Gérand, "Mesures et analyse du style: le cas du XIXe siècle français," Clermont-Ferrand II, http://www.chass.utoronto.ca.

[30] *DA* II.1.15, p. 80; AG, p. 546.

and all these educational precepts should form a coherent whole. We should not be surprised to find literary education cast as the basis of all moral education because this was the liberal conception of society and not Tocqueville's private view. Tocqueville's distinctive contribution was to recast this set of ideas and options in terms of aristocracy-democracy typology. Mme de Staël had previously adumbrated a similar approach.[31] Above all he forced the conflicts between romanticism and classicism into his own sociological mold. As he himself acknowledged in the chapters of the second volume of *Democracy in America* devoted to "literature," he spoke a great deal of France and very little about the United States. Furthermore, in his sociological interpretations of beauty, architectural splendor, "bombastic" oratory, and humanitarian poetry in democratic societies, he offered a critical revision of the optimistic views of the baroness of Coppet. His views were closer to those of Chateaubriand, who had become increasingly disenchanted with the progress of what he, too, called democracy. Tocqueville focused on the solitude and insignificance of the individual in a society of equals, and from this he derived a stylistic principle that we are now in a position to define.

DEMOCRACY IN AMERICA: A STYLE OF CONFLICT

Duality and Ambivalence

It is indeed remarkable that in his discussion of aesthetic creations, Tocqueville relied on poignant arguments concerning man's *disproportion*, to use Pascal's term—disproportion in relation not to nature and the two infinities but rather to the mass of his "fellow men" (*semblables*). The term *semblables* as Tocqueville uses it has a threefold meaning: it describes individuals equal in rights, equal before God, their common father, and similar to one another by virtue of their situation or through imitation. The theme runs through all the chapters we have been considering, sometimes boldly, at other times more covertly. For example, we read that "nowhere do citizens seem more insignificant than in a democratic nation."[32] Or again, in the chapter on poetry: "in democratic societies, where all men are insignificant and very much alike, each person looks at himself and instantly sees everyone else."[33] Similarly, in the chapter on writers

---

[31] Mme de Staël frequently compared literature's two modes of *social* existence. For instance, she examined the way in which democratic literature depends on competition among authors, whereas aristocratic writing is more likely to seek perfection because the author "always has his judges in mind" and in an eminent position: *De la littérature*, p. 137. See also her study of the age of Louis XIV, pp. 279ff.

[32] *DA* II.1.12, p. 67; AG, p. 536.

[33] *DA* II.1.17, p. 93; AG, p. 556.

and orators: "In democratic societies, each citizen is usually preoccupied with something quite insignificant: himself. If he lifts up his eyes, he sees only one immense image, that of society, or the even larger figure of the human race."[34]

The same explanation is given for democratic man's taste for *monumental* architecture: "insignificant" individuals construct grand edifices. These passages of Tocqueville are rather amusingly reminiscent of Jonathan Swift (Gulliver in the land of the Lilliputians), or of the utopian architecture of Étienne-Louis Boullée and Claude-Nicolas Ledoux, or of Robert Owen and his phylansteries. Tocqueville knew all these firsthand from his reading and relations. All revealed *tensions* in modern democracy—tensions that he sought to capture in his evenhanded style. Democracy might lack grandeur, but in compensation it fostered a sense of the human (he thought often of Lamartine). The risk of excess, bombast, and vulgarity[35] also allows for the poetry of humanity, striving for the infinite, and comprehension of "perfectibility," as Tocqueville discusses in chapter II.1.8, at the beginning of the series of chapters on aesthetics.[36] The same was true of oratorical art. Mme de Staël saw eloquence as an essential precondition for a free, that is to say, republican, state. She observed that although the Americans did not yet have a true literature, they were nevertheless familiar with "the most useful secrets of style" because their leaders had the ability to move, persuade, and mobilize the citizenry.[37] Tocqueville agreed on the subject of oratory and took the argument one step further: "Nothing is more admirable or powerful, in my view, than a great orator debating great affairs in a democratic assembly."[38] Yet he had just shown that parliamentary eloquence was completely spoiled by the presence of "mediocre men," who cannot be prevented from making "a spectacle of themselves whenever and wherever they can."

"Contrarieties," as Pascal would say: either too much or not enough.[39] The goal should be the mixed, the middle term, Aristotle's "middle way,"[40] so that

---

[34] *DA* II.1.18, p. 99; AG, p. 561.

[35] There is a formula of Pascal's that can be applied to Tocqueville: "I hate the clownish and the inflated equally." Fragment 503 of the *Pensées*.

[36] A perfectibility that Mme de Staël, as a disciple of Jean-Jacques Rousseau, made famous in a notorious conflict with Fontanes and Chateaubriand: the notion, which is central to *De la littérature*, immediately stirred controversy.

[37] It is interesting to note that Mme de Staël said of America what Rousseau said of Corsica in the *Social Contract*: "There is only one nation in the world to which these reflections can be applied at the moment: the Americans." See *De la littérature*, pp. 297–98, where, not yet daring to express hope for France (still subject to Napoleon), she turned to the United States, thirty-one years before Tocqueville. She dreamed of making the journey one day.

[38] *DA* II.1.21, p. 115; AG, p. 578.

[39] See part 3 above on Tocqueville as moralist.

[40] Aristotle recommended thinking of virtue as a middle way between two extremes: *Nicomachean Ethics*, II.6, 1107a5.

democracy corrects and limits itself. Democratic eloquence cannot be considered a good in itself because, in Tocqueville's view, democracy is not a good in itself. It is always pregnant with a variety of oppositions. Freedom of judgment, individual originality, diversity, sincerity of faith, defense of the law, minority rights—all these things, which democracy claims to promote, are threatened by their opposites. Democracy is nevertheless a relative good. It has its own form of progress, through the (providential) advance of equality: Tocqueville developed this theme primarily in connection with the oratorical art. Indeed, orators must "address the nation as a whole, and it is in the name of the nation as a whole that they speak. This enlarges their ideas and elevates their language. . . . The mind is obliged to adduce general truths derived from human nature in dealing with the particular affair at hand." Hence the truths that are expressed are of *general* import: "All men are interested in these debates because their subject is man, who is everywhere the same."[41]

This passage explains how a democracy of insignificant individuals and mediocre orators could, for the first time in history, reveal man as the bearer of universal rights and discover, or rather rediscover, Christianity.[42]

Ultimately the tensions of democracy have philosophical significance: the message of Rousseau, Montesquieu, Mme de Staël, and, less directly, Christian fraternity can be heard in the logic that Tocqueville describes (a logic whose content is at once social and historical). The ruse of history (I use this expression deliberately) is to make use of the disgraced and graceless forms described in the chapters we have been examining (II.1.9–21) to reach a conclusion that leaves Tocqueville with a certain hope for the future, namely, that man is everywhere the same. Tocqueville's style is a more complex version of Mme de Staël's: it alternates between, and in some mysterious way brings together, the illuminated and the dark side of things. It brings us to tremble in the face of a threatening future while at the same time adducing signs of progress and *perfectibility*. It is a style of conflict,[43] of even-handedness, a mixture of ever-renascent substances, very definitely of the school of Pascal: "Man is neither angel nor beast." Or, in more Tocquevillean terms, it is

---

[41] *DA* II.1.21, p. 115; AG, p. 578.

[42] Mme de Staël agreed: "We must attribute to the spirituality of Christian ideas and to the somber truth of philosophical ideas the art of bringing into the discussion even of particular interests touching and general reflections that grip all souls, awaken all memories, and involve the whole of man in each of man's interests." *De la littérature*, pp. 182 passim.

[43] This analysis is fairly similar to that of Laurence Guellec in "L'écriture de l'instable dans *La Démocratie en Amérique* de Tocqueville," in *Mélanges G. Benrekassa, Le Travail des Lumières* (Paris: Honoré Champion, 2002). See especially the analysis of paradox in Tocqueville, pp. 709–11. In another recent study Aurelian Craiutu showed the strong tensions in Tocqueville's thought: "Tocqueville's Paradoxical Moderation," *Review of Politics*, no. 4 (2005): 599–629. While searching for means of moderation, Tocqueville thought of himself as a man of most immoderate temperament.

because man is veiled from himself that he is poetic, that is, capable of the infinite—or, what comes to the same thing, the ideal. Staëlian perfectibility is therefore both a fact and a duty, a logic of history and an ultimate hope.

Tocqueville also deplored vagueness in writing, or what he calls the "ambulatory" style. He detested the strategic choice of democratic politicians to lull their listeners with words. Was he totally free of this vice himself? The following passage may be taken as both confession and absolution:

> Men who live in democratic countries will therefore often have vacillating thoughts; they need very broad expressions to contain them. Since they never know whether the idea to which they are giving voice today will fit the new situation in which they may find themselves tomorrow, they naturally develop a taste for abstract ideas. An abstract word is like a box with a false bottom; you can put in any ideas you please and take them out again without anyone being the wiser.[44]

Tocqueville knew, of course, that he himself had curiously altered the terms "equality," "democracy," "decentralization," and "association" and thus introduced areas of ambiguity into speculations about the modern world. Yet he continued to think that writing and speech that chose not to speak the truth in order to garner a majority constituted "democratic fraud." He therefore depicted himself as an author assuming his responsibility by revealing the tensions inherent in democracy, refusing florid language (or "boilerplate," as we might say today) and writing as a polemicist.

I will limit myself to a single example because Tocqueville's stylistics deserves a work in its own right. In the next section we will consider how Tocqueville contrasts the way in which a wealthy American merchant behaves in his own home with the way he behaves in the street. This is a portrait in the style of La Bruyère, which depicts a tension, a divided discourse that reveals the human consequences of a socially conditioned cleavage.

La Bruyère in America: The Sense of a Style

The passage in question occurs near the beginning of the second part of volume 1 of *Democracy in America*.[45] In other words, it comes before Tocqueville discusses the way in which the people govern everything, including the tyranny of the majority over thought. The passage is a sort of vignette,

---

[44] *DA* II.1.16, p. 89; AG, p. 552.

[45] *DA* I.2.2, p. 262; AG, p. 204. See another portrait in the manner of La Bruyère in *DA* II, p. 277, concerning the self-satisfaction of certain of Tocqueville's interlocutors, convinced that "America is best." Also cited in Benoît, *Tocqueville moraliste*, p. 471.

a colorful preface to the study of a society in which only "remnants of the aristocratic party" still exist. It is a sketch of "character" in the manner of La Bruyère, or, in other words, a portrait of an individual that also describes a moral type of more general import:

> Do you see this opulent citizen? Does he not resemble a Jew of the Middle Ages, afraid lest anyone suspect his riches? His dress is simple, his demeanor modest. Within the four walls of his home, luxury is adored. Into this sanctuary he allows only a few select guests, whom he insolently calls his equals. There is not a nobleman anywhere in Europe who is more exclusive in his pleasures than this man or more jealous of the least advantages conferred by a privileged position. Yet this same man leaves home to go work in a dusty hole in the business district downtown, where anyone is free to call on him. On the way there he passes his shoemaker, and the two men stop and begin to converse. What can they be saying to each other? These two citizens are discussing affairs of state, and they will not part without shaking hands.
>
> But beneath this conventional enthusiasm, beyond this obsequious politeness toward the dominant power, it is easy to see that the rich feel a deep disgust with their country's democratic institutions.

This account may put us in mind of an engraving (a composition somewhere between Rembrandt on the quays of Amsterdam and Hoggart in London), or perhaps of a puppet show. Of particular interest is the role of the person who speaks in the text, who *recounts* the portrait and thereby signals his own presence. The off-screen voice of the "showman" addresses the spectator directly and tells him what to look at and what to think about what he sees: "Do you see . . . Does he not resemble . . . It is easy to see. . . ." The rich man's enthusiasm is merely "conventional," and his respect for the power of the people is "obsequious."

The author (who is also the "showman") knows the secret of his marionettes. "What are they saying?" asks the spectator. Fortunately the showman is there to relay the inaudible dialogue and its important message: "These two citizens are discussing affairs of state." A very grand subject for a very ordinary encounter: the effect of contrast is deliberate. In an 1834 letter to Charles Stöffels, Tocqueville defined style as "a certain way of seizing the attention of the reader." Here, the style is clearly that of a puppeteer inviting the audience to participate in the show.

Why did Tocqueville choose to proceed in this way? Why did he impose this particular tempo on the show: "Yet this same man leaves home . . ."? He seems determined to warn his readers that falseness and hypocrisy reign in

American society, where wealth is considered to be legitimate only if it seems to serve the community.[46] This is because he is about to examine the moral, intellectual, and religious effects of popular sovereignty on civil society, but he must first warn the reader that these effects do not fail to leave individual souls divided and individual and collective psyches repressed (to use today's terminology). Indeed, the canvas is divided: at home, the rich man indulges in luxury and inequality (like a "nobleman in Europe"), but in the street or in his "dusty hole" of an office, this millionaire humbles himself to relate to his shoemaker on equal terms. The democratic bond is the basis on which the two men can claim the same relationship to "affairs of state." Their different situations and different mentalities are illuminated by the final, implacable sentence of the moralist-showman: the rich (plural) feel "deep disgust" with democracy. In short, Tocqueville is saying that, as he will soon show, there is something to admire in popular sovereignty, which exists in America without the disorder that has accompanied it in France, but first I will show you the price to be paid, which you may not care for—and neither do I.

❧

When inspired by La Bruyère, a writer whom Tocqueville had loved since his school days, Tocqueville's style gained in intensity from the tension it rendered. American hypocrisy could not be overcome. It was too closely linked to Puritanism and to the general, almost metaphysical problem of willing acceptance of servitude to the majority.

The issue of hypocrisy addressed in this passage comes up again elsewhere in relation to subjects treated in different stylistic registers because Tocqueville's writing was linked to paradox, as Laurence Guellec has shown, and to division, not only because of its subject matter, the psychology of the Americans, but also because its moral vision was Pascalian. For Tocqueville, as he indicated to any number of correspondents, man was a divided being, to a degree enigmatic to himself,.

I would add that if, as Tocqueville's credo would have it, "man is everywhere the same," if his divided character is indeed universal, and if Tocqueville's own personality was reflected in his writing, then we are indeed dealing with a writer. There is a learned ambivalence in his major work, as

[46]Chateaubriand spoke candidly of Americans as he saw them. In his view they exhibited "a self-interested spirit and mercantile immorality," which disguised itself as social service. He described "a society of greedy merchants, without warmth or sensibility, who never answer yes or no and never have two prices because their monopoly of certain goods forces you to buy at the price they wish to sell. In short, they are coldhearted actors who enact a farce of honesty calculated to serve a vast self-interest, and among whom virtue is something to be haggled over." *Essai sur les révolutions*, pp.148 ff. of La Pléiade edition.

he himself recognized, and he knew that this calculated ambiguity would disturb the parties, schools, and critics of his time. "Nobody likes me," he said proudly when the first volume of *Democracy in America* was published. He had turned what François Furet called his existential problem into authorial vanity.

Hence *Democracy in America* is also a portrait of Tocqueville, via the anamorphosis of the art of writing, just as Mme Bovary is a portrait of Flaubert. The force of the work of art lies in its ability to dissimulate, and indeed the work is still taught in American schools as an accurate portrait of America.[47] The two aspects of the work are clearly not incompatible.

Silvestre de Sacy, a Liberal Upset by Tocqueville's Writing

It is interesting to note that Tocqueville's style of tension and ambivalence triggered an allergic reflex in one well-known representative of the liberal school, Samuel Silvestre de Sacy, who published a review of the two volumes of *Democracy in America* in the *Journal des débats* of October 9, 1840.[48] A much displeased Tocqueville counterattacked in a letter, in which he said that his *intentions* had been misunderstood: his aim was not "to prove that a return to an aristocratic social state was necessary," nor to show that the dangerous tendencies of democracy were "irresistible," but rather to teach. He wanted "to make people afraid" of those tendencies "by vividly describing them so as to encourage the voluntary inward effort that alone could combat them and teach democracy to know itself and thus to guide and discipline itself."[49]

Here we do indeed recognize the goal that Tocqueville said he had set for himself in the introduction to *Democracy in America*, and his hope that laws would be loved, that appreciation of the chief of state would be a "reasoned and tranquil sentiment," that trust would develop among the classes,

---

[47] In 1986 James Schleifer observed that in the nineteenth century American schoolchildren "learned about their institutions from abridgments of Tocqueville's book. *Democracy in America* became a civics textbook in the United States." See interview with François Ewald, *Magazine littéraire*, no. 236 (December 1986): 41.

[48] The son of a prominent Orientalist and descendant of a well-known Jansenist family, Samuel Ustazade Silvestre de Sacy (1801–79) was of Tocqueville's own generation and the editor of the *Journal des débats*, which had a circulation of 13,000 in 1830, making it the second of the leading dailies after *Le Constitutionnel*. The periodical was later taken over by the elder Bertin. Sacy became a permanent staff member in 1828 and was a respected critic and future academician and senator. I cite from the anthology in which the review was later reprinted (after comparison of the two texts): *Variétés littéraires, morales et historiques* (Paris: Didier, 1858), 2:107–18. See appendix 2.

[49] Tocqueville, unpublished letter to Silvestre de Sacy, October 18, 1840, annotated thus: "I do not know if this letter was ever sent."

that associations would develop, and so on.[50] But instead, he observed, the critique published in the *Journal des débats* presented him as someone who wished to return to aristocratic rule, a misinterpretation that was difficult to allow, he explained on two occasions, since the critic was an eminent constitutional liberal writing in a liberal newspaper.[51]

The problem is that Sacy did not say this, nor did he even suggest it. On the contrary, he complained that Tocqueville was too complacent about the dangers of democracy and the reality of America, which Sacy himself had described and criticized numerous times. Thus there was a misunderstanding, and what is interesting is that it was a result of the way in which Tocqueville expressed himself. When we look closely at Sacy's review, we see why the critic saw Tocqueville as an obscure, embarrassed, and embarrassing writer.

Sacy wrote that he "regarded [*Democracy in America*] as one of the most solid books to have appeared in many years, yet I must confess that I am not at ease while reading it. It suffocates me. I am looking for the sun and air of the ideal" (p. 113). If we recall that Tocqueville hoped to spiritualize social relations in democracy, he apparently failed.[52] What Sacy took from Tocqueville's portrait was the absence of liberty: "Is man free in a country where the rich hide in order to enjoy their wealth,[53] where intelligent men must pretend to be stupid lest their superiority cost them votes, and where everything, even sentiments and beliefs, is ruled by the majority? I say that such arithmetic liberty is a harsh form of slavery, the harshest of all, namely, moral slavery" (p. 114).

Furthermore, Sacy could not accept the idea that religion may be "useful" and that self-interest can never be forgotten, and he asked the reader, "When everyone in the crowd is insignificant, can a people be great? . . . Isn't the mass necessarily what individuals are?" (p. 113). He criticized Tocqueville for taking America as *the* model of the democratic *idea* rather than one illustration of that idea among others (which he did not name). But his main complaint was that Tocqueville wanted to teach the French to imitate others: "American democracy in France? America's selfish and self-interested ways here? Oh! That is something else again." On the other hand, the Americans "are fine just where they are." They were in fact accomplishing a providential

---

[50] See *DA* I, introduction, p. 64.

[51] Which confirms that in practice Tocqueville knew who the literary "authorities" were in democracy, as discussed earlier.

[52] "Extreme efforts that the legislator in democracies must make to spiritualize man . . . Reveal heaven even by way of the worst instruments." Nolla II, pp. 115–16, n. n.

[53] Tocqueville's portrait of the rich man, which we just examined, clearly did not escape Sacy's notice, but he offers Tocqueville no compliments on his style in the review.

mission thanks to their wealth, their conquest of the "wilderness," and so on. Neglecting the warnings and denials that Tocqueville scattered throughout the two volumes of *Democracy in America*, Sacy apparently believed that he was out to Americanize France.

Clearly, Sacy did not dwell on the *dualities* that Tocqueville described: the contrasts between American reality and the French monarchy, the disparity between what Americans said about themselves and the mores and practices revealed by a sophisticated sociology, and so on. Unlike Villemain (whose review appeared in the *Journal des savants*), Sacy, who was also an heir of Jansenism, failed to understand that the discussion of America was a *figure*; more precisely, he saw it as an unacceptable apology. So much for Tocqueville's subtleties and ironies. For Sacy, he was a scion of legitimism who was dismissive of France's national heritage.

Yet even if Sacy failed to divine the dualism of *Democracy in America*, he was aware of the author's inner conflict: "It seems to me that M. de Tocqueville sees much more than he says.... His denials notwithstanding, he represses thoughts that occur to him. Some aspects of his subject apparently frighten him. I suspect that he may be afraid of not being as much of a democrat as he would wish to be if he were to follow the implications of his own ideas" (p. 111).[54]

Sacy then delivered his final blow: "There is no conclusion," which was unacceptable. The reader was "frustrated" at not being told whether or not democracy is superior to aristocracy. Tocqueville was afraid, and perhaps ashamed, to offer his judgment as he should have done: "The reader puts down the book and asks himself anxiously, 'Is that really democracy?' By demanding equal rights and abolition of privileges as we did, and as we paid for with blood and tears, might we have leveled man's sentiments and debased his heart?" (p. 112).

If this was what the reader felt, then he did not see the other side of the work, what Tocqueville called the "marvels" of democracy. He did not embrace the *metanoia* for which the writing's embrace of tension, veiled meaning, and paradox laid the groundwork. Sacy wanted a final judgment,[55] and he offered his own: yes to democracy, but only if tempered by limited suffrage. Tocqueville, for his part, never intended to deliver a final judgment. Within the terms of his book, there could be none, whether implicit or

---

[54] Tocqueville fastened on this sentence, in which he saw the same judgment that had been leveled at him as a candidate: that he was a legitimist in disguise. In fact, Sacy did not go that far.

[55] "And why be afraid, in the end, to give one's final judgment of aristocracy and democracy?" (p. 114).

explicit, because aristocracy was a regime of great crimes and great virtues,[56] while democracy was a system of liberties always on the verge of suppressing liberty.

Unlike Guizot, who rejected the term "democracy" as inapplicable to the modern era, Sacy was a subtle thinker, but he suspected that Tocqueville, in his style and indeed his whole approach to the subject, was so inwardly conflicted that he was *not in control* of what he said and did not say, which inevitably left the reader uneasy. Tocqueville's answer was that even if he had chosen the wrong subject, he had nevertheless tried to remain *independent* of contending schools of thought.[57] He offered this mordant comment: "It would have been easier and more certain to have written a fierce critique of equality or its apotheosis."

Why was Tocqueville hurt by Sacy's review? Because in criticizing Tocqueville's style, Sacy had touched on his inner wound. Tocqueville certainly did not advocate a return to aristocratic power, yet his aristocratic bias was clear in his insistence on independence, which protected his intellectual labors and his penchant for self-medication. He blamed his critic for understanding him all too well and for diverting the public's gaze from the work to the author.

CONCLUSION: TOCQUEVILLE, SPHINX OF DEMOCRACY

On "Tocqueville in literature," we have followed a trajectory that took us from his own question—"Is a kind of authority possible in democratic literature?"—to a consideration of the context in which that question was raised: the rise of Romanticism, the logics of individualism, the debate about "speaking well," and the new aspirations of modern society. It turned out that the "circle" (in the social and sociological sense) filled the gap between the claims of the individual and the pressure of the collective, reproducing the same situation that we encountered earlier with respect to "public opinion." As observer, as advisor to democracy, and even as a writer, Tocqueville worked against the grain: he set before his era values that it no longer recognized. We glimpse this in a jocular note to Gustave de Beaumont: "No idea

---

[56] See a letter to his wife, which I cited previously, on the castles of Warwick and Kenilworth and the ambience of Walter Scott: "We have virtually nothing in France to remind us of feudal times, of those centuries of liberty and oppression, of great crimes and sublime virtues . . . that will live in man's imagination as long as the least vestige of poetry remains on this earth." *Lettres choisies. Souvenirs*, pp. 291–92. As we will see again in part 5, in the comparison with Chateaubriand, the aristocracy that Tocqueville admired was that of feudalism (between the twelfth and fourteenth centuries).

[57] "The subject, you say, was poorly chosen. I grant this" (Tocqueville's letter).

should be exhibited in a state of undress. If it is to be welcomed, it must be presented in very few words of impeccable quality." Such values are no longer current because the state of undress suits the effusiveness of the *ego*. At the age of thirty, Tocqueville did assume a position of authority in *Democracy in America*, but he was under no illusion as to his power to regulate or dictate to the living language. To a society of which he disapproved but in which he had to live, he posed a disturbing question, the question of a fascinating Sphinx: "What authority will you unwittingly tolerate?"

May we then conclude that the *question* he raised defined his originality?[58] That question was not new, however. It had already been clearly formulated by Lamennais and his followers, most notably in a current of *Le Mémorial catholique* that was at once Bonaldian and Mennaisian: "On the Principle of Authority in Literature" was the title of a lengthy essay published by Salinis in 1824.[59]

The journalist's answer was that, yes, there exists an authority in the realm of literary *taste*: this was "common sense" as Lamennais described it, that is, the authority of the human race, which was also the "Catholic principle": what everyone, everywhere, has always believed is true.[60] As Salinis put it, "the agreement of our judgments with the judgments of the majority" is the criterion of truth and must be considered authoritative in matters of taste. Tocqueville, for his part, showed that this is indeed the de facto *rule*, but that does not make it an explicit criterion as Lamennais and his followers wished, believing as they did in a curious mixture of authoritarianism and democratism. What Tocqueville described as submission to the judgment of the majority (whether express or implied) was for Lamennais and his disciples respect for Catholic authority, itself representative of the "human race" in its perpetuity.

As was common in the school of Lamennais, Salinis's arguments authorized a series of very general and very dogmatic propositions whose concrete application remained vague. Of course the target of *Le Mémorial catholique* was Protestantism, because Protestants rejected the authority and universality

---

[58] It was a question that led ultimately to the idea that there is no true aesthetic canon in democracy, and aesthetics must be replaced by a *sociology* of art, mass taste, etc.

[59] Louis-Antoine de Salinis, "Du principe d'autorité en littérature," in *Mémorial catholique*, vol. 1 (Paris: Imprimerie Lachevardière, 1824). Salinis (1789–1861) was a priest during the Restoration who later became a bishop. He was by turns an impassioned royalist, a liberal, a republican, and a Bonapartist. In *L'Individu effacé*, pp. 226–27, I describe Montalembert's anger with him during the reign of Napoleon III. He was one of the founders of the *Mémorial*, which was intended to combat the young liberals of the *Globe*.

[60] Using the famous precept of Jean de Lérins, the criterion of the Church in regard to tradition: *id teneamus quod ubique, quod semper, quod ab onmnibus creditum est.*

of the Catholic Church.[61] Hence there was a kind of truth in art: "We will always be intolerant in literature, as in religion, philosophy, and politics, because there is truth and error in everything" (p. 57, n. 1). Romanticism rejected this consensus notion of truth. It emphasized singularity (for Salinis, there were as many Romantics as there were authors). It was also schismatic: Romanticism was "the Protestantism of literature" (p. 163). This theme runs throughout the 1824 article: authority versus individualism, Catholicism versus Protestantism—the habitual categories of the Bonald group were applied to literature without a great deal of subtlety.

It is both surprising and not surprising to read these arguments about the principle of authority. On the one hand, there is today no generally recognized authority, and no institution can compensate for this lack.[62] On the other hand, there is an authority—that of society as a whole, which is identified with the "human race" in temporal affairs. Readers of *Le Mémorial catholique* already found this idea in Lamennais, who had published the final volume of the *Essai sur l'indifférence* the year before.

In his critique of literary individualism, Lamennais reached the same conclusion as Tocqueville, namely, that writers profit from a series of petty frauds: "They twist words and denature their meaning, and each one invents his own idiom, of which he alone possesses the secret" (p. 165). The consequence was that there was no more unity in Romanticism than in Protestantism: "literary Protestantism is no more a literature than religious Protestantism is a religion."

Thus we see how Tocqueville mulled over the material that he deals with in the first section of volume 2 of *Democracy in America* in the light of his reading of Lamennais, whose thought was monarchist yet steeped in the "authority of the social." As he did with Bonald and Maistre, however, Tocqueville framed his answer in terms of the typology around which he organized the entire work: the contrast between aristocratic society and democratic society. But even that typology was not wholly original: in *De la littérature* Mme de Staël had already contrasted the two types of society and their respective norms. She laid the groundwork for an idea that Tocqueville made his own: that there is a "democratic" literature that can and should be studied sociologically—or, as Mme de Staël put it, that should be examined "in its relations with social institutions."

---

[61] "Catholic" of course means "universal," and for Bossuet it was also "invariable." See *Histoire des variations des Églises protestantes*.

[62] Tocqueville says nothing about the academies, cénacles, and "magi" studied by Paul Bénichou.

Tocqueville's strength lay in the way in which he combined the contribution of two major works of the day,[63] which deeply influenced the romantic sensibility yet managed to turn their message against Romanticism. Once again we see how unclassifiable and ambivalent a figure he was: Conservative? Liberal? Admirer of a bygone era yet prophet of a democracy that he hoped could be turned in a spiritual direction? *Democracy in America* was an object of fascination for many but deeply disturbing to some, such as Silvestre de Sacy. It remains so today when one recognizes the historical challenges that the work and its readers had to confront. Tocqueville assumed the role of democracy's Sphinx.

---

[63] *De la littérature* appeared in 1800, and vol. 1 of the *Essai sur l'indifférence* appeared in 1817.

PART FIVE

The Great Contemporaries

MODELS AND COUNTERMODELS

Tocqueville and Guizot

TWO CONCEPTIONS OF AUTHORITY

> At bottom, Madame, I have not lost my arrogance. I am still certain that power belongs to people of intelligence, of the greatest intelligence, and cannot fail to return to them. But we pass from the scene so quickly, whether intelligent or not! We have so little time to wait.
>
> —Guizot, to the princess de Lieven, 1837

> There is [today] no aristocracy in the proper sense of the word, but what there is is something other than democracy.
>
> —Guizot, *De la démocratie en France,* 1849

DISAGREEMENT CONCERNING THEORY AND HISTORY

Schoolchildren are often asked to compare Corneille and Racine, who supposedly could not understand each other because the latter depicted men "as they are" and the former "as they ought to be."[1] A similar exercise might be proposed for Tocqueville and Guizot, since both men represent the same important historical and intellectual moment and both are indispensable for understanding the French spirit. To be sure, they did not belong to the same generation: nearly twenty years separate the two men. Yet they continually observed each other, encountered each other in public life, and disappointed each other repeatedly. Although Tocqueville, the younger man, learned from his elder, particularly from the lectures on the "social state" that Guizot delivered between April 1829 and May 1830 (and later published as *Civilisation en France*), he nevertheless treated him as a prime target in his manuscript and correspondence. Tocqueville could not tolerate the disparity between the professor and writer whom he had admired and the conservative politician

---

[1] La Bruyère, "Des ouvrages de l'esprit," sec. 54, in *Les Caractères* (Paris: La Pléiade, 1941), p. 104.

who stood against the tides of "democracy." To Royer-Collard and Beaumont he wrote that he despised both Guizot and Thiers, whom he refused to support as a young deputy despite his ambition for a political career.[2]

Tocqueville was also exasperated by what he took to be Guizot's excessive and hypocritical emphasis on "morality,"[3] whereas he admired Royer-Collard and appreciated Broglie and Rémusat. But is it fair to say that the clashes between the two personalities were superficial and did not involve their fundamental ideas? Especially in view of the fact that both were actors in the events of July 1848, even if one profited from the fall of the regime (Tocqueville would become a minister of the prince-president), while the other was obliged to flee to England before attempting an electoral comeback in 1849 and failing miserably?[4] Both became members of the Académie Française,[5] Guizot in 1836 and Tocqueville in 1841; both wielded intellectual influence, albeit at different times and in different forms; and both eventually joined the broad group of liberals hostile to the coup d'état of 1851.

In fact, however, there was a fundamental divergence between them, which involved an issue that was central to Tocqueville's thinking and one of the major questions of the day: What type of *authority* was possible in the society to which Guizot often referred as "the new France"? The young Guizot in fact targeted this very question in the years 1816–22, when he was beginning to formulate his political philosophy.[6] Tocqueville addressed the same issue in *Democracy in America* but from a diametrically opposite direction. To simplify, Guizot favored the English model (and therefore looked for the "new aristocracy" that he believed was destined to govern France), while Tocqueville favored the American model, which he believed represented a "dispersion of power." Should distinguished individuals be concentrated at the summit, or should the means of governing all the people be dispersed among the people? Both options involved a sociology of power, and it was certainly Guizot who led the way in this regard. But whereas Tocqueville

[2] Tocqueville observed in the fall of 1841 that "there is no power in parliament today without joining these two men or using one of them," which he refused to do. "Both are fundamentally antipathetic to my way of feeling and thinking. I despise them." See letter to Royer-Collard, *OC* XI, p. 107. See also letter to Beaumont, *OC* VIII-1, p. 449.

[3] "M. Guizot's *morality* is beginning to bore me more than I can say.... When I read him, I always want to snatch away his great philosophical overcoat and leave him naked with his ambition" (to Corcelle in 1838 during the debate about secret funds, *OC* XV-1, p. 98). This sally was aimed at both Guizot's speeches in the Chamber and his political writings.

[4] Guizot obtained 166 votes in his electoral college out of some 90,000 electors.

[5] Tocqueville was a member of two academies, Guizot of three (including Inscriptions and Belles-lettres).

[6] The 1816 Lenormand edition of Friedrich Ancillon, *De la souveraineté et des formes de gouvernement*, translated and annotated by Guizot, was his first contribution to political theory at the age of twenty-one.

accepted the new deal in politics, which might be called "the authority of the social," Guizot rejected democracy and popular sovereignty.

The one constant thread that runs through all of Guizot's writing from 1816 to the 1870s[7] was the idea that popular sovereignty is absurd, a false concept, which in reality was raised as a banner by those who wished to destroy rather than build (as in 1789 and 1793).

What emerges from this fundamental divergence—Guizot as proponent of elitist government and Tocqueville of subdued popular sovereignty[8]—is that one man became the theorist of governability by the intellectual and administrative elite and the other the theorist of mass society. From the vantage point of the twenty-first century, it might seem that Guizot lost the match (property-limited suffrage is today a forgotten antique), while Tocqueville "saw the future." Yet if Guizot was fairly clear about what he wanted (power to the bourgeoisie, which needed to be improved by better education and strict discipline), Tocqueville was less certain because his thinking was imbued with a certain nostalgia for a moral aristocracy genuinely concerned with the welfare of the people. What Tocqueville called democracy should therefore be compared with Guizot's highly critical version thereof in his analysis of "representative government," which he took to be the ultimate achievement of European history and the pinnacle of the civilizing process. It is remarkable that while Guizot spent his life praising the parliamentary regime in its constitutional monarchical form, Tocqueville had little to say about this because it apparently did not interest him.

Various commentators have noted that Tocqueville did not believe in mixed political forms, but none has asked why he remained silent about the most common contemporary regime type. To be sure, he confessed in an 1831 letter that he did not believe that this political form would last.[9] This open contempt for constitutional monarchy had roots in the alliance between Carlists and republicans. Among royalists, this made all the difference

---

[7] See esp. the *Mélanges politiques* of 1869, in which Guizot reprinted a number of texts to which he remained committed: *Du gouvernement représentatif en France* (1816), *Des conspirations et de la justice politique* (1821), and *De la peine de mort en matière politique* (1822), along with a number of others, including a short but revealing article from the *Archives philosophiques, politiques et littéraires*, "De la situation politique et de l'état des esprits en France" (1817).

[8] That is, popular sovereignty "subdued" by a two-stage voting process. In an 1849 letter to Eugène Stöffels, Tocqueville said that universal suffrage remained the only way to hold together a society that had all but dissolved. By contrast, conservatives such as Renan would later describe universal suffrage as turning society into a "heap of sand."

[9] To Ernest de Chabrol: "As you know, I have always believed that constitutional monarchies would end as republics," to which he added that Protestantism would end in natural religion. *Lettres choisies. Souvenirs*, p. 244.

between old-line monarchists and someone like Chateaubriand, who tried in *La Monarchie selon la Charte* to domesticate English constitutional forms. In Tocqueville's part of the political spectrum, everyone was interested in constitutional monarchy,[10] but he scorned this sort of constitutionalism as much as he scorned the "parvenu king" Louis-Philippe, whom he characterized with savage venom in his correspondence and in the pages of the *Souvenirs*. Clearly the *principled* difference between Tocqueville and Guizot stemmed from their different views of America. Guizot, unlike Tocqueville, was interested mainly in the "aristocratic" aspects of American society.

The two men also had different conceptions of authority in France, to which each devoted a brilliant book. They held opposing views of the Ancien Régime, feudalism, and absolute monarchy. Tocqueville not only attended Guizot's lectures but also read him and admitted to being dazzled by him. During his travels he asked his family to send him work by Guizot so that he could profit from his analysis of the United States.[11] But some twenty years later, in *The Ancien Régime and the Revolution*, he returned to his basic disagreements with the older historian.[12] To simplify their disagreement once again, whereas Guizot was grateful to Louis XIV for subduing the nobility, Tocqueville was critical of the "leveling kings" (to use a formula that he and Guizot shared) for having eliminated not only feudal liberties but also the mores and manners of the nobility and the morality that went with them. Guizot was conscious, moreover, of two other crucial points on which he and Tocqueville disagreed: the choice of democracy and the opposition to absolutism. On the first point he relied on allies such as Carné, a legitimist who had come over to Guizot's side, and Alletz, as we saw earlier. Politically he responded to Tocqueville's more or less direct attacks. In addition, he spoke of their disagreements on at least two occasions: in a letter to Tocqueville about *The Ancien Régime* and, later, when he welcomed Lacordaire to the Académie Française as Tocqueville's successor. Fundamentally what separated these two thinkers was the question of legitimate modes of authority,

[10] On debates about the Charter, see Pierre Rosanvallon, *La Monarchie impossible* (Paris: Fayard, 1994). Interestingly, prior to the coup d'état of 1851, Tocqueville believed and hoped that the Orléans dynasty might make a comeback, in opposition (once again) to Guizot, who had recently explained to his friend Nassau Senior that he was working for "fusion" and hoped to see Henri V accede to the throne. The two rivals had thus switched sides. For the remarks of Guizot and Tocqueville as reported by Senior, see *OC* VI-2, pp. 369–72.

[11] In 1829 he outlined his winter reading plans to Gustave de Beaumont. He would reread all of Guizot's historical work, including his lectures and his *Essais sur l'histoire de France*. "It is prodigious for its dissection of ideas and propriety of language, truly *prodigious*." *OC* VIII-1, p. 80.

[12] In this work Tocqueville refrained, however, from mentioning Guizot's *Histoire de la civilisation en Europe* and *Histoire de la civilisation en France*, which had been huge successes in the 1830s and 1840s.

yet they were still capable of common diagnoses of their society and times. In regard to constitutional matters, Benjamin Constant anticipated the dispute in many ways.[13] Tocqueville not only revived the conflict but envenomed it by taking up the defense of Guizot's bête noire: the government of the people by the people, or the democratic, not to say republican, regime.

POLITICAL THEORY

Diverging Views on the Locus of Authority

To understand where Guizot began, it is important to look at his notes on Friedrich Ancillon and the lectures on representative government that Guizot gave in 1820–22.[14]

THE NOTES ON ANCILLON

Guizot published his translation of Ancillon when he was working in the administration and hoped to influence the Richelieu government. This government, which ruled from September 1815 to December 1819, had to contend initially with the so-called Chambre Introuvable, which was dissolved on September 5, 1816. The young Guizot began as secretary-general to the minister of the interior, Montesquiou, for whom he wrote a report on the state of the country in 1814.[15] In 1816 he became secretary-general to the minister of justice. It was at this point that he drafted his notes on the work of Ancillon. In late 1816, after being appointed *maître des requêtes* at the Conseil d'État, he published *Du gouvernement représentatif et de l'état actuel de la France* in reply to the leader of the Ultras, Baron de Vitrolles. Finally, in 1819, Descazes named Guizot director-general for communal and departmental administration. Hence there can be no doubt that the young Guizot's predilections and ambition had led him to a place at the heart of the French administrative machine. In the realm of constitutional ideas, he worked to strengthen royal prerogatives against the pretensions of the Ultras, who sought to "draw the government into the Chambers," to speak the language of the period. In the

---

[13] See the chapter on Guizot and the Doctrinaires in *L'Individu effacé*. Here I will not examine the clash between the school of Staël and Constant and the Doctrinaires.

[14] Guizot translated Ancillon's *De la souveraineté et des formes de gouvernement* (Paris: Le Normant, 1816) and provided translator's notes (his name does not appear, but his contribution has been confirmed). For the lectures, see Guizot, *Histoire des origines du gouvernement représentatif en Europe* (Paris: Didier, 1851). This edition corrected copies of the lectures that were already in circulation (thanks to the popularity of Guizot's lectures among the youth of the period) and included later texts as well (such as the *Essais sur l'histoire de France* of 1823).

[15] See "Exposé de la situation du royaume," *Le Moniteur*, July 13, 1814, pp. 771–74.

upside-down battle that followed,[16] the Ultras took England as their model, while Guizot searched for a French path to representative government.

It is interesting to note that Guizot shared the diagnosis of popular sovereignty that Tocqueville would propose fifteen years later: what this term meant in France was in fact the sovereignty of the people's *representatives*.[17] This little game had begun with the Revolution, which inaugurated a tradition: "People became accustomed to thinking of their representative not as a person with a special function for a specific and limited purpose but rather as endowed with vague and sacred qualities that entitled him to speak in the name of the nation and to consider himself an authentic interpreter of the nation's views, a natural defender of its interests, and a repository of its rights."[18]

For Guizot, the origin of this vision, which paved the way to despotism, was popular sovereignty itself. Unlike Tocqueville, he was not interested in finding a different way of organizing popular sovereignty. He rejected it completely, once and for all: "The idea of popular sovereignty corrupted the idea of representation."[19] To reinforce state power in the new France envisioned by Louis XVIII, no support could be given to popular sovereignty. The state must not derive its *authority* from the people if it wanted that authority to be liberal (in the sense of protecting liberties).

Guizot's diagnosis of France was thus similar to Tocqueville's in regard to the confusion of state and society, but his conclusion was the opposite: America, Guizot argued, *was necessarily a bad model*. Authority must be developed at the top—by a good governing class—rather than searched for and implanted at the base. He therefore delivered a lengthy diatribe against *municipalities*, which at the time were taking all sorts of initiatives in areas that "have nothing whatsoever to do with them." These might seem to be unimportant matters (such as complimenting deputies and giving rewards to defenders of the fatherland), but "all these measures sow disorder and are tantamount to usurpation." There must be no "sudden transfer to local authorities of a certain measure administrative power over their localities" because they would then "set themselves up as so many lesser centers of power, from which they would try to exert influence over all of France." There must

[16] See, for example, René Rémond, *Les Droites en France* (Paris: Aubier-Montaigne, 1982), and the great classic of S. Charléty, *La Restauration*, vol. 4 of *Histoire de France*, ed. Ernest Lavisse (Paris: Hachette, 1911).

[17] "Little by little, the sovereignty of the people passed entirely into the hands of the people's delegates." See Ancillon, *De la souveraineté et des formes de gouvernement*, p. 130, Guizot's n. 1.

[18] Ibid.

[19] Ibid., p. 129.

not be another round of reformist efforts in the wake of recent divagations of French policy (of which Guizot offered a rapid summary), lest "higher authority" be destroyed and replaced by "a multitude of petty local despotisms, which individual passions and special interests would seize upon." It would be a mistake to play the lottery in the hope that "a more regular and tranquil federal system might someday emerge."[20]

By contrast, there was no risk in calling upon "the authority of the king," because the king was no Bonaparte: in concert with the chambers, he would assure "the empire of laws."

Hence there were no grounds for placing one's hopes in the sovereignty of the people, which inevitably leads to disorder. Nor would there be any reason to loosen *administrative* authority in the foreseeable future. The government was clearly the locus of authority: in the same text Guizot called for what he would later (in 1820–21) call "government as head of society."[21] The government of 1816 had not only the means but also the duty to prove that authority belonged to it. It should aim to organize currents of public opinion, which Guizot called parties: "It is up to the government alone to create and organize a truly national party, and only by creating such a party can the government assure its independence and power. If the government raises its own banner . . . national interests, moderate opinions, and exclusively patriotic sentiments will rally around it."[22]

In the year after Waterloo, with foreign occupation weighing heavily,[23] the liberal government, composed of Constitutionals and Doctrinaires, was obliged to organize from the top down. There was no expectation that "parties" would form within civil society. They had to be deliberately instituted.

---

[20] Ibid. pp. 154–57, Guizot's n. 4.

[21] The formula can be found in particular in *Moyens de gouvernement et d'opposition* and, at the same time, in the writings of Auguste Comte.

[22] Ancillon, *De la souveraineté et des formes de gouvernement*, p. 161. In fact by 1816 one began to discern three parties among the deputies (Ultras, Constitutionals, and Independents). See G. de Bertier de Sauvigny, *La Restauration* (Paris: Flammarion, 1955), pp. 140–46. On the debate of ideas and the place of the Doctrinaires (who were advisors to the government but not ministers), see E. de Waresquiel and B. Yvert, *Histoire de la Restauration* (Paris: Perrin, 1996), pp. 198–234.

[23] Guizot says nothing about this foreign occupation, but it obviously influenced political debate. In 1818, when foreign troops quit French soil, "toasts to their departure" were poured from the excellent vintage of that year (according to Bertier de Sauvigny). France paid 265 million francs in war indemnities. It rejoined the concert of European nations in November 1818 at the Congress of Aix-la-Chapelle. The Napoleonic era seemed definitively over. In fact the feeling of humiliation would prove durable and explains many Bonapartist and republican attitudes of the next thirty or thirty-five years. In the middle of the century, another Bonaparte would appear, disrupting first the July Monarchy and then the Second Republic. The legitimist Victor Hugo probably grasped this point better than a liberal like Tocqueville or an Orleanist like Guizot.

Three years later Royer-Collard had a similar idea about the press. The parties that France needed (democrats, legitimists, and centrists) could not do without two or three newspapers, "since newspapers constitute opinions[24] in society and in a sense govern them, it is in the interest of the parties to be constituted ... on the same level as the society to which they belong."[25]

Newspapers would be party newspapers, and they would be tied to the governing elite. Thus in 1816 Guizot wrote in praise of a certain French idea of power, liberal and reformist to be sure yet partaking of a tradition that Tocqueville would criticize from standpoint of the United States. According to Guizot, if the people, who followed the wrong leaders during the Revolution, are treated decently, "they will soon become docile and make concessions ... and will submit wholeheartedly to authority, which, having learned to understand them, need not fear to make use of them."[26] *Make use?* Guizot liked this phrase, which he would use again in *Moyens de gouvernement et d'opposition*, where he observed that Bonaparte "did not neglect individuals. This [*sic*] too is worth caring for. But he was mainly concerned with the masses." But he added this: "Never was a man more surrounded by such a cortege of individual interests."[27] The case of Napoleon confirmed the axiom that Guizot developed at the time and would put into practice under the July Monarchy: "To act on the masses and through individuals is what is called governing."[28] But for Tocqueville, the future deputy, this axiom was too cynical and Machiavellian (to put in writing, at any rate).

WHAT IS REPRESENTATIVE GOVERNMENT?

Guizot's 1820–22 lectures on representative government will enable us to form a more accurate view of the differences between his view and Tocqueville's. To begin with, the two men had very different attitudes toward *time*. In everything that Guizot wrote during the Restoration, he clearly believed that *power was there to be taken*, hence that the future was open. Guizot's position was shaped by his belief that the bourgeoisie's time had come and that through his personal intervention the promise of 1789 would be realized:

---

[24]Note the use here of the term "constitute," borrowed from the counterrevolutionaries: what one "constituted" was artificial yet necessary.

[25]Royer-Collard, speech on the licensing of newspapers, May 3, 1819, in Barante, *La Vie politique de M. Royer-Collard*, 1:486.

[26]Ancillon, *De la souveraineté et des formes de gouvernement*, p. 166, Guizot's n. 6. These are the final words in the book. Guizot wished to correct the Prussian Ancillon's judgment of the French Revolution, which he thought too harsh for French national pride to accept. Ancillon was well-known in France, and many of his works were translated into French.

[27]Guizot, *Des moyens de gouvernement et d'opposition* (Paris : Ladvocat, 1821), pp. 131–32.

[28]Ibid., p. 130.

the "new France" needed him, and as he told Barante in a famous letter, "unemployed superiorities" existed everywhere in the provinces. Tocqueville saw not a promise but a certainty that the future would be "democratic" because of some mysterious providential design, which was nevertheless a source of deep anxiety. Above all, the past was very important to Tocqueville—a past that needed to be mourned.[29] The only way to accomplish that necessary mourning was to show that certain aristocratic values (actually values of the feudal nobility) could be transfused into the blood of democracy.

For Guizot, moreover, it was not only the future that called to the present but also a past that was *ready to hand*: in England, representative government had existed since the thirteenth century and had "hovered over Europe ever since modern states were founded."[30] This simplified matters: if the French Revolution was a rupture, the development of the representative idea outside of France exhibited a reassuring continuity: "We do not need to rely on some possibly incomplete and dubious philosophical hypothesis to ask what the political tendency of European civilization was."[31] In other words, we do not need Rousseau and his theory sanctifying the general will and the sovereignty of the people.[32]

Tocqueville, on the other hand, wrote that the principle of popular sovereignty "to some extent *underlies* nearly all human institutions" (emphasis added) but "is ordinarily wrapped in obscurity. People obey it without recognizing it."[33] This almost Thomist formulation was known to the scholastics of Salamanca, but Guizot regarded it as a major error, and it was an important reason for his later hostility to *Democracy in America*. Indeed, there was an

[29] Concerning what one might call Guizot's desires for the future, recall that he stated that his life did not begin until he was eighteen: "My memories go back no further. It was only then that I began to live." Citing this statement, his daughter wrote: "His mother's will and sovereign guidance filled his life exclusively." See Mme de Witt [Henriette Guizot], *Monsieur Guizot dans sa famille et avec ses amis* (Paris: Hachette, 1880), pp. 13, 11. Recall also that Guizot's father, a brilliant lawyer, was guillotined in 1794. His mother moved to Geneva in 1799 and oversaw her two sons' severe upbringing. She would later confide to Guizot's second wife Elisa that "for twenty years I spent all my nights seated on my bed crying." Quoted by Jean Schlumberger, Guizot's great-grandson, in *Lettres de François Guizot et de la princesse de Lieven* (Paris: Mercure de France, 1963), 1:xxi. Note that both Guizot and Tocqueville had parents who suffered tragically during the Revolution, and both had mothers who were very present and very affected by those events. While Mme Guizot displayed calm authority and took care of the three young children left by Elisa, Tocqueville's mother survived the Terror with a host of durable psychological problems, which affected those around her.

[30] Guizot, *Histoire des origines du gouvernement représentatif en Europe* (Paris: Didier, 1851), 1st lecture, December 7, 1820, 1:18.

[31] Ibid., p. 16.

[32] Guizot would attack Rousseau's theory directly in subsequent lectures, e.g., the 10th lecture of the first year, entitled, "Rousseau's Theory Denying Representation in the Name of Individual Sovereignty."

[33] *DA* I.1.4, p. 117; AG, p. 62.

error in the basis of Tocqueville's assertion about what constitutes the locus of authority. For Guizot it was the government of the representative elite that "underlies all general needs, all the enduring tendencies of European society."[34] Furthermore, he had a whole theory of "generality": whenever important men *agreed* among themselves and stipulated charters, confederations, or functions of authority for the collectivity they headed, they revealed a more general interest and advanced toward the representation of "general needs." When one *ascended* to power, rising above the basic community level (of family, clan, or fief), *one created authority by creating representation*. It was therefore a fundamental error to turn to the base, toward those same "natural" communities, in the hope of finding there the seeds of public authority. Popular sovereignty, Guizot explained in the seventh lecture, is "never a means of founding liberty." It can be useful momentarily for destroying what is unjust, such as "excessive inequality or absolute power."[35] Or, to put the point even more strongly, "all legitimate power comes from above."[36]

It follows that what "constantly hovered over Europe" was certainly not democracy, despite the example of the Greeks in Athens. Representative government was the real fact of civilization, exactly as Sieyès pointed out when he contrasted it with crude and primitive "democracy."[37] Tocqueville thought that popular sovereignty had existed to one degree or another in the medieval commune and that it had been transported to American soil where it flourished as the New England town. If one plays on the very senses of the term "authority,"[38] one can say that for Tocqueville the people "dispersed" among the various American states *authorized* their governments, which derived their legitimacy from the people alone.

Recall that for Tocqueville, "the people reign over the American political world as God reigns over the universe."[39] Indeed, *Democracy in America* represented an uncompromising response to Guizot on this point. The sovereign people is at once the base and the summit, immanent and supreme, as the

---

[34] Guizot, *Gouvernement représentatif*, 1:18.

[35] Ibid., p. 114.

[36] Ibid., 25th lecture of the first year, 1:357.

[37] See, e.g., Sieyès's speech of September 7, 1789, on the royal veto or the *Délibération à prendre dans les assemblées de bailliage*, in Sieyès, *Œuvres* (Paris: EDHIS, 1989), 1:61–62. Democracy is comparable "to the raw materials and basic foodstuffs that nature everywhere offered man" and which need to be processed and refined.

[38] With reference to Hobbes in *Leviathan* as well as to Bossuet, one might say that the representative is "authorized" to act because he is the fictional *actor* of individual *authors* (who "authorize"), whom he transforms and unifies into a political people. In the same spirit, Tocqueville wrote that in America the civil jury exercises "the authority of society." *DA* I, p. 377.

[39] See *DA* I, p. 120; AG, p. 65; and part 1 above on the gap between French and American views of power.

American example proved. In this respect, popular sovereignty in America bore very little resemblance to what was called popular sovereignty in France.

For Tocqueville, all legitimate power comes from below—which goes some way toward explaining the Carlo-republican alliance under the July Monarchy, whose periodic revivals Guizot sought to prevent. Guizot boldly embraced the thesis of the absolutists, the followers of Bonald: "All power comes from God."[40] Of course, representative power must authorize itself by way of a social *legitimation* (e.g., via limited suffrage, public opinion, and separation of powers, at least in theory),[41] but the important thing was that this legitimation required the people to consent to the action of the government rather than *delegate* sovereign authority to their representatives. Or, as Guizot put it, "power proves its legitimacy, that is, its conformity to eternal reason [*sic*], by gaining the recognition and acceptance of the people on whom it is exercised through the free use of their reason."[42]

In Guizot's eyes, an even more serious objection to the concept of popular sovereignty was that it denied the essential *inequality* that divided the governed from the class of individuals suitable to govern.[43] Indeed, one feature of the "true principle of representative government" was aristocracy, an absolutely intrinsic element of government.[44] What did "aristocracy" mean in this context? First, genealogically, it referred to "the rule of the strong." Later it meant "the rule of the best": "It is the wish and predilection of society to be governed by the best, by those who know best and most steadfastly desire truth and justice."[45]

As Guizot saw it, between the pitiless reign of the strong and the moral power of the best there intervened a long historical aberration, the hereditary nobility. Representative government wanted no part of this because

---

[40] As we shall see, he congratulated Hamilton in the United States for having understood that the authority and the right to command always come from above.

[41] In 1816 Guizot argued that all powers would soon be dissolved into the chambers (king and government, deputies, peers), after which there would be no further disputes about where legislative initiatives should come from. See Ancillon, *De la souveraineté et des formes de gouvernement*, p. 136, Guizot's n. 2. In fact, Guizot always dreamed of a fusion of powers in favor of the leader-king, although he accepted party pluralism and the right of opposition.

[42] Guizot, *Gouvernement représentatif*, 1:152.

[43] Not a class a priori but a group of diverse origins that gradually set itself apart and revealed itself as the "natural aristocracy."

[44] The thesis, widespread today, that representation is an aristocratic form (defended most notably by Bernard Manin, *Les Principes du gouvernement représentatif*) may well come from Guizot by way of Carl Schmitt (*Theory of the Constitution*). There are also American sources from the debate over federalism in the 1780s. For another approach to the question, see my essay "La représentation: une fiction malmenée," *Pouvoirs*, no. 120, special issue "Voter," pp. 5–16.

[45] Guizot, *Gouvernement représentatif*, 1:100.

the noble caste lacked political and moral authority. What was needed instead was a fully authorized authority (to repeat my earlier formulation), or, in Guizot's words, "an authentic and legitimate aristocracy drawn from the bosom of society, by which society has the right to be governed and which has the right to govern society."[46] One might speak of an effective right, for such is the authorization that society bestows on its elite, but there is no *delegation*, as there is with the supposed sovereignty of the people, who are obliged to elect and thus create their representatives and thereby to renounce themselves. A sovereign who obeys, a power that is not sovereign but commands! For Guizot, this was the absurdity implicit in the concept of popular sovereignty.[47]

Implicit in Guizot's notion that aristocracy should be "drawn from the bosom of society" was the idea that what was involved was the *recognition* of an objective reality, of those who were naturally the best. The "born electors" of whom he spoke in some of his theoretical writings had to be found.[48] As he frequently explained, his doctrine of capacities was not formulated in terms of *rights*. It depended rather on supposedly objective attributes (such as wealth and education), although individuals possessing these attributes could only be presumed to possess the capacity to govern as well. As Royer-Collard remarked, the theory of capacities did not really identify those who were apt to vote but rather *excluded* those who, taken collectively, would constitute the most dangerous of all sovereignties, that of the multitude.[49]

Ultimately, for Guizot, the truth of representative government was that it translated the institutions of "natural superiority" into the realm of *legitimate inequality*. The "principle of popular sovereignty, that is, the equal right of individuals to exercise sovereignty . . . violently introduces equality where there is none and violates legitimate inequality."[50] To Tocqueville this

---

[46] Ibid.

[47] Guizot saw clearly that sovereignty originated in monarchy. This was the strong point of his argument. He did not want to admit that it could be achieved in some other way (pluralist, decentralized, or via the logic of subsidiarity).

[48] See "Elections" (1826), reprinted in *Discours académiques* (Paris: Didier, 1861), p. 384: "In society there are natural, legitimate electors, ready-made electors, whose existence precedes the thought of the legislator and whom he must simply seek to discover."

[49] The oligarchy of wealth was "the most absurd of oligarchies," Royer-Collard also said that day, adding: "The political law [i.e., the articles of the Charter regarding the vote] is not attributive of capacity but merely exclusive of incapacity. These are our inexpugnable guarantees against both oligarchy and democracy." April 13, 1818, in Barante, *La Vie politique de M. Royer-Collard*, 1:411.

[50] Guizot, *Gouvernement représentatif*, 1:108. In the same period that he was publishing *Washington*, Guizot repeated to the Chamber of Deputies that "what has often doomed democracy was its inability to accept any hierarchical organization of society. Liberty was not sufficient for it; it wanted leveling." Guizot, *Histoire parlementaire de France*, 3:107.

language was intolerable. It revealed an appetite for power that led Guizot to exalt the bourgeoisie, notwithstanding his qualifications on this score. For instance, Guizot said that the "sovereignty founded on reason and right"[51] had never been realized in any actual government: in this world, all governments are fallible. Only the naïve or indulgent could be taken in by such subterfuges. Furthermore, it was obvious that Guizot's concept of authority was incompatible with democracy—not with its elitist reality, perhaps, but with its principle and fundamental tenets. If we compare Guizot's democracy with Tocqueville's, it is clear that in the former there is nothing like "the authority of the social." And there is no "day for universal suffrage,"[52] for to have one would be to want *the inferior* to govern. For Guizot, apart from those who occupied the seat of power, there was no such thing as "authority" (force, legitimacy, moral prestige).

In Guizot's eyes, the tragedy of M. de Tocqueville was that what he said during the July Monarchy resembled what Lamennais, the republicans, the radical democrats, and even the socialists said. Although he hailed from the legitimist camp, he was doing the work of the opposite camp. For whom was he writing, moreover? This was a question that Guizot certainly asked himself, as a man who, in introducing the periodical review *Archives*, which he founded in 1817, announced that he wished to speak on behalf of power and not the people governed:

> I am not among those who would hide from the people the situation in which they find themselves. They must know, because the means of salvation are in their hands alone. But it is not the people who are called on to say how those means ought to be used. In all the affairs of society, it is up to the government to lead and take the initiative. To address the government is to recognize it. To address the people is to allow them to believe that they ought to take the place of the government.[53]

This is perfectly clear: authority must be recognized for what it is, where it is. Authority is situated above society, and it is the former, not the latter, that must be addressed. Tocqueville, of course, did not share this view. In receiving Lacordaire at the Académie, Guizot pointed out, not without acrimony, that Tocqueville had been a "loyal and moderate opponent" of

---

[51] Guizot contrasted *"souveraineté de droit"* (founded on reason and right) with *"souveraineté de fait,"* de facto power.

[52] A celebrated remark that Guizot hurled in the face of Ledru-Rollin.

[53] Guizot, "De la situation politique et de l'état des esprits en France en 1817," *Archives philosophiques, politiques et littéraires*, no. 1, reproduced in *Mélanges politiques*, p. 89. Guizot was remarkably attentive to how his speeches would be received by different audiences. See ibid., pp. 86–87.

the government, all the more readily so because he was exempt "from all responsibility for events." By contrast, when he published *The Ancien Régime and the Revolution*, he had been a minister, and one could see how much he "had learned in such a short time from the difficult work of government and the weight of responsibility." The audience understood immediately that Guizot was settling scores with Tocqueville, as Louis de Kergorlay indicated at the time in a letter to Tocqueville's widow.[54]

Rémusat's Intervention: Would There Be Any More Great Men?

It is easy to understand why Guizot wished to pay special homage to George Washington, the hero of the American Revolution and a leader with a great deal of personal charisma who had been able to instill a spirit of authority in American institutions.[55] He then served two terms as president of the republic he had helped to establish. At Le Val-Richer, during a period of leisure, Guizot wrote a biography that appeared in 1839: *Washington. Fondation de la république des États-Unis d'Amérique*, which accompanied a six-volume French translation of Washington's letters.[56] At the time, Washington was much respected in France and admired for having resisted the temptation to convert his military glory into despotic personal power. He nobly retired to Mount Vernon, refusing to run for president for a third time as some hoped he would. To contrast Washington and Bonaparte had become a veritable classroom exercise. In 1800, three months after the coup d'état of Brumaire, Louis de Fontanes became famous for his eulogy of Washington, delivered at the Invalides at the behest of Bonaparte. The parallel became almost inevitable. Yet Fontanes seems to have been somewhat irreverent: General Washington had been clever enough to refuse to govern until the United States had equipped itself with proper institutions. "He fled authority when its exercise might have been arbitrary. . . . A character such as his would have done

[54] For the Guizot quotes and Kergorlay's letter, see *Mélanges, OC* XVI, p. 344, and Françoise Mélonio's n. 14 on p. 345.

[55] Washington recognized that the Union lacked what a state required in order to count internationally: an army, a system of national finance, and a diplomatic arm. He therefore worked actively to ensure that a constitutional convention would be held in Philadelphia under his chairmanship in 1787.

[56] *Vie, correspondance et écrits de Washington*, 6 vols., 1839–40. In his *Mémoires*, 4:315–23, Guizot recounted how he had been assigned the task of selecting letters to be translated into French from Jared Sparks's American edition of the letters of Washington. I cite from the edition of Cornelis de Witt (Guizot's son-in-law), *Histoire de Washington et de la république des États-Unis* (Paris: Didier, 1855). Guizot's text appears there under the title *Washington. Étude historique*, pp. i–civ. For the various editions of Guizot's text, see Maurizio Griffo in F. Guizot, *Washington. Fondazione della replica degli Stati Uniti d'America* (Soveria Mannelli, 2004), pp. 53–54.

honor to Antiquity in its most glorious days. One doubts... that anything like it has appeared in our time. It is easy to believe that one has stumbled upon the lost life of some illustrious figure of old, like those whose portraits Plutarch so ably painted."[57]

Guizot in 1839 seized the opportunity to state his opinion about the United States and to suggest implicitly a number of differences with Tocqueville, whose second volume of *Democracy in America* was eagerly awaited. He also wanted to show that Washington as president had, like Guizot, defined himself as *juste-milieu*[58] and demonstrated his personal talents. For Guizot, the American general "had the instinct and natural gift of authority," on top of which he had "no taste or tolerance for democracy."[59] Guizot was thus able to compare himself with the successful Washington, and in his memoirs he went so far as to say that in July 1830 he and his friends had faced a challenge similar to Washington's. Furthermore, it pleased him to say that he had understood the character of the United States so well that a number of enthusiastic Americans had congratulated him on his text.[60] Finally, the Americans had decided to have Guizot's portrait done for eventual hanging in the Library of Congress.

This brings us to the heart of Guizot's theory of government, of the forms of government appropriate to France, and of the general requirements of authority. In his *Washington,* he hailed one of the Founding Fathers, Alexander Hamilton, for his sound understanding: "His superiority consisted in the knowledge that power naturally and in keeping with the inherent law of the world stands at the head of society, that it must be constituted in accordance with this law, and that any system or effort contrary to this will bring trouble and weakness to society itself."[61]

He thus reaffirmed, twenty-three years after the fact, his guiding intuition of 1816: everything depends on "the head of society." To weaken the authority of the state—for it was the state that was at issue, even if the notion of

[57] Fontanes, "Éloge funèbre de Washington," in *Œuvres de Louis de Fontanes* (Paris: Hachette, 1839), 2:154.

[58] To justify this, Guizot relied on a letter from Washington to Lafayette: see *Washington. Étude historique*, p. lxviii. In his memoirs, Guizot reproduced a lovely December 1839 letter from Louis-Philippe concerning his book. The king, who had known Washington well during his time in the United States, portrayed him as a man of *juste-milieu* moderation and confirmed Guizot's view of him, though he had not had the time to read the book. *Mémoires*, 4:322–23.

[59] Guizot, *Mémoires*, 4:319. In these extremely interesting pages, Guizot reviewed the period 1838–40 at length, explained why he wanted to compare the constitutional monarchy in France with the American republic, and so on, but said nothing about Tocqueville's book.

[60] "Twenty-five prominent Americans" told him that America was grateful to him for depicting "the true nature of our revolution and the inherent superiority of its hero." Ibid., 321, 478.

[61] Guizot, *Washington*, p. lxx.

state was French—was to weaken "society itself." Hence there was no room for the distinction (of legitimist origin) that Tocqueville had popularized between political centralization and administrative decentralization. This, too, was a purely French distinction, proving that then as now the debate about America was really a debate about France.

Before delving into Guizot's text, it is therefore worth pausing a moment to note the way in which Charles de Rémusat tried to leaven the hostility in the relationship between the two observers of America. In a review of Guizot's *Washington* for the *Revue des deux mondes*, Rémusat reflected on the relation between democracy and great men.[62] Democracy, he argued, was the regime of the masses, and if people now said that "the world lacks great men," they were simply stating the law of the future. He added, however, that great circumstances would inevitably recreate the strong historical figures they required. Furthermore, no nation can live forever in the exceptional situation of ending a revolution and refounding the state: "The people have things to do other than cheer on triumphant heroes."

Still, Rémusat continued, there were reasons to worry about the future of both the United States and France. The issue was complex, and it would be "the subject of a beautiful book, because this is the question that Monsieur de Tocqueville will deal with in the continuation of his work."[63] For Rémusat, all things considered, both rival authors were right: Guizot because he articulated the *ideal* and because nations need to honor the memory of great men; Tocqueville because he described the reign of the masses and the new conditions of social peace and prosperity. It was the old antithesis between men as they are and men as they ought to be.

In fact Rémusat's article ended with a flourish, and one wonders whether the reviewer was speaking of the authority of notables or that of M. Guizot the historian: "Today, as conventions have crumbled and men seek to be governed by reason alone, truth alone is sovereign in this world, and superior intelligences are the ministers of truth."[64] In any case, the sovereignty of intelligence was incompatible with Tocqueville's idea of a social repository of authority. Democracy must be transcended and not left to its own devices.

[62] Charles de Rémusat, "Vie, correspondance et écrits de Washington," *Revue des deux mondes*, vol. 22 (January–March 1840), reproduced in Rémusat *Passé et Présent*, new ed. (Paris: Didier, 1859), 2:139ff.

[63] Rémusat, "Vie," p. 22, and *Passé et Présent*, 2:164. This passage confirms that the rivalry between Tocqueville and Guizot was apparent to the reader of 1840 even if it is not apparent today. Tocqueville's book came out in April, a few months after Rémusat's review of Guizot.

[64] Compare with two articles on Lamennais, rewritten and reprinted in *Passé et Présent*, 1:401. Only the elite knows and proves that it is enlightened and bestows the benefits of its enlightenment on the governed. As with Guizot, "superiorities" are justified by their position as reason immanent in society, but they are not delegated by society.

A Controversial America: Natural Aristocracy According to Guizot

Tocqueville and Guizot shared one methodological principle for the study of America: "Never forget the point of departure." They applied it differently, however. For Tocqueville the point of departure was the transplantation of the commune, which became the New England town, infused with the spirit of the Puritan pioneers. For Guizot, the relevant starting point was rather the American Revolution and the fact that there was "no struggle between aristocracy and democracy, between an old aristocratic society and a new democratic one."[65] Or, to put it another way, there were "no social spoils to share, no ancient and deep-seated passions to satisfy."[66]

In other words, Guizot directly compared the two revolutions and from this comparison deduced that events in America had been guided by an *aristocratic principle*, whereas in France, the hatred of privilege and the conflict between the revolutionaries and the king had given the principle of popular sovereignty the upper hand. Whenever Guizot returned to the American Revolution, his thesis was the same: the movement had been led by gentlemen. He recalled Washington's advice for selecting officers in the Revolutionary War: "Take gentlemen. They are the most trustworthy as well as the most capable."

Guizot judged the social conditions of the American Revolution to be ideal for republican government:

> Indeed, it was among the leaders, in the front ranks of the party, that enthusiasm and commitment persisted [after the initial battles]. Elsewhere, in an analogous situation [i.e., the French revolutionary wars], the impetus for perseverance and sacrifice came from the people. In America, it was the enlightened and independent classes who had to support and revive the flagging spirit of the people in the great battle waged in the country's name.[67]

Republican government required precisely this, moreover: it "needs the cooperation of all classes of citizens. If the mass of the population does not warmly adopt it, it is without roots. If the upper classes reject or abandon it, it is without repose. . . . Because the republican authorities are weak and precarious, they must draw much of their moral force from the disposition

---

[65] Guizot, *De la démocratie en France*, p. 37. It is amusing that Tocqueville said almost the opposite: when the word "gentleman" arrived in the new world, "people applied it indiscriminately to all citizens." Tocqueville concluded that "its history is the history of democracy." *ARR, OC* II-1, p. 148.

[66] Guizot, *Washington*, p. xx.

[67] Ibid., p. xxi.

of the social order."[68] In the United States "the country's natural and national aristocracy" served as "the head of the revolution and the republic." Among the crucial social categories (Guizot called them "classes") were judges, wealthy planters, important merchants, and army officers: "By virtue of their wealth, education, and habits," these people "brought the most natural authority, tranquil independence, enlightenment, and leisure to public affairs. Only under such conditions can a republic durably establish itself."[69]

Guizot developed the same thesis in the 1850 preface to his *Histoire de la révolution d'Angleterre.*[70] England's American colonies were already republican, he argued, and neither the social order nor the political order was disturbed by independence, which the wealthy had favored: "The people marched, and the event took place under the leadership" of the wealthy.[71] In fact Guizot oversimplified debates among republicans about English sovereignty and the notion of sovereignty in general.[72] He also discounted the controversy over how much democracy and how much aristocracy should be permitted, which attained its peak in 1787 because anti-Federalists suspected that a "hidden aristocracy" might favor the establishment of a monarchy in the newborn United States.[73]

Furthermore, Guizot believed that the American Revolution and the Glorious Revolution were both the work of elites. Indeed, "the revolution of 1688 was aristocratic in execution," and it showed that "aristocracy and democracy can live and prosper together, mutually supporting and disciplining each other."[74] For the leader of the Doctrinaires, a good revolution was thus one carried out by "men of order and government" (and Guizot maintained this wording even in the 1850 edition, thus after the revolution

---

[68] *Démocratie en France*, p. 38.

[69] Ibid., pp. 37, 39. See also *Washington*, p. xxi.

[70] Guizot began working on this book during the Restoration, and it was published in two volumes by Béchet in 1826 and 1827. He added to it after 1848, with four new volumes published between 1854 and 1856. It was published with a new "Discourse on the History of the English Revolution," which first appeared in print in 1850. Citations here are to *Histoire de la révolution d'Angleterre* (Paris: Victor Masson, 1850).

[71] Guizot, "Discours sur l'histoire de la révolution d'Angleterre," p. 161.

[72] See Gordon Wood, *The Creation of the American Republic, 1776–1787* (Chapel Hill: University of North Carolina Press, 1998). See also the references in Thierry Chopin, *La République "une et divisible"* (Paris: Plon, 2002), p. 20, n. 2.

[73] One particularly vehement critic published articles under the name "Centinel." See Chopin, *La République*, p. 87. Hence I cannot agree with Pierre Rosanvallon that "the term 'natural aristocracy' had . . . none of the repulsive connotations in the United States that it inevitably had in France at the same time," i.e., during the French Revolution. See *La Démocratie inachevée* (Paris: Gallimard, 2000), p. 29. Defenders of the elite attempted to prove that its superiority was "natural," but they encountered firm opposition.

[74] *Histoire de la révolution d'Angleterre*, 1:149.

of 1848). Like Tocqueville, Guizot proceeded by comparison with France in order to show, in the wake of 1848, "why the English Revolution succeeded." But their analyses diverged. Not only was the class struggle not the driving force in the English or American Revolutions (on that point they agreed), but the American Revolution was not in Guizot's eyes primarily *democratic*. France was turned upside down by the principle of popular sovereignty, which Guizot considered fallacious and destructive, and it could not distinguish a democratic regime of popular sovereignty from a republic. In Guizot's view, this confusion was central to understanding the Second Republic of 1848.

Consequently, what was distinctive about America was very different from what many people believed. As Guizot explained in 1849, "the United States of America are the world's model of a republic and a democracy. Did the Americans ever dream of calling themselves a 'democratic republic?' I am not surprised to learn that they did not." Indeed, "there was no clash between aristocracy and democracy" in America, and this explained everything.[75] Democracy corrected by aristocracy—or, in other words, an alliance between the lower orders and the natural aristocracy—was for Guizot the healthy and durable form of a republican regime.

Thus everything depends on what one is supposed to understand by "natural aristocracy." Or, to put it another way, what *institutions* corresponded to the social, political, intellectual, and moral preponderance of this supposed natural aristocracy? Did Guizot, in forming his views, draw on American authors? One might think so, because American leaders in the period 1770–1800 discussed "the natural aristocracy" a great deal, but in fact, as we shall see, Guizot did not draw the expected consequences in regard to institutions; in any case he was at best unclear about them.

Indeed, if we turn to John Adams's celebrated *Defense of the Constitutions of Government of the United States of America*,[76] we find that the question of the new aristocracy was directly linked to the organization of government. In Adams's view, there are always "gentlemen" and "simplemen," the former being those who have received a "liberal education" by virtue of either family tradition or the fact of issuing from the class of "merchants, mechanics, or

---

[75] *Démocratie en France*, pp. 36–37.

[76] Published in 1787, French translation in 1792. Adams wrote in response to Turgot and Condorcet and in support of the idea of mixed government, which was based on a faithful reproduction of the existing classes of society. See Denis Lacorne, *L'Invention de la république* (Paris: Hachette, 1991), pp. 175ff. On Adams's theory of the balance of powers, see M. Lahmer, *La Constitution américaine dans le débat français* (Paris: L'Harmattan, 2001), pp. 13 passim.

laborers."[77] It was natural for simpler folk to seek the support and protection of gentlemen, but Adams explained that there were two dangers to be avoided: first, that the elite created by birth, education, services rendered, and recognized merit be allowed to appoint itself to office, and second, that the elite would have the power to intervene directly with the executive branch that makes such appointments. Hence there should be separation of powers in the state governments (and later the federal government): *interests should be set against interests* to serve the general interest. In other words, the executive branch should have a rival for power in the senate (the chamber of gentlemen) and an ally in the other chamber, that of the common people.[78] This balance of power, reflecting the contending social forces, was supposed to draw the best from the natural aristocracy, which Adams described as both a boon of Providence (given its enlightenment, habits, and family and historical experience) and the gravest danger to a well-constituted state.[79] In another remarkable passage, Adams indicated that, in the interest of liberty, this natural aristocracy should be neither too united nor too divided. If the elite formed a compact corps, it might become despotic, but if it were too divided, it would give rise to factions that would clash on many issues and thus destroy the commonwealth. Since the ideal was a "government of laws" and not a "government of men"—the great principle of modern constitutionalism—the elite must be put to good use, but its pretensions had to be checked.[80] Thus Adams was no mere apologist for the social elite. He had some fairly sophisticated ideas about the way in which it was formed.[81] Only if the mechanism of government were properly contrived could one

[77] For the details of Adams's argument, see the excellent anthology by Philip Kurland and Ralph Lerner, eds., *The Founders' Constitution* (Chicago: University of Chicago Press, 1987), 1:348.

[78] Adams was attacked on this point by "Centinel" in 1787 (no. 1). The pamphleteer insisted that this structure of government would not be viable because institutionalized disparity would lead to stalemate. Furthermore, it was based on a mistaken philosophy, according to which "the happiness and well-being of the community were the result of opposing and discordant interests" (Kurland and Lerner, *The Founders' Constitution*, 1:349). As an anti-Federalist, "Centinel" favored a society of equal small proprietors and believed in the virtue of the citizenry as well as in a unicameral legislature. Similarly, Jefferson believed in natural aristocracy, which he contrasted to the "artificial aristocracies" of the European monarchies, but he rejected the idea of a legislative chamber to represent it. He argued that the people themselves would be able to choose an aristocracy of virtues and talents by way of elections. See letter to John Adams, October 28, 1813, "The Natural Aristocracy," University of Virginia Library, Electronic Text Center.

[79] "It forms a body of men which contains the greatest collection of virtues and abilities in a free government, is the brightest ornament and glory of the nation, if it be judiciously managed in the constitution. But if this be not done, it is always the most dangerous; nay, it may be added, it never fails to be the destruction of the commonwealth." See Kurland and Lerner, *The Founders' Constitution*, 1:543.

[80] See ibid., 1:544.

[81] See ibid., 1:541. Adams indicated that over the course of several generations, three or four families in each New England town provided the justices of the peace and even the state representatives.

ensure that the intellectual and moral attainments and ambitions of this elite would benefit rather than threaten the community: the natural aristocracy must not become a triumphant bourgeois oligarchy.

Guizot did not do justice to these debates in his writing about the United States, nor did he adequately convey the ingenuity of American constitutional arrangements (or the subtlety of *The Federalist*, which is still a lively topic of discussion in American studies). Nor did he clarify the differences between France and the United States by treating the French middle class as an aristocracy of "superiorities" with a vocation for representative government. Despite certain concessions concerning the need for a balance of powers,[82] Guizot sought to *unify* the middle class and to set it as a powerful and coherent unit at the summit of the state: this was the very principle of the property-limited suffrage.

Although Tocqueville was prepared to admit that "the aristocracy" exerted a powerful influence in the American colonies—most notably among southern planters, thanks to the system of entails exported from England—he insisted on the rise of the people, especially after the "republicans" (or, more properly, Democratic-Republicans) won the presidency against the Federalists, who had elected the first two presidents, Washington and Adams. He wrote that "America is the land of democracy. The Federalists were therefore always in the minority, but their ranks included nearly all the great men to come out of the War of Independence, and their moral power was considerable."[83] The election of Jefferson on March 4, 1801, marked a turning point: "From that moment on, the Republican, or Democratic, party marched from conquest to conquest and eventually took complete control of society." Despite all the achievements of the Federalists, they "fought against the irresistible penchant of their century and their country. Their theories, whether sound or flawed, suffered from being inapplicable in their entirety to the society they wished to govern; what came to pass under Jefferson would therefore have come to pass sooner or later in any case."

It is interesting to note that Guizot apparently responded directly to this passage: "Ever since that day the Democratic Party has governed the United States. Is this a good thing? Could it have been otherwise? What were the consequences of the Democratic Party's triumph? . . . These are vast questions, difficult to answer . . . [even] for nationals, and surely impossible for a foreigner."[84]

---

[82] In the *Histoire du gouvernement représentatif*, Guizot had little to say about the balance of powers and far more about the competition between the government and the opposition.

[83] *DA* I.2.2, p. 258; AG, p. 200.

[84] Guizot, *Washington*, pp. ci–cii.

Along with all his contemporaries on both sides of the Atlantic, Tocqueville saw Jackson's America as the triumph of "democracy" of the least distinguished sort, and he believed that great men would be unlikely to run for office. Rémusat echoed this idea in the 1840 article I cited earlier. For Tocqueville, the only aristocracy that remained was that of "jurists" (lawyers and judges), who, as Hamilton had remarked long before, had particular skills and highly specialized knowledge. But this aristocracy was apparently of no interest to Guizot.

Neither in 1839 nor in 1848 nor later on did Guizot wish to speak of what had become predominant in America, namely, democracy in Tocqueville's sense. He argued that a true republic was not democratic and that many people were confused about America. In 1839 he wrote that he himself was living proof that great individuals could still lead nations. His portraits of Peel in England and Washington in the United States embodied this idea and this desire, which often come up in his correspondence.

AUTHORITY AND LIBERTY IN THE ANCIEN RÉGIME: TWO INTERPRETATIONS

With regard to the Ancien Régime, Tocqueville and Guizot held different ideas of *society*.[85] Guizot believed that French history from the birth of feudalism to the Revolution was best analyzed in terms of the social bond, which was strong at times but at other times nonexistent. By the end of the Roman Empire, society was in ruins. Under feudalism it did not yet exist because personal bonds between one man and another predominated. It was under the rule of a strong central power that "society" was reborn: first Louis XIV and then Bonaparte rebuilt a society that had been decimated by religious or political conflict. We must therefore focus on the concept of society as

[85] I use the following editions: Guizot, *Essais sur l'histoire de France*, 13th ed. (Paris: Didier, 1872) (1st ed., 1823); *Histoire de la civilisation en Europe*, new ed. (Paris: Didier, 1846) (lectures 1827, 1st ed., 1828); *Histoire de la civilisation en France*, new ed. (Paris: Didier, 1857), 4 vols. (lectures 1828–29 and 1829–30) (neither the volume number nor the pagination is consistent among the numerous editions of these lectures). Tocqueville, *ARR, OC* II-1, 1964 (1st ed. 1856; 1st ed. of *OC*, 1952), is cited here as *ARR* I. The manuscripts, edited and annotated by André Jardin in 1953, published as *OC* II-2, are cited here as *ARR* II. The Gallimard edition (edited by J.-P. Mayer for *ARR* I and A. Jardin for *ARR* II) is based on the fourth edition, published in 1858 (but dated 1859). (Where possible, page references to the English translation by Arthur Goldhammer, *The Ancien Régime and the French Revolution*, published in 2011 by Cambridge University Press, are cited as AG2.) This edition includes many corrections and modifications by Tocqueville to his 1856 text and to the second edition (also 1856) and third edition (1857). It was Kergorlay who suggested these changes. The thousands of pages of Tocqueville's notes and manuscripts have been studied exhaustively by Robert Gannett Jr., *Tocqueville Unveiled* (Chicago: University of Chicago Press, 2005). This work is little concerned with the view adopted here, even in Gannett's comparison with Guizot (pp. 18ff).

Guizot used it, in service of a teleological vision in which what emerged from society, reconstituted in such a way as to manifest its essential qualities, was ultimately the *French nation* and *civilization*. For Guizot, these two terms marked the apogee of the historical process. French civilization revealed itself socially and culturally in the power of the bourgeoisie and politically in the rise of the state, which was nothing other than society's representative and administrator. Louis XIV and Napoleon were the two heads of state who had elaborated the French administration and laid the groundwork for, or at any rate consolidated the triumph of, modern equality.

It is easy to see why the conclusions that Guizot drew from his historical analysis would inevitably displease Tocqueville, whether in 1835–40 or in 1856, because Guizot was arguing that political *authority* had to pass through a despotic phase in order to achieve social and national unity. If so, then why shouldn't the Terror have been necessary to create a regenerated nation, as Lezay-Marnésia had argued in his controversy with Constant under the Directory?

Tocqueville attempted to construct a different history of France, according to which, in the words of Mme de Staël, "liberty is ancient and despotism is modern."[86] He, too, privileged the idea of society, which he opposed to that of isolation. Prior to the eighteenth century, one still observed a "common" life in France: "Although inequality existed, isolation did not, and even ineligibility for office (*incapacité*) was less absolutely determined by birth. Little by little, occasions to act in common in common affairs ceased to exist. The noble's need of the commoner, and in general and local affairs, the commoner's need of the noble, ceased to make themselves felt."[87]

This is the leitmotif of Tocqueville's analysis of the Ancien Régime: the explanatory key of the work is "acting together," class rapprochement, and bonds of subordination and benevolence (patronage). On the eve of 1789,

[86] Kergorlay recognized this connection and quoted this sentence to Tocqueville after receiving his book (see *OC* XIII-2, p. 300). Note that historians of political though, especially in the United States, have been attempting for some time to show that Guizot and the Doctrinaries influenced Tocqueville's analysis of the Ancien Régime. I have not found much useful in this work because it does not touch on the question that I am raising here, namely, the inherently conflicting choices made by the two historians. Furthermore, the idea of "the social state" as a fundamental determinant (discussed in part 1 above) was not limited to the Doctrinaires; indeed, it was a commonplace at the time. Furthermore, it disappeared from *ARR*. See the documents in *History of European Ideas* 30 (1) (2004), which reflect recent debates on liberalism and society, including the Guizot-Tocqueville comparison: see the articles by Melvin Richter, "Tocqueville and Guizot on Democracy: From a Type of Society to a Political Regime," and Cheryl Welch, "Tocqueville's Resistance to the Social." On Tocqueville as historian, I consulted Harvey Mitchell, *Individual Choice and the Structures of History* (Cambridge: Cambridge University Press, 1996), in addition to the work of Robert Gannett cited previously.

[87] *ARR* II, p. 361.

comparing France to Europe, he says that "nowhere [were] citizens less prepared to act in common,"[88] even though "men had become more similar to
one another" (title of chap. II.8). To be sure, Tocqueville continued, unity
was present,[89] but it was a unity of generalized rivalry, of "collective individualism" (to borrow an expression of Tocqueville's), which was a preparation
not for liberty but for despotism.

For the author of *The Ancien Régime and the Revolution*, the French both
desired authority and chafed under it because aristocracy had been eradi-
cated from society. For Guizot, on the other hand, it was by overcoming "a
multitude of petty nations and petty sovereigns"[90] that the kings created a
true *society*, one that conformed to the concept of society. Clearly Guizot
had adopted the point of view of the bourgeoisie, the beneficiary of the unity
forged by the kings and by Napoleon, whereas Tocqueville was describing
a process of dispossession (of the aristocracy and of communes deprived of
their liberties) and of the creation of a *factitious* nation, the creation of absolutism, which put offices up for sale, centralized the administration, and
forced the nobility to live at Versailles and beg for favors.

*The Comparison of France and England:
Disagreement about the Fourteenth Century*

In 1856 Tocqueville's comparative model was no longer America but England. As he saw it, both England and France had passed through similar historical stages, and it was not until the fourteenth century that "the destinies
of the two nations diverged."[91] He tried to show that in the old social constitution of Europe, feudal dues, guilds, fiefs, and taxes, "everything was alike."[92]
King Charles VII introduced a caesura in French history by establishing a
tax without consulting the nation and imposing it solely on the third estate:
"The nobility was cowardly enough to allow the third estate to be taxed provided that it remained exempt."[93] From then on, the contrast between France

---

[88] *ARR* I, p. 143.

[89] "Local life in the provinces had long since been extinguished. This had contributed greatly to making the French more alike. Through the various forms of diversity that still existed, unity was already
apparent; uniformity of legislation revealed it." Ibid., p. 143.

[90] Guizot, *Civilisation en France*, 3:209.

[91] *ARR* I, p. 160; AG2, p. 94.

[92] Ibid., p. 92. It was to this passage that Tocqueville referred when he indicated that the decisive break
had occurred in the fourteenth century (p. 160).

[93] Ibid., p. 160; AG2, p. 94. Indeed, according to Olivier-Martin, *Précis d'histoire du droit français*
(Paris: Dalloz, 1938), pp. 343–44, the king originally created the personal *taille* in the image of the sei-
gneurial *taille*. In 1439 Charles VII eliminated the *taille* on lords. The historian writes that the nobility
"would never have agreed to pay a tax that had previously been levied on [the king's] subjects."

and England increased steadily, and Tocqueville laid the blame squarely at the door of the French nobility: "In the eighteenth century in England, it was the poor man who enjoyed the tax privilege; in France it was the rich man. There, the aristocracy took the heaviest public responsibilities on itself so that it would be allowed to govern; here it retained the tax exemption to the end to console itself for having lost the government."[94]

Guizot's analysis was quite different because he did not claim that France and England had initially evolved in parallel. French feudalism never constituted a society because, in Guizot's terms, it was a system in which "individuality" dominated. "Society as such, . . . meaning the commonality of a certain portion of the lives, fates, and activities of individuals, was quite minimal and limited."[95] Individual independence cannot by itself create the social bond, which depends on submission to a common law. In feudalism, the common was one of "isolation more than liberty," and this fact would continue to influence the French aristocracy, which was *incapable of behaving as a body*: "By contrast, in England after the Norman conquest, everything was collective."[96] To resist the Anglo-Saxons, the Norman barons acted as a body. Similarly, in confronting the king of England, they behaved like "a true aristocracy." This was not true of the French nobility: "From the founding of the monarchy to the fourteenth century, everything was individual—forces, liberties, resistances, and oppression." The principal social force in France was thus fragmented. Most feudal lords thought of themselves as petty sovereigns and behaved accordingly. Fortunately, according to Guizot, a third estate, unique in Europe, was able to emerge with royal support. Thus the crucial difference emerged before the fourteenth century and not after, as Tocqueville maintained. For Tocqueville, the crucial process took place between the fourteenth and eighteenth centuries: the monarchy leveled local disparities, and the nobility surrendered to the king and to its own selfish attitude toward society. For Guizot, England chose a different course from the beginning, whereas for Tocqueville, the monarchy and aristocracy committed a true moral *error*, in which the French aristocracy, unlike the English, ultimately transformed itself into a "caste."

As will be clear from the foregoing, Tocqueville adopted the stance of a committed historian, who set out to compile an indictment against what he considered to be the guilty parties: *The Ancien Régime and the Revolution* is from beginning to end a polemic, as Tocqueville's friend Kergorlay

[94] *ARR* I, p. 160; AG2, p. 94.

[95] Guizot, *Civilisation en France*, 4:78. Seen already in his *Essais sur l'histoire de France*, the fifth essay, entitled "Du caractère politique du régime féodal."

[96] Guizot, conclusion of *Essais sur l'histoire de France*, p. 435.

immediately recognized.[97] Guizot set out to be ecumenical and conciliatory. He told a story of success rather than decadence and foretold the future rather than lament the past.

The Role of the State in France: Absolutism

Getting back to the idea of society, Guizot argues that society exists when three factors are united: (1) a form of union within the sphere of civil society; (2) unity achieved at the level of political power; and (3) the development of a moral identity shared by individuals.[98] Charlemagne was important because he brought an "external political unity" to France, but if we look at "the moral condition of men themselves," "unity was completely lacking" owing to diversity of laws, traditions, and languages. From the tenth century on, progress in this area was still hard to see, but "the tendency toward national unity and therefore political unity became the dominant character, the most important fact, in the history of French civilization, the general and persistent fact around which our whole study will revolve."[99]

The French nation, still called "French civilization," was for Guizot the result of this process, which began in the tenth century. He brilliantly traced its history through many stages, which I will not recount here, except to note that the legal advisors to the king in the late thirteenth century were the instrument that made it possible to impose regulations on the communes of France. Although this was an important step, Tocqueville condemned this expansion of monarchical power, which he deemed odious.[100] Similarly, the government of Louis XIV played a positive role in Guizot's analysis, as in that of Pellegrino Rossi.[101] Although the Sun King was a great reformer, he failed

---

[97] Upon receiving the book, Kergorlay proclaimed that "it is the most terrible censure of the *ancien régime* ever published" (*OC* XIII-2, p. 306). Tocqueville replied that he found himself committed to a far more stringent critical process than he had anticipated: "I discovered . . . that no more awful collection of documents about this period had ever been collected. Indeed, this seemed to me so much the case that I was led to this result in a sense against my will and original intention, which was rather the opposite." Furthermore, "The rather violent effect that the truth had on me gave it an impartial character" (*OC* XIII-2, pp. 309–10).

[98] *Civilisation en France*, 3:207.

[99] Ibid., p. 208.

[100] Tocqueville discussed this point with young Alexis Stöffels, who was studying law at the time: "It was with the aid of Roman law and its interpreters in the fourteenth and fifteenth centuries that the kings succeeded in establishing absolute power on the ruins of free medieval institutions. . . . Your professors will not tell you this." *Œuvres*, Beaumont ed., 5:468.

[101] The correspondence with Kergorlay shows that Tocqueville and his cousin wanted to follow Rossi's lectures in constitutional history, which were circulating in various forms. Tocqueville was surely familiar with them.

to reform French political institutions,[102] and it was this contradiction, as well as the struggle between "free examination" and "pure monarchy,"[103] that led to the crisis of the monarchy in the eighteenth century. Nevertheless, the reign of Louis XIV inspired a new *society*, "a society that witnessed important advances in wealth, might, and intellectual activity of all kinds. But alongside this society of progress, [there stood] an essentially static government."[104]

In 1818, in a review of the complete works of Rousseau, Guizot credited Louis XIV with a "new constitution of society," as well as with establishing a principle of equality before the law, which became "the essence of French society."[105] Although he no longer conceived of the nobility as a product of the Frankish conquest (in the line of Boulainvilliers), the Guizot of 1828–30 was clearly prefigured in this interesting 1818 text. The argument he developed there could not have pleased Tocqueville and most likely exasperated him: "The independence of the nobility ceased to exist [in the seventeenth century], and its hierarchy disappeared. Royal authority acquired the power and the duty to ensure that justice, lawful order, and protection—in short, the best for all citizens—emanate directly from it. . . . The reign of Louis XIV witnessed the peaceful and settled enjoyment of this new constitution of society."

Tocqueville knew that Guizot and Augustin Thierry, who quoted and corrected each other constantly, shared the same opinion about Louis XIV. Thierry wrote that the king "worked to complete the political unification of the country and unwittingly laid the groundwork for the great single and sovereign national community."[106]

In the view of Tocqueville, the great-grandson of Malesherbes, the parlements were the school in which the French nation learned about law and justice—though Tocqueville had important reservations about the parlementaire ideology. He observed that litigation and a taste for legal formalities and judicial habits had become widespread on the eve of the Revolution.

---

[102] Guizot of course traced the history of the English Parliament in his *Histoire du gouvernement représentatif en Europe*.

[103] A struggle that Guizot studied in *Civilisation en Europe*.

[104] Ibid., p. 392.

[105] Guizot, *Archives philosophiques, politiques et littéraires* (1818), 4:200–205.

[106] Augustin Thierry, *Essai sur l'histoire de la formation et des progrès du tiers-état*, new ed. (Paris: Garnier, 1875), p. 296. For Thierry, as for Guizot, the king and state marked indispensable stages and mediations in the advent of the nation. Rossi, an immigrant proud to teach at the Collège de France, argued that "under [Louis XIV], the French principle, of which he was the eminent representative, developed in all its forms—literary, scientific, artistic, and political. And this French principle developed so rapidly that it spread beyond the borders of France and into neighboring countries." See *Cours de droit constitutionnel*, Guillaumin (1866), 1:227. For Rossi, who was in the line of Guizot, "material and moral unity through civil equality—this was the civil and political religion of the new France" (ibid., p. 245).

"Only in this one respect did the Ancien Régime contribute to the education of a free people."[107] The parlementaire revolt of 1770, which was supported by lawyers associated with the sovereign courts and by the Cour des Aides (Malesherbes drafted their remonstrances), exemplified a spirit of liberty greater than the French or American Revolution: "In all the history of free peoples, I know of nothing greater than what took place on that occasion."[108] By contrast, Guizot saw nothing in the parlements but corporatist prejudices.[109]

Could Louis XIV really be portrayed as the liberator of society from feudalism, the founder of equality, and the protector of arts and of the new society? Tocqueville could not accept such a causal argument: royal despotism, which had muzzled the parlements[110] and stifled local liberties, could not account for the cultural achievements or great minds of the age. In a manuscript contemporaneous with *The Ancien Régime and the Revolution*,[111] he wrote at length about the illusions associated with the Augustan age or the age of Louis XIV. In the tradition of Mme de Staël, particularly in *De la littérature*, he wrote that "nearly all the masterpieces of the human spirit have been produced in centuries of freedom.... When we look closely at what happened in these [other] periods, we find that absolute governments had inherited the forms, the intellectual activity, and the freedom of imagination created by free mores and institutions." Indeed, he continued, "*feudal liberty*, which remained alive in the midst of wars of Religion and the Fronde," could explain the flourishing of the arts under Louis XIV.[112] Furthermore, under Augustus, under the Medici in Florence, and as a despotic regime emerged under Louis XIV, "these presumed effects gradually disappeared, and the nature of things reasserted itself in the form of a tranquil and sterile despotism."

[107] *ARR* I, p. 175; AG2, p. 109.
[108] Ibid., p. 174; AG2, p. 109.
[109] See Guizot's review of the historian Lémontey in *Archives philosophiques* (1818), 5:266.
[110] Recall that Louis XIV ended the Fronde by entering the Parlement of Paris in boots, whip in hand. He withdrew the right of remonstrance and forbade the parlements to refer to themselves as "sovereign courts." Nothing more was heard from the parlementaires during his long reign, much to the dismay of Saint-Simon and other exponents of the ancient liberties of the nobility. Boulainvilliers and Saint-Simon were two authors whom Tocqueville refrained from citing because their aristocratic liberalism was all too apparent.
[111] *ARR* II, p. 345: "That the means of reviving literary life is not to destroy political life."
[112] Italics added. Tocqueville developed the same idea in another passage of the manuscripts in which he explicitly quotes Mme de Staël as an opponent of Napoleonic despotism and a champion of human rights. See Tocqueville, *The Old Regime and the Revolution*, trans. Alan Kahan (Chicago: University of Chicago Press, 2001), 2:259. Tocqueville uses the idea of *feudal liberty* to explain the successes of the supposed age of Louis XIV.

Clearly, feudal liberty explained many things for Tocqueville, so powerful was his nostalgia for an era that existed more in his dreams than in the
historical record.[113] He did not believe in the education of the nation that
Guizot attributed to state authority under Louis XIV. He did not apply
the term "society" to what the theorist of "representative government" was
looking for, namely, the union of the state with bourgeois power.[114] By contrast, one of Tocqueville's goals was to incriminate the *demiurgic* character of
monarchical power, which Louis XIV had heated to incandescence. It was
this conception of state authority that Tocqueville would indict in volume
2 of *Democracy in America*. Its sociological aspect must now be examined.

Bourgeoisie and Centralization

As we have seen, the key to the differences between Guizot and Tocqueville
lies in the idea of society: for Guizot, it was a maximal spiritual and political unity that made the nation a society, whereas Tocqueville believed that
society should be analyzed in terms of "common action" and "sharing." In
this respect, and contrary to Guizot, the eighteenth century marked the cul-
mination of a social crisis. Perhaps the darkest chapter of *The Ancien Régime
and the Revolution*[115] sums up the dramatic desocialization that Tocqueville
believed he had observed: "But when the poor man and the rich man share
virtually nothing in common, neither common interest nor common complaints nor common affairs, the darkness that hides the mind of one from the
mind of the other becomes unfathomable."[116]

[113]Cf. François Furet's remark: "The French nobility was never the 'aristocracy' of which Tocqueville
dreamed, in the sense in which sixteenth-century Venice, say, was an aristocracy governed by its senate."
See Furet, *Penser la Révolution française*, p. 199.

[114]Bear in mind that Guizot pursued his own project of *raising the cultural level* of the French bourgeoisie of his time. In launching an *Encyclopédie progressive* (which lasted only a few months in 1826), he
spoke of the "bourgeoisie of the intellectual world" and of "the rich who are also looking for intellectual
riches" (quoted by Pierre Rosanvallon in *Le Moment Guizot*, p. 244). As minister of public instruction,
he complained to parents of students about the low level of conscientiousness and educational standards,
as I showed in *L'Individu effacé*.

[115]"How, Despite the Progress of Civilization, the Condition of the French Peasant Was Sometimes Worse in the Eighteenth Century Than It Had Been in the Thirteenth," chap. II.12. As we will
see, Tocqueville the moralist reappears in this chapter, and this was a role that Guizot did not seek to
play. The chapter is the last in book 2 and in fact covers more than just the condition of the peasantry: it
deals with the role of classes. That is why Tocqueville wrote the following sentence, which has often been
commented on: "One could no doubt find individuals who did not fit this description, but I am speaking
here of classes, which ought to be the sole object of the historian's interest." *ARR* I, p. 179; AG2, p. 113.

[116]Ibid., p. 188; AG2, p. 123.

The essential accelerant of desocialization (or, as Bonald would say, "de-constitution") was the sale of municipal offices at the end of the seventeenth century by express order of the king: "In each town the king sold to a small number of residents the right to govern the others in perpetuity.... I see no feature of the Ancien Régime more shameful than this."[117] This shameful feature (the moralist is speaking here) put an end to the "municipal patriotism that had worked such wonders in the Middle Ages." Here we find again the vocabulary of *Democracy in America*, where Tocqueville spoke of the "wonders" of which democracy was capable. Indeed, he was all the more keen to evoke vanished or surviving municipal liberties[118] because doing so enabled him to repeat the admiration he had expressed twenty years earlier for the New England town: "I recall that when I began my research on parishes in the Ancien Régime in the archives of one *intendance*, I was surprised to find in these poor subjugated communities several of the features that had struck me so forcefully in the rural towns of North America, features that I wrongly thought at the time were peculiar to the New World."[119] This was followed by the celebrated passage in which Tocqueville was able to judge France in relation not only to the English aristocracy but once again to American democracy: "Transported at a stroke far from feudalism and granted absolute dominion over itself, the rural parish of the Middle Ages became the New England town. Separated from the lord but gripped in the powerful hand of the state, what it became in France I will now describe."[120]

Here we see clearly the structure of the problem that Tocqueville set for himself in *The Ancien Régime*: the lord has been removed from the scene and replaced by the prebendal state. Here we see the emergence of a sort of Boulainvilliers (or even Montlosier).[121] Guizot interpreted the rise of the bourgeoisie differently: it was the bourgeoisie that "destroyed in France the communes in the proper sense of the term [i.e., self-administered political units]," for the purpose of providing the king with officers.[122] He also dated the beginning of the process to the end of the thirteenth century, thereby

[117] Ibid, pp. 115, 116; AG2, pp. 47, 48.
[118] See chap. II.3 on administrative tutelage.
[119] *ARR* I, p. 119; AG2, pp. 51–52.
[120] Ibid., p. 120; AG2, p. 52.
[121] Jean-Jacques Ampère, Tocqueville's great friend and corrector of his manuscripts, grasped the fact that this was the principal thesis of the work: "True municipal representation disappeared everywhere after Louis XIV put municipal offices up for sale: this was a great revolution accomplished for no political purpose but solely to raise money, which, as M. de Tocqueville rightly says, is truly worthy of history's scorn.... On reading these things, one wonders what the Revolution changed and why it was made." Review in *Le Correspondant*, June 1859, passage reproduced in *ARR* I, pp. 430–31.
[122] Final lecture of *Civilisation en France*, 19th lecture of the second year.

challenging before the fact Tocqueville's choice of 1692 (during the reign of Louis XIV). Furthermore, Guizot also maintained that the monarchy's choice of centralization "increased the importance and stature of the bourgeoisie and made it steadily wealthier, more creditworthy, and more powerful within the state."[123]

Did Guizot regret the loss of municipal liberties? At first yes, but after analyzing "the clash of petty interests" in Holland (for which he drew on a historian of law),[124] he concluded that "all in all," centralization was the far better choice.

The discordance of views between Tocqueville and Guizot, despite frequent agreement about the facts, is quite striking.[125] The two men clashed about the site and role of authority. How, in the final analysis, should this disagreement be characterized? As a consequence of class difference, as Marxist orthodoxy would have it? Was Tocqueville "feudal," as Althusser alleged of Montesquieu?

Moralist More than Historian: Tocqueville Judged by Guizot

It is interesting to see how Tocqueville presented himself in the foreword to *The Ancien Régime*. What we find there is what we said earlier about the moralist. As we have seen, Tocqueville set out to judge mores and to propose reforms. Taking on the role that La Bruyère rejected, he sought to "play the legislator." In this respect, Tocqueville's later work consists of the reflections of a moralist whose method is comparative, as in *Democracy in America*; it is not the work of a historian. Furthermore, the parallelism of certain passages is significant. In 1835 he wrote: "I confess that in America I saw more than America. I sought an image of democracy itself, its penchants, character,

---

[123] Guizot, *Civilisation en France*, 4:274.

[124] See Guizot's lengthy quote of Meyer in ibid, p. 275 (a page and a half). Interestingly, the passage anticipates Tocqueville's description of the petty local jealousies among rival corps, which ultimately made a true and healthy taste for liberty impossible.

[125] In *État social et politique de la France*, published in 1836 (and written for John Stuart Mill), Tocqueville, echoing Guizot, said that "the French nation, before and more completely than others, had abandoned the medieval system of fractioning and feudal individuality. The Revolution completed the unification of all parts of the country and molded them into a single body" (reproduced in *ARR* I, p. 65). The "feudal individuality" that Tocqueville missed was the very same term that Guizot used. Note, too, that in this 1836 essay, Tocqueville was already in possession of his thesis that the Revolution concealed continuity: "Everything that the Revolution did would have been done, I am sure, without it. It was simply a violent rapid process that helped adapt the political state to the social state, facts to ideas, and laws to mores." This passage from 1836 would eventually turn into this one from 1856: "The sudden and violent end to a work to which ten generations had contributed."

prejudices, and passions."[126] Similarly, in *The Ancien Régime*: "I confess that as I wrote about . . . the old society, I never entirely lost sight of the new."[127] This confession points to a light veil, which the reader is invited to lift (as in a story by Voltaire or Montesquieu). Tocqueville explains that the question he is asking about the Ancien Régime, so near and yet so far, is, "How might it have escaped death?"

On this point, most commentators have called attention to Tocqueville's concern with historical events and randomness, but it is the moralist who has a greater claim on our attention. How might the Ancien Régime have escaped death? In other words, how might the Revolution have been avoided? To answer this question, Tocqueville was led to paint *portraits*, to mark turning points in mores, and to assign *responsibilities*. Ultimately this strategy leads him to insist on royal actions that were entirely deliberate yet counterproductive—which is a curious thing, since, as a philosopher of history, Tocqueville was sensitive to the contingent as well as the unintentional. "The division of the classes was the crime of the old monarch."[128] The nobility was "cowardly" to allow the third estate to be taxed alone. Yet abolishing that nobility during the Revolution "inflicted a wound on liberty that will never heal."[129] The kings of France were "the most active and constant of levelers" (as he had said previously in *Democracy in America*). And one could multiply examples easily.

In his foreword, Tocqueville warns us that he will be presenting an indictment, but this time the moralist was no longer calling for a reform of mores, or perhaps no longer believed in the possibility. His goal was rather to pinpoint what had been lost. With implacable assurance, he paints a portrait of irremediable decadence.[130]

Tocqueville, who was more a moralist and *memorialist of ancient mores* than a historian, wrote in his foreword that "my goal was to paint a portrait that would be not only strictly accurate but also perhaps educational. Thus,

---

[126] *DA* I, p. 69. Similarly, he wrote about a specific point. "These topics, which touch on my subject, are not part of it. They are American but not democratic, and it is above all democracy that I wish to portray." *DA* I, p. 426. Indeed, in the school of Le Play and Claudio Jannet it is said that Tocqueville describes America by way of democracy rather than democracy by way of America.

[127] *ARR* I, p. 73; AG2, p. 5.

[128] Ibid., p. 166; AG2, p. 101.

[129] Ibid., p. 170; AG2, p. 105.

[130] Cuvillier-Fleury wrote to the duc d'Aumale that the book was admirable but "rather dispiriting" and that it was unable to "indicate the remedy for the disease" (quoted in ibid., p. 341). The four articles by Pierre Boutang in *Aspects de la France*, September–October 1952, do a good job of capturing the attitude of the acerbic nobleman that Tocqueville adopted here. Reprinted by S. Giocanti in Pierre Boutang, *La Source sacrée. Les abeilles de Delphes II* (Paris: Editions du Rocher, 2003).

each time I discovered in our forefathers one of those manly virtues that we so desperately need but no longer possess . . . , I tried to call attention to it." The question that particularly concerned Tocqueville was that of liberty as "independence." He singled out this independence for praise in both *The Ancien Régime*[131] and the 1836 text. More than that, he was aware of praising an aristocratic virtue—what Guizot called "feudal individuality"—and not "true liberty," meaning the obligation to submit to the common law.[132] Hence this confession in a note added to *The Ancien Régime*: "It is wrong to confuse independence with liberty. There is nothing less independent than a free citizen."[133] Pierre Boutang offered an excellent analysis of how "the vacillating Tocqueville dreamed of the feudal liberty of yesteryear yet anxiously threw in his lot with the democratic liberty of tomorrow."[134] He also showed that the individual value that Tocqueville saw in the Ancien Régime was not the juridical individualism of the moderns.[135] It was closer to what Guizot analyzed as feudal individuality.

The "common action" that Tocqueville nostalgically traced can also be interpreted as a reflection of the moralist, which is why historians who have studied Tocqueville have paid little attention to it, even though it forms the leitmotif of the work. One might wager (although it is difficult to prove) that, for Tocqueville, this theme was a continuation of the theme of *honestum* (or *l'honnête*) as collective utility, whose treatment in *Democracy in America* we have already examined. If, today, we can see "common action" as the mark of a political philosophy close to that of Hannah Arendt, this is because both Arendt and Tocqueville drew on a common source, namely, ancient philosophy, and, more precisely, Cicero's *De Officiis*, which inspired European humanism generally.

---

[131] See the discussion in chap. II.11, "On the Kind of Liberty to be Found under the Ancien Régime."

[132] This form of liberty within a collectivity was defined in the introduction to *DA* I, p. 64: "I then conceived of a society . . . ." In this Tocquevillean utopia, special interests are not pursued at the expense of the general interest, the law is just and beloved, etc.

[133] *ARR* I, p. 302, note to p. 176.

[134] Boutang, *Aspects de la France*, October 10, 1952. Boutang's analysis relies primarily on Tocqueville's 1836 essay, and in this respect there is in fact no rupture. Here is further confirmation that the historian's archival research reinforced preconceived ideas and that the pained surprise of which he spoke to Kergorlay ("this sort of violence on myself") was in fact a discovery about himself—the discovery of a truth that he was now more fully prepared to embrace.

[135] Here is the crucial passage that Tocqueville wrote in 1836 but could have acknowledged as his own twenty years later: "This aristocratic notion of liberty produces in those who have *received* it [emphasis added: a concept transmitted by upbringing] an exalted sense of individual value, a passionate taste for independence." *État social et politique de la France*, in *ARR* I, p. 62. Also commented on by Raymond Aron, *Essai sur les libertés* (Paris: Pluriel, 1976), pp. 25–29.

Tocqueville's contemporary Villemain wrote that Cicero's work was "the finest treatise on virtue inspired by purely human wisdom."[136] The Restoration era was particularly attuned to the study of Cicero, not only because he was a classic but also because of the discovery of *De Republica*, which was published in Italy by Cardinal Mai in 1825. The same Villemain brought out a French edition of the work, which caused quite a stir.[137]

We know, moreover, from the testimony of Charles de Grandmaison as well as Tocqueville's correspondence, that when Tocqueville rented a house near Tours[138] to begin work on *The Ancien Régime*, he placed a set of works by moralists in his writing studio.[139] It was certainly not exclusively for the style of those authors that he did so as he sat down to write his new book: form implies substance, as Benjamin Constant said in a text that Tocqueville admired.[140] What emerges once again in *The Ancien Régime* is the preoccupation of the moralist and the culture of "*l'honnête*" as the form of collective "utility"—in other words, the *Ciceronian theory of politics*, which one encounters across a vast range of literary sources, from Montaigne to Voltaire and the Scottish moralists of the eighteenth century.

A lexicographic analysis shows that the phrases "*agir en commun*" (acting in common) and "*agir ensemble*" (acting together) occur in four or five strategic contexts in *The Ancien Régime*. Tocqueville expresses his deep regret most fully in the chapter on the "separation of classes" deliberately maintained by the state: "It is no small undertaking to bring together citizens

---

[136] Villemain, "Notice sur Cicéron," reproduced in *Études de littérature ancienne et étrangère* (Paris: Didier, 1854), p. 51.

[137] Abel Villemain, *La République de Cicéron ... avec un discours préliminaire et des suppléments historiques* (Paris: Michaud, 1823). Tocqueville owned the revised and corrected edition published by Didier in 1858, shortly before Tocqueville's death.

[138] Tocqueville rented a house 3 km from Tours both for reasons of health (a relapse of tuberculosis) and so that he could study the archives of the Généralité of Touraine. See his June 1853 letter to Sedgwick, *OC* VII, p. 151, n. 2.

[139] To Corcelle, in 1853, he expressed his admiration for Bourdaloue (especially the sermon "On False Consciousness"), and he repeated this the following year (as noted earlier). He explained his return to his literary roots in the following terms: "I brought with me a volume of the works of all the great writers of our language. I haven't a single text that isn't a century or so old. From time to time I read a little of one and a little of another. The company is illustrious and fine." See *OC* XV-2, p. 89. This was written as he was beginning work on *The Ancien Régime*. The archivist Charles de Grandmaison, who visited Tocqueville in this house several times, confirmed these facts in an article published in the *Correspondant*.

[140] Benjamin Constant, *De la force du gouvernement actuel*, from which Tocqueville copied a passage he admired: "How true and even profound this is and, what is more, well said!" *Œuvres*, La Pléiade, 3:676. A little earlier in the same text, on the same theme, Constant wrote: "Forms bring on substance," in morality as in politics, and "forms perpetuate the mind." See *De la force du gouvernement actuel et de la nécessité de s'y rallier*, in Constant, *Œuvres complètes*, vol. 1, "Écrits de jeunesse" (Tübingen: Max Niemeyer, 1998), p. 369.

who have lived for centuries as strangers or enemies and teach them to *take joint responsibility* [Fr.: *conduire en commun*, emphasis added] for their own affairs."[141] In *Democracy in America*, we find the phrase *agir en commun* four times, characteristically where individualism is being examined (exclusively in the second volume, parts 1 and 2), and only once in the rest of the book (in the second part of volume 1).

෨

We find none of this line of argument in Guizot, who of course had his own philosophy of liberty and social organization but who aimed to be more precise and factual and to follow his sources more closely in presenting his detailed analysis of the Middle Ages. To be sure, he, too, intended his approach to be "philosophical" (as he said at the very beginning of his lectures), but in *Civilisation en France* he chose to emphasize the role of *class struggle* in the formation of the nation from the tenth century on.[142] His notion of "society" depended on this. One might compare the preface that Guizot wrote for a new edition of his work in 1856,[143] before Tocqueville's foreword to *The Ancien Régime* appeared. In his view, the French nobility and bourgeoisie had never found a way to unite, and he says in his preface that he will confine himself to showing how this lasting conflict was the result of two forms of egoism. Just as partial as Tocqueville, Guizot is careful to give the impression that his choice is determined by history, not his own preferences. In Tocqueville, the cruel animus of certain passages had already found expression in the *Souvenirs*, which for that reason would not be published until after his death.

෨

It happens that we know Guizot's opinion of *The Ancien Régime and the Revolution* because he acknowledged reception of the work and shared his opinion of it—a mixture of politeness and cruelty—with the author. If my hypothesis is correct—in other words, if *The Ancien Régime* can be read as a response to Guizot's lectures of 1828–29 and 1829–30—then in fact Guizot was simply repaying Tocqueville in kind.

What did Guizot say in his letter? To begin with, that the book was "excellent," "as true as it is useful and as useful as it is true; firmly of its own

[141] *ARR* I, chap. II.10, p. 167; AG2, p. 101. The chapter title is: "How the Destruction of Political Liberty and the Separation of Classes Caused Nearly All the Maladies That Proved Fatal to the Ancien Régime."

[142] As is well known, Marx said that he found the concept of the class struggle in Guizot (as well as in Mignet and Thierry).

[143] *Civilisation en France* (1857), 1: esp. iv–v.

time yet independent of the spirit of the age." But he added that he found it as biased as *Democracy in America* by its author's inclinations. "I find in your book the same character that struck me in your great work about the United States of America. You describe and judge modern democracy as a vanquished aristocrat convinced that his vanquisher is right."[144] Just as Tocqueville was wrong to paint the democratic aspects of America in too rosy a light (as we have seen), so, too, did he give too much credit in *The Ancien Régime* to . . . whom, exactly? The bourgeoisie? Not really, because his tone toward parvenus is highly critical. Rather, he once again showed his allegiance to democracy, which *he confounded with the power of the bourgeoisie*. Guizot had a different idea, and it accounts for the divergence of the two political theories: for Guizot, democracy denied the inevitable *inequality* of talents, chances, and situations. In the remainder of his letter to Tocqueville, he explained his view, not without malice toward what he takes to be the uneasy embarrassment of the Norman aristocrat: "Perhaps you have been too habitually inclined to think about the historical aristocracy, which really was vanquished, and not enough about the natural aristocracy, which can never be defeated for long and will always reclaim its rights in the end. Perhaps, if you had more consistently distinguished between the two, you would have felt more comfortable in accepting democracy while challenging what was illegitimate and unsociable in its victory."[145]

So Guizot's answer to Tocqueville was that the latter refused to recognize the rights of the "natural aristocracy" in both America and France, in the past and in the present. Tocqueville, hostile to the bourgeoisie, seemed to have a real personal problem with his own class, whose cross he bore: he judged its aspirations to be outmoded and obsolete, yet he continued to be nostalgic about them.[146] Guizot tells him that he would have been more comfortable had he thrown in his lot with the rising bourgeoisie, as did Louis de Carné, who was the same age as Tocqueville and came from the same background.

Guizot, who poured all his venom into these few lines, continued to do so when he received Tocqueville's successor at the Académie Française. In

[144]Guizot, letter from Le Val-Richer, June 30, 1856, Tocqueville archives, partially reproduced in the doctoral thesis of Françoise Mélonio and in Tocqueville, *OC* XVI, p. 343, n.

[145]The end of the letter (communicated to me by Françoise Mélonio) comes close to insolence: Guizot invites Tocqueville to stop at Le Val-Richer on the way to his chateau. "We would argue; we would agree; and I would tell you about my pleasure in reading you something quite different from what I am writing." Apparently this friendly invitation was not accepted.

[146]Contrary to what any number of authors say on the basis of reading *Democracy in America* by itself, divorced from any context, and without considering the hermeneutics and stylistics of Tocqueville's two major works.

1861, in his speech welcoming Lacordaire to Tocqueville's chair, he not only humorously evoked the days when other disciples of Saint Dominic might have sent Guizot, a Protestant, to the stake, but also savored the pleasure of speaking of Tocqueville when the latter could no longer answer him. Guizot feigned surprise: "How, then, was it possible that in public life we nearly always found ourselves in opposite camps and, despite our mutual esteem, devoted our time and energy to fighting each other?"[147]

Let us be as political as Guizot, who had a long memory: behind these words looms the specter of the Carlo-republican conspiracy, whose ominous power Guizot evoked at length in his memoirs.[148] "Vanquished aristocrat?" Tocqueville came close to acknowledging the accuracy of the portrait. For instance, he confessed to Nassau Senior that his most spontaneous sympathies bore a marked social stamp: "When I speak with a gentleman, even though we haven't two ideas in common, and even though his opinions, wishes, and inclinations are opposite to mine, I feel immediately that we belong to the same family, speak the same language, and understand each other. It may be that I prefer a bourgeois, but I sense in him a stranger."[149]

Commenting on this sincere effusion, Luis Diez del Corral remarked that Tocqueville's "obvious antipathy to the values and human type represented by the bourgeoisie led him to neglect the crucial role that the bourgeois class played in contemporary France." For Diez, this explained the ambivalence of the word "democracy" in Tocqueville's texts, because he saw political reality "with bifocals, as it were," which allowed him to see unusual features and yet also created certain blind spots owing to his partiality.[150] Indeed, Tocqueville's own correspondence from these years confirms that he harbored his own personal myth of a mild and paternalistic feudal nobility. After doing some research in family archives, he wrote to his nephew Hubert in 1857: "I rubbed shoulders with four centuries of the family line, all of them still here in Tocqueville. . . . Three hundred years ago, we served as godfathers to many

---

[147] Tocqueville, *OC* XVI, *Mélanges*, p. 342.

[148] On the ceaseless efforts of the legitimists and republicans between 1840 and 1848, see Guizot, *Mémoires de mon temps*, 6:344.

[149] Written in 1849 to Nassau William Senior, *OC* VI-2, p. 256. The same sentiment is expressed in the *Souvenirs*, where Tocqueville explains that the nobility is a sort of freemasonry whose members can recognize one another via invisible signs, so that he was able to reach an understanding with people he did not like at all, such as Count Falloux, a "not very scrupulous man" and "an uncommon but very effective scoundrel." *OC* XII, pp. 222–23. Tocqueville could be as tough as Saint-Simon when he chose to speak freely. I will have more to say about his judgment concerning legitimists below.

[150] See Luis Diez del Corral, "Tocqueville et la pensée politique des doctrinaires," *Alexis de Tocqueville. Livre du centenaire, 1859–1959* (Paris: Editions du CNRS, 1960), pp. 64–65.

of the villagers—further proof of the mild and paternal relations that still existed in those days between the upper and lower classes."[151]

As Proust says at the end of *Le Temps retrouvé*, the true paradises are the ones we have lost. It was this attachment to a vanished past that motivated the author of *The Ancien Régime*. The historian was partial; the moralist sought to rationalize his passion.

☙

Tocqueville was familiar with a certain register of moralistic reflection, of which he made sustained use in *The Ancien Régime*. It was a moralism derived from a theological interpretation of history. At least one passage in the book is a palimpsest of the celebrated final page of Bossuet's *Discours sur l'histoire universelle*.[152] Indeed, in the chapter in which Tocqueville most fully describes the ideological illusions of each of the classes of society, he offers as a conclusion, almost a peroration, the promise that he will introduce us to "one of the greatest of God's laws governing the conduct of societies."[153] The law in question concerns historical action, which aims at a certain purpose but produces undesired effects that may even be the opposite of what the actors were expecting. In the following passage, I have italicized each reiteration of the idea of deluded actors:

> Nobles ultimately allowed themselves to be exempted from most of the public charges to which they were subject. They *imagined* that they would retain their eminence while avoiding these burdens. . . . But soon . . . they grew poorer as their immunities grew more extensive. . . . Nobles who *had not wanted* bourgeois as partners or fellow citizens now had to face them as rivals, before long as enemies, and ultimately as masters. . . . Since they continued to march at the head of every procession, *they believed that they were still leaders*, and indeed they continued to be surrounded by men to whom they referred in official documents as their *subjects*. Others were referred to as their vassals, their tenants, and their farmers. *In reality*, they had no followers. They were alone, and when people at last rose up against them, they had no choice but to flee.

Tocqueville continued by showing that the bourgeoisie, which also chose to separate itself from the peasantry, suffered a similar blindness and would

---

[151] Tocqueville, *OC* XIV, p. 328.

[152] When we compare Chateaubriand and Tocqueville, we will see that the latter also invoked divine providence in the case of Louis XVI, the enigmatic martyr-king.

[153] *ARR* I, p. 189; *AG2*, p. 123.

also be in store for the rude awakening that God had prepared. For a historian who often declared his dislike for the "fatalist school," this passage was clearly intended to draw the attention of the reader and express a wrenching emotion: Tocqueville the moralist liberated himself in and through the writing, or, if you prefer, by mounting a Christian pulpit. As an inveterate reader of Bossuet, he obviously had in mind the final chapter of the *Discours sur l'histoire universelle*, whose title is "Everything Must Be Linked to Providence." Bossuet also emphasized the blindness of the actors, but in the imperfect rather than the present tense that Tocqueville uses, because his goal, unlike Tocqueville's, was not to dramatize the current situation:

> Alexander *did not believe* that he was working for his generals or destroying his dynasty through his conquests. When Brutus instilled an immense love of liberty in the Roman people, *he did not dream* that he was sowing the seeds of that outrageous licentiousness by which the tyranny that he *wished to destroy* would one day be restored harsher than ever under the Tarquins. When the Caesars flattered their soldiers, *they had no intention* of imposing masters on their successors and the empire. In short, there is no human party that does not serve, *in spite of itself*, purposes other than its own. God alone can reduce everything to His will.[154]

Clearly, Tocqueville the historian wanted his contemporary readers (for whom Bossuet was a classic) to understand that French history was worthy of being interpreted in Christian providentialist terms. Although Guizot confessed in his letters (especially to his daughter Henriette) that he believed in the intervention of Providence in history (but found it very difficult to make it out in individual lives), he would never have allowed himself to adopt the *style* that Tocqueville used to express the tragic qualities that he discerned in the present and their irremediable consequences. Guizot no doubt accurately gauged his rival's penchant for the tragic register.

By way of epilogue to the difficult dialogue between the two men, let me mention another detail. In the speech he gave on joining the Académie Française, Tocqueville, speaking of his predecessor in the academic chair (the Count de Cessac, an imperial official), was willing to say that Napoleon had been able to bring forth "from beneath the ruins of the Revolution . . . a new society, which was more tightly knit and stronger than the old." Guizot, upon reading this speech, hastened to write to his new colleague: "Why do

---

[154] Bossuet, *Discours sur l'histoire universelle*, in *Œuvres* (Paris: La Pléiade, 1961), p. 1026.

we not think alike? I see no good reasons."[155] Never mind that there were bad reasons! In any case, it did not escape Guizot's notice that on this occasion Tocqueville was willing to admit the demiurgic, institutionalizing character of a strong central government: it could create a "new society." In *The Ancien Régime and the Revolution*, however, he would no longer speak this way about either Napoleon or Louis XIV.

[155] Letter from Guizot, April 26, 1842, archives of Saint-Lô (AT 1664). Tocqueville gave his speech on April 21 (see *OC* XVI, p. 258; cf. *ARR*, manuscripts: *ARR* II, p. 316).

⊘⊙ 13

Tutelary Figures from Malesherbes
to Chateaubriand

> ... the man who, in our own time, has perhaps best preserved the spirit
> of the old races, M. de Chateaubriand, to whom I felt close owing to
> many family ties and childhood memories.
>
> —Tocqueville, *Souvenirs*

> Hugging the wall of the Meaux cathedral, I repeated to Bossuet his
> own words: "Man goes to his grave trailing after him a long chain of
> disappointed hopes."
>
> —Chateaubriand, *Mémoires d'outre-tombe*

> There is an important analogy between the tyranny of all and the
> tyranny of one. The despot is a leveler, as are the people.
>
> —Chateaubriand, *Discours et opinions*, 1826

THE THREAD LINKING THE TWO DESPOTISMS

We have already learned a great deal about Tocqueville's social and intellectual milieu, enough to show that his attitude toward that milieu was compounded of allegiance alloyed with dissidence. Now it is time to look more carefully at important thinkers on the monarchical side, who served him as references, boundary markers, or counterexamples. First and foremost among these was Chateaubriand, whose legacy Tocqueville often found irritating but could not ignore. Intellectually, Chateaubriand helped to nurture Tocqueville's intuition and what we might even call his personal myth, which can be summed up as follows: (1) the French monarchy was *despotic*, indeed a model of what administrative power could accomplish in the way of rationalized despotism; and (2) this despotism could recur in the modern era: history was likely to repeat itself in a new form if democracy did not equip itself with institutions to slow and counterbalance the power of the central government, representing the majority.

In regard to the pessimism of the Breton viscount Chateaubriand, Tocqueville added one important element: that factors to moderate democracy could be found by looking to the feudal aristocracy as a source of inspiration. For instance, associations are important collective "personalities" that never die and can play the role of countervailing powers, the same role that seigneurs played vis-à-vis the king before they ended up as losers in the power struggle.

Tocqueville's view was thus a curious one in which past and present came together and perhaps achieved a kind of reconciliation in the consciousness, as well as the unconscious, of the author: on the one hand, the past must not be allowed to repeat itself because kings from Philip the Fair on really had oppressed the country, while, on the other hand, it would be a good idea to revive "French liberties" and recover some of the feudal patronage of which Tocqueville had written to his nephew in a letter cited previously. Tocqueville's transmutation of historical "memory" into a present-day program of reform can be seen in the final chapters of volume 1 of *Democracy in America*. Tocqueville asks whether it might be possible to transfer American inclinations and mores, while the text subtly shifts toward the Ancien Régime, parting the American veil: certain worthy people (Hervé de Tocqueville, perhaps), "preoccupied with their memories,... judge absolute power by what it once was and not by what it could be today. *If absolute power were once again to establish itself* among the democratic peoples of Europe, I have no doubt that it would take a new form and exhibit features unknown to our fathers."[1] In other words, it is possible for the past to return but wearing the mask of modernity. Why did Tocqueville ask about absolute power *if it were once again to establish itself*, if not because he was following his strongest intuition: namely, that democratic despotism is *analogous* to the monarchical despotism of Louis XIV? The only difference, as we have seen, was that democracies have learned the art of "dematerializing" despotism.[2] Thus the two great ideas that animated all of Tocqueville's thought came together here: the resurgence of despotism and the advent of equality. These two ideas were in fact one, because royal despotism was the demiurge of equality. Hence the return of the despot suggested both continuity and change, with the latter clearly and effectively favoring a society of equality.[3] If there was remarkable continuity between the Ancien Régime and the Revolution—which was of

---

[1]*DA* I.2.9, p. 421; AG, p. 360. Emphasis added.

[2]"Democratic republics transform despotism into something immaterial." *DA* I.2.7, p. 352; AG, p. 292.

[3]"Absolute monarchies brought dishonor to despotism. Let us be wary lest democratic republics rehabilitate it and make it less odious and degrading in the eyes of the many by making it more onerous for the few." Ibid., p. 354; AG, p. 294.

course the key idea of Tocqueville's 1856 opus—there was also remarkable continuity between *the two forms of despotism*.

Tocqueville was raised in the monarchical culture of the Restoration by a family that had suffered in the Terror, yet Robespierre mattered less to him than Louis XIV or Napoleon. This was because "despotism" as he conceived it marked a profound departure from Montesquieu's version.[4] Despotism is not so much a regime of physical and moral violence as a government with equalizing effects that produces passive and complacent citizens. By way of Chateaubriand, who wrote in 1831 that "the age of Louis XIV was the magnificent catafalque of our liberties," Tocqueville harked back to *aristocratic liberalism*, which advocated pluralism and independence of intermediary bodies, whether privileged corps or entities to which specific rights had been granted (as when charters were issued communes). These collective organisms resisted the centralizing and homogenizing tendencies of royal power. For Tocqueville, one word summed up this view: leveling. Guizot in his lectures and Chateaubriand in his writing in the period 1830–34 had given Tocqueville the key to his fundamentally aristocratic liberalism: namely, the need to consider leveling in France in terms of a periodic, cyclical logic.

"The return of the despot": if this was indeed Tocqueville's personal myth, it is easy to understand why the question of authority arose in every area he looked at. In regard to institutions, society, morality, religion, and literature, he investigated the new nature of authority—an authority whose future he did not doubt.

A second point bears emphasizing. In his youth, Tocqueville was surrounded by people who were entirely monarchical and even legitimist in their outlook: his parents, his uncles (apart from the regicides among them), his two brothers, his cousin Kergorlay, his friend Gustave de Beaumont, and correspondents such as Ernest de Chabrol, to name a few. To be sure, he had acquaintances who were less committed (such as Bouchitté, who was more Catholic than royalist, and the Stöffels brothers), but setting them aside, how can one avoid asking how people from this milieu looked at authority? At two points in his life, Tocqueville experienced a crisis that caused him to take his distance from these relations: the first came with his discovery of the eighteenth-century *philosophes* at the age of sixteen,[5] and the second began with the revolution of 1830, which inaugurated a long phase of detachment

[4]Which was based primarily on fear.
[5]Tocqueville's long letter of February 26, 1857, to Mme Swetchine is often cited. In it he confessed the magnitude of his adolescent crisis and the despair he experienced.

and reflection that ultimately ended in writing, "self-medication" via ratiocination, and the American "detour."

It will be useful to press our inquiry further in order to appreciate more fully the type of choice that Tocqueville felt forced to make, as well as to understand his complex relationship with Chateaubriand, a self-styled defender of "legitimacy" who nevertheless formed an alliance with republicans such as Carrel.

In 1845, in the midst of a polemic about freedom of instruction, Tocqueville shared a secret with his friend Corne: "I broke with part of my family and turned my back on cherished relationships and precious memories to embrace the cause and the ideas of 1789. Having made such sacrifices for my opinions, I will not renounce them now out of fear of malevolence in the press, etc."[6] Those opinions, which cost Tocqueville a great deal in terms of struggle with himself and with those close to him, had become firmly established thanks to intellectual labor, writing, and the *metanoia* he proposed to monarchists.

TOCQUEVILLE AND HIS FAMILY ENVIRONMENT

Tocqueville's father Hervé de Tocqueville cannot really be classified as an Ultra of the Restoration,[7] especially if we base our judgment not on the policies he adopted as prefect, which were often tough, but rather on the ideas he set forth in two works of history, *Histoire philosophique du règne de Louis XV* and *Coup d'œil sur le règne de Louis XVI*. It is true that Polignac elevated him to the peerage in 1827, which he had requested four years earlier, without anticipating that he would benefit from a turn to the right in a system in which the nomination of peers was intended to counter liberal opinion. Tocqueville noted this somewhat sadly to his friend Kergorlay: "So my father has become a peer. Four years ago he earnestly desired and asked for this recognition. Today, although he was no longer seeking the honor, he was included in the list. Such is the way of the world. He expressed his disapproval of the measure before it was decided. He has not changed his opinion since, and I am convinced that he is right."[8] In retracing the career of the prefect Hervé de Tocqueville, André Jardin conceded that after entering the Chamber of

---

[6] Letter dated November 13, 1845, according to Jardin, *Tocqueville*, p. 377.

[7] André Jardin does call him an Ultra, but by his own definition of the term: "Insofar as the 'ultracism' of 1835 was a temperament more than a doctrine, a combination of love of the sovereign and old-fashioned liberties, he was essentially an Ultra." See Jardin, *Alexis de Tocqueville*, p. 37.

[8] *OC* XIII-1, p. 118.

Peers, Hervé did not join the Ultra faction but instead sought out the more moderate group headed by the duc de Mortemar.

Politics, understood as service to the community, was Hervé de Tocqueville's abiding ambition until the July Revolution forced him to renounce. In 1829 the Polignac government nominated him to preside over the electoral college in La Manche, which leads Jardin to the conclusion that he "was seen as a leader of the legitimist party."[9] In fact, Hervé de Tocqueville's views seem to have coincided with prevailing monarchist opinion at the time. His notes on the manuscript of *Democracy in America*, which can be consulted in the Nolla edition, show that he believed that a writer must be extremely cautious in expressing political opinions. It comes as no surprise, either, that he was keenly interested in the notion of honor. Not only did he respond to Alexis's request that he look into the definition of honor,[10] as did Kergorlay, but he also reserved a key place for the idea in his study of the reign of Louis XV. There he wrote the following, citing Montesquieu:

> There is great danger in a monarchy that honor in the nobility may degenerate. That is what happened during the Regency, and we ascribe most of the blame to the system. Honor prefers glory and renown to money. The ignoble passion for gold is incompatible with lofty ideas. Thus the nobility of that era sacrificed its principle when it succumbed to the unrestrained greed that the system encouraged. It then ceased to inspire respect and could not recover it.... Wealth began to be respected as much as birth; before long it was more respected.[11]

This scorn for the relations and hierarchies created by money, voiced here in regard to the system of John Law, as well as the idea that "democracy" emerged from the attenuation of hierarchy[12] and the corruption of mores, are not alien to the thought of Hervé's son Alexis. The latter wrote rather warmly to Kergorlay that he did not regard money as his primary concern in life.[13] Accordingly, he refused to heed the wishes of his cousin, who wanted to arrange "a good marriage" for him.

Broadly speaking, Hervé de Tocqueville organized his historical analysis around the events of 1789. More often than not he adopted the standpoint of the future anterior: "Such and such had to happen in order that

---

[9] *OC* VII-1, correspondence with Beaumont, with Jardin's n. 6 on p. 343.

[10] See letter to his son dated January 17, 1838, Nolla II, pp. 200–201.

[11] Hervé de Tocqueville, *Histoire philosophique du règne de Louis XV* (1847) (Paris: Librairie d'Amyot, 1874), 1:153.

[12] See ibid., p. 156.

[13] Unpublished letter of November 8, 1831, written from America.

these other things would happen later." His writing therefore has the tone of historical necessity: "The transformation that was ultimately to produce a revolution was already evident toward the end of the reign of Louis XV."[14] As we have seen, such backward-looking teleological reasoning was not always foreign to his son Alexis's way of thinking, despite what some scholars have affirmed. In any event, the goal that the elder Tocqueville set for himself was not without interest for his son, whose study of the administrative archives of the Ancien Régime would, however, be a major contribution to the subject: "This philosophical investigation of causes that persisted throughout much of the eighteenth century and disposed the people to make the great revolution that marked its end is worthy of our study."[15] Hervé de Tocqueville's study of the prodromes of the "great revolution," though inadequate from an institutional point of view, suggested a certain acceptance of the Revolution, given the failings of the pre-1789 ruling class. We have seen the force of this idea in *The Ancien Régime and the Revolution*, the work of a moralist who similarly castigated the ruling class. André Jardin, too insistent on setting Tocqueville on a pedestal, offered a rather harsh judgment of his father, which other commentators have generally followed.[16] As we have seen repeatedly, Tocqueville also drew on the commonplace ideas of his time. He was more artful in reformulating them, however, even when he borrowed from the same sources as his father.

Hence it is worth pausing to ask how Tocqueville viewed his father, to the extent that he was willing to reveal publicly. When Count Hervé died, Tocqueville confessed to Corcelle that, other than his wife, there was no one to whom he felt closer. Above all, he saw Hervé as a picture of deep but unostentatious religious feeling.[17] As always, one should be cautious in interpreting what Tocqueville says in his correspondence. Corcelle, who was the son of a deputy of the extreme Left, had gone from political radicalism to a militant Catholicism for which Tocqueville had little sympathy when, as minister of foreign affairs, he saw Corcelle, then serving as France's representative in Rome, take a position on the Roman question that Tocqueville believed was too favorable to the pope. So Tocqueville may have been laying it on a bit

[14] Hervé de Tocqueville, *Histoire philosophique du règne de Louis XV*, 1:4.

[15] Ibid., preface, p. ii.

[16] The elder Tocqueville's efforts were, according to Jardin, "works of a cultivated man with a rather banal and boring philosophy." See Jardin, *Tocqueville*, p. 36.

[17] "I saw in my father, and to date in no one else, the pervasive influence of religion in the smallest acts of life and at every moment. Without making a show, religion infused all his thoughts, all his feelings, and all his actions." June 18, 1856, *OC* XV-2, p. 162.

thick,[18] but the portrait seems truthful and the emotion genuine. Furthermore, all signs are that Tocqueville's image of his father was closely bound
up with his father's veneration of Malesherbes, a totemic figure for the entire
family, whose granddaughter Hervé had married in the trying circumstances
of 1793. A defender of Jews and Protestants, author of the "Réclamations de
la cour des aides," and protector of the *Encyclopédie*, Malesherbes was not only
a great and liberal-minded administrator but an illustrious representative of
the Enlightenment.[19] His most admirable gesture was to return to the public
arena, which he had abandoned because of the Revolution, to offer himself
as attorney for Louis XVI. For this loyalty to the king he ultimately paid with
his life, along with his family. After the trial, he returned home and made no
attempt to hide. He was arrested and guillotined along with Chateaubriand's
brother and sister-in-law.[20]

Recall that Tocqueville issued on his father's side from the nobility of the
sword and on his mother's side from the nobility of the robe (the Lamoignons). One of Malesherbes's daughters, Marguerite de Lamoignon de
Malesherbes, married Louis Le Peletier de Rosambo, an important judge in
the Parlement of Paris. Their daughter was Tocqueville's mother. The couple were guillotined in April 1794. One of their daughters, Aline-Thérèse,
married Chateaubriand's brother, and they were also guillotined that April.
Their two children, Louis and Christian de Chateaubriand, were raised by
Hervé de Tocqueville and his wife alongside Alexis, Édouard, and Hippolyte
Clérel de Tocqueville, at the château of Verneuil-sur-Seine (which belonged
to a sister of Malesherbes). There, Chateaubriand visited with his nephews.[21]
Guests diverted themselves with games and theatrical performances (a true
family passion, to which Alexis would remain faithful throughout his life),
and, according to Tocqueville, reading aloud from recently published books.
The château in Verneuil was, in Chateaubriand's chilling phrase, a "legacy of

---

[18]When he wrote: "My poor father's life and death were for me the greatest proof of the excellence
of religion."

[19]He warned Diderot a day ahead of time that he would be obliged to send the police to seize the
writer's papers. According to Diderot's daughter, Malesherbes ordered that the manuscripts collected
for the continuation of the *Encyclopédie* be stored in his house. On this story and other cases in which
Malesherbes, as director of the book trade, protected the *Encyclopédie*, see Roger Chartier, introd. to
Malesherbes, *Mémoires sur la librairie* (Paris: Imprimerie Nationale, 1994), pp. 12–15.

[20]See the account taken from the *Mémoires* of Hervé de Tocqueville in Manzini, *Qui êtes-vous M. de
Tocqueville?* pp. 12–13. The entire text from the *Mémoires* concerning the arrest and captivity can be
found in *Commentaire*, no. 110 (Summer 2005), and 111 (Fall 2005): Hervé de Tocqueville, "Épisodes de
la Terreur. Souvenirs inédits." Hervé de Tocqueville was twenty-two years old at the time.

[21]See Chateaubriand, *Mémoires d'outre-tombe*, part 2, book 5, ed. Levaillant, pp. 184–85.

the scaffold" from Mme de Sénozan, Malesherbes's sister, who, at the age of eighty-some years, was guillotined on May 10, 1794.

Tocqueville's mother owned this château for fourteen years, and Alexis spent his summers there in early childhood. Books, objects, and memories of all sorts from both the Malesherbes and Tocqueville sides of the family were therefore familiar to him.[22]

In Hervé's mind, Malesherbes thus figured indelibly as a martyr who had died in the service of the nation and in fidelity to his sovereign. The count had been imprisoned alongside the great jurist and came close to being guillotined himself. He was able to transmit this image of Malesherbes to his son Alexis.[23] A note in the Tocqueville archives contains the following passage:

> As to the question of why I should have felt more obliged than others to speak out and say these things, my answer is clear and precise. I am the grandson [sic] of M. de M[alesherbes].[24] No one is ignorant of the fact that M. de M[alesherbes], after defending the people before King Louis XVI,[25] defended King Louis XVI before the people. I have not forgotten and will never forget these two exemplary actions.[26]

Another fragment in the Tocqueville archives bears the following mention: "It is because I am the grandson [sic] of M. de Malesherbes that I have written these things."[27]

In 1833, when Tocqueville served as Kergorlay's lawyer in the case of the duchesse de Berry and published a protest against her illegal imprisonment, he had his illustrious forebear in mind. In recalling the circumstances ten years later, he once again invoked the familial example: "I know that I am

[22] For more details, see the fine portrait by Françoise Mélonio, "Les années de formation," in *Lettres choisies. Souvenirs*, pp. 99ff.

[23] Hervé de Tocqueville wrote an eloquent letter of thanks to Dupin for a speech at the Académie in praise of Malesherbes: "I married under his auspices at Malesherbes in 1793, shortly after the king's death, and he was willing to entrust his granddaughter to me in that time of danger and alarm.... Having lived with M. de Malesherbes for eighteen months, and having been imprisoned with him and honored by his friendship, I retain bittersweet memories of the final glorious period of his life." See *Mémoires de M. Dupin* (Paris: Plon, 1861), 4:555–56.

[24] In fact, Tocqueville was Malesherbes's great-grandson via his mother. When invoking this tie, he often made the same mistake (a sign of emotion, perhaps?).

[25] Tocqueville is alluding to the celebrated *Remontrances de la cour des aides* of 1775, under Louis XVI. But there were also remonstrances in 1771, under Louis XV. The remonstrances of 1775 included an analysis of the "despotism" and "clandestine administration" that weighed upon France. Text in Élisabeth Badinter, *Les Remontrances de Malesherbes* (Paris: UGE 10/18, 1978).

[26] Text in Manzini, *Qui êtes-vous M. de Tocqueville?* p. 13.

[27] Contrary to what André Jardin wrote (*Tocqueville*, p. 39), which all other commentators have followed, this was not a reported comment but a handwritten note: it ends with the words "these things," and does not say what they were.

the grandson [*sic*] of a man who defended Louis XVI in irons and who is today honored by all parties."[28] The important point, however, is that the lesson in parlementaire liberalism that Tocqueville took from his ancestor had to do mainly with Malesherbes's analysis of "administrative despotism." He and Chateaubriand both drew on this *critique of absolute monarchy*. Like the youthful Chateaubriand (who consulted Malesherbes about his journey to America), Tocqueville nursed the project of writing a book about his great-grandfather. Neither one did write that book, but both drew on the same source: a liberalism that preferred the aristocracy, or intermediary bodies, to royal state power.

This point bears further elaboration: contrary to what is sometimes said, Tocqueville did not discover the effects of centralization when he worked on the Ancien Régime.[29] Beyond the chapters of *Democracy in America* that prove the contrary, there is the evidence of note K, added to the first edition of the first volume: "It is not accurate to say that centralization originated with the French Revolution; the French Revolution perfected but did not create it. The French penchant for centralization and mania for regulation date from the period when legists first joined the government, which takes us back to the time of Philip the Fair."[30]

Interestingly, the remainder of this note analyzes the effects of centralization with the aid of Malesherbes's remonstrances of 1775. This critique of administrative monarchy was the theoretical model that guided Tocqueville, all the more so because its author was also a moral model. With the final sentences borrowed from his ancestor, Tocqueville points to the idea that the French spirit was shaped not by liberty but by habits of dependency and submission: "It is by means such as these, Sire, that every last vestige of municipal spirit has been snuffed out in France, including, when possible, the sentiments of the citizens. The entire nation has in a sense been declared *incompetent* and placed in receivership."[31]

[28] *Discours et écrits politiques, OC* III-2, p. 71. The note from which I am citing was handwritten in 1842, at a time when Tocqueville had to defend himself against charges of dissimulated legitimism, especially before his electors.

[29] To be clear, Tocqueville himself *believed* that he had discovered the phenomenon, which he in fact began speaking about as early as 1835. See André Jardin's introduction to *ARR, OC* II-2, p. 149, on the beginning of Tocqueville's research. In his manuscript notes, Tocqueville expresses "surprise that this centralization, which he believed typically Napoleonic, already existed in the eighteenth century." Jardin does not correct Tocqueville's self-delusion on this point, which has to do with the difficult question of Tocqueville's family antecedents and, more generally, the monarchist past.

[30] *DA* I, p. 557, n. k, p. 165; AG, p. 853, n. x.

[31] Ibid., p. 558; AG, p. 854.

In the period during which he reflected on and wrote about his American travels (between the fall of 1833 and the end of 1834), Tocqueville was thus already in possession of the keys to his analysis *thanks to family tradition*: these included a critique of the monarchy, the contrast between the death of the municipal spirit in France and the vitality of the New England town, and a vision of what "citizen sentiment" might be. He was able to incorporate all of these elements into his argument all the more decisively because in doing so he was conscious of paying his respects to his forebears. Indeed, although *The Ancien Régime and the Revolution* was not published until 1856, its shape was foreordained, even though in the author's own mind, *the final* (albeit incomplete) *text* was the result of a lengthy process involving painful conflicts and diligent research.

In the end, Tocqueville acknowledged what he already thought, but only in an unpublished letter that he wrote at the end of his life: that no French king had loved the people.[32]

⁊

Loyalty to Malesherbes thus came to Tocqueville through his father. In his mother, who was Malesherbes's granddaughter, we find rather a naïve and sentimental loyalty to the monarchy combined with political attitudes more rigid than her husband's. In a passage reminiscent of the fantastic tone of Nerval's *Filles du feu*, Tocqueville evoked a family evening in which his mother sang a song in honor of the king. Written in the troubadour style by Gabriel-Joseph d'Eaubonne in 1792, the lyrics recounted the sadness of Louis XVI's captivity. Tocqueville had alluded to this scene in an 1853 letter to Corcelle, but he sent a more evocative version to a British writer whose work on the English Revolution he admired, Lady Thereza Lewis. After noting the disappearance of "the sort of idolatry of royalty that once lent nobility to obedience" (in the seventeenth century), he gave free rein to his feeling:

> I recall as if it were yesterday a certain evening in a château in which my father was living at the time, to which a family occasion had brought quite a number of our close relatives. The servants had been dismissed. The whole family was gathered around the fire. My mother, who had a sweet, affecting voice, began singing a tune that was famous in our time of civil troubles, the words of which had to do with the misfortune and death of King Louis XVI. When she stopped singing, everyone was in tears, not because of what each of them had suffered personally,

---

[32] Letter to Bouchitté, August 9, 1856 (unpublished correspondence).

nor even because of the many relatives they had lost in the civil war or on the scaffold, but for the fate of a man who had died fifteen years earlier, and whom most of the people whose tears were flowing had never laid eyes on. But that man had been the king.[33]

This pious attitude toward the martyred king had been instilled in Tocqueville by his tutor, Abbé Lesueur. The eight-year-old Alexis wrote to the abbé after shouting *"Vive le roi!"* during a parade. Numerous letters and documents confirm Tocqueville's affection for his tutor, a former refractory priest who heartily disapproved of liberals as "an accursed race."[34] He hoped to see the old monarchy restored. Tocqueville therefore did not have to search far from home to learn what total rejection of the Revolution looked like or what Ultras thought. Recall, too, that Abbé Lesueur had long been associated with the Tocqueville family and had been Count Hervé's tutor as well. He became a sort of nurse to the count's wife, who took to her bed as a permanent invalid after surviving the ordeal of imprisonment.[35]

Unlike his two brothers, Alexis was able to come to terms with all this and, after a series of painful renunciations, free himself from this world, at times hiding the truth from his tutor.[36] He was able to distinguish between his attachment to individuals and between ideas that he accepted and those he rejected, while continuing to recognize the role that certain values played in his thinking.

---

[33] Compare Gérard de Nerval, *Sylvie*, in *Œuvres* (Paris: Gallimard/Pléiade, 1952), 1:264–65. The text features a young woman, Adrienne, "with a fresh and affecting voice, rather thin, as girls' voices tend to be in that misty region ... [who] sang one of those old romances full of love and melancholy, which are always about the misfortunes of a princess confined to a tower by her father as punishment for having loved." Earlier in the text, Nerval wrote: "I imagined a château of the time of Henri IV, with a pitched slate roof and a reddish façade with parapets of yellow stone." *Les Filles du feu* is a work "in search of lost time," of youth retrieved in memory, and it appeared in the same period in which Tocqueville engaged in his act of memory. *Sylvie* appeared in the *Revue des deux mondes* on August 15, 1853, and Tocqueville's letter was written on May 6, 1856: *OC* VI-3. Cf. his letter to Corcelle, in a different style, *OC* XVI-1, pp. 86–87, December 1853.

[34] Letter from Lesueur to Édouard de Tocqueville, 1822: cf. Benoît, *Tocqueville moraliste*, p. 62. This work contains information about Tocqueville's upbringing as well as some of Lesueur's letters.

[35] In an earlier comparison with Mme Guizot, I mentioned that Tocqueville's mother was permanently scarred by the ordeal of awaiting execution, while her husband's hair turned instantly white. They were saved by the fall of Robespierre.

[36] For instance, when he discovered the philosophes of the eighteenth century in his father's library at the prefecture of Metz, and when he lost his faith thereafter. Also, his amorous experience: he fathered a child with a servant employed by the prefecture in 1822 and had a passionate relationship with Rosalie Malye, whom he finally gave up under pressure from friends and family (Kergorlay played an important role). He also fought a duel over Rosalie.

ARISTOCRATIC FAMILY VALUES: FIDELITY AND REASSESSMENT

Dino Cofrancesco has examined a set of values to which Tocqueville adhered and which can be characterized as constituting an "aristocratic cast of mind."[37] Aristocratic liberty, Cofrancesco argues, consists of four things: the virtue of disinterestedness, participation in jointly exercised power, power over oneself and especially one's prejudices, and finally what he calls *autarkeia*, that is, power over one's own domain and the sense of not depending on anyone. There is some reason to doubt the third item in this list, since honor according to both Montesquieu and Tocqueville is in fact a strongly maintained prejudice. More precisely, the first two pages of the chapter on honor in the United States and in democratic societies in *Democracy in America* are literally based on Locke's treatment of the "law of opinion or reputation": "Honor is nothing other than a particular rule based on a particular state that a people or class uses to assign blame or praise."[38]

Tocqueville, like Locke, insisted on the way in which social and historical conditions give rise to "a form of honor" that becomes more specific over time. Indeed, Tocqueville wrote that "whenever men gather to form a particular society, a characteristic form of honor immediately springs up among them, that is, a distinctive set of opinions regarding what is to be praised or blamed."[39] Hence aristocratic honor was not defined by capacity to master one's prejudices. It was rather Tocqueville who adopted this concept, because it seemed to correspond to the new face of personal *independence* under democracy. The "honor" of Tocqueville the moralist and writer was no longer a sign of belonging to a group but rather of his claimed ability to remain detached and impartial—as, for example, in opposition to Silvestre de Sacy's review. The honor that Tocqueville proposed for himself—a survival of aristocratic honor or caste prejudice—was thus intellectual honor: he refused to place his thought at the service of any party. Ultimately the crux of the difficulty of *Democracy in America* lies in the author's choice to position himself

---

[37] See Dino Cofrancesco, "La 'libertà aristocratica.' Considerazioni su Alexis de Tocqueville," *Trimestre* 22 (2-3-4) (1989): 167–89. See also Cofrancesco, "'Assieto sociale' e dominio aristocratico," in *Il teatro della politica*, ed. F. Mioni (Reggio Emilia: Edizoni Diabasis, 1990).

[38] *DA* II.3.18, p. 286; AG, p. 726.

[39] Ibid., p. 290; AG, p. 730. Compare Locke, *Essay Concerning Human Understanding*, II.28.10: "Virtue and vice are names pretended and supposed everywhere to stand for actions in their own nature right and wrong: and as far as they really are so applied, they so far are coincident with the divine law above mentioned. But yet, whatever is pretended, this is visible, that these names, virtue and vice, in the particular instances of their application, through the several nations and societies of men in the world, are constantly attributed only to such actions as in each country and society are in reputation or discredit."

counter to democracy's evolution.[40] The book played upon an ambivalence that was supposed to resonate in the conscience of the reader and help him make up his own mind. That is what Tocqueville meant by "enlightening democracy about itself." In this connection, the final lines of the chapter on honor, despite their pessimistic ring, call on the reader to resist succumbing to pessimism, no matter how well founded: "So, to sum up all my thinking in a single formula, it is dissimilarities and inequalities among men that created honor; the importance of honor fades as those differences diminish; and it will presumably disappear when they do."[41] The "presumably" in the final clause is telling: it opens a door halfway, inviting the reader to fill in what the author has left blank.

If one needs to be convinced that Tocqueville observed the values of his own family closely yet maintained his distance from them, it may be useful to consider a rather minor yet revealing fact from June 1848. Tocqueville wrote to the marquis de Blosseville about correcting an error in *L'Union* (a monarchist newspaper) concerning his brother Hippolyte:

> An article published [in the paper] stated that all men belonging to old families who happened to be in Paris during the June Days fought energetically in the ranks of the National Guard. Concerning my legion, the first, the article mentioned the names of several relatives or friends of mine but omitted that of my brother Hippolyte de Tocqueville, who resigned as captain after the July Revolution. He nevertheless spent four days and four nights in arms and found himself in some of the hottest situations. This omission distresses me.[42]

Why was Tocqueville so keen to point out that his brother had taken up arms against insurgent workers in June 1848? Because it was a matter of defending the honor of the "old families" of the French aristocracy. In *Souvenirs* he paid homage to the aristocracy's martial spirit of resistance. In the following passage he is speaking of volunteers from the department of La Manche who were not able to reach Paris (owing to a shortage of trains) until the civil war was in its fourth day:

> I was moved to see among them landowners, lawyers, physicians, and farmers —my friends and neighbors. Nearly all the old nobility of the country had taken

---

[40] Just as we saw in the previous part of the present work that Tocqueville's style resisted the tendencies of democratic language.

[41] *DA* II.3.18, p. 298; AG, p. 737.

[42] Letter to the marquis de Blosseville, June 1848. Unpublished correspondence but included in Louis Passy, *Le Marquis de Blosseville. Souvenirs* (Évreux: Charles Hérissey, 1898).

up arms on that occasion and joined the column. The same was true throughout most of France. From the muddiest country squire in the depths of his province to the elegant and idle heirs of the great houses, all remembered in that moment that they belonged to a ruling warrior caste, and everywhere they set an example of initiative and enthusiasm—such is the great vitality of these old aristocratic corps. For they retain a trace of themselves even though they seem to have been reduced to dust already, and on several occasions they have risen up from the ghostly realm in which ultimately they will find their eternal rest.[43]

This bravura passage can almost be read as a funeral homage, since these "old corps" have no future, but one nevertheless senses Tocqueville's respect for the values they were defending: namely, order and legality, in the face of an uprising of "red" workers. Tocqueville himself took up arms on two occasions: first in July 1830 against the "armed mob," even though he regarded the Bourbons as "cowards" who did not deserve the blood that was shed on their behalf;[44] and again in 1848, but in April, not June: "During the whole of yesterday," he wrote to Nassau Senior, "I had a rifle in hand rather than a pen."[45]

This remark aptly portrays Tocqueville's awareness of carrying on the values of the aristocracy, by force of arms if necessary. On August 17, 1830, he wrote to Marie Mottley that it pained him to have sworn allegiance to the House of Orleans, and he recalled having hoped for civil war. "Now that the first step has been taken, where will I stop? Oh! How right I was to have wished for civil war! How simple it would have been to proceed if only duty had coincided with all the prods of honor."[46]

❧

By the same token, war did not frighten him, including war for the health of democracy. Like Hegel, Tocqueville believed that the drama of war could restore the unity of society: "War almost always enlarges the thought and ennobles the heart of a people. There are cases in which war alone can halt the excessive development of certain penchants to which equality naturally gives rise, and in which it must be considered a necessary corrective to certain deep-seated afflictions of democratic societies."[47]

[43] *OC* XII, p. 177.
[44] Letter to Marie Mottley, July 30, 1830, *OC* XIV, pp. 375–76.
[45] *OC* VII-2, p. 103. See F. Mélonio in *Œuvres*, La Pléiade, 3:1198. Note that Tocqueville did not mention this episode in the *Souvenirs*.
[46] Letter of August 17, 1830, *OC* XIV, p. 377.
[47] *DA* II.3.23, p. 329; AG, p. 765.

He was careful, however, to indicate that a democracy that engaged in war would face new dangers, most notably from "warlike princes," factious generals, and those who "sought to destroy liberty" and found an opportunity to do so in war. The army is a permanent problem for any democracy. The chapter from which the quote above is taken is entitled "Why Democratic Peoples Naturally Desire Peace and Democratic Armies Naturally Desire War." Hence Tocqueville cannot be described as an apologist for rule by force, but his aristocratic roots, no less than the type of political and geostrategic analysis he favored, led him to look upon armed struggle as one avenue of human progress. As Dino Cofrancesco points out, Tocqueville wrote that "the feudal aristocracy was born in war and for war."[48] In his view, the aristocracy was *in essence* a warrior caste, and in this respect he agreed with writers such as Montlosier, who during the Restoration defended the myth that the French nobility stemmed from a race of barbarian conquerors.[49]

In the case of Algeria, Tocqueville had several opportunities to set forth his ideas about the war "that began all the conquests," followed by politics, "which made them durable," as he said in an 1846 letter to Lamoricière. Some scholars have given quite polemical accounts of Tocqueville's attitude during the colonization of Algeria. The subject deserves a study of its own because his thought evolved continually and should not be interpreted in the light of a few "sensational" quotes from various letters and texts or of his support at one point for Bugeaud's *enfumades*.[50] Another passage from Tocqueville's letter to Lamoricière may be helpful in clarifying the equilibrium he hoped to achieve:

> Having committed the huge *violence* of the conquest, I think that we must not shrink from the lesser instances of violence that are absolutely necessary to consolidate our victory. But in the interest of establishing our hold, it is very important

---

[48] See Dino Cofrancesco, "Alexis de Tocqueville. L'archetipo aristocratico e il 'primato della politica,'" *Il Pensiero politico*, no. 2 (1989): 433–61. The quote is from *DA* II.3.22.

[49] Among Montlosier's celebrated works, see *De la monarchie française depuis son rétablissement jusqu'à nos jours*, 3 vols. (Paris: Nicolle, 1814), and *De la monarchie française depuis le retour de la maison de Bourbon, jusqu'au premier avril 1815* (Paris, Nicolle, 1815). Tocqueville wrote, for example, that "all the aristocracies of the Middle Ages were born of conquest. The victor was the noble, the vanquished the serf." *DA* I, p. 523.

[50] The word *enfumade* refers to the use of fire and smoke to asphyxiate Algerians who had fled to caves seeking refuge from French troops. For a careful, nuanced assessment, see Françoise Mélonio, "Le choc des civilisations: Chassériau et Tocqueville en Algérie," in *Chassériau. Un autre romantisme* (Paris: La Documentation française/Musée du Louvre, 2002), pp. 171–96. See also the introduction by J.-J. Chevallier and A. Jardin to Tocqueville's numerous writings on Algeria in *OC* III-1.

to persuade the natives, insofar as possible, that we have the law on our side, and if the law fails, then at least humanity and a measure of respect.[51]

In the same vein, although Tocqueville believed that European civilization was superior to Arab or Kabyle civilization (and he did regard both as civilizations), he remarked in one of his parliamentary reports that "we have made Muslim society far more miserable, chaotic, ignorant, and barbarous than it was before it encountered us." The course he recommended was not to crush existing hierarchies or force assimilation but to allow native structures to develop, as the English had done in India: "Do not force the natives to come to our schools, but help them to improve theirs, to increase the number of teachers in them, and to train men of law and religion, whom Muslim civilization can no more do without than ours can."[52]

Finally, it is worth recalling that dueling, to which Tocqueville devoted an essay when he was a young magistrate,[53] did not frighten him either. Indeed, during his stay in Metz, he fought at least one duel, probably having to do with his relationship with Rosalie Malye, and was seriously wounded. During his convalescence, he contrived with help from his father to conceal the fact from Abbé Lesueur.

As these various texts and actions suggest, Tocqueville remained faithful in certain respects to the values of his milieu while searching for ways in which those values might find a new lease on life in a democratic world. His moment of greatest distress came during the July Days of 1830, which led to division in his family between those who agreed to swear the oath of allegiance to the new regime and those who refused, including both his father and his uncle Louis de Rosambo, who were peers of France. Two interesting letters to Henrion reveal the complexity of Tocqueville's feelings.[54] Henrion, a friend of Tocqueville's in Metz to whom his father took a liking, spoke of "baseness" in regard to Louis-Philippe and showed the letter of reproach to Tocqueville's mother to increase the pressure on the "turncoat." On October 17, 1830, Tocqueville explained himself at length in a letter written in a cold rage. He acknowledged having been in open resistance to the four executive decrees of Charles X, even in his official function as magistrate, but denied participating in insurrection or the overthrow of the dynasty: "I said that I would participate in the civil war if there was one." He thus confirmed

---

[51] Letter to Lamoricière, April 5, 1846, *Lettres choisies. Souvenirs*, pp. 561–67.

[52] For these two quotes, see "Rapport sur le projet de loi relatif aux crédits extraordinaires demandés pour l'Algérie" (1847), *OC* III-1, pp. 323, 325.

[53] See "Discours de rentrée des tribunaux sur le duel," 1828, in *Mélanges, OC* XVI, pp. 49ff.

[54] See Jardin, *Tocqueville*, pp. 42, 59.

what he had written earlier, in August, to Marie Mottley. "Baseness," he added, would have been to serve his own self-interest in a time of national crisis. Indeed, "at the point we had reached," he wrote, the salvation of France "seemed to me to depend on keeping the new king. I therefore promised to support him without making a secret of the fact that I was not doing it for him."[55] Tocqueville added that if the new dynasty acted against the interest of the country, his oath would be nullified: "I would conspire against it."

The point of this controversy is clear: it bears on the question of opportunism and its inconsistency with honor. Tocqueville maintained that he had made his choice not to save his career—and in his October letter he emphasized the fact that he had just refused a promotion—but to serve a more general interest than the (future[56]) legitimist cause, namely, the interest of France. His position rested on a calculus of the contending forces: because civil war had been forestalled thanks to the efforts of Thiers and others who urged the duc d'Orléans to take the throne, it would have been irresponsible to reject this pact and this pacification of a volatile situation. Honor, as Tocqueville understood it in these circumstances, was subordinate to an appreciation of public order and the general interest in a time of great confusion. Nevertheless, as he would explain subsequently, his decision to go to America was intended in part to gain some breathing room and weigh his options: would the new regime manage to survive? To be sure, its legitimacy was highly uncertain, but for Tocqueville, who had already moved a long way beyond the prejudices of his milieu, a whole system of unquestioning loyalty and obedience had already succumbed forever. He had decided to defend a different value: independence of judgment for the individual and the citizen in the face of the new despotism lurking in the term "democracy." To true legitimists, such a "conversion" could seem shocking.

Tocqueville discussed all this at length in a letter to Charles Stöffels. He insisted that his behavior had been guided by loyalty not to the monarchy nor the values of aristocracy but to France:

> I swore an oath to the new government. In doing so, I thought I was doing my strict duty as a Frenchman. In our current state, if Louis-Philippe is overthrown, it will certainly not be in favor of Henri V but rather to establish a republic and

[55] Letter to Henrion, October 17, 1830, partially unpublished. A second letter, dated November 19, continued the polemic because Henrion had tried to involve Tocqueville's mother. Parts of these letter were included in French in Vittorio de Caprariis, *Profilio di Tocqueville* (Naples: Edizioni Scientifiche Italiane, 1962), pp. 80–83, but with an erroneous attribution giving Kergorlay as the addressee, who was in fact far from France and from the events of July because he was serving in the army in Africa.

[56] The term "legitimism" was not really used until after the fall of the Bourbons.

anarchy. Anyone who loves his country must therefore openly support the new government, since it alone can save France from itself. I feel contempt for the new king and believe that his claim to the throne is dubious at best, yet I will support him, I think, more steadfastly than those who paved the way for him but who will soon become his enemies.[57]

ᘒᘙ

Toward legitimism as a political movement, which was in reality essentially a parliamentary movement, Tocqueville cultivated a resolutely pragmatic attitude. He repeatedly stated that the legitimists were unrealistic, outdated, and often ridiculous (the ill-fated coup attempt of the duchesse de Berry being a case in point). There is no need to cite evidence of this here, as the point has often been made. Aristocrat by emotion and democrat by reason,[58] Tocqueville's personal reactions and perceptions of social relations were inevitably divided. Politically, however, he harbored no illusion about one crucial fact: the French peasant remained haunted by the tithe, the corvée (compulsory labor service), the possible loss of *biens nationaux* (property confiscated during the Revolution and distributed to the peasantry), and so on.[59] A return to the past was therefore unrealistic and inconceivable in France, just then beginning its industrial takeoff, all the more so because mystical veneration of the king's person had all but disappeared. As for what was then called "legitimacy," Tocqueville himself, unlike his kinsman by marriage Chateaubriand, never expressed the slightest flutter of emotion at the idea of "the national will maintained and personified in a family." He did not share the myth of the "primitive popular mandate, granted by the nation to his race," which Louis XVIII had supposedly renewed by "granting" the Charter of 1814.[60]

Tocqueville thus made his peace with the Carlo-republican electoral alliance when it was to his advantage to do so. For instance, in 1837 he clearly found it useful to play a double game. In a letter to Mathieu Molé, the prime minister and a relative of Tocqueville's, he rejected the support of the prefect

[57] Letter of August 26, 1830, *Lettres choisies. Souvenirs*, pp. 155–56. Included in Caprariis, *Profilo di Tocqueville*.

[58] As Tocqueville wrote in a handwritten note on which I commented in part 1, based on the version given in Rédier, *Comme disait M. de Tocqueville*.

[59] On the recurrent fears of a return of "feudalism," he wrote: "That is enough for me. For me, the proof is given and the system has been judged." *OC* II-2, p. 287. The passage begins ironically: "Some fine minds have recently tried to rehabilitate the Ancien Régime."

[60] The quotes are from Chateaubriand, *De la nouvelle proposition relative au bannissement de Charles X et de sa famille* (1831), in *Grands Écrits politiques*, 2:655.

in his campaign to win election as deputy for Valognes. "I am not an enemy of the government in general," he wrote, "nor of those who are currently governing in particular,"[61] but he added that he held to an "independent position." Earlier, however, he had asked Molé to name Élie de Beaumont to a post as magistrate. Furthermore, in the same month of September 1837, he wrote to Blosseville that it was essential to reach agreement as quickly as possible with Berryer, the leader of the legitimists: voters would "have an interest in my entering the Chamber because they are quite sure ... of my independence and know that on many points I think as they do."[62] His position was thus one of calculated ambiguity: he was not an adversary of the Orleanist government but "on many points"—one would very much like to know which ones—he was sympathetic with the government's opponents. It is easy to see why suspicion of his motives remained, even though Tocqueville pretended to be irritated by it.

CHATEAUBRIAND, THE PRECURSOR: THE MONARCHY AS "LEVELING" AND DEMOCRACY AS "DELUGE"

According to one unpublished source, Tocqueville sent a copy of *Democracy in America* to Chateaubriand two weeks after it was published, accompanied by a long letter of homage to "the greatest writer of his century" in which he discussed what he personally hoped to accomplish with the work.[63] The letter was clearly drafted in accordance with the conventions of the genre, with lavish compliments to its recipient, but as always with Tocqueville, there remained an element of authenticity. He indicated that he had three reasons for writing to the paladin of Legitimacy: to pay homage to the writer, to recall the family ties between them, and to respond in advance to the charge he was sure to face of "working for the destruction of the monarchy" in order to make room for democracy. To this list Tocqueville added one further point, which is of the utmost importance to us, namely, that Chateaubriand was the preeminent analyst of the democratic revolution:

> You are not only the man who painted the past better than anyone else but also the most prophetic about the future.[64] Standing at the place where two great revolutions came together, one ending and the other beginning, you shed equal light

[61] Letter to Molé, September 12, 1837, partially reproduced in *Lettres choisies. Souvenirs*, p. 390, n. 179.

[62] Letter to Blosseville, unpublished correspondence, but included in Passy, *Le Marquis de Blosseville*, p. 171. Blosseville, a friend of Tocqueville's youth, had become a political writer in the legitimist camp.

[63] Letter to Chateaubriand, draft with variants, unpublished correspondence, January 1835.

[64] Variant reading: "There is no one, Sir, who has portrayed the coming of democracy as well as you."

on both sides of this vast canvas. No one has described the progress of democracy in the Christian world as you have done. The purpose of this book is to explain the effects of this same democracy in a country that witnessed its arrival at the end of its journey and observed the peaceful establishment of its empire.

Leave aside the uncharacteristically stiff style of this missive, which can be explained by Tocqueville's awareness that he was posing a respectful challenge to his elder, and focus instead on the central assertion: was Chateaubriand in fact a precursor of *Democracy in America*? Tocqueville was not simply flattering his illustrious uncle. He had every reason to make such a claim.

The revolution of 1830 had been a dramatic moment for Chateaubriand as well as for Tocqueville, and he subsequently published at least five or six pieces describing the "democratic" turn (taking the word "democratic" in one of Tocqueville's senses).[65] All these texts were much discussed, either because they were comments on political events of the day or because Chateaubriand chose to publish them either in well-known journals such as the *Revue des deux mondes* or in new ones whose inception drew the attention of readers, such as *La Revue européenne*. Finally, the volumes of the *Études et discours historiques*, which included the end of Chateaubriand's "Rational Analysis of the History of France," were a widely remarked contribution to the study of the Ancien Régime, intended to follow the work of Guizot, Thierry, Lémontey, and others cited in the introduction.

In a pamphlet on the law aimed at Charles X, Chateaubriand stated his guiding intuition: no matter what differences existed among the nations of Europe, the continent as a whole was proceeding in a single direction, toward democratic "leveling." "Europe is but a single family. . . . Only in England was the aristocracy powerful enough to preserve its privileges. Europe will be leveled in the modern era as it was leveled in the Middle Ages. France will not remain in social contradiction with surrounding states. Such isolation is not possible."[66] Here the main point stands out clearly: the aristocracy is the quintessential focal point of resistance to leveling, hence leveling is a characteristic of democracy.

---

[65] Here is a list of the most important texts, all prior to *DA* I: last speech to the Chamber of Peers, August 7, 1830, reproduced in *Mémoires d'outre-tombe*; *De la Restauration et de la monarchie élective*, March 1, 1831, in J.-P. Clément, ed., *Grands Textes politiques* (Paris: Imprimerie Nationale, 1993), 2:569ff.; *De la proposition relative au bannissement de Charles X*, October 31, 1831, in ibid., 2:609ff.; "La France de 1830 et ses futuritions," in *La Revue européenne*, December 15, 1831; "Avenir du monde," very important article in *Revue des deux mondes*, April 15, 1834, reproduced in *Mémoires d'outre-tombe*, ed. Levaillant, appendix 25, 4:781ff.; "Analyse raisonnée de l'histoire de France," in *Études ou Discours historiques* (1831), vol. 4.
[66] *De la proposition*, 2:621.

Or is it rather characteristic of despotism? In this regard, it is interesting to examine another text, that of March 1831 entitled *De la Restauration et de la monarchie élective*, which preceded the one I just quoted, conceived as its continuation. In the earlier piece, despotism was portrayed as one possible end point of democracy:

> We are headed toward a general revolution: if the transformation that is under way proceeds on course and encounters no obstacle; if popular reason continues its progressive development; if the moral education of the intermediate classes suffers no interruption; then nations will be leveled to a condition of equal liberty. If this transformation is halted, nations will be leveled to a condition of equal despotism.[67]

Finally, in 1834, in the *Revue des deux mondes*, Chateaubriand published a text on "The Future of the World," in which he summarized his two main ideas: "Europe is hastening toward democracy," and, before the age of popular government can be realized, "Europe must first be leveled into a single system."[68]

Now, what does the penultimate chapter of the first volume of *Democracy in America* have to say about the "importance of the foregoing in relation to Europe?"[69] That the various barriers against "the organized force of the government" have been blown away. Those barriers included "religion, love of the prince by his subjects, the prince's goodness, honor, family spirit, provincial prejudices, custom, and public opinion."[70] Once there were despotic princes and liberal mores. Tocqueville reviewed the transformations endured by honor (which remains a capital theme in his eyes), by municipal liberties, and by a public opinion that can no longer rely on association as a source of strength.[71] He then asked this question, which for him encapsulated what was at stake in democracy: "If complete equality were ultimately inevitable, would it not be better to choose to be leveled by liberty rather than by a despot?"[72]

---

[67] *De la Restauration et de la monarchie élective*, 2:569.

[68] Cf. *Mémoires d'outre-tombe*, appendix 25, pp. 781, 783. This text was also published in a work entitled *Lectures des Mémoires de M. de Chateaubriand, ou Recueil d' articles publiés sur ces Mémoires* (Paris: Lefèvre, 1834). The readings were organized at the Abbaye aux Bois, orchestrated by Sainte-Beuve for the benefit of the local idol.

[69] *DA* I.2.9, pp. 420–25; AG, pp. 360–64.

[70] Ibid., p. 421; AG, p. 361. The enumeration in "feudal" style is typical of Montesquieu.

[71] Reference to art. 291 of the Penal Code, which Guizot had tightened in 1834: freedom of association was drained of its content.

[72] *DA* I.2.9, p. 424; AG, p. 364.

This may be a bit too much of a rhetorical question (the proposed choice is hardly a choice), but in reality it serves as a mirror for what has been said previously about the French monarchy, to which Tocqueville would return in the second volume. The new despotism, which led to "leveling by liberty," was the heir of monarchical despotism. "It was the absolute kings who did most to level ranks among their subjects."[73] In the same vein, the introduction of 1835 had heralded the same theme: "In France kings proved themselves to be the most energetic and constant of levelers."[74] The whole European process is described in the introduction as having been promoted by royal governments to create "factors" of equality among individuals: "Every newly discovered process, every newly conceived need, every new desire ... marked further steps toward universal leveling."

In lending support to "democracy" (in Tocqueville's sense), "the king invited the inferior classes of the state to participate in government in order to humble the aristocracy."[75] It was possible for some authors to view such monarchical despotism as a good thing because it served the interests of the majority of the population: "Some kings served democracy through their talents, others through their vices. Louis XI and Louis XIV tried hard to equalize everyone below the throne, and ultimately Louis XV descended with all his court into the dust."[76] One might almost imagine that this was Hervé de Tocqueville castigating the vices of the ruling class and the weaknesses of royalty.[77] We may therefore suppose that Tocqueville took from Chateaubriand the theme of modern "leveling" as a revival of the leveling visited upon the aristocracy. To be sure, the same theme can be found in the work of Restoration historians such as Guizot and Augustin Thierry. Michelet, who followed Guizot's lectures, adopted the same argument: "The long years of leveling by the monarchy created a deep gulf between France and England, with which some writers insist on comparing our homeland."[78] Michelet perfectly summed up Guizot's idea, that the French monarchy was "the arm of the nation against aristocracy, the shortest route to leveling."

---

[73] *DA* II.2.1, p. 122; AG, p. 584.

[74] *DA* I, introduction, p. 59; AG, p. 4.

[75] Ibid.

[76] Ibid.

[77] Both Hervé and Édouard de Tocqueville made marginal comments on Louis XV in the manuscript: see Nolla I, p. 5, n. m. In places, the comte de Tocqueville suggested that his son tone down his remarks on "leveling kings." Always think of the reader! This was a family precept, a matter of politeness and breeding.

[78] Michelet, *Introduction à l'histoire universelle*, 1831, in Michelet, *La Cité des vivants et des morts*, ed. Claude Lefort (Paris: Belin, 2002), p. 131.

Once again, then, Tocqueville echoed a theme he did not invent. As we
have just seen, he turned it in a direction that made the value of liberty quite
ambiguous. What did it mean to say that the fate of Europe was "to allow
itself to be leveled by liberty?" It could only have meant to diminish the pride
and accomplishments of *the individual*: it was on this point that Tocqueville
was deeply sympathetic to Chateaubriand's thought and sensibility. In "The
Future of the World," the latter did indeed say that the fate of democracy was
to fabricate hives and anthills. A society that produces individualization is
not a society that encourages individual wealth, however.

> How will fortunes be leveled? How will wages be apportioned to labor? How
> will women achieve legal emancipation? I have no idea. Until now, society has
> proceeded by *aggregation* and *family*. What will it look like when nothing re-
> mains but the *individual*, as present tendencies suggest, and as we already see
> happening in the United States? The *human race* will very likely be greater, but
> it is to be feared that *man* will diminish, that certain eminent faculties of genius
> will disappear, that the imagination, poetry, and the arts will die in the cells of a
> hive-society in which each individual will be but a single bee, a cog in a machine,
> an atom in organized matter. If the Christian religion were to vanish, liberty
> would lead to the same social petrification that China has achieved through
> slavery.[79]

In this disturbing scenario, it is clear that the process of equalization can
lead to despotism without a leader or king. The power to dominate society
(or the "human race") comes from society itself. It is fairly obvious, then,
that Chateaubriand anticipated Tocqueville's idea of "generality" as a characteristic of democracy and of the taste for "general ideas." He also anticipated
Tocqueville's expansive view of man as a "general being." As his correspondence shows, Tocqueville was capable of mocking the pride of his illustrious
elder, yet he was well aware that Chateaubriand had helped him discover
what can only be called the aristocratic tendency of his own thought.[80]
Furthermore, the dialogue between the two men continued after the publication of *Democracy in America*. As Marc Fumaroli suggests, we can also detect signs of influence in the other direction, of Tocqueville on his uncle: for
example, in the 1836 *Essai sur la littérature anglaise*, and again in a chapter

[79] Chateaubriand, "Avenir du monde," 4:784.
[80] To believe a letter quoted by Pierre-Roland Marcel, *Essai politique sur Alexis de Tocqueville* (Paris:
Félix Alcan, 1910), p. 191, n. 126, Chateaubriand, shortly before the publication of *DA* I on January 11,
1835, confirmed to Tocqueville that he had gotten things right: "We are undoubtedly entering the democratic era. The democratic idea is everywhere. It is undermining thrones and ruining aristocracies.... No
matter what one does or says, the ultimate victory will belong to it."

written between 1837 and 1840 that was to have served as a conclusion for *Mémoires d'outre-tombe*: "Liberty, a spirit of leveling and incredulity, hatred of superiority, anarchy of ideas—in a word, democracy found its way into literature as into the rest of society."[81]

ফ

Chateaubriand did not suspect how much Tocqueville actually owed him. Indeed, the author of *Democracy in America* prepared a draft introduction that he did not keep because it so closely imitated the great champion of aristocratic liberty. If one compares parallel passages, it is hard to say which of the two men was the author. Consider first this excerpt:

> Fatal march of democracy. Democracy! Don't you see that these are the waters of the Deluge? . . . Already they cover the countryside and the cities, they are breasting the ruined parapets of stalwart castles and lapping at the feet of thrones. . . . Rather than build useless dikes against the flood, let us build a saving ark instead. . . . [In the fourth century, when the Barbarians invaded], no one anticipated the universal advent of the feudal system, which was the consequence of the destruction of Rome throughout Europe.

And now compare this, which, though less agitated in style, is astonishingly similar in content:

> The boldest doctrines concerning property, equality, and liberty are proclaimed morning and night to the face of monarchs who tremble behind a triple line of suspect soldiers. The flood of democracy has overtaken them. They climb from story to story, from the ground floor to the palace attic, from which they will hurl themselves into the tide that will swallow them up.

The style, the length of the sentences, and the descriptive intent might suggest that the second passage is by Tocqueville, while the first, which recounts the flood in more breathless tones, seems more likely to have come

---

[81] The same passage is found in both works: *Essai*, vol. 15 of *Œuvres complètes* (Paris: Administration de librairie, 1853), p. 197, and *Mémoires d'outre-tombe*, 2:703, appendix 2. Note that the *Mémoires* quote Tocqueville in several places, both for biographical details and to correct what was deemed to be an overly positive view of America. See 4:586 and 1:353: "A chrysogenic aristocracy is ready to appear with love of distinctions and a passion for titles. Some imagine that a general level prevails in the United States. This is completely wrong." In January 1839 Chateaubriand came to Tocqueville's château and insisted on hearing passages from the still-unfinished second volume of *Democracy in America* read out loud. He heaped praise on Tocqueville, which the latter then mocked in a letter to Beaumont, *OC* VIII-1, pp. 337–38. See the very detailed study by Marc Fumaroli, "Chateaubriand et Tocqueville," *Revue des deux mondes*, January 2003, pp. 23–78.

from the pen that wrote *Atala* and *René*. The opposite is true, however.[82] So impressed was Tocqueville by the metaphor of the democratic deluge in "The Future of the World" that he borrowed the theme to express the frightening aspect of the spectacle. The 1835 introduction retained only the image of "leveling." The flood imagery appears at several points in the book but in a very different sense (the new humanity that is born in America apparently comes after total destruction has taken place).

☙☞

Ultimately Tocqueville had to face any number of questions that Chateaubriand, even more than his father, had bequeathed to him, whether he was conscious of the legacy or not. Like Chateaubriand, he, too, was a "swimmer between two banks." The opening lines of *Mémoires d'outre-tombe* say a great deal in a few words: "I was born a gentleman. In my own mind, I capitalized on the accident of my birth and retained the steadfast love of liberty that belongs primarily to the aristocracy, whose final hour has rung."[83] Both authors claim the same privilege: a better understanding of liberty as the "temperament" of a social class. This could hardly fail to arouse the ire of republicans like Edgar Quinet, who saw it as a mark of haughty superiority. In his notes on *The Ancien Régime and the Revolution*, Quinet protested: "Is aristocracy really necessary to liberty? See the United States! What did Tocqueville see there anyway?"[84]

Unlike Tocqueville, the Breton bard did not shrink from saying that, all things considered, Bonaparte, whom he had hated, admired, combated, mourned, and almost loved, was the incarnation of *individuality*: "He will be the last of the great individual existences. Nothing will ever again dominate our petty, leveled societies."[85] The shared aristocratic vision of both authors is evident in the obsession with "leveling" and the comparison of the leveling effected by the king with that accomplished by the people.

It is worth noting that the term came from the English Revolution and its "levelers" and was applied in France to the left wing of French revolutionaries, the *enragés* and *sans-culottes* of 1793–94, as linguists have demonstrated.[86] In

---

[82] For the first text: Tocqueville, *Œuvres*, La Pléiade, 2:937–38, n. a. For the second: Chateaubriand, "Avenir du monde," 4:782 (and *Revue des deux mondes*, April 15, 1834). The Tocqueville excerpt is mentioned in Aurelian Craiutu, "Tocqueville's Paradoxical Moderation," *Review of Politics*, p. 617.

[83] *Mémoires d'outre-tombe* I.1.2, ed. Levaillant, 1:15.

[84] Quoted in François Furet, "Quinet et Tocqueville," *Commentaire*, no. 26 (Summer 1984): 347.

[85] *Mémoires d'outre-tombe*, 3:666, and 1:703, appendix 2.

[86] See Ferdinand Brunot, *Histoire de la langue française*, vol. 9-2 (Revolution and Empire), p. 705. The levelers were hotheads dreaming of an "equality of scarcity," according to Camille Desmoulins. The

other words, the metaphor was heavily laden with meaning when used by kin of Malesherbes. Ampère, who once again served as a link between the two writers, fully grasped the essential character of the "return of despotism" theme. In the (rather poor) poem that he composed in Tocqueville's honor in 1840, he made the point clearly:

Ah! C'est le mot fatal qui vous remplit d'effroi;
Oui! que cet ennemi s'appelle peuple ou roi,
Ce despote...

[Ah! That is the fatal word that fills you with terror;
Yes! Whether the enemy is called people or king,
that despot...][87]

Consciously or not, Tocqueville, when he arrived in America, was already seeing with Chateaubriand's eyes. Surely it is in this sense that one should understand his famous words to Camille d'Orglandes: "For ten years now I have been thinking about some of the things about which I shall soon tell you." This statement led François Furet to say in his preface to *Democracy in America* that "there is a mystery of origin about Tocqueville's journey to America."[88] By the time Tocqueville was twenty (in 1825), Chateaubriand had already expressed Ultra views in praise of aristocratic values, which monarchs since Louis XI had failed to recognize or even scorned. As we saw earlier, the Orleanist usurpation had led him to write that "we are headed toward a general revolution" in Europe (*De la Restauration et de la monarchie élective*, March 1831). On June 29, nearly four months later, Tocqueville wrote from America to Kergorlay: "We are headed toward an unlimited democracy..., we are being driven there by an irresistible force."

Chateaubriand, a monarchist "swept up" by the idea of a liberal republic, was strongly suspected of being in league with the friends of Armand Carrel.[89] To believe the memoirs of Alton Shée, he even proposed to Berryer that they work together on behalf of the republic because "legitimacy is dead,

---

newspaper *Le Néologiste français* recorded the term in 1796, and it entered the supplement to the *Dictionnaire de l'Académie* in 1798.

[87] *OC* XI, p. 142.

[88] *DA* I, preface by F. Furet, p. 7. The quote from the letter to Orglandes (wrongly attributed to Kergorlay) is in *DA* I, p. 9.

[89] The newspaper *La Mode* wrote in September 1831 that republicans had joined with legitimists such as Chateaubriand around the idea of appealing to the people over the head of the government. See Clément, *Grands Écrits politiques*, 2:707, n. 82. Indeed, Chateaubriand became a friend of Béranger and Carrel and joined in plots uncovered by the police; he proposed a restoration of Henri V to be followed by ratification by the people with universal suffrage. See *De la nouvelle proposition relative au bannissement de Charles X*.

completely dead." Meanwhile, Tocqueville continued to gravitate toward the idea of a republic shorn of myths bequeathed to French republicans by the Terror, or else toward a constitutional monarchy not far from that proposed by Chateaubriand in *La Monarchie selon la Charte*.[90] Like his uncle, he detested the man to whom Chateaubriand referred as "Philippe" and shared the following ferocious judgment, which has since become famous: "What we have today [in 1831] is I know not what: neither a republic nor a monarchy, neither legitimate nor illegitimate. It is an almost thing, which partakes of everything and nothing, which does not live and does not die; a usurpation without a usurper, a day without a yesterday or a tomorrow."[91]

Tocqueville would make similar statements in later discussions with Nassau Senior. Yet both of these scions of the French nobility, Tocqueville and Chateaubriand, confronted the same difficulties: to accept "democracy," albeit without enthusiasm; to favor liberty while rejecting the power of money; to hope for an enlightened elite that would educate and enrich the people while detesting the bourgeoisie.

To this we must add a consideration that is more irrational, perhaps, but by no means insignificant: both men came to believe in God's presence in history. Family tradition had initiated them in the mystery of the martyred king, guillotined in 1793. It is quite interesting to discover that both treated this sacrifice as an inscrutable enigma. In the *Mémoires*, Chateaubriand had this to say about the king's death: "Louis XVI's qualities did not redeem the sins . . . that his forebears had left for him to expiate, but it is on the sin that the blows of Providence fall, never on the man: God abridges virtue's days on earth only to prolong them in heaven."[92] Virtue, because in Chateaubriand's eyes as in Tocqueville's, Louis XVI was *the only French king who loved the people*.[93]

Similarly, Tocqueville indulged in a lengthy meditation on the mystery of the king who was sacrificed despite being a good and just ruler:

> I see only one [French monarch] who passionately loved men for themselves . . . and that king—who can say his name without trembling—was Louis XVI. Such are the inexplicable judgments of God, or perhaps one should say that only the other world can make sense of this one. We must acknowledge that while God's

[90] Note for the comte de Chambord, January 14, 1852, published by *La Gazette de France*, November 23, 1871, ed. in S. Rials, *Révolution et contre-révolution en Europe* (Paris: DUC/Albatros, 1987), pp. 162–66.

[91] Chateaubriand, *De la nouvelle proposition*, 2:629.

[92] *Mémoires d'outre-tombe*, conclusion of book 12, 4:578.

[93] I pointed out earlier that Tocqueville seems to have forgotten this in his (unpublished) letter to Bouchitté, in which he says that no French king loved the people.

designs are visible in the conduct of the race, they become obscure and all but invisible in the fate of the individual.[94]

In the end, the published text of *The Ancien Régime* is more cautious and less emphatic because the expiatory cult dedicated to the memory of the martyred king had too strong a political and ideological resonance.[95] To be sure, Tocqueville and Chateaubriand shared a common reference when it came to the influence of Providence in history: Bossuet was one of their most beloved authors. But more than Bossuet, they shared the symbol of "Malesherbes, a man of ancient virtues and novel opinions," as Chateaubriand characterized him. Was this not precisely the ideal that Tocqueville adopted?

[94] *Œuvres*, La Pléiade, 3:1074, note on a manuscript of *ARR*.

[95] The kings did not seek to bring the classes together. "I am wrong: one and only one did want do and even lent his whole heart to the task, and that one—who can fathom the judgments of God!—was Louis XVI." *OC* II-1, p. 166.

Conclusion

> I cannot believe that people don't see me clearly as a new kind of
> liberal.
>
> —Tocqueville to Eugène Stöffels, 1836

TWO DEMOCRACIES OR TWO DESPOTISMS?

As is often the case with liberal thinkers (such as Locke, Montesquieu, and Constant), Tocqueville's thought is truly a deconstruction, or at times a circumvention, of the idea of *sovereignty*. This concept, which played such an important role in the building of the European nation-state, has the property of clearly defining the locus of power: the sovereign is he who can issue commands with the authority of law and who thus decides the specific content of the general interest at any given moment.

As we have seen, however, Guizot, in the *Origines du gouvernement représentatif*, showed what was paradoxical about modern representative democracy, in which the people are supposed to be sovereign yet obey. The sovereign is governed: that is the paradox. Originally, sovereignty was in fact a monarchical (and pontifical) idea, ill-adapted for transplantation to a democratic setting. Those who govern *exercise* sovereignty, while the people "possess" it. These ambiguities, which Rousseau only reinforced, gave rise to a great deal of confusion and conflict, and indeed to Jacobinism itself, during the French Revolution.[1] Tocqueville was able to sidestep or defuse the problem thanks to his intuition of an "authority of the social," which was borrowed from Lamennais's "authority of common sense." For one thing, in America (or, more precisely, in New England), the sovereignty of the people was exercised in local assemblies that wielded a judiciously "dispersed" form of power (as we saw in part 1). For another, the power to which one had to pay attention in democracy was not sovereign power but the way in which the public at large exercises an authentic form of authority. Tocqueville

---

[1] See the appendix on Rousseau and sovereignty at the end of *La Liberté et la loi*.

attached several names to this authority of the people over itself: the tyranny of the majority, the power of public opinion, and the common faith:

> There is reason to believe that the intellectual ascendancy of the majority would be less absolute in a democratic nation subject to a king than in a pure democracy, but it will always be quite absolute, and regardless of what political laws men are subject to in ages of equality, we may anticipate that faith in common opinion will become a sort of religion, with the majority as its prophet.[2]

He thus shifted attention from the classical problem of sovereignty (separation of powers, decentralization, federalism, etc.) to a more redoubtable question: not that of the danger represented by the state (the problem of classical liberalism) but rather the way in which a democratic people might protect itself from itself, from its own penchants, *which originate and reverberate within civil society, or what Tocqueville called "the social state."*

In this book I have tried to show that what sharpened Tocqueville's perception of these ever-present perils was his aristocratic culture, which he translated into the structuring myth of *Democracy in America*: namely, the return of the despot. In this light, it is possible to reconsider a problem with which students of Tocqueville have long grappled: Is the "soft" tutelary despotism described at the end of volume 2 incompatible with the view of American democracy set forth in volume 1? Are there in fact "two democracies" and indeed two distinct books, one in conflict with the other?

Indeed, the end of volume 2 of *Democracy in America* describes a power *external* to society based on untrammeled administrative centralization, something that resembles a combination of Hobbes' Leviathan and Bossuet's Providence: looming above a society of similar and equal men "stands an immense tutelary power, which assumes sole responsibility for securing their pleasure and watching over their fate. It is absolute, meticulous, regular, provident, and mild. It would resemble paternal authority . . . but on the contrary . . . seeks only to keep them in childhood irrevocably. . . . Why not relieve them entirely of the trouble of thinking and the difficulty of living?"[3]

By contrast, Tocqueville in volume 1 insisted on the tyranny of the majority, the factors of stability introduced by Christianity, and the way in which the American people act by themselves and on themselves. Some commentators on the work have therefore concluded that Tocqueville's view had changed between 1835, when volume 1 was published, and 1840. In fact,

[2] *DA* II.1.2, p. 18; AG, p. 492.
[3] *DA* II.4.6, p. 385; AG, p. 818.

as Francesco de Sanctis has shown, the situation was a good deal more complex because the issue in volume 1 was that of an *incarnate* despotic power,[4] whereas in volume 2 it was a question of society's oppression of itself.[5] Indeed, it is in volume 2 that one finds the passage on "the principal source of beliefs" that I just quoted. The commentators who contrast the two volumes of *Democracy in America* as though they were two different books have not read the text in the light of Tocqueville's *overarching* question: What metamorphoses will *authority* undergo? In what respects will authority supplant the traditional role of sovereignty?

⊘⊙

It is nevertheless true that, in stylistic terms and in his introduction of the question of authority, Tocqueville conveyed a difference of approach. In volume 1 he wrote: "If absolute power were once again to establish itself among the democratic peoples of Europe, I have no doubt that it would take a new form and exhibit features unknown to our fathers."[6] The words "once again" resound as a signal: apparent innovation conceals a hidden historical repetition. I have argued that Tocqueville sees both an analogy and a filiation with "leveling" monarchs. The emphasis in the second volume is different, however: "If despotism were to establish itself in today's democratic nations, it would probably have a different character. It would be more extensive and more mild, and it would degrade men without tormenting them."[7] In this passage he seems to have given up on the idea of a resurgence of the past. Indeed, he adds the following: "I search in vain for an expression that exactly reproduces my idea of it and captures it fully. The old words 'despotism' and 'tyranny' will not do. The thing is new, hence I must try to define it, since I cannot give it a name.'"[8]

If one takes this passage literally, Tocqueville has moved to a new paradigm on the question of despotism: what he has in mind here is the ultracentralized

---

[4] The president of the United States might become a monarchical despot of the European type: "American officials could keep their indefinite power yet cease to be answerable to anyone, and it is impossible to say where tyranny would then end." *DA* I, p. 522; AG, p. 460.

[5] See Francesco de Sanctis, *Tempo di democrazia. Alexis de Tocqueville*, new ed. (Naples: Editoriale Scientifica, 2005), pp. 91ff. Authors who have contributed to this controversy include Seymour Drescher, "Tocqueville's two 'Democracies,'" *Journal of the History of Ideas* 25 (2) (1964); Lamberti, *Tocqueville et les deux Démocraties*, which advances the idea of a split within *DA* II itself between part 4 and the preceding parts; A.-M. Battista, "Il primo Tocqueville sulla democrazia politica," 1981, reprinted in Battista, *Studi su Tocqueville*. See also Schleifer, who finds a fundamental continuity in regard to the theory of despotism in *The Making of Tocqueville's Democracy in America*, p. 285.

[6] *DA* I.2.9, p. 421; AG, p. 360.

[7] *DA* II.4.6, p. 384; AG, p. 817.

[8] Ibid., p. 385; AG, p. 818.

welfare state, concerned with the well-being of its citizens. Yet when we consider the *remedies* that he proposes in volume 2, an objection to this interpretation arises. One of these remedies is to establish intermediary bodies, defined as free associations (rather than compulsory guilds) that form within and at the behest of civil society:

> I am firmly convinced that aristocracy cannot be reestablished in the world. But ordinary citizens, by associating, can constitute very opulent, very influential, and very powerful entities—in a word, they can play the role of aristocrats.
>
> In this way one could obtain several of the most important political advantages of aristocracy without its injustices or dangers. A political, industrial, commercial, or even scientific or literary association is an enlightened and powerful citizen that cannot be made to bow down at will or subjected to oppression in the shadows, and by defending its rights against the exigencies of power it saves common liberties.[9]

This is very strange if one remains within the terms of the debate about the "two democracies." The argument would then be that Tocqueville posed a different question in 1840 than in 1835 but proposed the same answer: associations playing the part of "aristocratic individuals." This is not credible.

What is needed is therefore an *interpretation* of the text, such as the one proposed in this book. Tocqueville was indeed pursuing his intuition about a "return of despotism," which he took from the culture of aristocratic liberalism (Malesherbes). In the first volume of *Democracy in America*, he spoke of centralization as a fact that the French Revolution did not invent and which was therefore not a minor aspect of what remained vital in the legacy of the past.[10] In the future the general tendency of democracy would be to *return to centralization* by means and in circumstances that could not be predicted, apart from the passivity of citizens infantilized by the consumption of "material satisfactions." This completes the overall argument.

Thus Tocqueville did not change paradigms within a mere five years' time, nor did he conceive part 4 of the second volume in opposition to parts 1 through 3. He rather modulated his intuition, fraught with personal anxiety, by giving greater consideration to the way in which the state could gain the affection of society by enhancing its material well-being. In that respect, the welfare state would accomplish something similar to the royal

---

[9] *DA* II.4.7, p. 391; AG, p. 824.

[10] This is n. k (in the Garnier-Flammarion ed.; n. x in the AG translation), which I quoted previously and which contains the lengthy quotation from Malesherbes.

administration of Louis XIV, which did so much to lay the groundwork for *equality* in France.[11] Furthermore, in volume 2, before the introduction of "mild despotism," there are many passages that repair the broken links in the temporal chain. For instance: "Hence it is natural for love of equality to grow steadily with equality itself; by satisfying it, one fosters its growth.... Any central power that follows these natural instincts loves equality and encourages it, because equality markedly facilitates, extends, and secures the action of such a power."[12]

Clearly the point is not to set the growth of equality apart from the growth of "centralized" government. Indeed, Tocqueville offers a pessimistic prophecy that is not far removed from fatalism: "In the democratic centuries that are about to begin, I think that individual independence and local liberties will always be a product of art. Centralization will be the natural form of government."[13]

Indeed, Tocqueville did not describe two democracies but rather two despotisms, that of absolute monarchy and that of absolute democracy. The latter is not a *different* democracy but rather the corruption of the democracy described in the first part of this book (just as, in Aristotle, each pure form of government has its corresponding pathological form).

Worse yet, according to the passage quoted above, absolute democracy, the democracy of administrative centralization—so favorable to "equality in everything" (as Montesquieu might say)—is the more natural form.[14]

On Equality: The Gaze of an Aristocratic Moralist

In part 3 of this book we examined the source of pessimism in Tocqueville's writing, namely, the Pascalian discourse that haunts the text of *Democracy in America*. The author's Jansenist tendencies and aristocratic outlook come out most clearly in relation to the question of equality.[15] When he asked "why Americans seem so restless in the midst of their well-being," one can

---

[11] On this point Tocqueville agreed with Lémontey, Guizot, Rossi, and Chateaubriand, the liberal historical school of the Restoration.

[12] *DA* II.4.3, p. 361; AG, p. 795.

[13] Ibid., p. 362; AG, p. 796.

[14] The "natural government" of the future would be centralized. Silvestre de Sacy was right to question Tocqueville's optimism about democracy and his actual feelings toward it. In case anyone thinks my reading of Tocqueville is too dark, I recommend rereading these passages, which Tocqueville placed in a prominent position at the end of his book. To be sure, one can always apply to Tocqueville Gramsci's maxim, "Pessimism of the intellect, optimism of the will."

[15] In his manuscript notes, Tocqueville links Jansenism with aristocracy: for him, Pascal embodies an aristocratic type of thought.

almost hear the words of a sermon: "Having destroyed the obstructing privileges enjoyed by some of their fellow men, they run up against universal competition."[16] Long before, Pascal, the seventeenth-century Augustinian, had said that men want to live remote from God and run up against the tyranny of amour-propre.[17]

How, too, can one fail to see history exacting its own revenge, as Tocqueville not very discreetly pointed out. By abolishing aristocracy in 1789 and inflicting a wound that (as he put it) would never heal, society deprived itself of the means of moderation that it now so sorely lacked:

> The form of the obstacle has changed, but the obstacle remains. When men are nearly alike and all follow the same route, it is quite difficult for any of them to move ahead quickly and break through the uniform crowd that surrounds them and presses in upon them.... It is possible to imagine men achieving a degree of liberty that satisfies them completely. They will then enjoy their independence without anxiety or ardor. But no equality instituted by men will ever be enough for them.

Never? Tocqueville maintains this pitiless tone throughout lengthy passages in which, as we saw in part 3, he transposed the Pascalian concept of *"divertissement."* Human desire, aroused in and through the pursuit of *greater* equality, conceals the fact that what moves society is the hunt, not the quarry. A powerful misapprehension continually spurs the machine on: "When inequality is the common law of a society, the greatest inequalities do not call attention to themselves.[18] When everything is more or less on a par, the slightest inequality becomes an eyesore. That is why the desire for equality becomes ever more insatiable as the degree of equality increases."[19]

Hence there is no solution. Here is a "new kind of liberal," as Tocqueville wrote in his celebrated letter to Stöffels, because he regarded equality not as a foundational norm issuing from 1789 but rather as an imaginary quality, an *illusion* inherent in modernity.

True, the aristocrat Tocqueville also tried to convince himself. This, we know, was one of the purposes of his very complex style. Since the egalitarian passion could not be extinguished, he set against it a counterweight to

---

[16] *DA* II.2.13, p. 173; AG, p. 627. And in *The Ancien Régime and the Revolution*, the same "punishment" is applied to nobles: "Not having wanted the bourgeois as either partners or fellow citizens, they would find in them rivals, before long enemies, and ultimately masters." *OC* II-1, p. 189.

[17] G. Ferreyrolles sums up this idea as follows: "Man did not want to obey the Lord, so he obeyed his equal. The political order is a penal order." See "Politique et dialectique dans les*Pensées* de Pascal," p. 40.

[18] This is Tocqueville's view, which we may doubt.

[19] *DA* II.2.13, p. 174; AG, p. 627.

be derived from equality itself, a "remedy in the disease" (as in Domat): "I admire equality when I see it deposit an obscure notion of, and instinctive penchant for, political independence in every man's heart and mind, thereby preparing the remedy for the ill that it provokes."[20]

Is this a solution? In reality, Tocqueville forces us to hesitate with respect to the remedy that he adumbrates in this passage because he also tells us that equality leads to centralization, democracy's "natural" passion. Particularly since the chapters that follow this suggestion of a "remedy" deal with democracy's propensity to restore or reinforce centralization until "mild despotism" is achieved.[21] After describing the features of the "immense power" that was coming into being, moreover, Tocqueville added this summation: "Equality paved the way for all these things by preparing men to put up with them and even to look upon them as a boon."[22]

Reading Tocqueville was therefore a somewhat disturbing experience for his contemporaries, or at any rate for those who hoped that liberty might survive under democracy. As twenty-first century readers, we have been able to detect a Pascalian "postulation" in the text: this is essential if we wish to grasp the dual character of the work before us while at the same time taking note of the warning issued in 1840. In a preface to the second volume, Tocqueville warned that he had been "quite severely critical" of democracy for the following reasons: "It is because I am not an enemy of democracy that I sought to deal with it in a sincere manner. People do not receive the truth from their enemies, and their friends seldom offer it. That is why I have told it as I see it."[23]

What this seems to say is that Tocqueville wished to be physician to a society that was in fact alien to him. He was not a philosopher in the classical tradition, such as Kant.[24] The writer who speaks in the text in such harshly critical terms about equality-as-mirage is the *moralist*. Could contemporary readers grasp all this? There are reasons to doubt it, although it is true that discourse that imitated sacred eloquence was an oratorical genre of the period.[25]

[20] *DA* II.4.1, p. 354; AG, p. 788.
[21] See the titles of *DA* II.4.2–6, which speak volumes.
[22] *DA* II.4.6, p. 386; AG, p. 818.
[23] *DA* II, preface, p. 6; AG, p. 480.
[24] One might compare the Pascalian "postulation" in Tocqueville (see part 3) with the Kantian idea of the republic: an idea that is indispensable to reason yet without adequate empirical realization, unlike the "concept."
[25] See Frank Paul Bowman, *Le Discours sur l'éloquence sacrée à l'époque romantique* (Geneva: Droz, 1980).

As an aristocratic moralist, Tocqueville had an acute eye for the confusion with which the societies of his time were grappling, and he tried to hold up a mirror in which they could see themselves. His pitiless tone nevertheless revealed a worrisome *delectation*. The author's famous claim of impartiality is thus undone by his style: the critic's delight, with its Pascalian echoes, works counter to the author's strategy, which was to remain impartial.

In fact, the style of *Democracy in America* is not one of impartiality but rather of tension and conflict—or what Pascal would have called "contrarieties": either too much or not enough, too close or too distant, too dark or too bright. One should take care not to confuse impartiality with the *cleavage* that Tocqueville believed he had found in the object of his study (liberty, equality, democracy, the finitude and the infinitude of human desire) and which was reflected in the shimmering meaning of his text. Because he took this position, he was able to *displease everyone*. He was not impartial but unclassifiable, "between right and left," as Mario Tesini has written.[26]

It is easy to see why the Right in the nineteenth and twentieth centuries found *Democracy in America* unsatisfactory: it was too complacent toward progressive myths (the rights of man, the law of progress, morality in politics). Maurras called Tocqueville a "malefactor." But it is just as easy to see why the Left could only be wary of or irritated by a writer who described the dialectic of liberty and servitude: liberty was the basis of economic development, economic development increased man's taste for "material pleasures," and these in turn exacerbated imaginary equality, which "revived" administrative centralism, sweeping government regulation, and generalized surveillance of individuals by one another and by the state.

⚏

In the gallery of "masters of suspicion"—Marx, Nietzsche, Freud—one portrait has long been missing: that of Alexis de Tocqueville.

[26] Mario Tesini, *Tocqueville tra destra e sinistra* (Rome: Edizioni Lavoro, 1997).

The Use of Anthologies and Summaries in Tocqueville's Time

Writers in this period were fond of painting portraits of great authors and summarizing their work. It is interesting to compare Tocqueville's portrait of Pascal with that of Jean-Baptiste Maigrot, *Illustrations littéraires de la France*, 2 vols. (Paris: Lehuby, 1837).

Tocqueville wrote:

> Seeing him, as it were, wrest his soul from life's concerns so as to devote himself entirely to this research, only to die of old age at forty, having prematurely ruptured the bond between soul and body, I stand amazed in the knowledge that no ordinary cause could have produced such extraordinary efforts. [*DA* II.1.10, p. 56; AG, p. 525]

In Maigrot's anthology we find the probable source of this text, which is striking for its suggestion that Pascal was old at forty:

> He had barely achieved the age at which other men attain their full strength, yet already he felt all the infirmities of a premature old age. Apparently, the vigor and energy of the moral faculty in him had sapped his physical strength before its time. He died at thirty-nine, with all the signs of decrepitude. The constant tension of his mind had seemingly exhausted his brain. [From the Ducrocq one-volume edition of 1860, p. 286]

APPENDIX 2

Silvestre de Sacy, Review of *Democracy in America*

M. de Tocqueville wanted to complete his work on American democracy.[1] The first two volumes, which came out two years ago to widespread and legitimate acclaim, dealt primarily with political institutions and, before our eyes, as it were, took apart the mechanism of this entirely elective government. These two new volumes, which M. de Tocqueville published a few months ago and which I regret to be so tardy in reviewing, consider the effects of those institutions on the heart of man, on his penchants, tastes, and mores, and on the nature of his ideas about art, literature, philosophy, religion, and the family—in short, on society itself. It is a portrait of democracy in action, of the intimate life of democracy, and, as it were, of democracy undressed. It is an immense, difficult, and often sad subject, which touches us closely enough to be frightening, and into which, I hasten to say, M. de Tocqueville has been able to delve deeply.

I have one criticism to make, however. The title of the book is misleading. It isn't really about democracy in America but about the future of democracy in the world and particularly in France: that is the title that would have done justice to M. de Tocqueville's thought. How, indeed, can one live in Europe, in the midst of old and crumbling social organizations; how can one live in France, which has been so deeply shaken by fifty years of revolution and whose future remains shrouded in menacing obscurity; without coming back to the same lugubrious and overwhelming thought: Where is the world headed? What unknown form of government, what new society, and which men will emerge from the confused and shattered rubble of the old society? What is the meaning of these periodic shocks, of these howling tempests that at times seem to be receding only to loom again suddenly on the horizon? Is it liberty? Is it despotism? Is it a hierarchy based on merit? Is it unbridled equality? Is it human happiness or unhappiness, glory or shame

---

[1] André Jardin quoted parts of this letter in *Alexis de Tocqueville*, pp. 260–61. He cut it after the second sentence without any indication and changed the wording at several points. Here I restore the original text, together with the half of the letter that Jardin omitted. Two illegible passages are indicated with dashes.

that democracy will bring forth—the very democracy of which France has for fifty years been the ardent hearth? Indeed, with our proverbial impetuosity, we did indeed shred our old laws and mores. Religion fell with the ancient monarchy. All order and all classifications vanished in the same storm that swept away the last vestiges of feudal nobility. We have laid bare society's bones and muscles, as it were. Property and family stand uncovered, without protection. To be sure, we have proclaimed some magnificent principles, but what are principles without mores? We recognize only one rule, justice. But will we be wise enough and strong enough to apply that rule to ourselves without the aid of faith? Ancient history has few examples to offer us. The world has rarely tried democracy on so vast a scale. Everything is new: the earth on which we walk, the sky that shines above, our civil and political organization, the relations between man and man and between the government and everyone!

The problem is everywhere: a hidden power is undermining even those societies whose surface has changed the least and which remain tranquil in appearance. In France, there is open debate, in the public square, about the awesome question of what we shall become, because to be honest it must be said that to date we are nothing. We have laws that no one obeys, not even those who made them or are charged with executing them. We have authorities that quake in the presence of their subordinates. We have opinions, because each man is sovereign over his own opinions, accepting or rejecting at will. We have no public morality. We believe that we have fulfilled our duty to society and conscience when we have said, "That's how I see it." To be sure, mores cannot be remade in a day. Mores are the habits bequeathed to the present by the past and passed on to the future. They are like a torch that each generation hands on to the next. When that torch goes out, the world stumbles and thrashes about in profound darkness for quite some time. Even the glimmers that appear from time to time have something dark and sinister about them. Yet society cannot take definite shape or form without a stable moral foundation. Laws and constitutions, I confess, worry me to some extent. In these times they provide but a temporary shelter, an unsafe harbor in which one seeks refuge for want of anything better, but not a true port. When mores are ripe, laws make themselves. What will our mores be? That is the question on which our future greatness or vileness depends.

From what I have said about M. de Tocqueville's new work, the reader will have grasped that it is this great question, the greatest that any writer can tackle today and of the most palpitating interest for all of us, that he has undertaken to resolve. American democracy is merely one type at which M. de Tocqueville glances from time to time so as not to allow his imagination to run too wild in the portrait he paints of the future organization and mores of democracy in general and of French democracy above all. America is before his eyes; France is in his thoughts. He mentions us often; he implicitly deals with us at every turn. The anxieties and hopes that he expresses are fundamentally patriotic, and this betrays his secret preoccupation. This is not the narrative of an unruffled and indifferent traveler who is describing the mores of a foreign nation. I fear only that, in obedience to his title, M. de Tocqueville has gone too far in taking American democracy as the model for all possible democracies. I regret that he has not frankly admitted to himself the true purpose of his book. Instead of placing American democracy in the foreground, he would have done better, perhaps, to use it to illustrate and confirm his general ideas about democracy. He would then, I believe, have seen more clearly the essential differences that prevent one from drawing rigorous conclusions about Europe on the basis of America, or about France on the basis of Carolina or Virginia. He would have given a more accurate account of our national character and our situation in Europe, because of which France will always be at least as much a military democracy as a commercial one, and he would have rendered more fully the long past that all the revolutions one might imagine will never entirely erase. There would not have been a perpetual combat, if I may put it this way, between the specificity of his title and the grandeur of his subject.

I may be mistaken, but it seems to me that M. de Tocqueville sees many more things than he writes about. He holds back; he restrains himself. He rejects thoughts that come to his mind, despite his denials. One might say that certain aspects of his subject frighten him. He may, I suspect, fear that if he were to surrender to the implications of his ideas, he might discover that he is not as much of a democrat as he wishes to be. Often, perhaps too often, the effects of aristocracy are compared to those of democracy. Which of the two social forms is better, all things considered? Which does greater honor to the human race? Which is more favorable to the development of all the noble instincts, literary genius, the love of glory, and the taste for the great and the beautiful in all things? Pointless questions! exclaims M. de Tocqueville. Good or bad, aristocracy's day is done. The popular torrent that has been in full flood for the past fifty years cannot be stopped. Any dikes that one might put in the way of its irresistible force would only swell the current. The times said: Let there be democracy, and there was democracy. Accept it as a work of God. Study it in order to guide it, if possible. —I beg M. de Tocqueville's pardon, but an author is not entitled to prune his subject at will. If the reader is somewhat fatigued by the perpetual comparison he makes in his book between the mores of aristocracy and the mores of democracy, the real problem is that the conclusion is missing, and the mind becomes impatient when its expectations are frustrated. The question that M. de Tocqueville evades with a care that shows how much it preoccupies him nevertheless reappears despite his efforts on every page, in every line. Try as he might to get rid of this nagging issue, the subject brings him back to it. The reader puts the book down and wonders anxiously: Is this really democracy? In demanding equal rights and the abolition of privileges and paying for them with our blood and tears, did we level sentiments and debase the heart of man? Was not aristocracy, with all its injustices but also its lofty ideas, superior to this democracy of jobbery, cheapness, and selfishness? When the crowd is petty in every respect, can a people be great? However much one multiplies petty interests and petty sentiments, can one achieve heroism? Is not the mass necessarily what individuals are?

Call these questions pointless too, if you will. They nevertheless stem directly from M. de Tocqueville's subject, and no one can read his book without asking a hundred others like them. The practical man can reconcile himself to things as they are. Yet I have little taste for practical men who scorn the philosophical and ideal aspect of things. Still, when a writer, an observer, a philosopher contents himself with telling me, "This is how things are!" he leaves me cold and saddens me. My body can bear the yoke; my imagination cannot. It indomitably yearns for something better. The human spirit is too noble to submit to the weight of the factual, no matter how oppressive. I appreciate the merits of M. de Tocqueville's book. I admire his infinite sagacity and rare delicacy of observation. Throughout one senses a righteous heart and a warm love of humanity. I certainly consider it to be one of the most solid books to have appeared in many years, yet I must confess that I am not at ease in this book; I find it stifling. I search for the air and sun of the ideal. I feel overwhelmed by the weight of the masses, which impose on me not only their laws but their crude tastes and frequently foolish ideas. M. de Tocqueville himself seems to have surrendered, to have resigned himself, and, his heart filled with sadness, he is trying to turn a bright face toward the terrifying democracy he describes. I do not wish, God forbid! to ferret out his secret feelings. What I know is that he has the air of a traveler who, having courageously set sail upon the stormy seas of the future, finds it difficult to wrench himself away from the tranquil and majestic shores of the past. In the end, though, why should he be afraid to say his final word about aristocracy and democracy? Why does democracy appear in a disadvantageous light in M. de Tocqueville's book? In my opinion, the problem is that he focuses too exclusively on American democracy, which he takes to be the type and model of universal democracy. Is this what repels our national ideas and instincts?

Here, a word of explanation is in order. On several occasions I have expressed my limited liking for American institutions and mores. I love liberty—liberty that elevates the soul, that fortifies the character, and that stems more from the independence of the heart than from public guarantees. And from all the books that I have read about America, starting with M. de Tocqueville's, I have come away with the sad conviction that what America lacks most is liberty. Is one free in a country where the rich hide in order to enjoy their wealth; in which men of intelligence pretend to be stupid lest their superiority cost them a few votes; and where everything, including feelings and beliefs, is ruled by the majority? I call such arithmetic liberty a harsh form of slavery—the harshest of all: moral slavery. Already I see too many signs of this among us. How often have I heard the abjection of the servants of popularity characterized as courage and independence? In a democratic age, one must stiffen one's soul in order to be oneself. One readily escapes the yoke of the court and great lords and flees into obscurity. But how does one escape the domination of the crowd, which is everywhere? In America, the despotism of the crowd is crushing. That is the source of my repugnance. I do not deny, however, that the Americans are a great people. They are fine where they are, granted. God has assigned them a mission that they are fulfilling admirably, to till a vast territory and summon it to civilization. Their restlessness, their ardor, their love of wealth, which they lose as readily as they gain, is in some sense providential. One cannot reproach a people that marches toward its goal with such a resolute step and virile air.

But American democracy, with its selfish and self-interested mores, in France? Oh! That is something else. That, I confess, is the idea against which my soul rebels. If one were to give a general characterization of the detailed portrait that M. de Tocqueville draws of democratic mores, would it not be, if I may put it this way, a universal debasement of hearts and minds? Consider. In letters, no more pure devotion to art. Factories turning out books, novels, and poems conceived in gigantic boldness but without taste and contemptuous of form—the form which, begging M. de Tocqueville's pardon, is quite simply the essence of beauty in literature and in art. In the sciences, the abstract, philosophical, sublime side of things neglected in favor of the utilitarian aspect, for trade. Religion, whose essential purpose is to detach man's heart from this world, treated as a means of living a more comfortable existence here below. Christianity, with its severe law of penitence and mortification, transformed into a subtle sort of epicureanism. A more equitable distribution of well-being, no doubt, but an ardent thirst for pleasure, an astringent selfishness in pursuit of wealth. Every man a king in his own castle, and every man for himself! Mildness in manners but no dignity or independence of character. Purity in marriage, regarded as a contract. Fewer faults of conduct, but less nobility as well, less delicacy, less sensibility. Man's spiritual side stifled, as it were. Modesty replaced by early lessons in defending oneself. A sort of realism, fundamentally crude, disenchanting the world, with the useful everywhere dethroning the beautiful. Is this not a fair summary of democratic mores as M. de Tocqueville describes them?

And this is supposed to be the future of democracy in France, which loves, extravagantly perhaps, the brilliant and majestic—true grandeur, and, failing that, false grandeur? No, I do not think so. I do not believe that the France of the crusades and the Italian expeditions, the France of Louis XIV and Napoleon, can ever forget itself to that degree. I know, and hasten to say, that M. de Tocqueville expresses reservations about the differences from time to time, but I think that the differences are fundamental enough to ensure that French and American democracy would have few traits in common. In regard to French democracy, my fear is not that it will fall into America's moral apathy. I fear its impetuous enthusiasms, its impassioned bounds. I am afraid that France does not know how to confine itself to liberty and may leap again from anarchy to despotism. That is its tragic fate. This idea has not escaped M. de Tocqueville's notice. A sincere friend of liberty, he is not unaware of the dangers to which democracy subjects it. He has called attention to these with a great deal of force and eloquence in his fourth volume. May all farsighted men read and meditate upon M. de Tocqueville's reflections! It is so convenient for despotism if everything is in the hands of the people! Only one deed of sale then needs to be signed. The people abdicate for the benefit of one man, and that is all there is to it. That man then oppresses them and mocks them as well, saying, "This is what you wanted. Here is your contract, duly signed and sealed." This is what the Roman emperors did with their so-called royal law, as did another emperor, whose glory and misfortunes prevent me from calling him by name, with his plebiscite and four million votes. In my own mind I have no doubt: the best guarantee of liberty in France is the *cens* [the property qualification for voting], which establishes hierarchy and order in the electoral process itself. Thanks to the *cens*, one rises by degrees through work, thrift, morality, and enlightenment to the acquisition of the sovereign right. The numerical principle will lead the nation to only one result: tyranny!

To conclude, I ask myself whether I may unintentionally have been too harsh on M. de Tocqueville. If so, I regret it. Every writer has a certain cast of mind. It is not impossible that some of the ill humor that American institutions and mores have always inspired in me spilled over onto M. de Tocqueville's book. May he pardon me! No one has greater esteem than I for his talent and his character. I do not know whether these final two volumes will enjoy as wide and popular a success as the first two. What I do know is that they will maintain M. de Tocqueville in the very high place that he occupies among our political thinkers and writers.

Letter from Alexis de Tocqueville to Silvestre de Sacy

Based on Tocqueville's draft, filed in a sleeve bearing the following note: "Letter written to M. de Sacy on October 18, 1840. I do not know if this letter was ever sent."[1]

Sir,

I have just received the issue of the *Journal des Débats* containing your article on my book. I cannot refrain from sharing with you the painful impression that it made on me.

Not that this article does not contain any number of very flattering judgments of me and several parts of my work, with which I ought to be and am satisfied. On the most important point, the basic premise, the seminal idea of the work, however, it does not do me justice, and justice on that point is what I expected especially from you, Sir.

I pointed out that, in our own time, [the] new social state that had produced and is still producing very substantial goods also gave rise to a certain number of very worrisome tendencies. These germs, if left to grow freely, seem to me likely to lead to a steady decrease in intelligence, materialism in mores, and ultimately universal subjugation. I believed that I saw, not without terror, the human race heading in this direction in recent years, and therefore believed that all men of heart must lend a hand to stop it. To my knowledge, few friends of the Revolution of 1789 dared to point out these most worrisome tendencies, a chimerical undertaking that I would not wish to follow even if I thought it practicable. Those who saw it and were not afraid to speak of it, being among those who condemn the democratic social state as a whole and in all its details, were more likely to irritate than to lead.

---

[1] André Jardin quoted parts of this letter in *Alexis de Tocqueville*, pp. 260–61. He cut it after the second sentence without any indication and changed the wording at several points. Here I restore the original text, together with the half of the letter that Jardin omitted. Two illegible passages are indicated with dashes.

The intellectual world was divided between democracy's blind friends and its enraged detractors.

My purpose in writing [my] book was to reveal the frightening prospects in store for our contemporaries, not to prove that they must return to an aristocratic social state, nor to predict, as you seem to believe, and it is a great error, that these —— are irresistible. But in order to make them fearsome by depicting them in vivid colors so as to obtain the inward and voluntary effort that can alone combat them, teach democracy to know itself and thus to guide itself and restrain itself. To show our contemporaries that in order to prevent this equality, which we rightly hold dear, from becoming the leprosy of the human race, one must work tirelessly to sustain the flight of ideas, to lift souls toward —— and —— to show that in the democratic age that is just beginning, political liberty is not only beautiful but also necessary for nations to become great and even to remain civilized. That, Sir, is the idea of my book, which alone sustained me in the face of the perhaps insurmountable difficulties of the subject and against criticisms that I anticipated, because I knew that in writing a book based on such an hypothesis, I was not following in the wake of any party.

The subject was ill-chosen, you say. I grant you that. But I nevertheless tell myself that it took a certain amount of energy and devotion to choose it. It would have been easier and safer to write either a bloody critique of equality or its apotheosis. Nothing, Sir, in the article I have just read indicates that you so much as glimpsed this purpose of the author.

This, I repeat, is what pained me. For among the men who were kind enough to review my book, you were the one—I can say this now without giving the appearance of self-interested flattery—who seemed best prepared by virtue of his sentiments and ideas to appreciate my point of view or at least to recognize and explain it.

I hope, Sir, that you will find in the style of this letter nothing that suggests the bitterness of an author stung by criticism. Any such feeling is far from my mind. You will see here only the legitimate sorrow of a man who, believing that he has done something courageous and honest, finds that he has been neither appreciated nor understood.

Reproduced with the authorization of the comte d'Hérouville. Letter to appear in the Œuvres complètes *(Gallimard).*

Index

absolutism in France, 276–79
academician, Tocqueville as, 222–23
Adams, John, 269–70
Alain, Émile-Auguste Chartier, 164, 165,
  231n21
Algeria, 12, 305–6
Alletz, Édouard, 47, 49, 50, 254
Althusser, Louis, 281
ambulatory style, 208n39, 238
American Democrat, The (James Fenimore
  Cooper), 144
American Revolution, 24; natural aris-
  tocracy and, 268–69. *See also* United
  States, the
Americans. *See* United States, the
amour-propre, 40n81, 145,149, 150–51,
  176–81, 324
Ampère, André-Marie, 50n116, 167n30,
  199, 213n58, 226n3, 280n121, 316
Ancien Régime and the Revolution, The
  (Tocqueville), 3–4, 11, 12, 13, 18, 40,
  181, 199, 254, 264, 275, 283, 300, 318;
  bourgeoisie and, 280; concept of society
  in, 272–74; duality of soul and body
  and, 174; foreword to, 281–82; "generative principle" used in, 111; Guizot on,
  285–88; Jansenism and, 168, 169; preface to, 19, 56; Quinet on, 315; reforms
  of Louis XIV and, 276–79
Ancillon, Friedrich, 252n6, 255, 258n26
anthologies, 232–33
antideterministic reasoning, 102
antifederalism, 24–25
architecture, monumental, 236
Arendt, Hannah, 283
aristocracy, 85–86, 275; aristocratic liberalism, 11, 243–44; democracy and, 82–87;
  309–14; family values, 302–9; individualism and, 122; legitimate inequality and,
  262–63; manners and, 122, 127–28;

masters and servants in, 126; moralistic
  reflection, 288, 323–26; natural, 267–
  72; politics of language and, 194–95;
  relationships among, 127; sociology of
  art and, 220–21; women and, 118
Aristotle, 152, 236
Arnauld, Antoine, 164
Aron, Raymond, 14, 103, 158n52,183
authority: Michel Chevalier on, 52–53;
  of common sense, 319; democratic
  literature, 244–47; different conceptions
  of French, 254–55; Guizot on locus of,
  255–58; l'honnête and, 181; individualism versus collective, 137–42; intellectual, 66–72, 77–78; Jansenism threat
  to, 165; legitimism and, 35–44, 63;
  liberty and, 41; moral, 77–78; mores as
  new form of, 52; newspapers and, 258;
  popular sovereignty and, 73–74, 319–
  20; psychology of, 34–35; of the public,
  65–66, 70–72, 92–93; reason and, 75–
  76; religion and, 79–80, 96–97; of the
  social, 10–11, 71, 76, 96–97, 123–24,
  195, 319; sociological rules of democracy supplanting, 219–25; spiritual,
  181–84; the state as an agent of industry
  and, 53–55; traditionalists on, 60–64;
  visible, 219–25; will of all and, 91. *See
  also* democracy; social authority
Avenir de la science, L' (Renan), 8, 61, 176

baccalaureate, 229–32
Ballanche, Pierre-Simon, 214–15, 218, 233
barbarism, 224
Barthes, Roland, 230
Battista, Anna-Maria, 13, 80
Baudelaire, Charles, 212
Beaumont, Gustave de, 7, 12, 32, 46, 200,
  223, 244–45, 252, 293

Béchard, Ferdinand, 39–44, 68
Béguin, Albert, 202
Bénichou, Paul, 224
Benoît, Jean-Louis, 16n2, 117n8, 169n41
Benrekassa, Georges, 103
Besoigne, Jérôme, 166
Biran, Maine de, 115, 116
Blanc, Louis, 36, 44
Bonald, Louis de, 75, 78, 97–98, 107, 108, 117, 227–29, 246; on power of the collective, 116–17; on republics, 112; social metaphysics of, 115
Bonaparte, Louis-Napoléon, 264, 272–73. *See also* Napoleon III
Bonapartism, 54–55
Borel, Pétrus, 233
Bossuet, Jacques-Bénigne, 163, 199, 215, 288, 289, 318, 320
Boullée, Étienne-Louis, 236
Bourbons, 21
Bourdaloue, Louis, 199
Bourdieu, Pierre, 126
bourgeoisie, the, 32–33, 39, 50–51, 85; centralization and, 279–81
Boutang, Pierre, 283
Broglie, Gabriel de, 117
Bruneau, Charles, 215n67, 217n72, 218, 233

Caprariis, Vittorio de, 13
Caractères ou les mœurs de ce siècle, Les (La Bruyère), 145
carbonarism, 47–48
Carné, Louis de, 6, 35, 44, 50, 83, 170n43, 286
Carrel, Armand, 33, 316
Catholicism: authority rejected by Protestants, 245–46; common sense and, 75; individualism and, 96–97, 143; political traditionalism and, 115–16; reconciliation with modern society, 131; as repository of truth, 92; self-government in France and, 53–55, 60–61; social authority in, 140–41; in the United States, 68. *See also* Protestantism/Christianity; religion

centralization and despotism, 321–23
Cerquiligni, B., 198
Cessac, M. de, 117
Chabrol, Ernest de, 180, 187, 202, 293
Champaigne, Philippe de, 209
Changy, Hugues de, 42
Channing, William Ellery, 142, 143
Charlemagne, 276
Charles VII, 274
Charles X, 306, 310
Charmettes, Le Brun de, 232
Charter of 1814, 16
Chateaubriand, François-René de, 8, 9, 14, 82, 197, 200–203, 205, 211–12, 291, 297, 299; on democracy and despotism, 311–14; on English constitutional forms, 254; frustration with democracy, 234; influence on Tocqueville, 291–92, 309–14, 314–15; on the monarchy, 316–17; on natural Christians, 213–14; relationship to Tocqueville, 297
Chevalier, Jacques, 185
Chevalier, Michel, 63, 83; critiques of America, 47–57; rivalry with Tocqueville, 45–47, 49
Childe Harold, 220
Christianity. *See* Protestantism/Christianity
churches of prosperity, 86
Cicero, 151–52, 231, 234, 283–84
Cid, Le (Corneille), 85, 214
civic education, 26
civic spirit, 40, 66–67
civil disobedience, 143–44
civil equality, 16–19, 71–72
Civilisation en Europe. See Histoire de la civilisation en Europe
Civilisation en France. See Histoire de la Civilisation en France
Cochin, Augustin, 57, 61
Code Civil (France), 104, 106
Cofrancesco, Dino, 13, 103, 302, 305
Collard, Angélique, 168
Collard, Paul, 168
collective consciousness, 72
collective constraint, 123–24; voluntary adherence to, 125–28

collective logic, 98–99

common sense, 75, 319

communal life, 41–43

competition, 88, 161–62

Comte, Auguste, 48, 72, 97

conformism, social, 142–44

consent, secret and tacit, 124

Constant, Benjamin, 8, 30, 48, 90, 103, 111, 142, 231, 319; Tocqueville's disagreement with, 130–37; views on religion, 129–30, 132–37

Constituent Assembly, 228–29

constraint, collective, 123–24; voluntary adherence to, 125–28

contractual adherence, 125

contractual consent, 98

Cooper, James Fenimore, 9, 144

Corneille, Pierre, 251

counterrevolutionaries, 111–12, 128

Coup d'œil sur le règne de Louis XVI (Hervé de Tocqueville), 294

Cousin, Victor, 8, 155n43, 177n74, 199, 209, 210n45, 211n49, 231

Craiutu, Aurelian, 103n10, 237n43, 315n82

Cromwell (Hugo), 212, 216

cult of the One, 69

culture of absolutism, 11

D'Eaubonne, Gabriel-Joseph, 300

decentralization, 20; antifederalism and, 24–25; Catholicism and, 53–55, 60–61; favored by Tocqueville, 44–45; Guizot on locus of authority and, 255–58; local independence and, 30, 42; monarchists and, 36–37; public opinion and, 40–41

Defense of the Constitutions of Government of the United States of America (Adams), 269

De finibus (Cicero), 151

de Gaulle, Charles, 22

De la charité et de l'amour-propre (Nicole), 145, 177

De la démocratie en Amérique. See *Democracy in America*

De la démocratie en France (Guizot), 251

De l'administration de la France (Béchard), 40

De la littérature considérée dans ses rapports avec les institutions sociales (Staël), 205, 226, 231

De l'Allemagne (Staël), 215

De la religion (Constant), 132, 133

De la Restauration et de la monarchie elective (Chateaubriand), 316

delegation through representatives, 262

De l'Église gallicane (Maistre), 165

De l'esprit de conquête et de l'usurpation (Constant), 90

De l'esprit géométrique (Pascal), 203

De l'état du paupérisme en France et des moyens d'y remédier (Béchard), 39

de Maistre, Joseph. *See* Maistre, Joseph de

democracy: aristocracy and, 82–87; authority and, 34–35; Bonapartism, 54–55; as both a way of life and a mode of thought, 18–19; Michel Chevalier on, 49–50; civic education and, 26; civil equality and, 16–19; communal life and, 41–43; competition within, 88, 161–62; danger inherent in modern, 19–20; democratic language as spume of "perpetual motion" in, 203–9; despotism and, 18–19, 311–12; duality and ambivalence in, 235–38; duality of soul and body and, 174–76; equality through, 84–87, 104; family and, 117–21; l'honnête and, 151–58; human finitude and, 170–72; importance of Protestantism in, 129–30; legitimism and, 35–44; leveling through, 309–18; living, 27–28; local, 24–26, 42; material pleasures and, 18–19, 82–84, 87–91; meaning through images in, 184–87; the middle classes and, 16; moderated through religion, 79; modern meanings of, 15–20; participatory, 28; politics of language in, 193–98; popular sovereignty in, 21–28, 253–55; public opinion and, 40–41, 43–44, 52, 125–28; as religion, 20, 66–67, 86–87, 97, 109; social authority and, 74; as a social state, 33–35, 50–51, 71–72, 95–99; sociological rules of, 219–25; spiritual authority and, 181–84; traditionalists and, 57–58, 60–64; uniformity in, 122–23; universal

democracy (*continued*)
suffrage and, 31; women and, 117–21.
See also authority; decentralization
Democracy in America: Doctrinaires and,
46–47; French liberalism and, 5–7;
introduction, 314–15; levels of meaning
in, 6–7; literary debate over, 227–29;
preface to the French edition of, 14;
reviews of, 101–2, 328–34; themes of,
8–9; Tocqueville's reasons for writing,
1–5, 11. *See also* Tocqueville, Alexis de
democratic spirit, 83
De officiis (Cicero), 283
De Republica (Cicero), 284
De Sanctis, Francesco M., 12n31, 13, 321
Descartes, René, 67, 76, 113, 139, 164, 203
Des intérêts matériels en France
(Chevalier), 49
despotism, 54, 89, 90, 154, 195–96, 221,
311, 316; centralization and, 321–23;
democracy and, 18–19, 311–14; mild,
323, 325; popular sovereignty and, 256;
two forms of, 291–94; tyranny of the
majority and, 321–22
Diderot, Denis, 91, 93
Diez del Corral, Luis, 158n52, 287
Discours et opinions de Chateaubriand, 291
Discours sur l'histoire universelle (Bossuet),
288
dispersion of power and Romanticism,
214–19
distraction and dissatisfaction, 162–63
dogma, 21, 114, 143
Domat, Jean, 176, 184
Douay-Sublin, Françoise, 229–30
Druon, Maurice, 198
duality of soul and body, 174–76, 177
Du Contrat social (Rousseau), 91
Dufaure, Jules, 13
*Du gouvernement représentatif et de l'état
actuel de la France* (Guizot), 255
Duvergier de Hauranne, Prosper, 167
Dumas, Alexandre, 207
Dupont-White, Charles, 30
Durkheim, Émile, 72, 95, 97, 99, 116, 120,
122, 124, 130, 221; on mobs, 127; on
public opinion, 126

eccentricity, 123
education, civic, 26
egoism, 179, 180
Elias, Norbert, 28–29
elitism, 262–63; natural aristocracy and,
267–72
eloquence, 229–32, 237
Emerson, Ralph Waldo, 143
England: democratic leveling in, 310,
312; feudalism in, 274–75; fourteenth-
century, compared with France, 274–76;
Glorious Revolution, 268–69
enigma of man, 172–73
Entretiens au bord de la mer (Alain), 164
equality: aristocratic moralism and, 323–
26; civil, 16–19, 71–72; leveling and,
313–14; modernity and, 105, 110; as
a norm and a passion, 104; passion for,
161–62, 179; representative government
and, 261–62; through democracy, 84–
87; of women, 117–21
Essai sur la centralisation administrative
(Béchard), 39
Essai sur la littérature anglaise (Chateau-
briand), 313
*Essai sur la manifestation des convictions
religieuses* (Vinet), 138
Essai sur les institutions sociales (Ballanche),
214
Essai sur l'indifférence en matière de religion
(Lamennais), 72, 75
Étapes de la pensée sociologique, Les
(Aron), 14
État et ses limites, L' (Laboulaye), 15
États-Unis contemporains, Les (Jannet), 58
Études et discours historiques (Chateau-
briand), 310
Européen, L', 39
Everett, Edward, 101

family and democracy, 117–21
family environment of Tocqueville,
294–301
Febvre, Lucien, 7, 8
Federalist, The, 6, 271
Ferry, Jules, 31, 131

feudal individuality, 283
feudalism, 274–79, 287–88
Fiévée, Joseph, 25
Figaro, Le, 198
Filles du feu, Les (Nerval), 300
finitude, human, 170–72
Fleurs du Mal, Les (Baudelaire), 212
Fontanes, Louis de, 264-65
France, 330, 333; absolutism in, 276–79; acceptance of republicanism in, 316–18; anti-Americanism in, 59–60; appointment of mayors in, 25–26; bourgeoisie of, 32–33, 39, 50–51, 85, 279–81; Catholicism and hierarchical government in, 53–55; Code Civil, 104, 106; concept of society in, 272–74; Constituent Assembly, 228–29; corruption in, 32; decentralization of power in, 25, 36–37; despotism in, 291–94; different conceptions of authority in, 254–55; feudalism in, 274–79, 287–88; legitimism in, 35–43; local administration in, 24–26; locus of authority in, 255–58; middle class of, 271; monarchists versus traditionalists in, 57–58; moralistic reflection on history of, 288–90; National Assembly, 24; people substituted for the king in, 57–58; politics of language in, 197–98; popular sovereignty in, 21–28, 36–37; sovereignty of the people in, 23; fourteenth-century, compared with England, 274–76; Third Estate, 25, 82; universal suffrage in, 37; women of, 118. *See also* Restoration, the
free institutions, 33–34
French Revolution, the, 3, 4–5, 16, 18, 322; civil equality and, 16–17; moderates in, 23
Fumaroli, Marc, 199, 202n17, 203, 211n51, 229n12, 313, 314n81
Furet, François, 3–4, 14, 241, 279n113, 315n84, 316; on French moderates, 23

Gambetta, Léon, 31
Gautier, Théophile, 233
Gazette de France, 37–38

generative principle of republic, 107–8, 110–14, 113–14
Génie du Christianisme, Le (Chateaubriand), 211
Genoude, Antoine-Eugène de, 36–37
Girardin, Émile de, 207
Girondins, 25
Globe, Le, 48, 218
Glorious Revolution, 268–69
God, 108–9, 112; "benefits" to democracy, 157–58; duality of body and soul and, 177; as hidden, 186. *See also* Catholicism; Protestantism/Christianity; religion
Grancey, Eugénie de, 15
grandeur, 153, 176; in architecture, 236
Grandmaison, Charles de, 199, 284
"Great Revolution" of 1789, 3
Guellec, Laurence, 16n2, 199n2, 237n43, 240
Guizot, François, 8, 10, 11, 14, 17, 50, 60, 217, 251, 319; on absolutism in France, 276–79; on *The Ancien Régime and the Revolution,* 285–88; on bourgeoisie and centralization, 279–81; on concept of society in French history, 272–74; disagreement with Tocqueville, 251–55; on local interests, 25; on locus of authority, 255–58; on natural aristocracy, 267–72; political theory of, 255–72; on representative government, 258–64; Tocqueville judged by, 281–90; Tocqueville's rivalry with, 33; on George Washington, 264–65

Hamilton, Alexander, 265, 272
Hauranne, Duvergier de. *See* Duvergier de Hauranne, Prosper
Hazareesingh, Sudhir, 30n40
Heliogabalus, 176
Helvétius, Claude-Adrien, 147, 149, 150, 156, 178
Hernani, 197, 218
heroism, 153–54
Herriot, Édouard, 153
Histoire de la civilisation en Europe (Guizot), 254n12, 272n85, 277n103

Histoire de la civilisation en France (Guizot), 11, 75n44, 251, 254n12, 272n85, 274–76, 280n122, 281n123, 285
Histoire de la révolution d'Angleterre (Guizot), 268
Histoire des Origines du gouvernement représentatif en Europe (Guizot), 255n14, 259n30, 319
Histoire philosophique du règne de Louis XV (Hervé de Tocqueville), 294
Hobbes, Thomas, 320
honnête, l', 147, 151–58, 166, 174, 178–79, 181, 223
honnêteté, 178
honor, 151–58
Hugo, Victor, 8, 197, 198, 207, 212, 216, 217, 222, 228
human finitude, 170–72
humanism, 233–34
Hume, David, 179
humility, 68
hypocrisy, 239–40

Iliad, The (Homer) 213
images, meaning through, 184–87
Imitation de Jésus-Christ, L', 189
individual reason/individualism, 75–76, 98, 99, 108–9, 113–14; antideterministic, 102; aristocracy and, 122; Catholicism and, 96–97, 143; collective authority versus, 137–42; feudal individuality, 283; Jansenism and, 166; Protestantism and, 129–30; religion and, 96–97, 131, 135–36, 245–46; social individuality, 155–56; society of, 106–10
Individu effacé ou le paradoxe du libéralisme français, L' (Jaume), 6
inequality, 261–62, 286; legitimate, 262–63
intellectual authority, 66–72, 77–78
invisible things, 185–86
Irving, Washington, 144
Islam, 132, 170, 306

Jackson, Andrew, 8, 50, 54, 111, 144, 272
Jacobins, 22

Jannet, Claudio, 58, 59
Jansenism, 66, 84, 92, 112, 131, 137, 158, 323; amour-propre and, 149, 150, 176–81; individualism and, 166; influence on Tocqueville, 168–87, 189–90, 208; meaning through images and, 184–87; moralism and, 146; representations in Tocqueville's time, 163–68; spiritual authority and double aspiration in, 181–84
Jardin, André, 11n28, 14, 77n32, 117n8, 169n42, 214, 226n3, 294–96, 298n27, 299n29, 328n1, 335n1
Jefferson, Thomas, 6, 60, 271
Jerôme, Saint, 176
Jerusalem Delivered (Tasso), 213
Jocelyn (Lamartine), 142
Journal des débats, 4, 46, 241, 242, 335
Journey to Lake Oneida (Tocqueville), 200
judicial power, 58
July Revolution of 1830, 3, 104–5, 163, 167, 231, 263, 306, 310

Kant, Immanuel, 107, 325
Kergorlay, Louis de, 5, 7, 37, 154, 159, 199, 264, 293, 294, 295, 316; Tocqueville as lawyer for, 298–99
knighthood, 213–14

La Boétie, Étienne de, 69
Laboulaye, Édouard, 15, 21, 55n137, 130n6, 131, 142
La Bruyère, Jean de, 145–46, 238–41, 281
Lacordaire, Henri-Dominique, 8–9, 254, 287
Lamartine, Alphonse de, 8, 142, 198, 220
Lamennais, Félicité Robert de, 9, 10, 11, 72, 75–81, 98, 108, 114, 245–46
language and literature: authority in democratic, 244–47; eloquence in oratory and, 229–32; instability of, 207–9; moral training and, 233–35; platonism in art and, 209–12; politics of, 193–98; as a sacred function, 206–7; as spume of "perpetual motion," 203–9; Tocqueville's

view on the mission of, 224–25. *See also* Restoration, the

Lanjuinais, Victor, 13, 167

La Rochefoucauld, François de, 149, 150–51, 158, 184

law of inheritance, 106

law of opinion, 124

Ledoux, Claude Nicolas, 236

Leçons de littérature et de morale ou Recueil en prose… (Noël and Delaplace), 232

Lefort, Claude, 69, 188n121

legitimate inequality, 262–63

legitimation, social, 261

legitimism, 243; aristocracy and, 85–86; authority and, 35–44, 63; education and, 234; as a political movement, 308–9

Le Gros, Nicolas, 166

Leibniz, Gottfried Wilhelm, 164

Lémontey, Pierre-Édouard, 195–96, 310

Leonardo da Vinci, 211

Le Peletier de Rosambo, Louis, 297

Le Play, Frédéric, 57, 59, 60–64, 103n12

Leroux, Pierre, 48, 72

Leroy-Beaulieu, Paul, 47, 54

Lesueur, Abbé, 159, 169, 301

Lettres persanes, Les (La Bruyère), 145

Lettres sur l'Amérique du Nord (Chevalier), 46

leveling, 309–18

Lévi-Strauss, Claude, 202

Lewis, Thereza, 300

liberalism, 77, 216, 222; aristocratic, 11, 243–44; Bonapartism and, 54–55; French, 5–7; Romanticism and, 197–98; Silvestre de Sacy and, 241–44

Lieber, Franz, 15

living democracy, 27–28

local administration. *See* Decentralization; Democracy

Locke, John, 124, 231, 302, 319

logic of the collective, 98–99

logic of the social, 95, 125

Lorrain, Claude, 210, 211

Louis-Philippe, 21, 104, 111, 254, 306

Louis XI, 312, 316

Louis XIV, 4, 82, 165, 197, 204–5, 290, 312, 323; arts and oratory during

time of, 213, 216, 221, 229, 231, 333; concept of society under, 272–73; despotism under, 292–93; nobility subdued by, 254; reforms under, 276–79

Louis XV, 205, 221, 295, 296, 312

Louis XVI, 23, 297, 298, 300–301, 317

Louis XVIII, 36–37, 45, 256, 308

Lourdoueix, Honoré Lelarge, 37

Luther, Martin, 113, 139

Lutteroth, Henri, 138

Maigrot, Jean-Baptiste, 147n2, 327

Maire, Catherine, 92n30, 163n13, 165, 169n40, 185n107, 186n112,

Maistre, Joseph de, 72, 73–75, 78; as counterrevolutionary, 111–12; on individual reason, 113; individual reason and, 107–8, 109; Jansenism and, 165–66, 169; on people as childish, 110

Malebranche, Nicolas, 109, 164

Malesherbes, Chrétien Guillaume de Lamoignon de, 297–301, 316, 318

Malye, Rosalie, 306

Manent, Pierre, 70, 108n12

manners, 122, 127–28

Manzini, Charlotte, 14, 127n42, 297n20, 298n26

Marc, Yann-Arzel, 13

Marx, Karl, 98

Massillon, Jean-Baptiste, 163, 199

master-servant and voluntary adherence, 125–28

material pleasures, 18–19, 82–84, 85–86, 326, 332–33; duality of body and soul and, 174–75; as motivation and self-delusion, 87–91; respectable materialism and, 154–55

Matteucci, Nicola, 13

Maurras, Charles, 38, 59, 326

Maximes, Les (La Rochefoucauld), 149

meaning through images, 184–87

megachurches, 86

Mélonio, Françoise, 13, 14, 32, 36n64, 159n2, 185, 191n130, 298n22, 305n50

Mémoires d'outre-tombe (Chateaubriand), 201, 291, 314, 315

Mémorial catholique, Le, 96, 166, 245–46

metanoia, 195, 197, 243, 294
Méthode sociale, La (Le Play), 60
Michelet, Jules, 312
middle classes, 16, 271
Mignet, François, 224
mild despotism, 323, 325
Mill, John Stuart, 26, 224
mission of literature, 224
modernity and equality, 105, 110
Molé, Mathieu, 308–9
Molière, 145, 166, 204
Monarchie selon la Charte, La (Chateaubriand), 254
monarchists and monarchy, 57–58, 97–98, 243–44, 254; Chateaubriand on, 316–17; despotism of, 291–94, 312–14; republicanism and, 111
Montalembert, Charles Forbes René, comte de, 61
Montesquieu, Charles de Secondat, baron de La Brède et de, 59, 70, 82, 90, 92–93, 96, 121, 133, 159, 169, 237, 319; on equality, 162; influence on Tocqueville, 101–5; on religion, 134
moral authority, 77–78; l'honnête and, 158; spiritualism and, 175–76
Moralistes des seizième et dix-septième siècles (Vinet), 65
moralist(s): defined, 147–51; l'honnête and, 147, 151–58; moralistic reflection in interpretation of history by, 288–90; Tocqueville as, 145–46, 281–90, 323–26
moral training and literature, 233–35
motivation, material pleasures as, 87–91
Mottley, Mary, 182, 304, 307
Mun, Albert de, 57
Muséum littéraire, Le (Le Brun de Charmettes), 232–33

Napoleon, 4, 21, 22, 105, 117, 229, 231, 258, 290, 333; mayors under, 25–26
Napoleon III, 22, 54, 105
nationality, 58
natural Christians, 212–14
New England towns, 23–24, 26–27, 267; passions, interests, and authority in, 28–33

newspapers, 258
Nicole, Pierre, 145, 146, 176, 177–79, 189
Nolla, Eduardo, 19
Notions of the Americans Picked Up by a Travelling Bachelor (Cooper), 144
Nouveau dictionnaire d'économie politique (Say and Chailley), 46

obscurity: of popular sovereignty, 259–61; of sin, 210
Orglandes, Camille D', 16n2, 35n61, 78n59, 118n12, 181n91, 316
oratory, 229–32, 237
Owen, Robert, 236
Ozanam, Antoine-Frédéric, 57

pantheism, social, 139–40
Parrhasius, 211
participatory democracy, 28
Pascal, Blaise, 3, 92, 114, 122, 145, 187–88, 189, 199, 220, 233, 237, 324, 326, 327; influence on Tocqueville, 159–63, 172–73; on invisible things, 185–86; Jansenism and, 164–66; on man's disproportion, 235; as moralist, 146; on obscurity of sin, 210; three orders of people and, 180
patriotism, 30, 123–24
Paul, Saint, 183, 185–86
pauperism, 43
Pensées, Les (Pascal), 145, 161, 165, 173, 185–86, 210
Philip the Fair, 4
Pius XII, Pope, 91
Plato, 152, 155, 156, 176, 196, 231
Platonism, 209–12
Politian, 234
political power and nature of republics, 104
politics of language, 193–98
Pompidou, Georges, 198
Poor Law (England), 43
popular sovereignty, 20, 35, 109; authority and, 73–74, 319–20; despotism and, 256; in France, 21–28, 36–37; Guizot on, 253–55; judicial power and, 58;

legitimate inequality and, 262–63; monarchists and, 36–37; obscurity of, 259–61; traditionalists and, 73–74; in the United States, 21–28, 53

Port-Royal, 163–65, 167–68, 189, 212

Poussin, Nicolas, 209, 211

Pozzi, Regina, 13

Prix de Vertu, 222–23

Prix Montyon, 223

Producteur, Le, 103

Protestantism/Christianity, 69; authority of the Catholic Church rejected by, 245–46; critiques of social conformism, 142–44; grandeur and, 153; importance to democracy, 129–30, 132; l'honnête and, 189; monarchy and, 98; natural Christians and, 212–14; political traditionalism and, 116; social authority and, 96–97, 166–67; social conformism and, 142–44; as useful social practice, 166–67. *See also* Catholicism; religion

Provinciales, Les (Pascal), 165, 166

public opinion, 40–41, 43–44, 52, 320; authority and, 65–66, 70–72; collective authority and, 137–42; confidence in the public and, 67–68; sociology of, 72–81; voluntary adherence to, 125–28

Puritanism, 53–55

Quarterly Review, 47

Qui êtes-vous Monsieur de Tocqueville? (Manzini), 14

Quincy, Josiah, 57–58

Quinet, Edgar, 315

Rabelais, François, 212

Racine, Jean, 212, 251

Raphael, 210–11

reasoning: eloquence and, 230; Jansenism and, 163–64. *See also* individual reason

Récamier, Mme., 214–15

Réflexions diverses (La Rochefoucauld), 149

Règles de la méthode sociologique, Les (Durkheim), 126

Réforme sociale en France, La (Le Play), 60

Revue européenne, La, 310

religion: authority of the Public and, 92–93; Christianity and Catholicism in America, 69; collective authority through, 137–42; and creation of individual reason in man, 108–9, 112, 131; democracy as, 20, 66–67, 86–87, 97, 109; dogmatic beliefs, 21, 114, 143; God and self-government by individuals, 108–9; individualism and, 96–97, 129–30, 135–36; invisible things and, 185–86; l'honnête and, 189; megachurches and, 86; moderation of democracy through, 79; relationship to politics, 77–80; self-government and Puritan, 53–55; self-interest and, 130–37; social conformism and, 142–44; as a useful opinion, 69–70. *See also* Catholicism; God; Protestantism/Christianity

Rémond, René, 38–39, 52n124, 109n15, 212n53, 256n16

Rémusat, Charles de, 266, 272

Renan, Ernest, 8, 253n8

representation of self and others, 18

republican/representative government, 97–98, 279; defined, 258–64; French acceptance of, 316–18; generative principle of, 107–8, 110–14, 113–14; locus of authority in, 255–58; natural aristocracy in, 267–72; nature of, 104

respectable materialism, 154–55

Restoration, the: literature and moral training in, 233–35; rhetoric and the baccalaureate during, 229–32; rise of anthologies during, 232–33

Revue des deux mondes, 44, 191, 266, 311

Reynaud, Jean, 62

Rials, Stéphane, 36, 37n69, 38n71, 317n90

Richter, Melvin, 13, 19n18, 103n8, 10, 273n86

Robespierre, Maximilien Marie Isidore de, 156, 157

Rocard, Michel, 198

Romanticism, 8, 88, 195, 197–98, 246; American, 143; dispersion of power and, 214–19

Romantic Soul and Dreams, The (Béguin), 202

Rosambo, Louis de, 306

Rousseau, Jean-Jacques, 91–92, 93, 156, 157, 159, 200, 212, 237
Royer-Collard, Pierre Paul, 16, 131, 137, 153, 167–68, 252; on the press, 258

Sacy, Silvestre de, 4, 241–44, 247; letter from Tocqueville to, 335–36; review of *Democracy in America*, 328–34
Sainte-Beuve, Charles Augustin, 14, 163, 166, 188, 190–91, 218
Saint-Simon, Henri de, 45–48, 89, 166. *See also* Chevalier, Michel
Salinis, Louis-Antoine de, 245
Schleifer, James, 15
Scott, Walter, 8
Scottish Enlightenment, 204–5
Séché, Léon, 167
self-delusion, material pleasures as, 87–91
self-interest, 30, 34, 332; amour-propre and, 149, 150–51, 178–80; l'honnête and, 151–58; moralists on, 149; political and economic liberty and, 89–90; religion and, 130–37; virtue and, 152–53
self-knowledge, 172–73, 187–88
self-understanding, 172–73, 183–84
Semeur, Le, 116, 138
Seneca, 135
Senior, Nassau, 199, 304
Serre, Comte de, 16
Shée, Alton, 316
Sieyès, Abbé, 22
Simon, Jules, 46
Smith, Adam, 204–5, 206
social authority, 74, 76, 123–24, 195, 319; Catholicism and, 140–41; Christianity and, 96–97, 166–67; logic of the social and, 95, 125. *See also* authority
social bond, constraining essence of, 121–25, 123–24
social conformism, 142–44
social legitimation, 261
social pantheism, 139–40
social power, 216–17
society: amours-propres and, 149, 150–51, 176–81; concept in French history, 272–74; constraining essence of social

bond in, 121–25; of individuals, 106–10; social pantheism and, 139–40; social state and unified spirit, 101–5, 121; social wisdom and, 115–17; structure and democracy, 33–35, 50–51, 71–72, 95–99; and tension created by wealth, 238–40
sociology, 72
Socrates, 176
Souvenirs (Tocqueville), 291
spiritualism, 175–76, 181–84; hidden, 185–86
Staël, Germaine de, 8, 9, 137, 171, 197, 205, 215, 226–27, 233, 237–38, 278; on importance of eloquence, 229–30; on philosophy, 231; on two types of societies, 246
Stanhope, Lord, 231
Stöffels, Charles, 183, 193, 199, 202–3, 205, 239, 307, 319, 324
Stöffels, Eugène, 172
Strauss, Leo, 172
suffrage, universal, 31, 37, 59
Swift, Jonathan, 236

Taguieff, Pierre-André, 149
Tarde, Gabriel, 116
Tartuffe, Le (Molière), 166
Taveneaux, René, 165, 166n26
Temps, Le, 190
Temps retrouvé, Le (Proust), 288
Terror, the, 25
Tesini, Mario, 13, 128n44, 326
Théorie du pouvoir politique et religieux (Bonald), 97
Theory of Moral Sentiments, The (Smith), 205
Thibaudet, Albert, 31
Thierry, Augustin, 277, 310, 312
Thiers, Adolphe, 22, 35, 63, 224, 252, 307
Third Estate, 25, 82
Thoreau, Henry David, 143
Tocqueville, Alexis de: as academician, 222–23; as analyst of politics of language, 193–98; aristocratic family values of, 302–9; aspiration to be a

writer, 199–203; biographies of, 14; decentralization favored by, 44–45; disagreement with Constant, 130–37; disagreement with Guizot, 251–55; family environment of, 294–301; influence of Chateaubriand on, 291–92, 314–15; influence of Montesquieu on, 101–5; intellectual portrait of, 9–10; Jansenist leanings of, 168–87, 189–90, 208; judged by Guizot, 281–90; letter to Silvestre de Sacy, 335–36; Frédéric Le Play on, 60–64; meanings of democracy, 15–20; as moralist, 145–46, 281–90, 323–26; moralistic reflection by, 288–90; Blaise Pascal's influence on, 159–63; portrait of New England towns, 28–33; portrayal of Pascal by, 327; reasons for writing *Democracy in America,* 1–5, 11; rivalry with Michel Chevalier, 49; Charles Augustin Sainte-Beuve and, 190–91; sociology of, 95–99; unpublished correspondence of, 13; use of philosophical deductions and analogies by, 102; on war, 303–5; writing style of, 199–200. See also *Democracy in America*
Tocqueville, Édouard de, 2–3, 6, 297
Tocqueville, Hervé de, 6, 294–301
Tocqueville, Hippolyte de, 297, 303
Tocqueville et les Français (Mélonio), 14
towns, New England, 23–24, 26, 267; passions, interests, and authority in, 28–33
traditionalists, 57–58, 60–64, 97, 98; religion and, 115–16; sociology and, 72–81
Traité des lois (Domat), 177
transcendentalism, 143–44
Two Weeks in the Wilderness (Tocqueville), 200–201
tyranny of the public, 139, 320–21

unified spirit of Americans, 96–98, 101, 103
uniformity in democracy, 122–23
Union, L', 303

United States, the: anti-Americanism and, 59–60; Michel Chevalier's account of, 45–57; Christianity and Catholicism in, 69; critiques of Tocqueville, 142–44; generative principle of the republic, 107–8, 110–14; local administration in, 24–26; manners in, 122; middle class, 271; natural aristocracy in, 267–72; New England towns in, 23–24, 26; patriotism in, 123–24; popular sovereignty in, 24, 53; social structure in, 50–51; under George Washington, 263–64; unified spirit in, 96–98, 101, 103; wealth in, 238–40; wilderness of, 200–202. See also Jackson, Andrew
universal suffrage, 31, 37, 59
utilitarianism, 132, 133

Villemain, Abel-François, 8, 163, 164, 184–85, 187, 188, 229, 243, 284
Villeneuve-Bargemont, Louis-François, 175, 234
Vinet, Alexandre, 14, 65, 116, 129–30, 132–33, 230; antisociological spirit of, 137–42
virtue, 152–53
visible authority, 219–25
Voltaire, 136, 139, 193, 217, 222, 229
voluntary adherence, 125–28
voluntary servitude, 69
Voyage au lac Onéida (Tocqueville), 200, 201

war, 303–5
Washington, George, 231, 264–65, 267
Washington. Fondation de la république des États-Unis d'Amérique (Guizot), 14, 264, 266
wealth: leveling of, 313; tension created by, 238–40
Weber, Max, 102
Welch, Cheryl, 273n86
wilderness of America, 200–202
will of all, 91
women and democracy, 117–21